T0330740

Globalization and Defence in the Asia-Pacific

This edited volume examines the impact of globalization on the economies, security policies and military–industrial complexes of the Asia-Pacific region.

The work is structured into three main parts. The first explores globalization and its general effects on the policy-making of the nation-state; the second section looks at how globalization affects a country's threat perception and defence posture within the specific context of the Asia-Pacific region; while the third explores how it impacts on a state's allocation of resources to defence, and how economic globalization affects the defence industry, with specific reference to the procurement policies and practices of different states across the Asia-Pacific.

This book will be of much interest to students of Asian Studies, International Security, Defence Studies, Security Studies and Economics.

Geoffrey Till is Professor of Maritime Studies in the Defence Studies Department, Kings College London, and Director of the Corbett Centre for Maritime Policy Studies. He is author of many books on defence issues. **Emrys Chew** is Assistant Professor at the S. Rajaratnam School of International Studies, Nanyang Technological University. **Joshua Ho** is Senior Fellow at the S. Rajaratnam School of International Studies, Nanyang Technological University.

Contemporary security studies
Series Editors: James Gow and Rachel Kerr
King's College London

This series focuses on new research across the spectrum of international peace and security, in an era where each year throws up multiple examples of conflicts that present new security challenges in the world around them.

NATO's Secret Armies
Operation Gladio and terrorism in Western Europe
Daniele Ganser

The US, NATO and Military Burden-Sharing
Peter Kent Forster and Stephen J. Cimbala

Russian Governance in the Twenty-First Century
Geo-strategy, geopolitics and new governance
Irina Isakova

The Foreign Office and Finland 1938–1940
Diplomatic sideshow
Craig Gerrard

Rethinking the Nature of War
Edited by Isabelle Duyvesteyn and Jan Angstrom

Perception and Reality in the Modern Yugoslav Conflict
Myth, falsehood and deceit 1991–1995
Brendan O'Shea

The Political Economy of Peacebuilding in Post-Dayton Bosnia
Tim Donais

The Rift Between America and Old Europe
The distracted eagle
Peter H. Merkl

The Iraq War
European perspectives on politics, strategy, and operations
Edited by Jan Hallenberg and Håkan Karlsson

Strategic Contest
Weapons proliferation and war in the greater Middle East
Richard L. Russell

Propaganda, the Press and Conflict
The Gulf War and Kosovo
David R. Willcox

Missile Defence
International, regional and national implications
Edited by Bertel Heurlin and Sten Rynnin

Globalising Justice for Mass Atrocities
A revolution in accountability
Chandra Lekha Sriram

Ethnic Conflict and Terrorism
The origins and dynamics of civil wars
Joseph L. Soeters

Globalisation and the Future of Terrorism
Patterns and predictions
Brynjar Lia

Nuclear Weapons and Strategy
US nuclear policy for the twenty-first century
Stephen J. Cimbala

Globalization and Defence in the Asia-Pacific

Arms across Asia

Edited by Geoffrey Till, Emrys Chew and Joshua Ho

Routledge
Taylor & Francis Group

LONDON AND NEW YORK

First published 2009
by Routledge
2 Park Square, Milton Park, Abingdon, Oxon OX14 4RN

Simultaneously published in the USA and Canada
by Routledge
711 Third Avenue, New York, NY 10017, USA

Routledge is an imprint of the Taylor & Francis Group, an informa business

Typeset in Times by Wearset Ltd, Boldon, Tyne and Wear

British Library Cataloguing in Publication Data
A catalogue record for this book is available from the British Library

Library of Congress Cataloging in Publication Data
Globalisation and defence in the Asia-Pacific : arms across Asia / edited
by Geoffrey Till, Emrys Chew and Joshua Ho.
p. cm. – (Contemporary security studies)
1. Globalization–Pacific Area. 2. Security, International–Pacific Area.
3. Pacific Area–Foreign relations. 4. Pacific Area–Foreign economic
relations. 5. Military policy–Pacific Area. 6. Defense industries–Pacific
Area. I. Till, Geoffrey. II. Chew, Emrys. III. Ho, Joshua.
JZ6009.P16G56 2008
355'.03305–dc22   2008013407

ISBN10: 0-415-44048-3 (hbk)
ISBN10: 0-203-89053-1 (ebk)

ISBN13: 978-0-415-44048-6 (hbk)
ISBN13: 978-0-203-89053-0 (ebk)

Contents

Illustrations

Figure

Tables

Contributors

Rommel C. Banlaoi is the Executive Director of the Strategic and Integrative Studies Center, Inc. (SISC). His works appeared in *Contemporary Southeast Asia, Asian Affairs, Parameters, US Naval War College Review, Foreign Relations Journal, Asia Pacific Journal, Studies in Conflict and Terrorism, Intelligence and National Security, Indian Ocean Survey* among others. He has published six books to date and his most recent books are *War on Terrorism in Southeast Asia* and *Security Aspects of Philippines–China Relations*.

Renato Cruz De Castro is currently the chair of the International Studies Department, De La Salle University and the holder of the Dr. Aurelio Calderon Professorial Chair of Philippine–American Relations. He has written several articles on international relations and security that have been published in a number of scholarly journals and edited works in the Philippines, South Korea, Malaysia, Singapore, Taiwan, Germany, the United Kingdom, and the United States. He is currently a columnist in the *Manila Bulletin*, contributing his insights on U.S. foreign and defence policies as well as general strategic issues and trends that affect the Philippines. He also conducts courses and delivers lectures in the Foreign Service Institute of the Philippines and in the National Defense College of the Philippines.

Emrys Chew is currently Research Fellow of the S. Rajaratnam School of International Studies, at Nanyang Technological University in Singapore. He has written a series of articles for the Golden Web Project at the University of Cambridge, under the title 'Guns and Gems: The Sinews of War and the Ornaments of Peace in the Indian Ocean World'. In addition to his research interests, Emrys has taught undergraduate courses on Imperial and Post-colonial History at the University of Cambridge, examining cross-cultural interactions that have generated and shaped much of the modern world.

Guibourg Delamotte is Research Associate at Asia Centre, Paris. Her publications include *Japan Analysis – La Lettre du Japon*, a newsletter, which is issued five times a year and provides an analytical overview of Japanese current and foreign affairs; and chapters in *Ramses 2006* and *Asie 2006*. She lectures regularly at HEC Business school, Ecole des hautes etudes en sciences socials, and Inalco.

Arthur S. Ding is Research Fellow at the Division III (China Politics) of the Institute of International Relations, National Chengchi University in Taipei. His research focuses on China's security and defence policy, civil–military relations, defence industry, and international relations in East Asia. His published works include *China's Changing Military Theory, 1979–1991, PRC's Defense Industry Conversion*, and articles in numerous edited books and journals.

Joshua Ho is Senior Fellow at the S. Rajaratnam School of International Studies, Singapore and Coordinator of the Maritime Security Programme. He is a co-editor for several publications, and has had articles published in journals like *Asian Survey, Australian Army Journal, Defence Studies, Journal of the Australian Naval Institute, Maritime Affairs, Military Technology, Pointer*, and *Security Challenges*. He has presented papers at conferences and seminars organized by the *Asia-Pacific Economic Cooperation (APEC), Canadian Maritime Forces Pacific, Center for Strategic and International Studies, Washington DC*, among others. Joshua is a serving Naval Officer with 20 years of service and currently holds the rank of Lieutenant Colonel.

Christopher W. Hughes is Senior Research Fellow and Deputy Director at the Centre for the Study of Globalisation and Regionalisation, University of Warwick, UK. He is also Reader in International Politics, Department of Politics and International Studies, University of Warwick. He is the author of *Japan's Economic Power and Security: Japan and North Korea*; *Japan's Security Agenda: The Search for Regional Stability*; *Japan's Reemergence as a 'Normal' Military Power*; co-author of *Japan's International Relations: Politics, Economics and Security*; and co-editor of *New Regionalisms in the Global Political Economy*. He is joint editor of the *Pacific Review*.

Ron Matthews is Professor of Defence Economics and Academic Leader of the Masters in Defence Administration Course in the Department of Defence Management and Security Analysis, Cranfield University, UK Defence Academy. He has written and edited several books and numerous articles on defence industrialization. The most recent book co-edited with Jack Treddenick, Marshall Center, Germany, is entitled *Managing the Revolution in Military Affairs* and was published in 2001.

Deba R. Mohanty is Senior Fellow in Security Studies at the Observer Research Foundation (ORF), New Delhi. His writings on security studies have found place in prestigious publications like *Military Technology, Bulletin of Arms Control, Strategic Analysis, Air Power, Force* and *National Review*. Currently, he is a columnist for *Military Technology* and a commentator for *All India Radio*. He has also contributed extensively to many political and security risk firms like *Jane's Foreign Report and Oxford Analytica*. His Occasional Paper titled 'Arms Dynamic and Strategic Stability in South Asia' was published by South Asia Strategic Stability Unit, Department of Peace Studies, University of Bradford.

K.S. Nathan is currently Senior Fellow at the Institute of Southeast Asian Studies in Singapore. He is the current President of the Malaysian Association for American Studies , serves on the Editorial Board of the *Australian Journal of International Affairs* and is the Editor of the ISEAS journal *Contemporary Southeast Asia*. He has several publications including five books (both as author and as editor), including *Detente and Soviet Policy in Southeast Asia*; *Trilateralism in Asia*; *American Studies in Malaysia*; *North America and the Asia-Pacific in the 21st Century*; *India and ASEAN*; *The European Union, United States and ASEAN*; *Islam in Southeast Asia* and numerous articles in local, regional, and international journals.

Brian M. Pollins is Associate Professor of Political Science at the Ohio State University and Research Fellow at the Mershon Centre. His published research has focused on the effects of international political relations on global trade flows, global economic conditions and armed conflict, and the use of statistical techniques and computer simulation in the study of global politics. This work has appeared in journals such as *International Studies Quarterly*, *American Journal of Political Science Review*, *Journal of Politics*, *Journal of Conflict Resolution* and *American Political Science Review*.

B. Raman has served in the Ministry of Home Affairs as an internal intelligence analyst and in the cabinet secretariat as an external intelligence analyst. He was the head of the Counter-terrorism division of the Research and Analysis Wing, India's external intelligence agency, and is currently Director at the Institute For Topical Studies, Chennai. He was a Member of the Central Advisory Committee, ORF, New Delhi and a member of the Special Task Force on the revamping of the intelligence apparatus of the Government of India in 2000 and has served as a member of the National Security Advisory Board (NSAB) of the Government of India.

Vijay Sakhuja is Senior Fellow at the Observer Research Foundation, New Delhi, India. He was Research Fellow at the Institute for Defence Studies and Analysis, New Delhi, and United Service Institution of India New Delhi. He has authored a book *Confidence Building From The Sea: An Indian Initiative* and is the recipient of Vice Admiral S.L. Sethi Maritime Media Award, 2002. His research areas include South Asian security, maritime and naval developments and risk analysis.

Rizal Sukma is currently Deputy Executive Director at the Centre for Strategic and International Studies (CSIS), Jakarta. He is also the Chairman of International Relations Bureau, Central Executive Board of Muhammadiyah; member of the board at Syafii Maarif Institute for Culture and Humanity; a visiting lecturer at Post-Graduate School of Political Science at the University of Indonesia; and a member of National Committee on Strategic Defense Review, Indonesia's Ministry of Defence. He has published extensively in the field of security, conflict and terror within Indonesia and other areas. His books include *Indonesia and China: The Politics of A Troubled Relationship* and *Islam in Indonesian Foreign Policy*.

Geoffrey Till is Professor of Maritime Studies at the Joint Services Command and Staff College and a member of the Defence Studies Department, part of the War Studies Group of King's College London. He is the author of a number of books including *Air Power and the Royal Navy*; *Maritime Strategy and the Nuclear Age*; *Modern Sea Power*; and, with Bryan Ranft, *The Sea in Soviet Strategy*. More recently he has edited *Coastal Forces*; *Sea Power: Theory and Practice* and *Seapower at the Millennium*. Other titles include *The Challenges of High Command: The British Experience* with Gary Sheffield; *Development of British Naval Thinking* and *Seapower: A Guide for the 21st Century*. Geoffrey is currently working on *On Naval Transformation* and a major study of the impact of globalization on naval development.

1 Introduction

Joshua Ho

Globalization, once a rather nebulous concept, has become a buzzword and entered into mainstream dialogue and discourse. Globalization as a phenomenon in itself has attracted its fair share of supporters and detractors. Supporters have celebrated its virtues and its inevitability and emphasized that globalization is economically benign and increases economic prosperity by enlarging the economic pie. Supporters have also emphasized that globalization is socially benign, and that it diminishes poverty, gender discrimination, and protects both mainstream and indigenous culture. Detractors, on the other hand, have accused globalization of lacking a human face. They see globalization as the increase in the power and influence of the multinational corporation who will pursue profits at the expense of civil liberties and human rights. In particular, opponents have feared that the phenomenon of globalization might increase poverty or the rich–poor divide, increase the use of child labour, undermine democracy, harm the interests of women, dilute indigenous cultures, damage the environment, and encourage illegal flows of humanity that simultaneously fuel vices within industry such as prostitution and the consumption of drugs.

But when all is said, what is lacking is a clear, coherent, and comprehensive sense of how globalization works and how it can do better. Globalization can mean many things: it can mean economic globalization; cultural globalization, which can be affected by economic globalization; and the globalization of communications, which is one of the factors that deepen economic globalization. However, globalization in the context of this volume will focus largely upon *economic* globalization. Economic globalization constitutes the integration of national economies into the international economy through trade, direct foreign investment (by corporations and multinationals), short-term capital flows, international flows of workers and humanity, and flows of technology.

If the effects of globalization on civil liberties and human rights remain a continuing debate, the effects of globalization on defence in particular are even less well understood. What does the latest research tell us about the relationship between globalization and conflict or cooperation? How will globalization affect a state's revenue collection and, in consequence, how will it affect the way that a country allocates its budget to various priorities and to defence in particular? How will the international flows of workers and humanity, as well as technology, affect the state's procurement and acquisition policies? Will the increasing economic integration of national economies into the international economy through trade, direct foreign investment by corporations and multinationals as well as increase in short-term capital flows alter threat perception or will new threats arrive that need to be addressed? This volume addresses these and other questions in three main parts. The first part will establish theoretical frameworks for exploring the connections between economic interdependence and international conflict, thus examining whether greater economic interdependence that comes with globalization is likely to result in greater cooperation or exacerbate existing rivalries that could lead to conflict. At the more practical level, the second part will examine how globalization affects a country's threat perception and its defence posture, locating the debate firmly within the particular time–space context of an increasingly dynamic but volatile Asia-Pacific region. The third part will examine how globalization affects a state's allocation of resources to defence, and how economic globalization affects the defence industry, with specific reference to the procurement policies and practices of different states across the Asia-Pacific.

To begin with, the first part of this volume deals with the current scholarship on economic interdependence. Authors in this section will examine the latest globalization theories and expound the relationship between economic interdependence and conflict as well as cooperation. Will greater global economic interdependence result in greater cooperation or will it exacerbate existing rivalries that might culminate in conflict?

Moving from the more theoretical and general to the more practical and specific, authors writing in the second part discuss whether globalization has significantly altered traditional threat perceptions of different countries and entities in the Asia-Pacific region. Has globalization brought with it economic competition between states and between regions and as a result exacerbated inter-state competition and increased the perception of threat, or has globalization required greater integration with the global economy and reduced threat perception? For example, economic competition brought about by globalization could increase the competition for scarce natural resources such as oil and, in the process, exacerbate traditional rivalries; on the other hand, greater economic integration with the global economy may require greater interdependency and transparency and, as a consequence, encourage greater participation in multilateral institutions and, in the process, reduce threat perceptions. Another question that is examined is whether the phenomenon of globalization in itself has created new threats that the state will have to respond to, such as terrorism, illegal migration, drug smuggling, and crimes associated with the Internet? The authors shed new light on how respective states have coped with both the new and old threats brought about by globalization, by looking at the defence concept, posture, doctrine and missions allocated to the respective militaries, and how this is likely to continue or change in the context of the different sub-regions of Northeast, Southeast and South Asia.

Authors writing in the third part deliberate whether globalization has impacted the economies of the regional countries in a positive or a negative way, and whether the states concerned have been able to increase their revenue as a result of globalization. Have the regional and individual economies become more dynamic, allowing states to embark on a virtuous upward cycle, or has globalization resulted in net economic loss for the states and regions concerned, leading to a downward spiral? Consequently, on what basis have states allocated revenue resources for the purpose of defence? Has globalization brought about a different pattern of revenue resource allocation to the different sectors of government? For example, is defence spending increasing as a proportion of GDP, or increasing as a proportion of the national budget? What are some of the reasons for this resource allocation and how will countries continue to allocate resources in the future? Once again, such questions should be examined in the context of the different sub-regions of Northeast, Southeast and South Asia.

The third part will also examine globalization's impact on the defence industry. Economic globalization constitutes the integration of national economies into the international economy through trade, foreign direct investment (FDI) by corporations and multinationals, short-term capital flows, international flows of workers and humanity, and flows of technology. In order to remain competitive in the face of globalization, corporations have had to focus continuously on competitiveness and on areas where they have comparative advantage. Globalization has also forced corporations to establish global operations so as to be able to tap into the comparative advantages of the different countries, be it in terms of the labour pool, or access to raw materials or intermediate products. Traditional factors of production like land, labour and capital (and a more recent factor, intellectual capital) have become globalized; and firms do not have to be vertically integrated anymore but are able to have access to these different factors from the global marketplace. Have the pressures faced by profit-making commercial firms also affected the defence industry in the region? Have they had to diversify their operations into commercial activity as well to sustain operations? Will there be a scenario where we could expect a consolidation of the regional defence industry in a manner that has occurred in Europe with the creations of the European Aeronautic Defence and Space Company (EADS)? What impact would technology flows, capital flows, and human capital flow have on the defence industry in terms of its ability to harness the latest technology and hire the most talented individuals? What is the impact of such trends on defence acquisition and procurement policies? Will countries be able to maintain secret edge capability or will defence equipment and products be increasingly commoditized with similar look, feel and capability? These are just some of the questions that are addressed by the authors in the context of the different sub-regions of Northeast, Southeast and South Asia.

Part I Theories of globalization and defence

In the chapter, "Globalization and armed conflict among nations: prospects through the lens of international relations theory," Brian Pollins predicts the net effect of the positive and negative developments brought about by globalization. He begins by sketching those theories of International Relations that link aspects of economic growth, development, exchange and distribution to prospects for war and peace. They fall into three distinct groups: the first set examines how characteristics or trends within a national economy affect the interests and capabilities of the state; the second set focuses on the economic ties between two countries in order to explain their security relations; and the third set considers the characteristics of the global economic system as the driving force that shapes security relations among nations.

Pollins then examines those aspects of economic globalization that are most likely to impact on the security domain. They can be divided into two groups: new players and new forms of interconnectedness. By new players, Pollins refers to the rise of non-state actors such as inter-governmental and non-governmental organizations. Multinational corporations in particular can both impel and enable nations to move towards more peaceful relations in some cases, and towards conflict in others. In addition, globalization tends to redistribute economic assets and capabilities within the state system itself, leading to a change in the capabilities and interests of the states concerned. In terms of new forms of interconnectedness, these are the novel aspects of economic interdependence that distinguish this period of globalization from previous eras. These include the transnational reorganization of production, the content of trade flows and the dispersion of global capital centres.

In his final section, Pollins employs International Relations Theory to evaluate the economic shifts brought about by globalization in order to conclude as to whether or not the phenomenon will increase the prospects for peace in the twenty-first century. The key variables in such an analysis, isolated by many of the theories, are those relating to economic growth and stagnation. However, Pollins concedes that the field of International Relations is far from having all of the answers and more research remains to be done in a number of areas. First, more research is needed in order to ascertain whether or not the predictions of the theories are correct and which particular prediction is the more accurate. Second, additional research is needed to understand the mechanisms whereby interdependence discourages the resort to force in some circumstances but encourages conflict in others. Third, the relationship between the presence of a hegemon in the world system and the occurrence of war needs further investigation.

In the chapter, "Beyond interdependence: globalization, state transformation and security," Christopher Hughes gives an overview of the globalization–security nexus. He begins by stating his argument that there is indeed an interconnection between globalization and security, and that globalization's impact on national security can certainly be highly corrosive. This relationship can be most clearly explained by examining four inter-related themes. First it is necessary to define the concept of globalization in order to render it a useful analytical tool. Hughes offers a definition which views globalization not only as a quantitative change in the degree of social and economic interaction (i.e., increased economic interdependence and inter-connectedness) but also as a qualitative change in the nature of these flows, and in state capacities to respond to them.

Second, the concept of security must be more closely examined, in particular in order to understand how security has been traditionally generated. This will aid the analysis of how globalization may impact on national security. According to Hughes, security has been organized primarily around the role of sovereign states and that the main impact of globalization will be its ability to infiltrate and undermine the security prerogatives of sovereign states. To make his point, Hughes paraphrases and alters Charles Tilly's maxim: if the state can be remade or unmade under conditions of globalization, then so is remade the nature of war and security.

Third, it is necessary to examine how and under what circumstances globalization's impact on state sovereignty will result in the generation of specific security issues. It is possible to argue that the principle way in which this will take place is that globalization exacerbates the economic causes of traditional and non-traditional security issues. These causes feed off one another, often resulting in the generation of political violence. One way that this exacerbation occurs is that globalization can produce economic exclusion, which can lead to conflict. Hughes gives the example of North Korea to illustrate his point. Following the end of the Cold War, North Korea embarked on a policy of self-imposed isolation (this was supplemented by externally imposed exclusion) from the rapidly globalizing political economy of the region. The leadership of the state is currently aware that any economic liberalization at this point would expose its economy to the shocks of globalization and may threaten the stability of the ruling regime. The result is that North Korea has used its remaining military assets in what Hughes terms a strategy of brinkmanship, in order to extract economic concessions from the surrounding powers. Globalization can also impact on economic disparities within states, causing the disintegration of state structures and the potential for conflict.

Fourth, it is necessary to understand why globalization impacts in different ways on different sovereign states in different regions. This, Hughes explains, is a result of "geographies of national security." In other words, some countries or regions are more prone to insecurity linked to globalization than others. Hughes argues that it is in those states where sovereignty is weakest that globalization's impact and generation of insecurity is most strongly felt. These states are often located in the developing and post-colonial world. Globalization must be understood as an attack on state sovereignty and the ability of the state concerned to consolidate its sovereignty to limit globalization's impact.

Part II Globalization and defence policy in the Asia-Pacific

In the chapter, "Globalization and military–industrial transformation in South Asia: a historical perspective," Emrys Chew observes that the military–industrial configuration of South Asia is the globalized by-product of countless cross-cultural interactions that emerged out of a complex interplay between the motive forces of a changing world order and the crises of indigenous societies. In military–strategic terms, the transfers of military hardware and technology in South Asia have accelerated largely as a result of a world power seeking to enhance its military capabilities in order to maintain its hegemony and contain its rivals, or a South Asian power wanting to augment its military capabilities for both defence and offence. In political-economic terms, the development of the South Asian defence industry has been driven by Western (and in the most recent case, American-led) global expansion, as well as by regional trans-formation and indigenous crisis across Asia.

Shaped by these military–strategic and political–economic imperatives, the defence establishments of India and Pakistan were at first armed by foreign powers. But their strategic rivalry and pursuit of greater military–industrial self-reliance led progressively to "global diversification" of companies and corporations, the "internationalization" of supply networks, production systems, labour forces, management and financing. As the global military market unfolded across the subcontinent, the territorial boundaries of nation-states became more porous. This diluted and reconfigured national sovereignty and allowed for the arming of groups and individuals beyond the interstices of state power, and encompassed states in the wider South Asian periphery such as Sri Lanka and Afghanistan. According to Chew, the arming of South Asia has also manifested itself as a creeping militarization beyond the official jurisdiction of the state: the arming of local warlords, regional resistance groups and global terror networks. South Asia remains one of the world's most militarized zones not only on account of the global expansion of the West or great power rivalry in Asia; modern India and Pakistan are nation-states constructed out of myriad societies and polarized communities of the subcontinent whose growing sense of alienation, independent aspirations, and volatile ambitions have fuelled armed confrontation and conflict.

At the same time, Chew argues the importance of locating the processes of military–industrial globalization in South Asia within the dynamic military cultural context of the subcontinent's history. The chapter attempts to redress perceived imbalances in the contemporary emphasis of current debates about the nature and impact of globalizing supranational forces. Finally, it seeks to review possible implications of long-term globalizing trends and patterns for the present defence policies and future security of the region.

In the chapter, "Globalization's impact on threat perceptions and defence postures in Northeast Asia," Guibourg Delamotte focuses on Japan, China and South Korea, and globalization's impact on each of these countries' defence posture. As a starting point Delamotte quotes Peter Van Ness's definition which sees globalization as human activities that are reshaping the planet. She goes on to state that those security threats or human activities that have such an impact are failing states, rogue states, terrorism and weapons of mass destruction (WMD). In addition, the response deployed against these threats should also be taken into consideration for its reshaping impact. Thus, the US army's transformation and modernization is also a focus of the chapter.

Delamotte begins with a discussion of the various countries' responses to terrorism. She notes that both Japan and South Korea have committed themselves to the fight against terror. Both countries passed new anti-terror laws and both were in some way involved in the war on Iraq. Japan, through the contribution of a $5 billion assistance package and manpower to help the reconstruction of the devastated country, and South Korea, through its contribution of the third-largest amount of troops to the war effort after the UK and US.

China, on the other hand, has adopted a more controversial position with regard to the war on terror. China showed support for the fight against terrorism and the war in Iraq through its voting-in of the UN Security Council's resolutions related to these issues. However, it is thought that China saw an advantage domestically in supporting the war on terror; it has argued that Uighur separatists in Xinjiang received financial and material support from Al Qaeda in order to justify crushing this rebellion. The US war on terror has also impacted on US–China relations; China is no longer seen as the strategic competitor that it once was.

The next issue examined is the threat of nuclear weapons and the various defence policies of the three countries with regard to this threat. Japan is in a unique position in that it is the only country to have experienced a nuclear attack. Its pacifist constitution has led it to promote non-proliferation and disarmament actively. Despite the protection of Japan by the US's nuclear umbrella, Japan is very much aware of the threat from North Korea and recently agreed to start joint research with the US on a missile defence system. South Korea also feels threatened by North Korea. It started its own nuclear programme, and despite declaring it had officially stopped following US pressure, it continued clandestinely until 2000. The threat from North Korea has been the basis of its alliance with the US. Since the new president was elected in 2003, the threat has been played down somewhat and some South Koreans now feel that Japan is more of a threat in the region. China is gradually beginning to adhere to non-proliferation regimes, after a period in which it reportedly sold nuclear technology to Pakistan and Iran. However, its recent controversial declaration that the US could become a nuclear target caused some unease in US–China relations.

A further issue is the US's military influence on South Korea, China and Japan. The South Korea–US military alliance is increasingly seen as unequal by Seoul, particularly given the provision that the US would assume command during a conflict in the peninsula. Recent US withdrawal of its forces from South Korea has prompted it to seek accommodation with China and North Korea in the area of regional policy. Due to policy constraints, it is in Japan's best interest to appear as a trustworthy ally of the US. However, it does not wish to see its troops sent around the world to act alongside the US. Recently, Japan has been trying to gain a more influential position within the alliance in order to be relieved somewhat of US pressure. China has watched the US's military activities with increasing concern. It is eager to close what it perceives as the technology gap between its forces and those of the Western countries and has therefore, since the 1990s, been modernizing its forces. Delamotte concludes by highlighting a number of flash-points that could cause tension. These include the Taiwan question and future energy policies, particularly with regard to the South China Sea.

In the first part of the chapter, "Globalization's impact on threat perceptions and defence postures in Southeast Asia: two views," Rizal Sukma asks whether globalization produces security-enhancing or security-eroding effects on national, regional and international security. Sukma argues that globalization produces a combination of security-enhancing as well as security-eroding effects. In other words, globalization produces different security effects in different issue-areas and in different national and regional contexts.

As a case study, five member states of the Association of Southeast Asian Nations (ASEAN) were chosen. The discussion was divided into three sections: an overview of the traditional threat perceptions of the states concerned; an examination of the extent to which globalization has (or has not) altered threat perceptions within the region; and, finally, an analysis of the new security challenges facing these countries as a result of globalization. In terms of the traditional threat perceptions of the states, it was found that each had a preoccupation with internal security and in particular the preservation of sovereignty and political independence. There was a concern to maintain regime legitimacy, ensure domestic stability, and guard against external intervention in their domestic affairs. All of these concerns served as a basis for regional cooperation.

Globalization's impact on security in the region has been mixed. On the one hand it has led to cooperation on a regional basis and therefore reduces some of the concerns that had existed earlier. On the other hand, globalization has reinforced some of the concerns regarding national security. This is especially the case in relation to sovereignty, regime stability and the central role of the state in ensuring domestic order, all of which globalization threatens to weaken.

Globalization has also generated and perpetuated non-traditional security threats. These include piracy, disputes over fishing grounds, drug trafficking, arms smuggling, environmental degradation, terrorism, ethnic and communal violence, and transnational organized crime. There has also been an increasing concern over threats to human security, such as poverty, hunger, human rights abuses and diseases. Globalization will continue to shape and affect the security environment in Southeast Asia for the foreseeable future.

In the second part of the chapter, "Globalization's impact on threat perceptions and defence postures in Southeast Asia: two views," K.S. Nathan mentions that globalization has had a twin effect on security in the region. It is at once a security-eroding and security-enhancing phenomenon. Globalization is not easily comprehended; it has different impacts on different localities. However, what will remain a constant, in particular in Southeast Asia, is the central role of the state in regional security and cooperation. Nathan argues that globalization has actually strengthened the power and role of the state in many respects. In Southeast Asia, it is still necessary to view threats to security from a states-based perspective. This is what ASEAN has done and continues to do today. Security cooperation within ASEAN is intergovernmental, in other words, at the level of the state. Globalization has resulted in ASEAN increasingly seeing itself as a unique region. There is now a belief that what works in Europe works in Europe, and what works in ASEAN works in ASEAN. In Europe, cooperation tends to occur at a more supranational level as opposed to the governmental level, whereas in ASEAN, intergovernmental cooperation is still the primary form of interaction amongst states. Nathan goes on to point out that the US will remain an important actor. The US will be a facilitator in how we perceive threats and how we address them. The US is an important common denominator in terms of security cooperation in the region. This security cooperation leads to a kind of common security culture leading to security being seen in a certain way.

In the chapter, "Globalization's impact on threat perceptions and defence postures in Southeast Asia," B. Raman discusses the principle of interdependence that is promoted by globalization. He argues that interdependence works when it is between two countries that have a psychological sense of parity, either in terms of economic strength or strategic strength. Where the psychological sense of parity is not present, there is always a fear that the interdependence, would lead to the dependence of the weak on the strong. Interdependence between India and China is a prime example of where it has had a positive effect and a sense of parity is in evidence. India and China took the decision to develop their economic linkages in the early 1990s. The two countries have not allowed their political differences to prevent their economic cooperation. Since promoting economic linkages, the trade between the countries has boomed, from a low of US$2 billion to US$13 billion. However, according to Raman, what remains to be seen is how the fruits of globalization would be fed down to all sections of the population in the respective countries.

Part III Globalization and the defence economy in the Asia-Pacific

In the chapter, "Defence and the economy: an introduction," Ron Matthews states that globalization is a nebulous concept that represents a move from Keynesian to classical liberal economy. This has meant a big focus on wealth creation, cost reduction, and international industrial integration. Consequently, outsourcing and offsets have emerged as important elements of globalization. Matthews also observes that globalization is leading to enhanced civil–military integration particularly due to the changes in the nature of the defence economy. However, he adds that barriers to defence trade remain, as exemplified by the UK's 2005 Defence Industrial Strategy. Furthermore, protectionism in the defence sector continues even in the European Union. Countries like China continue to espouse self-reliance, even though the so-called Revolution in Military affairs (RMA) was making self-reliance difficult.

Matthews mentions that globalization of the defence sector has produced the new concept of "Defence Eco-Systems" that emphasizes a comprehensive national security framework and promotes civil–military integration to minimize any negative impact on the defence economy. According to him, civil–military integration reduces the burden of defence expenditure by promoting techno-logical sharing, supply chains, spin-on and spin-off technologies, and dual-use technologies. He cites the example of China's Plan 863 to highlight civil–military integration that helps defence industrialization.

In the context of the defence economies of Northeast Asia, Matthews notes that states face self-imposed or externally imposed embargoes like the respective cases of Japan and China have demonstrated. Both countries have also favoured self-reliance. China has looked upon foreign direct investment as a conduit to self-reliance, while Japan has aimed for self-reliance through the process of stra-tegic alliances and international consortia involving its defence firms. According to Matthews, the notion of reliance was built into the cultural aspect of these states. Given the rising costs of weapons systems, Matthews adds that states would have to pay greater attention to defence management issues including smart acquisition procedures. Although internationalization and regionalization of defence-industries were likely to be the wave of the future for the defence economies of Northeast Asia and beyond, work-sharing and technology-sharing were likely to remain sticking issues even between the closest of allies, as the Joint Strike Fighter project involving the UK and US would indicate.

In the chapter, "Globalization and defence industry in East Asia: seeking self-sufficiency and teaming up for dual-use technology," Arthur Ding observes two trends in Northeast Asia in the field of international relations. The first is that globalization and regionalization of the Chinese economy has been demonstrated best through its accession into the World Trade Organization (WTO) and the "ASEAN plus 3" process. However, there is another trend moving in the opposite direction: the growing tensions in Northeast Asia. This is embodied in US–China, China–Japan, and China–Taiwan tensions, as well the US–Japan alliance. Faced with uncertain political developments, China is likely to see a need to continue its military modernization in order to prepare for all eventualities.

China has understood fully that it cannot rely on foreign countries to support its military in the long term, and thus self-sufficiency remains the only way for China to go. There is no likelihood for China to form a regional defence consor-tium or to rely on the European Union (EU), Israel, or the US for defence technology. According to Ding, globalization has made dual-use technology more accessible than before and it remains the most feasible option for China to develop its own defence industrial capabilities.

Ding further mentions that joint ventures represent a feasible path for China to take. China's highly developed space industry had been invited for inter-national projects and China's participation in the EU's Galileo project was a typical case from which China could learn to manufacture navigation satellites of its own in the future for military use. Diversification into civilian production would be the other strategy China could adopt together with spin-on and cost-down measures. The end objective was to employ the state's limited resources for urgent military technology development and to let the civilian sector provide the innovative input required for arms development.

In the chapter, "Exploring Southeast Asia's twenty-first century defence economies: opportunities and challenges in the era of globalization, 1993–2005," Renato Cruz De Castro discusses how Singapore, Malaysia, Thailand, and Indonesia were managing their globalizing national economies, while at the same time maintaining viable and relatively autonomous defence economies. He states that globalization has not adversely affected the ability of these states to develop and maintain a viable defence economy. These four ASEAN states have proven that there is no dilemma in adopting the general economic strategy of an open and globalized economy, and the creation and management of a viable and functioning defence economy.

According to Castro, these states have not experienced any tension between their nationalistic conceptions of security as they built up autonomous defence economies while ensuring the globalization of their national economies. These states have found that economic liberalization and global division of labour in the generation of natural wealth complemented their preoccupation with developing and managing an autonomous and functional defence economy. According to him, this clear-cut thrust helped these states in the pursuit of their two very important goals in the globalizing world: ensuring economic development and prosperity, and enhancing national security in an anarchic international environment.

By opening their economies to the global market, these four countries have been able to generate the necessary wealth to finance their war preparation. Implementing a strategy of import-oriented industrialization and neo-liberal economic policies have assisted them with developing conventional armed forces that could be sustained by their existing defence economies. As a result, Castro states that these states have become skilled and seasoned practitioners of a new form of modern statecraft – neo-mercantilism. Analytically, Singapore, which has the most open economy in Southeast Asia, is also the country that could best afford to develop and manage the most advanced regional defence industry. Furthermore, statistical evidence suggests that these four countries could afford their defence economies without having to face a guns-versus-butter dilemma. Castro speculates that unless a global economic recession occurred in the next decade, these four ASEAN states would be in a position to finance and expand their functioning and relatively autonomous defence economies.

In the chapter, "Globalization's impact on defence industry in Southeast Asia," Rommel Banlaoi argues that although globalization had led to the internationalization of defence industries, the defence industries in Southeast Asia have remained rudimentary. With the sole exception of Singapore, ASEAN countries have failed to develop their domestic defence industries. Though most ASEAN countries have increased their defence spending in the aftermath of 9/11, the funds were used to purchase, rather than to produce, arms.

According to Banlaoi, ASEAN countries continue to be arms recipients rather than suppliers of weapons. ASEAN remains an important market for global defence industries. But the persistent lack of transparency in Asian defence procurement tends to resurrect fears that arms purchases would destabilize the region. Banlaoi reiterates the conclusion of many analysts that in the absence of more defence white papers and open-ended discussions about what arms purchases the regional states were making and why, the region is likely to be riddled with suspicions and tensions.

Banlaoi says that the globalization of the defence industry could provide ASEAN states with a key opportunity to invite foreign investors. However, this would require new thinking in ASEAN. This new thinking would call for the overcoming of sensitivities on defence issues and improving of governance in the security sector. Unless ASEAN states improve the functioning of their security sectors and overcame their sensitivities on issues pertaining to defence, Banlaoi argues that they are unlikely to be able to transcend the embryonic and rudimentary state of their defence industries.

In the first part of the chapter, "Globalization and the defence economy of South Asia: two views," Vijay Sakhuja observes that South Asia's experience with globalization and market reforms presents a mixed picture. He mentions that while the regional countries were conscious of cooperative and mutually beneficial economic benefits that accrued from globalization, they would go to great lengths to prevent any forces that questioned the sovereignty of the state. Sakhuja adds that the linkage between globalization and the defence economy were more apparent and forceful in the case of India; in India, the security function has increased with its liberalizing economy.

In the case of India, there appears to be a positive correlation between technological growth, national GNP growth, and defence expenditure growth, on the one hand, and defence industrialization, defence transformation, and the export of defence hardware, on the other. To a significantly lesser degree, Pakistan might have gained with globalization, but its defence expansion was driven more by its traditional animosity with India and more than three decades of military government. The impact of globalization has been varied for Bangladesh, Sri Lanka, Nepal, Bhutan, and Maldives; however, there was no tangible evidence to prove that they had expanded their defence economies on account of it.

Sakhuja notes that much of South Asia remains mired in conflicts and the mentality of partition continues to be pervasive. Given these facts, Pakistan has been unable to look beyond Kashmir and has often accused New Delhi of being a hegemon. Bangladesh has also aired similar views about New Delhi from time to time. There has been a general belief that as India gains in economic and military capability, it would attempt to gain a leadership role and that there would be a distinct possibility of conflict in the region. In Nepal and Sri Lanka, ethnic violence, insurgency, and terrorism are the major challenges that severely hamper economic development.

In the second part of the chapter, "Globalization and the defence economy of South Asia: two views," Deba Mohanty mentions that the defence industry, traditionally considered as a critical "national asset," has long been one of the more protected parts of national industries of many countries. Most countries prefer self-sufficiency in defence production and hence indigenous defence industries have been treated as critical to a country's security than simply as one more manufacturing sector. Even in market economic conditions, many of the states have preferred to keep their defence industries under state control. It is surprising then, how the forces of globalization as well as the end of the Cold War have challenged this once sacrosanct notion about autarky in defence production.

According to Mohanty, the end of the Cold War and the consequent disintegration of the Soviet Union has threatened to bring down the weapons emporium to the nadir of its existence. Military expenditures have plummeted from a high of $1,260 billion in 1987 to $704 billion in 1996. The same period between 1987–1996 witnessed an almost 35 per cent decrease in operational expenditure, 20 per cent reduction in equipment procurement, nearly 25 per cent decrease in military R&D investments and an almost 30 per cent reduction in demand for military weaponry.

The global defence industry tried to adjust itself to the new environment marked by considerable reductions in almost every aspect of military efforts. The adjustment process was most visible in the US. The US defence industry went in for a massive drive toward concentration, primarily through merger and acquisition (M&As) among defence manufacturers. It also adopted diversification strategies where many defence-dependent companies entered the civil market while quite a few became defence-dependent. Structural and other restructuring processes resulted in the emergence of a few giant defence manufacturers while many medium-sized and small units either merged with their bigger counterparts or were wiped out from the defence market altogether. What is most striking is the fact that many of the companies, that were earlier concentrated within the US, went beyond national boundaries to forge partnerships of different types, either in order to expand their business activities so as to grow further in the competitive defence business or just to survive in the contemporary market.

Although slower to follow suit in comparison to its US counterparts, the European defence industry also witnessed significant changes during the whole of 1990s and beyond. Both vertical and horizontal concentration efforts witnessed in the US defence industry were also witnessed in the European defence industry, which has been otherwise struggling with issues like structural and institutional processes related to the European Union, greater transatlantic military-industrial cooperation, formation of a single European defence industry and a common security and defence policy (known as ESDP).

However, sometime during the late 1990s, the available indicators started suggesting a different trend. Military spending started looking up again. The near decade-long peace dividend paved way for renewed efforts toward military modernization, force restructuring and military production. Evidence suggests that from roughly 1997–1998 onward, the decreasing trends slowed down fast and were consequently translated into a real term increase in a span of just a few years. This is attributed primarily due to renewed military efforts by the US, the impact of which has been felt the world over.

The chapter tries to explain some of the major challenges faced by the defence industry in the era of globalization and assesses the kind of impact it entails for the Indian defence industry. The chapter argues that relative consolidation, diversification and internationalization efforts witnessed in the defence industry during the whole of the 1990s were likely to continue well into the future, which in turn demands corresponding responses to such challenges from major arms producers. It further argues that a high degree of consolidation efforts by the US defence industry has also witnessed spill-over effects, especially in Europe, although the latter has been witnessing a slower pace of restructuring efforts. Such a scenario has prompted smaller producers like India to contemplate and undertake structural and policy related reforms in the defence industrial sector.

Part I

Theories of globalization and defence

2 Globalization and armed conflict among nations

Prospects through the lens of International Relations Theory

Brian M. Pollins

Introduction

While the effects of globalization appear to be wide reaching, should we expect them to have a significant impact on international security relations? Yes, most certainly we should. But just what are these effects likely to be? Here, the picture is less clear, for some of the shifts and trends engendered by the phenomenon of globalization can be expected to draw nations together, increase the costs of using armed force, and decrease the benefits of doing so. In short, certain aspects of globalization will have a pacifying effect in global politics. But other forces unleashed by economic globalization will increase tensions and fractious relations among states, while destabilizing political orders that themselves have pacifying effects, thereby increasing the prospects for armed conflict. Predicting the net effect of these positive and negative developments is most difficult.

The purpose of this opening chapter is to begin this very task, however difficult it may be to accomplish. The plan is to take an inventory. What do we know about the ways in which economic change affects security relations among nations? What are the most relevant aspects of globalization to study in order to understand its effect on security? How can our understanding of the political economy of security and likely economic trends allow us to envision possible, or even probable futures?

Subsequent sections of this chapter will take a first look at these questions. First, taking stock of theories in the field of International Relations, and sketching those that link aspects of economic growth, development, exchange and distribution to prospects for war and peace, the chapter will then look at those aspects of economic globalization that are most likely to affect the security domain. It will then offer an assessment of these economic trends in light of relevant International Relations Theory, and conclude with thoughts about our future prospects for conflict and peace.

Economics, armed conflict and war

The field of International Relations has been centrally concerned with questions of security throughout its history. Through much of the twentieth century, the field was dominated by a school known as Realists, who viewed international insecurity as resulting from the clash of nations with competing interests and varying capabilities in an environment of essential anarchy (given that there was no higher authority or effective means of enforcing peace between sovereign nations). Among the central theorists of this school – people like Hans Morgenthau, Raymond Aron, Hedley Bull and others – interest in economic production and growth was very limited to how a nation's economy could underpin its capacity to make war. Consideration of economic exchange as a determinant either of national power or of national interest was virtually absent. Despite the dominance of the school, a surprising number of scholars developed a rich and diverse body of theory which can shed light on the ways in which economic life can and often does have significant effects on security relations.

This section will briefly sketch a number of these theories, placed, for convenience, into three groups. The first set considers how characteristics or trends within a national economy affect the interests and capabilities of the state. The second group looks to a comparison of the economic characteristics of two states, or to the economic ties between them to explain their security relations. And the third set considers characteristics of the global economic system as an important force shaping the security relations among nations. Accordingly, these three levels of groups – the nation, the dyad, and the system – will be considered in order to see what each says about the influence of economic factors and trends on international security relations.

The nation

This is the level at which Realist scholars come closest to suggesting that economics matters to security. Very simply, Morgenthau and others discuss how the size and level of technological development of a nation's economy undergirds its war-making potential. The larger and more advanced a nation's economy is, the more effective that state is likely to be in war. The economy is a central pillar in the state's capability, and becomes even more important in more protracted conflicts when military assets at the onset of conflict will need to be replaced as they are lost in battle. But in the writings of these most mainstream realist scholars, there is nothing beyond this notion of capabilities – no sense that economic characteristics might somehow shape the state's diplomatic or strategic objectives. The "war chest" hypothesis of Geoffrey Blainey is one exception to this rule. Blainey felt that growing nations would tend to spend more on their military as time went by, and that such growth in their war fighting capability would come to create a mind-set that encouraged leaders to use the men and arms they had accumulated. So as the nation's war chest grew in size, it would be increasingly likely that the state would become involved in armed conflict.[1]

A much more fully articulated theory of the relationship between national economic growth and the propensity for armed conflict is offered by the theory of Lateral Pressure.[2] Choucri and North focus explicitly on national growth in three factors: population, resource usage, and technological development. They argue that as each or all of these factors grow, the propensity of society to expand its activities beyond its own borders also grows. At the same time, its capability to expand such activities also increases. Such increased activity abroad does not necessarily entail conflict with other nations (some needs of a growing society might be met through trade, investment or other cooperative activity) but there is always the possibility for the interests and activities of growing nations to come into direct conflict. Rivalries, arms races and crises can ensue. Even trade is not always peaceful. Growing commercial relations can also contain the seeds of armed conflict, as they did for the British and Dutch in the eighteenth century, or for Japan and the United States in the 1930s. For Choucri and North, then, economic factors are quite central to international security relations. Growth in population, resource use and technology, in their view, actually drive nations to interact with one another. Scarce resources and the need for market outlets make it likely that these interactions are competitive. And when such competition becomes heated, nations find that the very same dynamics that motivate their behavior also provide them with the materials to engage in armed conflict. National economic growth does not make armed conflict inevitable, but it does create a dangerously combustible mixture all around.

If economic growth can be dangerous, so can economic stagnation and recession.[3] Diversionary War Theory states that hard economic times can create public discontent for the government. The regime's hold on power may become threatened if the downturn in the economy is particularly severe or protracted. At such times, governments may provoke an armed crisis with a convenient rival in order to engender a "rally 'round the flag" effect in their mass public.[4] The ruling generals in Argentina in 1982, for example, provoked a crisis with Great Britain in order to shore up their eroding support at home. Of course it is not inevitable that governments will resort to this tactic, and recent work has been able to pin down the more limited circumstances under which governments are likely to adopt this destructive strategy. But the point remains that under particular circumstances, economic recession can also impel national leaders to undertake dangerous initiatives.

The dyad

Perhaps it is not growth in any particular, single nation that creates sources of conflict, but the *relative* growth of two or more nations. Or perhaps the economic ties between nations, like trade or colonialism, affect their chances for an armed clash? Such questions are addressed by theorists who employ the dyadic level of analysis.

Perhaps closest to classical Realist thought in this area would be Power Transition Theory as articulated by A.F.K. Organski and his student Jacek Kugler.[5] An independently developed but parallel argument is found in Robert Gilpin's *War and Change*.[6] Power Transition Theory concentrates exclusively on great powers, and seeks to understand the roots of major power war.

Economic growth in the leading power and in its largest, rising challenger turns out to be the key. Interests between these two top rivals are certain to clash, for one supports the status quo, while the other seeks to change the existing order in ways that reflect its rising status. As the economic and military gap between them narrows, the system leader feels growing pressure to contain or defeat the rising power. Security relations between them become increasingly tense and volatile and often result in war. Once again, economic growth is a chief, driving source of conflict, though Power Transition Theory tells us we must look at growth in two specific major powers to assess the global security situation.

Another interesting and more detailed treatment of these dynamics is offered by Charles Doran's Power Cycle Theory. Just as the Power Transition school does, Doran looks to the major power subsystem. But here the full set of major powers comes into play, not just the top two rivals. Doran shows that the *share* of all major power capabilities held by any one state over time always follows a cyclic pattern, rising and falling at regular, identifiable rates. The amplitude and periodicity of these cycles can differ from one great power to another, but we can always identify the pattern followed. Importantly, identification of this cycle for any particular power allows us to see those times when the power trajectory of that nation diverges most widely from the trajectory that leaders believe themselves to be on. It is in these periods of divergence that a nation is most likely to become involved in military conflict, Doran shows.[7] It is then that leaders are most likely to misperceive their situation, or to sense that their situation is changing markedly and requires drastic action to rectify. Transitional moments in the power cycle (and the term "moment" can be understood here in its mathematical as well as in its historical sense) is when armed conflict is most likely. According to Power Cycle Theory, differences in economic growth rates among all major powers is the factor introducing both dynamism and danger into global security relations.

Finally, bilateral or multilateral economic ties between nations may affect the likelihood of conflict between them.[8] It has long been an aphorism among liberal economists that "trade brings peace," and there is a large body of both theoretical and empirical research that supports this claim.[9] However, economic ties can also at times be exploitive, and thus conflict-generating. Or security concerns may arise when a country feels itself becoming too dependent on a particular partner (as President Bush expressed recently concerning dependence on Middle East oil). Research by Katherine Barbieri indicates that, in the main, bilateral trade ties are more conflict-generating than they are conflict-inhibiting as the liberals claim.[10] And because peace between two nations leads them to trade more with each other, it is entirely possible that the two correlate simply because peace brings trade, not because trade brings peace.[11] Recently published empirical work supports this very suspicion.[12] It seems that trade still follows the flag. This does, however underscore the point that security relations and international commerce remain intertwined in myriad ways that we should continue to explore.

The system

It may well be that the global economic and security systems are more than just the sum of actions taken by individual nations, or even more than the networks of bilateral and multilateral relations suggested by patterns of international trade, investment, alliances, etc. Theories at the systemic level of analysis suggest that the elements and relationships discussed above are part of larger, truly systemic phenomena, and that factors found at the systemic level must be examined if we are properly to understand prospects for conflict and peace. Two distinct but related theories are of particular importance for our present purposes: the theory of the Long Wave and the theory of the Leadership Cycle.

The theory of the Long Wave, first put forward by Russian economist Nikolai Kondratiev in the 1920s, claims that there are regular and repeated rhythms in global investment, production and prices. While not in lock step, each has a periodicity of roughly 50 years. Joshua Goldstein (1988) looked closely at these economic long waves for the period 1495–1980 and found them to be strongly associated with the size of wars among major powers. That is, very large wars among the largest powers occurred in synchrony with economic long waves. This led Goldstein to argue that periods of growth in the global economy led nations to build capabilities while also increasing both their friendly and their competitive interactions. Rising competition in the economic and security domains, coupled with rising military capabilities culminated, Goldstein claimed, in a system-wide war in which all major powers participated. Such conflagrations clearly affected the global economy – the occurrence of these great wars coincides with the price peak in the Kondratiev long wave, to mention but one clear consequence. So, there is an important reciprocal relationship between security and economy at the global level. Economic growth engenders conflict while large wars spur production, innovation and price inflation.

The theory of the Leadership Cycle tells a similar story. The authors of this theory, George Modelski and William R. Thompson, look primarily at the structure of the global political system. Specifically, they note that a single, pre-eminent power emerges roughly once every 100 years. This system leader holds a preponderance of key military capabilities (chiefly blue-water sea power, they argue) while also boasting the lead economy in terms of size and innovative energy. Regular rhythms in the global economy are related to the rise of this leading state. Just as importantly, key economic trends and the prospects for peace and war are found to be associated with the rise, ascendancy and decline of one system leader, and the struggle to produce the next one. The work by Modelski and Thompson (1996) shows a very strong association between pairs of 50-year long Kondratiev waves with the 100-year long Leadership Cycle. Waves of technological innovation ("leading sectors" in the global economy) are very much connected to the rise and decline of global political systems dominated by a hegemonic state.

As system level theories, Goldstein's Long Wave and the Modelski–Thompson Leadership Cycle do not tell us precisely who is likely to become embroiled in conflict. But they do describe in some detail the conditions in the global economy and in the global political system which lead us to expect large wars among major powers. Pollins builds upon and extends their findings beyond the major powers. Explicit connections between the Long Wave and the Leadership Cycle are established, and the joint effect of these two macro-processes correlate with the frequency of armed conflict among all nations, not just major powers. And by taking account of the effects of both the Long Wave and the Leadership Cycle, we find that lower levels of armed conflict (like crises and armed clashes) also correlate with their rhythms. Other forms of security-related behavior (e.g. alliance formation, colonial expansion) are also correlated with the Long Wave and the Leadership Cycle.[13] For our present purpose, what is most important in all this work is that there seems to be a clear association between specific conditions in the global economy and the system-wide prospects for war and peace.

There may also be important linkages across these three levels of analysis, since they obviously do not operate in isolation from one another. Global economic growth is likely to be associated with growth in some or all of the major powers in the system. This should generate effects in the behavior of individual powers, or in the patterns of interaction between them. One study[14] tries explicitly to link the various dynamics at national and systemic levels by looking at patterns for the US economy, US involvement in foreign conflicts, and the Long Wave put forward by Goldstein. Pollins and Schweller show that regular periods of expansionism and isolationism in US foreign policy coincide very strongly with periods of the Long Wave. This goes back to the founding of the US republic in 1789, long before the United States was a leading economy. Further, they find that US involvement in foreign clashes is more likely as the US economy grows, and that the probability that the US will become involved in armed conflicts reaches its peak shortly before downturns in the Long Wave.

Thus, when this large body of research is considered together, we have strong reason to believe that economic conditions within nations, differential growth between them, the economic ties they create, and economic trends in the overall global economy all have an impact on the security relations of nations. These relationships are complex, and there is a great deal we do not understand. But the work just discussed offers several clues about how changing economic conditions and new economic ties might make the world either a more peaceful or a more dangerous place. What, then, are the key changes and trends that we can expect to result from the phenomenon on globalization?

Globalization and shifts in economic life

Some observers consider current economic globalization to be an utterly unprecedented phenomenon in world history.[15] Others scoff at such characterizations and point to an earlier period when global interconnectedness was even greater than today.[16] The truth, as always, lies in between two extreme positions. Some key shifts, while not unprecedented, are significant nonetheless, while other, truly novel developments will indeed make the world of 2020 look importantly different from the world we know today. The changes that are most relevant and important to the prospects for conflict and peace form two groups – *new players* and *new forms of interconnectedness*.

"New players" refers to the fact that national economies will be less central to the organization of global economic life than they were in the twentieth century. The rise of non-state actors in the world economy like inter-governmental organizations (IGOs), non-governmental organizations (NGOs), and the "electronic herd" will create new players in the security arena. Just as importantly, globalization will redistribute economic assets and capabilities within the state system itself. New powers are rising while others fade, and some fear being left behind altogether. Such changes in the capabilities and interests of states have always been a source of dynamism in the politics of international security.

"New forms of interconnectedness" refers to the novel aspects of economic interdependence that distinguish this period of globalization from previous eras in which the global economy was highly integrated. Several scholars in the Realist camp, like Kenneth Waltz or his student John Mearsheimer[17] point to the period 1870–1914 as one during which levels of trade and investment were extraordinarily high, yet world peace did not ensue. Thus, they argue, we should not believe the contemporary liberal line that growing economic interdependence will result in more peaceful relations among nations. While this point deserves to be heeded, we should not infer (as far too many Realists do) that economic interdependence is irrelevant to security relations. This would be profoundly wrong in two ways. First, there are features of contemporary globalization that *are* truly novel and of unprecedented significance. These include the transnational reorganization of production, the content of trade flows and the dispersion of global capital centers. Second, while interdependence will not ensure peace as the liberals dream it will, it can and does have an effect on state interests that can be conflict-limiting in the right circumstances. We need to know just what these circumstances are. So let us look at these shifts in players and the forms of interconnectedness in closer detail.

New players

Economic globalization has dramatically increased the access of many nations to investment capital and innovative technologies. It is no surprise that such access has not been shared equally, nor is it a shock to discover that it offers great opportunities for some and dangers for others. Most centrally, the trends it has engendered are reshaping the distribution of state interests and state capabilities. Nothing could be more central to any forecast of future prospects for conflict and peace. "Miracle" stories from Korea to Ireland are easy to find. Others, from Botswana to Bolivia, have been left behind thus far. The rise of so-called "Big Emerging Markets" may be most significant from a security perspective, for it is these nations – including China, India, Indonesia, Brazil, and Mexico – that have the clear potential to become significant regional powers in the near term, or even global powers in the longer run. As they rise to that status, we should expect their interests to become more outward looking, following the pattern set by all countries which have occupied such positions in the past. And their capabilities to secure those interests will rise as well. Thus, for even the most traditional, Realist scholar, the effects of globalization on security in the state system should not be underestimated.

Neither should we ignore the significance of globalization for non-state actors. Multinational corporations have been a part of global economic life for centuries, but they have never been so large in number or in the resources they command and move around the globe. Their activities – in pursuit of their own interests, let us not forget – can both impel and enable nations toward more peaceful relations in some circumstances and toward conflict in others. Easy access to capital and technology is also empowering non-governmental organizations (NGOs) from Food for Peace to The Open Society Institute to Al Qaeda.

Domestic business interests now often meld with international business into what Thomas Friedman[18] has termed the "electronic herd." This bottom-up, emergent group can shape and constrain state actions on everything including commercial policy, investment policy, as well as security policy (namely Friedman's "Golden Arches" theory of conflict). Friedman is surely over-estimating the effect that market agents may have on security relations. But he is right to point them out, and we should do a better job of mapping just what these effects are, for they are surely there.

Finally, it is clear that rising economic interdependence provides a powerful impetus to the formation and strengthening of inter-governmental organizations (IGOs). Market forces desire openness, the recognition of property rights and the rule of law. This interest meets the interest of states for increased access to investment capital and technology. The result is an increase in the number of international institutions that seek to provide precisely these things. Such institutions include the WTO, the IMF and IBRD, the International Patent Rights Organization, a rising number of regional trade organizations (e.g. ASEAN, NAFTA, Mercosur) and many others. The number of such organizations is now orders of magnitude larger than at any time in history. And the enforcement powers of a number of these institutions is also rising. Interestingly, a number of trade agreements among developing nations now explicitly include exactly the same kinds of security provisions that we are used to seeing in military alliances and non-aggression pacts.[19]

New forms of interconnectedness

The volume of international trade and international capital flows has risen over the past 30 years at a truly amazing rate. But as many have pointed out, this may seem new to our time but it is not unprecedented historically. If those earlier "globalized" worlds dissolved into state dominated competitions of all-against-all, then there is no reason to expect the current period of globalization to be transformative in international security relations. While disintegration of today's global economy is certainly possible, its impact on security relations will indeed be transformative and therefore must not be dismissed. The key is to look not at what is similar about the current period of globalization and previous periods, but to identify and focus on those aspects that are different. On this count, two key features of our current period are unprecedented: the reorganization of production and the changing location of capital and technology.

The volume of capital flowing across national borders in the 1990s was broadly comparable to that witnessed during the earlier period of globalization, 1870–1914.[20] But in the pre-World War I era, the overwhelming share of transnational capital took the form of *portfolio* investment, while today the greater share of capital flows is *foreign direct investment* (FDI). Put very simply, the difference is between owning shares in a company or being an officer in that company. In the former case, one has an arm's length, partial ownership of the enterprise, and in the latter case, one is running the business. The implications of this difference are several, but the most important is that companies have already transformed their production processes so that many everyday items – from cars to computers – contain components manufactured in several countries. Importantly, these sub-components are manufactured by divisions of a single company owning factories in many countries. In other words, the production line making this car or that computer is owned and operated by one company, but it stretches across countries and even across continents.

The globalization of production is unprecedented, and it certainly deepens the connections among national economies in ways we are just beginning to understand. We do know, for example, that 30–50 percent of all "international" trade today is actually made up of component transfers from one factory within a given company to another of its operations in a different country. International trade is often no longer the arms-length exchange between independent entities based in sovereign national markets as it was in David Ricardo's time. The security implications of such interdependence is understood even less, although Stephen Brooks provides an admirable first look.[21] Brooks argues that the effects of globalized production should deepen peaceful relations among advanced, market economies. But he is more pessimistic about its effects in the developing world and sees mixed effects for relations between North and South.

In addition to the transformation of production, there are changes in capital markets themselves and in the production and diffusion of technology. In earlier periods of globalization and unipolarity, one nation served as the world's main capital exporter and chief technological innovator.[22] Modern advances in information processing and communication have coupled with transnational business interests to decentralize both in ways we have not seen before. The mobility of capital today greatly reduces the necessity of physical proximity for bankers, insurers, financiers. In some ways, it even militates against concentration (capital flows away from attempts to control it). Major banking centers are no longer found only in the financial capitals of the largest economies and the most technologically advanced nations. Historically, we find them in cities like Amsterdam, London, New York, and in more recent times in Frankfurt or

Tokyo. Today, they are also located in capitals of emerging nations like Brazil, as well as in nations with huge capital account surpluses like the United Arab Emirates, as well as in off-shore havens like the Cayman Islands.

As for technological innovation, past history exhibited a pattern in which most new technologies would tend to appear first in a single, leading nation and then disperse throughout the international system over a period of decades. But with unprecedented flows of FDI and transnational production, companies are locating major R&D activities in a much wider range of locations. Talented scientists and engineers are not found only in Western Europe, Japan and the United States. And sophisticated workers and consumers are found in many emerging as well as advanced markets. Thus the location of innovative activity, and the benefits which ensue from its production and use, are enjoyed in a wider array of nations than we have seen in previous periods of globalization. The possible implications of this dispersion of capital and technology for security will be examined later. For now it is enough to say that control of investment capital and new technology correlated historically with power, and in the past such power was concentrated in the hands of a very few nations (or even just one nation). No more. By no means do capital and technology flow across national borders with complete freedom. Far from it. But their ease of movement is greater, and their likelihood of concentrating inside the borders of a single country or region is less than ever before.

The importance of these shifts and trends especially for relations between the developed and developing worlds needs to be emphasized. The technological advances and economic shifts that we lump under the heading of "globalization" all serve to connect a larger portion of the world's population to modern rather than traditional sectors of the economy. This is unprecedented. This means that the South is less dependent on the North for economic growth than in the past. Indeed, it is now widely accepted that it was Third World economic growth, not growth in the then-moribund North that led the world out of recession in the early 1990s. This is certainly unprecedented. And notwithstanding financial crises such as Asia experienced in the late 1990s, or the normal dips and swings of the Business cycle, big emerging market economies (BEMs) like China, Brazil, Indonesia and others will be sizable and important players in the global economy by 2020. Indeed, all three *could* rank among the world's ten largest economies by that time. The hierarchy that has characterized the global economy for several centuries, and the associated top-down, bottom-up cycling of wealth and power appear to be fading away.

Mapping new economic trends onto theories of conflict and war

If we employ International Relations Theory to evaluate the important economic shifts brought about by globalization, should we be optimistic or pessimistic about the consequent prospects for peace in the twenty-first century? Simply put, we can expect important changes at every level. The security behavior of various state and non-state actors will be greatly affected. So too will the security relations between them. Finally, the global security system itself might well experience the greatest change of all. Let us consider each level more closely.

Globalization and the security behavior of players old and new

Globalization is clearly bringing additional efficiencies into the economies of very many nations, and growth is thereby enhanced. But, as is always the case, the costs and benefits of such change are not shared equally. So some national economies grow and develop more rapidly while others may stagnate or decline. New demands are created for food, energy, and consumer goods as well as basic needs like health care, housing and education. Living standards improve for many, but not for all. And the revolution in global communications provides everyone with unprecedented information on exactly who the haves and have-nots are, and how the gaps between them – whether imagined or real – may be widening.

Viewing these developments through the lens of International Relations Theory presents a worrisome picture. The traditional Realists among us will note that new, rising powers must be expected to challenge the status quo in the global political order. Growing war chests, especially among larger, emerging economies and regional powers, suggest we should not expect such challenges to remain solely in the realm of diplomacy. Jockeying for position in the international system has given rise to armed conflict in the past, and Realists will see no reason why this should be any different in the future.

Lateral Pressure theorists will also be concerned about such developments. Growth in population and technology will bring rising demands for resources. Nations will reach increasingly beyond their own boundaries to secure those needs. Their interests will sometimes conflict with others, and they will find their capability for engaging others in the system similarly increased. Their capacity for foreign engagement will involve non-military as well as military assets, so armed conflict is by no means inevitable. But rising needs and capabilities among nations do contain the seeds not only of competition, but of rivalry and war as well.

Prospects for economic stagnation and decline, as well as widening gaps between rich and poor, must add to the pessimism of this part of our assessment. During economic downturns, most nations refrain from armed conflict if only because the costs of military action cannot be borne in such times. But there are specific circumstances in which more desperate leaders will resort to diversionary conflicts in their attempt to hold on to power.

Non-state actors will play a larger role in the future than they have in the past, though the net effects of their growing number and participation in world politics must be studied further. The forces of globalization alone provide an impetus for the creation of new IGOs and NGOs. We can be confident that their numbers will proliferate simply because states are not the most effective organizations to manage the inherently transnational forces and problems that globalization brings. Intergovernmental organizations will often provide a forum and means to manage shared interests and resolve conflicts before they escalate to dangerous levels. But some IGOs serve to aggregate the interests and capabilities of particular groups whose objectives are not shared by all – NATO and OPEC are two examples – and thus the mere rise in the number of IGOs alone will not be sufficient to guarantee a more peaceful world. Similarly, the growth in number and resources controlled by NGOs does not point in a single direction toward conflict or peace. Many NGOs serve to satisfy basic needs in food, housing, health care or education, others work to relieve injustices aggravated by uneven economic development or war. As such, we can expect them to have a palliative effect and to decrease chances of conflict. But even when engaged in such humanitarian missions, their effect is not always pacific. NATO's involvement in the Balkan Wars of the 1990s raised concerns among some regarding a possible underlying Western, imperial agenda. And no small amount of firepower was unleashed by NATO members in their efforts to protect the vulnerable peoples of Serbia, Croatia and Bosnia. Hamas, to offer a second example, has worked to relieve suffering of many of the neediest in Palestine. But the same organization has also undertaken operations that lead many to label them as terrorists, and some of their central, stated objectives are anathema to many powerful states. Globalization increases the need for, and resources available to, Médecins sans Frontières. But it also empowers Al Qaeda. It simply is not clear that the rising numbers, activities and capabilities of IGOs and NGOs will lead us to peace rather than conflict.

Globalization and security relations among the players

The central and most significant aspect of globalization is that it ties national economies together more extensively than ever before, and in qualitatively new ways. This shift is so great that it leads some to question whether national economies can any longer be considered meaningful.[23] Even if such assessments are overblown, the networks of transnational production and finance in operation today are quite extensive, and they continue to grow, diversify and deepen. It is very difficult for all who watch these trends closely to accept the standard Realist claim that there is nothing really new here, and we should expect only more of the same as far as security relations are concerned. But if we reject this simple assessment, what then should we expect?

International Relations Theory is slightly more hopeful when considering economic relations among nations and their likely effect on conflict. When exchange benefits both parties, anything which threatens to interrupt that exchange – such as armed conflict – will be resisted.[24] Therefore, trade or any other form of mutually beneficial exchange will create "vested interests for peace" among those groups in society who benefit from this activity.[25] As described above, a large body of empirical work supports this claim.[26] With the volume of international economic exchanges rising so rapidly, there should be a growing number of groups within societies around the world who agitate against resort to armed force when disputes arise between their homeland and that of their exchange partner.

But we would be overly optimistic if we believed that this effect is universal, or if we believed such interests would trump all others when disputes arise. Brooks admirably details how the liberal claim that "trade brings peace" is bounded and limited.[27] Barbieri shows how trade may be conflict-generating when asymmetries create a dependency that is resented and resisted. Hegre presents solid evidence that the palliative effect of trade on conflict is limited to advanced, industrial nations.[28] In fact, he finds that trade may be conflict-generating among Lesser Developed Countries (LDCs). In both claims, he supports the findings of Brooks as well as Barbieri, not those of Russett and Oneal.

We should also note that the impetus for the creation and deepening of IGOs that is engendered by globalization could reinforce the pacifying effects of economic exchange. Russett and Oneal show that shared membership in IGOs reduces the likelihood of members to resort to force against one another. Mansfield and Pevehouse similarly show that shared membership in Preferential Trade Arrangements (PTAs) makes armed conflict less likely between co-signatories.[29] Powers, moreover, finds that PTAs created among developing nations are incorporating explicit security guarantees. These will hopefully make armed conflict in some Third World areas less likely.[30]

Taken together, these claims and findings suggest that the forces of globalization might reinforce the reluctance to use force among advanced, developed nations. At the same time, there is some reason for hope, but significant grounds for scepticism, that greater integration of national economies will bring peace in relations among developing nations, or between states in the rich North and the less affluent South.

Globalization and the international security system

Theories of the Long Wave and the Leadership Cycle bring us to the most speculative thoughts in this chapter, but also possibly to the most hopeful. Goldstein as well as Modelski and Thompson consider the political and economic systems they describe to be evolutionary in nature.[31] At what point does change in degree become change in kind? The cycles described by these scholars contain great change within them. There are periods of rapid and widespread growth, and times of wrenching economic depression. Leading technological sectors come and go, as do those nations whom we recognize as great powers and system leaders. Still, they show us, the same basic patterns repeat. Destructive and deadly practices like major power war occur with disturbing regularity even if the identity of those powers may change over the centuries along with the technologies they employ to battle one another. Might we not expect more of the same in the century to come?

The central role played by the hegemon in these theories, especially that of the Leadership Cycle, and by what globalization may mean for the nature of hegemony is certainly intriguing. During the hegemon's ascendance, the international system enjoys a period of relative peace (though the word "relative" must be underscored). The even darker side of the same coin, however, is that the biggest and bloodiest wars result from the struggle within the system to decide new leadership roughly once every century. If this is our future, then it is a grim one indeed. But consider the economic bases of past hegemonies, and compare those patterns to contemporary forces of globalization.

Over the past 500 years, periods of hegemonic ascendance were marked by a concentration in economic and military capability in the hands of a single, leading state.[32] The hegemon held not only a larger share of long range, power projection capability, that same state was the world's largest single market, the world's chief exporter of investment capital, and its fountainhead of innovation. That high concentration of economic assets provided a solid foundation for its military power in two ways. First, concentration afforded the possibility of imposing quasi-monopoly rents for access to its markets and its capital, and because technological leadership guaranteed market advantages for its products and manufacturing processes. Second, it provided political leverage in negotiations when it chose to forego those advantages with particular exchange partners.

Globalization, as we saw in the previous section, is working directly against the concentration of these very assets into the hands of any single actor or even small group of actors. With that deconcentration of economic assets could come a deconcentration of political power. Trade relations are less hierarchical today and the content of trade flows is more diversified than ever before. Capital centers have dispersed, as have centers of innovation. Capital mobility is very high, and technology diffuses more rapidly to multiple points in the global economy. To be sure, the United States enjoys a preponderance of military capability to match or surpass any previous hegemon.[33] But one wonders whether the special character of nuclear weapons, and the disturbing trend for such weapons to continue to proliferate, will act to check American power in ways not faced by earlier hegemons. And whether they do or not, it seems clear that the United States will not enjoy all the political and economic advantages of earlier system leaders, for the bases of economic dominance are becoming too diffuse for one nation to consolidate and hold such power. It is globalization that is bringing this about.

Does all this portend the end of hegemony? That is very difficult to say. But given that the largest wars of the past five centuries were connected to the struggle to determine a new system leader, then the end of this process, brought about by the considerable, decentralizing forces of globalization, could be a very hopeful development.

Conclusion: a more pacific or a more violent world?

Clearly, the consequences of economic globalization wash through the international system in numerous currents, rivulets and eddies, and they are changing the shape of the global political landscape as they flow. In some ways, globalization is strengthening the chances of peace, in others it pulls some states and non-state actors toward grievance, rivalry and war. On balance, can we say whether globalization is, or is not, a force for peace?

The field of International Relations is very far from having all the answers, but we saw there is a great deal of work that shows how upward or downward swings in production, exchange and distribution of economic values impels nations and other actors toward or away from war. Surveying these theories, we see that the key variables pertain to economic growth and stagnation, and how such growth is distributed among the world's nations; whether interdependence is rising, and whether those new connections are symmetric or asymmetric; and what the system-wide rhythms of growth and stagnation, including all this, portends for the production and reproduction of a hegemonic state standing above all others in world politics.

We can also see broad outlines of the changes in economic life being brought upon us by globalization. The finer points of this story will no doubt be important, but the complexity of these processes leaves such details obscure. Nevertheless, the larger trends alone allow us to develop expectations about the prospects for conflict and peace, even while they point us toward the areas most in need of additional research.

It is clear that economic growth has been and will continue to be surprisingly high for some actors, while others are left well behind. Such patterns of growth are danger signals to Realists who subscribe to Blainey's notion of rising war chests and the growing motivation it brings to employ armed force. Lateral Pressure Theory also cautions us to expect greater international competition as a result of such growth. To the extent that these patterns impact the sub-system of major powers (i.e. by changing the membership of that subsystem or the distribution of capabilities among its members) scholars within the Power Transition and Power Cycle traditions will also raise storm warnings. Are the fast-growers spending more on their militaries and other capabilities (shipping, finance) which enhance their capability to expand? Do we see evidence of growing confidence, if not hubris, regarding themselves and their foreign interests? New research on these questions should be undertaken to see whether the cautionary predictions of these theories appear to be correct or not.

A dramatic rise in the forms and levels of economic interdependence is another distinct feature of globalization that is very likely to continue for the foreseeable future. This will surely alter the motivations of some groups within some nations to steer their political decision makers toward cooperation with their exchange partners and away from the military option when disputes arise. In ways less well understood (though evidence for them is found in numerous empirical studies) growing interdependence will generate grievances and competition, especially among developing nations. Globalization also encourages formation of preferential trade agreements and other forms of international organization. While our knowledge of their effects is limited, the evidence that has been gathered to date suggests that such associations may, on balance, be a force for peace. Additional research is needed to understand the mechanisms whereby interdependence discourages the resort to force in some circumstances, but exacerbates conflict in others. Knowing macro-tendencies alone is not enough, for the evidence is clear that the relationship between interdependence and conflict can cut both ways. We need to know when and why. In addition, far too little is understood about the ways in which intergovernmental organizations might reinforce or complement the effects of economic ties on conflict.

Finally, it is most reasonable to assume that the global economy will grow at an uneven rate over time. ("It will fluctuate" is the ready answer of every stock-broker asked to predict the future course of the market.) It is less certain whether global growth will fluctuate with the regular rhythms identified by Kondratiev and others, and whether cycles of innovation, investment, production and prices continue to be tied to the rise and fall of an economic and militarily pre-eminent system leader. Because globalization disperses the control of capital, technology and markets as never before, it remains to be seen whether a single state can establish and maintain dominance in the global system on the basis of military might alone. More important for the prospects for peace, we need to know whether the presence of such a hegemon will again provoke the bellicose challenges to its dominance, the competitive arms build-ups and the formation of freshly armed counter-coalitions – for these are the very things which stirred and brewed into systemic war once in every century for the past 500 years. Answers to these questions will be most important to understanding the prospects for human survival, not least in Asia.

Notes

1 Blainey, Geoffrey. 1988. *The Causes of War*. 3rd edn. New York: The Free Press.
2 Choucri, Nazli and Robert C. North. 1975. *Nations in Conflict: National Growth and International Violence*. San Francisco: W.H. Freeman.
3 Russett, Bruce M. 1990. "Economic Decline, Electoral Pressure, and the Initiation of Interstate Conflict." In *Prisoners of War? Nation States in the Modern Era*, edited by Charles S. Gochman and Alan Ned Sabrosky. Lexington, MA: Lexington Books, pp. 123–140.
4 Levy, Jack. 1989. "The Diversionary Theory of War: A Critique." In *Handbook of War Studies*, edited by Manus I. Midlarsky. Boston: Unwin Hyman, pp. 259–288.
5 Organski, A.F.K. 1958. *World Politics*. New York: Basic Books; Organski, A.F.K. and Jacek Kugler. 1983. *The War Ledger*. Chicago: University of Chicago Press.
6 Gilpin, Robert. 1981 *War and Change in World Politics*. Cambridge: Cambridge University Press.
7 Doran, Charles, and Wes Parsons. 1980. War and the Cycle of Relative Power. *American Political Science Review*, 74, pp. 947–965.
8 Mansfield, Edward D. and Brian M. Pollins. 2001. "The Study of Interdependence and Conflict: Recent Advances, Open Questions, and Directions for Future Research", *Journal of Conflict Resolution*, 45, no. 6, December, pp. 834–859.
9 Polacek, Solomon W. 1980. "Conflict and Trade." *Journal of Conflict Resolution*, 24: pp. 55–78.
10 Barbieri, Katherine. 2002. *The Liberal Illusion: Does Trade Promote Peace?* Ann Arbor, MI: University of Michigan Press.
11 Pollins, Brian M. 1996. "Global Political Order, Economic Change and Armed

Conflict: Coevolving Systems and the Use of Force." *American Political Science Review*, 90, pp. 103–117.

12 Keshk, Omar M.G., Brian M. Pollins and Rafael Reuveny. 2004. "Trade Still Follows the Flag: The Primacy of Politics in a Simultaneous Model of Interdependence and Armed Conflict." *Journal of Politics*, 66 no. 4, pp. 1155–1179.

13 Pollins, Brian and Kevin Murrin. 1999. "Where Hobbes Meets Hobson: Core Conflict and Colonialism, 1495–1995." *International Studies Quarterly*, 43, pp. 427–454.

14 Pollins, Brian and Randall L. Schweller. 1999. "Linking the Levels: The Long Wave and Shifts in U.S. Foreign Policy, 1790–1993." *American Journal of Political Science*, 43, no. 2, April, pp. 431–464.

15 Ohmae, Kenichi. 2005. *The Next Global Stage: The Challenges and Opportunities in Our Borderless World*. Philadelphia: Wharton School Publishing.

16 Waltz, Kenneth. 1970. The Myth of National Interdependence. In *The International Corporation*, edited by Charles P. Kindleberger. Cambridge, MA: MIT Press; Waltz, Kenneth. 2000. "Globalization and American Power." *The National Interest*, Spring.

17 Mearsheimer, John J. 2001. *The Tragedy of Great Power Politics*. New York: Norton.

18 Friedman, Thomas L. 2000. *The Lexus and the Olive Tree: Understanding Globalization*. New York: Farrar, Strauss & Giroux.

19 Powers, Kathy L. 2006. "Alliance Obligations in Regional Trade Agreements and Dispute Initiation." *Journal of Peace Research*.

20 To make this comparison, volume is scaled as a share of total world production.

21 Brooks, Stephen G. 2005. *Producing Security: Multinational Corporations, Globalization, and the Changing Calculus of Conflict*. Princeton, NJ: Princeton University Press.

22 Modelski, George and William R. Thompson. 1996. *Leading Sectors and World Powers: The Coevolution of Global Politics and World Economics*. Columbia: University of South Carolina Press.

23 Wriston, Walter. 1992. *Twilight of Sovereignty: How the Information Revolution is Transforming our World*. New York: Charles Scribner's Sons.

24 Polacek, op. cit.

25 Arad, Ruth, Seev Hirsch and Alfred Tovias. 1983. *The Economics of Peacemaking: Focus on the Egyptian–Israeli Situation*. London: Macmillan for the Trade Policy Research Center.

26 Russet, Bruce M. and John R. Oneal. 2000. *Triangulating Peace: Democracy, Interdependence, and International Organizations*. New York: W.W. Norton.

27 Brooks, op. cit.

28 Barbieri, 2002, op. cit.; Hegre, Håvard. 2000. Development and the Liberal Peace: What Does it Take to be a Trading State? *Journal of Peace Research*, 37, pp. 5–30.

29 Russet and Oneal, op. cit.; Mansfield, Edward D. and Jon Pevehouse. 2000. "Trade Blocs, Trade Flows, and International Conflict." *International Organization*, 54, pp. 775–808.

30 Powers, op. cit.

31 Goldstein, Joshua S. 1988. *Long Cycles: Prosperity and War in the Modern Age*. New Haven, CT: Yale University Press.

32 Modelski and Thompson, op. cit.; Wallerstein, Immanuel. 1984. "Long Waves as a Capitalist Process." *Review*, 7: 559–575.

33 Wohlforth, William C. And Stephen G. Brooks. 2002. "American Primacy in Perspective." *Foreign Affairs*, 81, pp. 20–33.

3   Beyond interdependence

Globalization, state transformation and security

Christopher W. Hughes

Introduction: the globalization–security nexus

Globalization and national security vie for the status of the least well-conceptualized, most contested, but also most significant, of contemporary issues for academics and policy-makers. The interconnections between globalization and national security, arguably, have been even less well-studied and conceptualized to date. This is despite the growing sense of the importance of 'globalization's shadow'[1] or the negative effects of globalization on a variety of policy areas, and the readiness to ascribe problems of national insecurity to the onset of globalization. This sense of the seeming interconnection between globalization and national security has been enhanced post-September 11, with the talk of terrorist acts as some form of backlash against globalization, propelling the 'Clash of Civilizations', and the 'global reach' of terrorism. Nevertheless, it is perhaps fair to say that much of the discussion on globalization and security – in parallel fashion to much of the debate about globalization's impact on other policy issues – continues to struggle with the nebulousness of globalization as a concept. Globalization is always there, somehow lurking in the background of academic and policy analysis and explanation, and serves as a convenient phenomenon upon which to pin the origin of much of the world's ills and discontents. But this often indiscriminate attachment of insecurity to globalization can hinder more than help understanding of globalization's impact on national security.

Hence, globalization's potential complicity in the generation of international security clearly demands greater academic and policy investigation. For sure, there have been a number of initial studies that have attempted to link globalization with insecurity effects.[2] The objective of this chapter is to take these studies further and to offer a more integrated, but certainly not exhaustive, sampling and overview of what might be termed the 'globalization–security nexus'. This chapter seeks to argue that there is indeed an interconnection between globalization and security, and that globalization's impact on national security can certainly be highly corrosive. However, it argues that globalization's impact on security can perhaps most readily be elucidated by examining four inter-related themes.

First, this chapter seeks to investigate the actual concept and inherent qualities of globalization; for only by attempting to discover the very essence of globalization as a social force can its more amorphous and sometimes obfuscating aspects can be stripped away, and it then be rendered into a useful analytical lens that focuses our understanding on the potential linkages with national security. Specifically, a definition of globalization will be offered that includes, but is more than, economic interdependence, interconnectedness, liberalization and integration per se, and stresses the character of globalization as a phenomenon of trans-sovereign interaction. This therefore has fundamental implications for contemporary security structures founded upon national sovereignty. In short, globalization is not only a *quantitative* change in the degree of social and economic interaction on a global scale, but also, most importantly, a *qualitative* change in the nature of these flows amongst, and across, national boundaries, and in state capacities to respond to them.

Second, this chapter seeks to understand the interconnections between globalization defined in these ways and national security by looking more closely at the concept of security itself. Although the intention is, once again, not to rehearse all the definitional issues surrounding security, it is necessary to delve into this concept, and particularly the means by which security has traditionally been generated, in order to provide context for understanding the potential impact of the rise of globalization on national security. The fact that security has in large part been organized around the role of sovereign states in the modern era means that the key to understanding the analytical value-added of applying the term globalization to examining security is to appreciate its very ability to infiltrate and undermine the security prerogatives of sovereign states.

Third, this analysis will be taken forward by looking at where globalization's potential assault on state sovereignty may directly connect with the generation of specific security issues. Globalization's impact as a trans-sovereign phenomenon can be seen in: assisting the reactivation of a range of non-state actors as key rivals to sovereign state actors in the security realm; the exacerbation of the economic causes of traditional and non-traditional security issues, which in many cases feed off each other in the generation of political violence; and as impacting on the modes by which international conflict is played out.

Fourth, globalization may assist in understanding what might be termed as the 'geographies of national insecurity'. The argument is that globalization's essential nature is a trans-sovereign force, which helps to explain why it has a differential impact on different types of sovereign states in different regions, and thus why certain regions are more prone to globalization-linked insecurity. Those states and regions where sovereignty is weakest are those where globalization's impact as a potential force for instability is most strongly felt. Predictably, these regions are located in the developing and post-colonial world, where states faced with the task of acquiring sovereignty find this doubly difficult when pitted against the challenge of globalization.

Conceptualizing globalization

Internationalization, liberalization, universalization, Americanization

Globalization, as is well known, just like its counterpart security[3], is a notoriously 'slippery' concept and is subject to a wide variety of definitions. The most common understanding of globalization has perhaps been that of *internationalization*, implying the increasing density and interdependence of interaction amongst nation-states and their markets, or more accurately, given the common lack of congruence in many regions between state entities and their national populations, sovereign states. In turn, these increased flows of capital, personnel and knowledge in many cases exceed the process of internationalization, which essentially views states as moving closer together but remaining unchanged, and can produce a general lowering of state imposed barriers to the flow of economic forces, so giving rise to a process of *liberalization*, a second key definition of globalization.

A third prevalent definition of globalization is derived from the general notion of convergence in global economic, political, and social spheres of activity. The convergence thesis finds its most extreme form in the 'hyperglobalization' and 'end of history' literature.[4] This convergence thesis then feeds through into a definition of globalization that revolves around the *universalization* of standards of economic and social interaction; and indeed the Structural Adjustment Packages (SAP) advocated for many developing states by the international financial institutions (IFI) are a manifestation for many of this form of globalization. Globalization as universalization also gives rise to a fourth common and highly politicized definition relating to *Westernization* or *Americanization*. In line with this definition, the US is viewed as the principal power pushing for convergence of global economic standards that are essentially US standards and designed to reinforce US political and economic dominance. Globalization is thus used as a codeword for US hegemony or even empire. It is arguable that the conflation for some of globalization with Americanization has been an important driving force in anti-US feeling as in the case of September 11 terrorism.[5]

De-territorialization and the challenge to sovereignty

Internationalization, universalization, Americanization, and particularly liberalization as will be seen in later sections, are all key components of globalization. However, it is possible to conceive of globalization at a second, and perhaps higher, level, which can help to further elucidate its potential impact on international security. This is because the definitions already presented fail to capture fully the qualitatively different nature of globalization from other processes and phenomena associated with the interaction of social forces on a global scale. Globalization represents a qualitatively different process due to its essential de-territorialization, or stated in reverse, supra-territorialization of social interaction.[6] That is to say, globalization is a process which increasingly reconfigures social space away from, and beyond notions of, delineated territory, and *transcends* existing physical and human borders imposed upon social interaction. For instance, global financial transactions, facilitated by information technology, can now often operate without reference to physical territorial distance or human-imposed territorial barriers. Hence, globalization is a process facilitated by economic liberalization and new technologies, but it also goes beyond these in its functioning and outcomes. Once again, it is important to avoid the type of 'hyper-globalization' thesis which views the world as moving towards a condition of being totally 'borderless'.[7] For it is apparent that there is considerable territorial 'drag' upon the free-flow of globalization forces, that not all forms of economic interaction such as trade and labour migration are as fully globalized as finance, that there are wide disparities in the degree of globalization across different regions of the world. There is, moreover, both resistance to, and reversibility in, the process itself.[8] Nevertheless, globalization as a process of de-territorialization is increasingly affecting large sections of the world, and must be acknowledged as a markedly different (although certainly intimately related) process to those other definitions of social interaction noted above. Hence, even though universalization, internationalization, Westernization and liberalization may eventually result in globalization, the fact that they may not necessarily be entirely detached from territorialization means that they remain on a qualitatively different level to the inherently supra-territorial phenomena of globalization.

Globalization's challenge to sovereignty and the state

Globalization defined as supra-territorialization, and involving the reconfiguration of social space, poses significant implications for existing forms of social organization, and most importantly in the case of security, the dominant position of the state within the global polity.[9] Needless to say, the state, with its exclusive jurisdiction – or sovereignty – over a particular social and territorial space, delineated by a combination of physical geography and, most especially, human construction, has been the basis unit for the division of global space in the modern era. States in the past have attempted, in theory and practice, to exercise sovereignty over all forms of social interaction in the political, economic and security domains, both within and between their respective territorial borders. It is clear that not all states throughout modern history have been strong enough to exercise the same degree of sovereign control and authority over all forms of social interaction.[10] Nevertheless, sovereign states rooted in territorial notions of social space have been the prime unit for facilitating, mediating and impeding interaction between societal groups, organizations, and citizens and other categories of collective and individual societal units contained within their borders. Hence, to date, global social space has been primarily carved up into international, or inter-sovereign-state, social space.

However, the inherent quality of globalization as a process which transcends, overrides, and even erodes sovereignty as the dominant principle for the organization of social space now poses a fundamental challenge to the sovereign state as the basic organizational unit which exemplifies and supports this very territorial principle. Sovereign states must increasingly contend with the freer flow of social forces and actors on a global scale which move with declining reference to the previous limitations and channels imposed by state borders. Globalization conceived of in this way clearly challenges the capacities of states to cope with the action of social and economic forces within their borders. Moreover, it clearly has both integrative and disintegrative effects on social interaction. On the one hand, it is increasingly possible for new trans-national social movements to be initiated amongst societal groups, whilst on the other globalization can also lead to the atomization of societal groups and their disassociation from each other and the framework of the sovereign state.

This increasing porosity of state borders, relative decline in the de facto sovereign authority of states over social interaction, and corresponding increased exposure of 'internal' social groupings to 'external' forces indicates a number of outcomes for security. For, if global society has been primarily international or inter-sovereign-state space for much of the modern era, then the security order as one aspect of social interaction has been primarily built around the inter-state order. But it is clear that the security order is now pitted against the phenomenon of globalization which generates security issues diametrically opposed to, and often beyond the limits of, sovereign state authority.

Hence, the definition of globalization offered here strongly overlaps with, but also goes beyond, the idea of simply enhanced interdependence. It brings with it the concept that economic forces are not only enhancing integration amongst states, but that they are increasingly penetrating states, forcing them to remake themselves in order to respond to the challenge,[11] and in certain cases openly undermining the attempted monopoly of authority of states over social interaction. Simply put, globalization can spell the incapacitation and 'retreat of the state'.[12] The exact interconnections with, and consequences of, globalization understood in this way for security will be addressed in later sections, but in the next section it is first necessary to consider in more detail definitions and modes of security under the auspices of sovereign states. In this way, by understanding the central role of states in security, it then becomes possible to conceive of how globalization's potential to attack the state's central position has transformative consequences for security.

Conceptualizing security and sovereign states: the making and unmaking of conflict

In the modern era, as already noted above, global space has been organized around inter-sovereign space, and, correspondingly, global security has been centred around the inter-sovereign-state system. However, it is important to remember that this sovereign-state-centred security order has not been the 'natural' or eternal security order throughout much of the history of conflict.

Sovereign states have only risen to a central and arguably monopolistic position in controlling the instruments of violence since the late seventeenth century.[13] In fact, the rise and strengthening of the modern state itself, and its displacement of other competing actors for the governance of political, economic and security space – including, variously, city-states, religious groups, ethnic groups, private merchant companies, privateers, pirates and mercenaries[14] – has been intimately bound up with conflict or security[15]; or in Charles Tilly's famous phrase: 'states make war and war makes the state'.[16]

In the past, states' drive to mobilize resources for war-making led to their initial acquisition and consolidation of sovereignty and supremacy in conflict and security. In order to augment their power, states sought to centralize control over the material resources of the economy, banking and finance, taxation, and trade. States, furthermore, sought to professionalize their armed forces, to harness new military technologies, and to monopolize the means of violence. In turn, states as well as making external war needed to engage in the internal pacification of their own territory, the suppression of religious and ethnic insurgency, and the dismantling of other private forms of domestic and international violence.

The consequence of the rise by the twentieth century of the modern state was that, in theory and to large extent in practice, they had come to be seen as the supreme and legitimate actors in security, and had effectively eliminated or neutralized other forms of security actors. States had come to assume full responsibility for the security of all citizens within their sovereign territory. They had established strong, if not total, control over the means of violence; and thus violent conflict had become essentially inter-national, between sovereign nation-states. Moreover, sovereign states possessed, or increasingly strove to possess, the material resources to provide not only military security, but also other forms of security to their citizens, such as economic welfare.

It has to be acknowledged that in many senses this description of the state's central position in international conflict is an ideal type. As noted earlier and examined in more detail later on, not all states can fully govern security. In many instances, despite promises to deliver civility, security and peace, states have actually directed violence against their own citizens, or merely displaced violence to relations between states,[17] although these caveats are vital, there can be little doubt that by the twentieth century states came to dominate the global security scene. Given this reality, it is then also apparent that any challenge to the centrality of states, their sovereignty, capabilities, and material basis can also undo this system and generate significant change in the global security order. This change can include shifts in terms of who are the key and legitimate security actors, the types of security threats that are prevalent, and the means by which these sources of insecurity are responded to. Globalization is just such a challenge to the primacy of the state in security, or to re-phrase Tilly's maxim: if the state can be remade or unmade under conditions of globalization, then so can the nature of war and security.

Globalization, the state and security

Globalization, previously defined as the de-territorialization of social space accompanied by economic liberalization and assisted by new technologies, can be seen to be ranged against, and to pose a number of challenges and indeed potentially transformative challenges to, the existing international/sovereignty-based security order outlined earlier. Globalization's challenges can be encapsulated in two major areas. First, globalization is a force capable of operating with declining reference to sovereignty, that can penetrate state borders, and impact directly upon the internal societal groupings within states and thereby produce a new sense of insecurity. Second, globalization as a phenomenon, often spearheaded by economic liberalization, undermines the material capacities of certain states to respond to these trans-sovereign forces in the security arena.

Globalization's twin challenges to the sovereignty of the state impact specifically on security in two categories. These involve the *vertical* extension of the levels of actors involved in security, and the *horizontal* extension of the range of dimensions of security issues.

Types and levels of security actors

The study and praxis of security throughout much of the twentieth century and the Cold War has focussed on the state as the principal referent object[18] of security due to the concept that the security of the state can be equated with the security of its citizens, especially in the case of fully-fledged nation-states where there is a close fit and identification between the security fate of the states and its general citizenry. Indeed, this chapter has already outlined how the process of sovereign-nation-state formation involves the displacement and suppression of other potential security actors below the level of states.

Globalization, though, is a process which is capable of accentuating the divisibility between the security of the state and the security of its internal societal groups, thus revising understandings of the essential referent object of security. This is because globalization is capable of transcending territorial and sovereign state boundaries, and thus penetrates with relative ease the internal space of states and impacts directly and differentially on societal groups. For example, free flow of market forces across borders, the accompanying wealth creation and also economic dislocation that it engenders, undercuts the ability of the sovereign state to act as the principal arbiter of the economic welfare of its internal society. In turn, globalization's ability to strip away the supposed protection of the state from societal groups and citizens means that the state can be seen as an enfeebled or even irrelevant mechanism for providing security, and that attention turns away from the level of the security of the state to focus instead upon the security of societal groups, whether socio-economic, ethnic or religious, and towards the level of individual 'human security'.

The East Asia region's experience of the financial crises of 1997–1998 illustrates well many of these effects of globalization in activating an alternative range of referent objects for security and the knock-on effects upon conflict generation. The crises produced a set of economic costs for societal groups and individual citizens that many of the states of the region found themselves unable at first to mitigate and redistribute. In these circumstances, even though the governmental apparatus of the states of the region remained intact, societal groups and individuals began again to view certain states as redundant frameworks for the preservation of their economic and political security interests, and so looked to detach themselves from political dependence upon them.[19] The result for many of the states was to produce short and longer term crises of legitimacy. East Asian states have dealt with these challenges, generated by globalization, with varying degrees of success. Indonesia has seemingly coped least well with the impact of globalization,[20] and the centralized state has struggled to reassert its legitimacy in the eyes of various societal and ethnic groupings, thereby contributing to the problems of re-emerging intra-mural instability and violence.

Globalization's challenge in fracturing the state's role as the principal referent object of security further extends to undermining its role as the principal actor in the supply and denial of security. The retreat of state capacities to mitigate and redistribute the costs imposed by the direct penetration of their societies by global economic forces has opened up space for other actors to supplement or even supplant the role of the states as providers and deniers of security. Transnational corporations have increasingly assumed a key role as both providers and deniers of security in the economic and environmental dimensions of security. States unable to cope with demands of economic globalization, especially in the developing world, have also increasingly ceded their tasks in providing economic security and basic human needs to non-governmental organizations (NGO) and aid providers with a transnational composition, such as the Red Cross, Oxfam, and Médecins Sans Frontières. Globalization's penetration of sovereign state borders and its integrative and disintegrative effects have also fostered the activities of transnational organized crime groups – with implications for domestic and international security. Crime groups have skilfully exploited the economic networks and technology accompanying globalization to access new markets and facilitate their trans-national networks,[21] but at the same time have also found that those states with declining sovereign capacity to mediate the impact of globalization are the most convenient locations for their activities.[22] For instance in the 'stateless zones' of Colombia, the drug cartels have built up very considerable military capacities, facilitated by the weakness of the Colombian state and its penetration by global economic forces.[23] The re-emergence of piracy in Southeast Asia, although a multi-causal phenomenon bound up with issues of decolonization and the end of the Cold War, has also been attributed in part to the general enfeeblement of the Indonesian state apparatus following the financial crises, and the rise of new incentives to engage in crime for societal groups resulting from the general economic downturn in the region.[24]

Finally, states under conditions of globalization have increasingly shown an inclination towards, or at least acquiescence in, relinquishing their previous monopoly over the instruments of violence and to cede these to non-state actors. In the developing world, declining state capacities after the Cold War in the face of reduced economic aid and neo-liberal prescriptions for governance, including reduced central government deficits and privatization,[25] have ensured that many security functions have been transferred from state militaries to private military companies. In the developed world, there has also been a movement towards the privatization of certain key military functions. In certain cases, privatized militaries are seen as valuable assets for intervening in states in the post-Cold War era where national interests would not necessarily sanction the use and risk of lives of regular state forces;[26] in other cases the use of privatized military companies is seen as a means of achieving cost-efficiencies in the maintenance of high technical capabilities and logistical services, again the result of the financial strictures imposed by globalization and the conviction of the superiority of the market in providing public needs.[27] The result is the strengthening presence in the post-Cold War period of the private military company (PMC) to compensate for the decline of state capabilities in the security field. PMCs perform various functions ranging from frontline mercenary activities in Croatia and the Balkans and Sierra Leone; guarding transnational corporations' resource extraction activities in Angola and Sierra Leone; mine clearance in Kosovo; combat training for state forces in Saudi Arabia; and logistical support for the US forces in Iraq.

This 'privatization' of military force in fact may serve many useful functions by enabling states to acquire security capabilities otherwise beyond their reach and thereby contribute to regional and global security. But the essential point to note here is that globalization has contributed to the retreat of many states from their previous functions as referent objects and deniers and suppliers of security. The further consequence has been the 'restoration of private international violence,[28] or re-entry into the security arena of a range of non-state actors (ethnic groups, transnational movements, private corporations, mercenaries, pirates) previously suppressed by the centrality of the state, with thus potentially significant implications for the nature of contemporary conflict.

Globalization and the economic origins of conflict

Globalization, defined as de-territorialization, a fundamental challenge to state sovereignty, and state transformation, and therefore going beyond straight quantitative notions of increased economic interaction amongst states, provides another useful qualitative lens for understanding the interconnections between a globalizing economy, national insecurity, and the potential for conflict.

Globalization in the form of increased internationalization and interdependence is undoubtedly a key consideration driving contemporary security dynamics. This form of globalization is capable of driving high speed economic growth for states, but also of engendering concerns about relative gains, economic rivalry and mercantilist conflict over precious trade networks and resources.[29] China's economic rise and thirst for markets and energy resources has often been cast in terms of a potential source of conflict with its regional neighbours.

The flipside to this argument is that increased economic interdependence brings with it increased costs associated with conflict and can produce a form of 'Kantian' or 'democratic' peace.[30] These types of arguments are deployed to support the thesis that economic interdependence between China and Japan will ultimately deliver peaceful relations. This chapter takes no particular stand on either of these perspectives, other than to acknowledge that both are probably correct depending on particular circumstances and time periods. Other parts of this book will do so instead.

However, definitions of globalization as qualitative change in the nature and impact of economic flows, and the related implications of state transformation, compel us to consider additional ways in which economic interaction can influence the potential for conflict. The first of these ways is that globalization, as a force capable of challenging sovereignty, can actually produce economic exclusion rather than integration and that this can be a cause of conflict. In East Asia, this type of impact of globalization can be seen in North Korea's loss of access to the socialist economic sphere following the end of the Cold War, and its exclusion, both self- and externally-imposed, from the rapidly globalizing political economy of the region. North Korea has then been presented with a new security dilemma by the globalization–security nexus.[31] For, on the one hand, North Korea's reluctance to reform and integrate itself into the region will only exacerbate the deep-seated structural economic crisis that it has experienced since the latter stages of the Cold War which could lead to its political implosion. On the other hand, though, the North Korea leadership is also aware that economic liberalization even on a modest scale would expose its closed political economy to the shocks of globalization, transcend previously imposed sovereign barriers to the political control of its internal society, and also threaten the collapse of the regime. Hence, faced with the twin risks of this dilemma, the North Korean regime has attempted to steer a middle path with a limited policy of opening to the outside world but on terms that it has sought in part to dictate. In practice this has meant that North Korea has utilized its remaining military assets in a strategy of brinkmanship to extract economic concessions in the form of food aid, but also preferential access to energy, financial aid, investment and international economic institutions, from the surrounding powers.[32]

The second impact of globalization and its ability to penetrate state sovereignty and challenge state capabilities is the issue of economic disparities, not *amongst* but *within* states, and the generation of potential conflict. Globalization is capable of re-mapping economic and social space, with the frequent result that economic interdependency can pull actors and regions away from the defined territorial space of the sovereign state and towards regions incorporated within other states. In these instances, the rise of regionalization can lead to the disintegration of state structures, with unforeseen consequences for internal and external security. These problems in the Asia-Pacific are encapsulated in speculation about the breakaway from the Russia of its Far East provinces resulting from their desire for greater control over their own natural resources; and the possible 'deconstruction' of China as economic liberalization undermines the capability of the centre to govern the local provinces. Moreover, China's economic liberalization has created problems of security not only between centre and provinces, but also within the provinces themselves, as China's gradual abandonment of socialist principles erodes the basis for the 'iron rice bowl' which ensured political stability and was one of its greatest achievements in terms of providing human security for the bulk of its population.

Third, globalization's ability to penetrate state borders and to debilitate their capacity to provide economic welfare to their citizens can often result in economic dislocation, poverty, and financial crises. All this can lead to insecurity for states, societal groups and individuals, which can again feed into social instability. within and amongst states. and possible armed conflict. The discussion above of the problems of many ASEAN states in the wake of the financial crises of 1997–1998 provides examples of these types of security problems.

Globalization and modes of conflict

Globalization's trans-sovereign nature, as well as affecting the types of actors involved in security and the causation and types of emergent conflicts, has also produced a qualitative impact on the means and modes by which violent conflict has been pursued. This impact is multifarious, so the purpose of this section is to briefly outline two areas in which globalization is seen to have made a difference to contemporary conflict.

First, globalization and declining barriers to social interaction have not only led to the proliferation of security actors beyond the level of the state, but have facilitated and 'democratized' the means by which these actors practice violent conflict. Non-state actors, such as terrorists, organized crime, and ethnic groups have been able to exploit globalized transport and communications networks, in the same way as transnational corporations. They can use them in order to organize transnationally and to obtain access to various forms of low and high technology weaponry since states are increasingly less able to govern these networks.[33] The A.Q. Khan network originating in Pakistan is one example of the exploitation of globalization to proliferate weapons of mass destruction (WMD) technologies.[34] In certain cases, groups involved in the perpetration of conflicts have been able to arm and fund themselves through engaging in globalized 'shadow economies' and 'war economies'[35] accepting funds channelled across weakened state borders by external supporters, as in Bosnia; or trafficking globally in resources, such as diamonds to generate war funds, as in Sierra Leone.

A second impact of globalization on the modes of violent conflict has been the exploitation of the increasingly globalized media to exert leverage over adversaries.[36] Globalization of the mass media is perhaps the apogee of the globalization phenomenon, with the capacity, provided the technology is in place, to communicate information almost instantaneously across sovereign borders. The globalization of information has mixed effects on the nature of violent conflict. It can act as a final trigger for humanitarian intervention as with the 'CNN effect' and US intervention in Somalia in 1992, but also act as a trigger for withdrawal, as Somali militia groups exploited the global media to turn US public opinion against interventions. State actors may actually become more adept at exploiting the media in conflict situations, as with the use of 'embedded reporters' during the Iraq war which tightly constrained the style and extent of coverage of the war. But non-state actors may equally master the globalized media to exert leverage over the US and developed states,[37] demonstrated by the insurgents' current media campaign against the US in Iraq.

Globalization and the geography of conflict

Finally, we should now consider how globalization, defined as a qualitative change in transnational interaction and state capacities, helps us to understand the distribution of contemporary conflict. The previous sections have outlined a number of areas where globalization can be seen to affect security in general, but it is also clear that this varies amongst states and across regions. It is not the case that all states are affected to the same degree by globalization, and thus it is not the case that globalization will necessarily produce the same degree of insecurity in all parts of the globe. This section seeks to explain why this difference in the impact of globalization on security exists and thus to provide indicators of what conditions, particularly in regard to the nature of the state, need to be sought in order to understand the potential for conflict in various zones and regions. In addition, the provision of these indicators is useful in that it teaches us that economic interdependence and the more quantitative markers of globalization are necessary, but not sufficient, means to analyse the linkage between economics and conflict. For it is often the case that zones and regions with low levels of formal state-to-state economic interdependence are highly subject to conflict. Hence, the key to understanding patterns of instability again lies not merely in the quantitative degree of exposure of states to global economic forces but their ability to mediate the trans-border nature of these flows, or in other words the qualitative degree of solidity of their sovereignty.

In turn, this chapter argues that the key to understanding the qualitative degree of state sovereignty and their ability to deal with the qualitatively upgraded challenge of globalization is to examine the history of their positioning within the global political economy. The first set of states with the most readily identifiable degree of weak sovereignty are ex-colonial entities. This is due to the fact that they are recent creations, often delineated along former colonial borders drawn in arbitrary fashion, ignoring trans-border ties of ethnicity and religion. Such states suffer a number of internal contradictions and stresses that can only be suppressed or reconciled by advancing process of state building and demonstrating 'performance legitimacy'[38] to their citizens. The second set of states with relatively weak sovereignty, many of which overlap with the first set, are those states of the former communist sphere, or states closely aligned in client fashion with the US during the Cold War. The sovereignty of former states of the communist sphere is challenged in that they are structurally disadvantaged to deal with the pressures of globalized and neo-liberal capitalism.

Those states aligned with the US during the Cold War are arguably better equipped, given that for much of this period they were insulated from the full impact of liberal capitalism by the US's provisions of special economic dispensations including preferential access to markets, aid and technology.

However, in the post-Cold War period, post-colonial states and states from the communist and US-centred spheres alike have now been thrust more fully into an increasingly globalized economy, without the insulation offered by communist autonomy or US dispensations, and face full exposure to the stresses of neo-liberal capitalism. The result has been to demonstrate the essential vulnerability of many of these states to globalization because it has been able to penetrate their internal societies, to exacerbate the internal inconsistencies that are the legacy of colonialism, and to reveal the economic weaknesses of states previously tolerated by the international political economy during the Cold War. In extreme cases, the result of globalization's penetration and sapping of state capacity, combined with the legacy of colonialism and the end of the Cold War, has been to precipitate near state collapse and 'failed states'.

Hence, globalization's impact on the incidence of insecurity across the globe needs to be understood in terms of its essential attack on state sovereignty and the inherent abilities of states to consolidate their sovereignty in order to counter the effects of globalization. It is no accident that those states where international conflict is currently most often centred are those states where sovereignty is weakest and where they are unable to control the trans-border flow of globalization forces, and not necessarily those states where the degree of international trade or finance with other states is greatest. These are states such as Somalia, Afghanistan and the former Yugoslavia where transnational terrorism, ethnic strife, trans-national crime and religious extremism find a ready base. Once again, then, globalization's added value as an analytical term is found not just in quantitative measures of economic association, but in the ability of economic forces to contribute or detract from state sovereignty and thereby to influence the generation of conflict.

Conclusion: globalization's security impact felt beyond interdependence

This chapter has outlined a number of ways in which globalization can be viewed as impacting on international security – in terms of the range of actors involved in security, the economic origins of conflict, the means by which conflicts are pursued, and the particular geographical location of conflicts. Each of these is based on the argument that globalization's ramifications can only be fully understood by defining it as the de-territorialization of social space which carries significant qualitative implications for the maintenance of state sovereignty and capacity in dealing with the changing quality and quantity of flow of economic forces across borders.

Globalization defined in this way has significant implications for the primacy of the state as the referent object and denier/supplier of security in the modern period. States subject to the impact of globalization and the penetration of their internal societies have experienced increasing difficulty in conflating their own security with that of internal groupings, thereby expanding the range of referent objects of security. Similarly, states under conditions of globalization have faced increasing rivalry from, and been forced to cede a number of their security functions to, non-state actors. As the modern sovereign state system retreats under pressure from globalization, so there are signs of the re-emergence of privatized forms of violence.

Globalization has furthermore had an important impact on the economic origins of security. Its enhancement of economic interdependency is clearly one important impact. But globalization as de-territorialization and an assault on sovereignty goes beyond generating simple economic rivalry. It generates economic exclusion through states' fear of the loss of sovereignty which can drive military confrontation; it engenders economic disparities within rather than just between states, and gives rise to instability; and it creates economic dislocation and renders states incapable of dealing with the security fallout. Globalization has in addition affected the means by which conflicts are fought. Non-state actors now have increasing access to transnational flow of funding and armaments to pursue conflicts and can utilize the global media to enhance their capabilities.

Last, globalization clearly affects the geography of conflict. This is because its impact is felt most strongly in those regions where sovereign states are weakest, usually in post-colonial and former communist spheres and US client state regions. In sum, the essential argument is that globalization's connection with security can only be properly understood by examining the changing nature of states themselves rather than just economic flows and interdependence amongst them.

Notes

1 Devetak, Richard and Hughes, Christopher W. 'Globalization's shadow: an introduction to the globalization of political violence', in Richard Devetak and Christopher W. Hughes (eds) *Globalization and Political Violence*, London: Routledge, 2006.
2 Cha, Victor D. 'Globalization and the study of international security', *Journal of Peace Research*, 37 (3), 2000, pp. 391–403; Clark, Ian *Globalization and International Relations Theory*, Oxford: Oxford University Press, 1999; Coker, Christopher *Globalisation and Insecurity in the Twenty-first Century: NATO and the Management of Risk, Adelphi Paper 345*, Oxford: IISS/Oxford University Press, 2002; Hughes, Christopher W. 'Conceptualizing the globalization–security nexus in the Asia-Pacific', *Security Dialogue*, 32 (4), 2001, pp. 407–421; Hughes, Christopher W. 'Reflections on globalisation, security and 9/11', *Cambridge Review of International Affairs*, 15 (3), 2002, pp. 421–433; Kaldor, Mary *New and Old Wars: Organized Violence in a Global Era*, Oxford: Polity, 1999; Scholte, Jan Aart *Globalization: A Critical Introduction*, Basingstoke: Polity, 2000.
3 Buzan, Barry *People, States and Fear: An Agenda for International Security Studies in the Post-Cold War Era*, Hemel Hempstead: Harvester Wheatsheaf, 1991, pp. 1–12.
4 Fukuyama, Francis *The End of History and the Last Man*, Harmondsworth: Penguin, 1992; Ohmae, Kenichi *The Borderless World*, London: Fontana, 1990.

5 Hughes, 2002, op. cit., p. 429.
6 Scholte, Jan Aart, 1997, 'Global capitalism and the state', *International Affairs*, 73 (3), 1997, p. 431.
7 Ohmae, op. cit.
8 Hughes, Christopher W. *Japan's Economic Power and Security: Japan and North Korea*, London: Routledge, 1999; Hirst, Paul and Grahame Thompson, *Globalisation in Question*, Cambridge: Polity Press, 1999.
9 Higgott, Richard and Ougaard, Morten 'Introduction – beyond system and society: towards a global polity', in Morten Ougaard and Richard Higgott (eds) *Towards a Global Polity*, London: Routledge, 2002, pp. 1–20.
10 Krasner, Stephen *Sovereignty: Organized Hypocrisy*, Princeton: Princeton University Press, 1999; Rosenberg, Justin *The Follies of Globalisation Theory*, London: Verso, 2000, pp. 27–41.
11 Held, David, McGrew, Anthony, Goldblatt, David and Perraton, Jonathan *Global Transformations: Politics, Economics, and Culture*, Cambridge: Polity, 1999.
12 Strange, Susan *The Retreat of the State: The Diffusion of Power in the World Economy*, Cambridge: Cambridge University Press, 1996.
13 Ruggie, John G. 'Territoriality and beyond: problematizing modernity in International Relations', *International Organization*, 46 (1), 1993, pp. 139–174.
14 Hirst, Paul *War and Power in the 21st Century*, Cambridge: Polity, 2001, pp. 44–78.
15 Cheeseman, op. cit.
16 Tilly, Charles 'War making and state making as organized crime', in Peter Evans, Dietrich Rueschemeyer and Theda Skocpol (eds), *Bringing the State Back In*, Cambridge: Cambridge University Press, 1985. Tilly, Charles *Coercion, Capital and European States AD 990–1990*, Oxford: Blackwell, 1990.
17 Devetak and Hughes, op. cit.
18 Buzan, Barry, Waever, Ole and de Wilde, Jaap *Security: A New Framework for Analysis*, Boulder, CO: Lynne Rienner Publishers, 1998, p. 36.
19 Hughes, 2001, op. cit.
20 Huxley, Tim *Disintegrating Indonesia? Implications for Regional Security* Adelphi Paper 349, Oxford: IISS/Oxford University Press, 2002, pp. 9–10.
21 Andreas, Peter 'Transnational crime and economic globalization', in Mats Berdal and Monica Serrano (eds), *Transnational Crime and International Security: Business As Usual?*, Boulder, CO: Lynne Rienner Publishers, 2002, pp. 37–52.
22 Flynn, Stephen E. 'The global drug trade versus the nation-state', in Maryann K. Cusimano (ed.) *Beyond Sovereignty: Issues for a Global Agenda*, Boston and New York: Bedford/St. Martin's, 2000, pp. 44–66.
23 Singer, Peter W. *Corporate Warriors: The Rise of the Privatised Military Industry*, Ithaca, NY: Cornell University Press, 2003.
24 Abbott, Jason and Renwick, Neil 'Piratical violence and maritime security in Southeast Asia', *Security Dialogue*, 30 (2), 1999, pp. 183–196.
25 Singer, op. cit., p. 55; Leander, Anna *Wars and the Unmaking of States: Taking Tilly Seriously in the Contemporary World*, Copenhagen Peace Research Institute Working Paper 2002. Online, available at www.ciaonet.org/wps/lea06/lea06.html.
26 Shearer, David *Private Armies and Military Intervention*, Adelphi Paper 316, Oxford: IISS/Oxford University Press, 1998.
27 Singer, op. cit., p. 66.
28 Bull, Hedley *The Anarchical Society: A Study of Order in World Politics*, New York: Columbia University Press, 1971, pp. 268–270.
29 Grieco, Joseph M. 'Anarchy and the limits of cooperation: a realist critique of the newest liberal institutionalism', *International Organization*, 42 (3), pp. 485–429.
30 Russett, Bruce M. and Oneal, John R. *Triangulating Peace: Democracy, Interdependence, and International Organizations*, New York: W.W. Norton and Company, 2001.

31 Sheehan, Michael *International Security: An Analytical Survey*, Boulder, CO, Lynner Rienner Publishers, 2005, p. 75.
32 Hughes, 2002, op. cit.
33 Flynn, 2000, op. cit., p. 45.
34 Joyner, Dan 'International legal responses to weapons proliferation', in Richard Devetak and Christopher W. Hughes (eds) *Globalization and Political Violence*, London: Routledge, 2006.
35 Andreas, 2004, op. cit.; Ballentine, Karen and Sherman, Jake *The Political Economy of Armed Conflict: Beyond Greed and Grievance*, Boulder, CO: Lynne Rienner Publishers, 2003; Duffield, Mark *Global Governance and the New Wars*, London: Zed Books, 2001, pp. 136–160; Keen, David, *The Economic Functions of Violence in Civil Wars*, Adelphi Paper 320, Oxford: IISS/Oxford University Press, 1998; Pugh, Michael and Cooper, Neil *War Economies in a Regional Context: Challenges of Transformation*, Boulder, CO: Lynne Rienner Publishers, 2004.
36 Ignatieff, Michael *Virtual War: Kosovo and Beyond*, London, Chatto and Windus, 2000.
37 Lentini, Pete 'Beheading, hostage taking and "the new terrorism": the transformation of tactics and the globalisation of violence', in Richard Devetak and Christopher W. Hughes (eds) *Globalization and Political Violence*, London: Routledge, 2006.
38 Stubbs, Richard 'Performance legitimacy and "soft authoritarianism"', in Acharya, Amitav B. Michael Frolic and Richard Stubbs (eds) *Democracy, Human Rights and Civil Society in South East Asia*, Toronto: Joint Centre for Asia Pacific Studies, 2001, pp. 37–54.

Part II

Globalization and defence policy in the Asia-Pacific

4 Globalization and military–industrial transformation in South Asia

A historical perspective

Emrys Chew

> Oh, East is East, and West is West, and never the twain shall meet,
> Till Earth and Sky stand presently at God's great Judgment Seat;
> But there is neither East nor West, Border, nor Breed, nor Birth,
> When two strong men stand face to face, tho' they come from the ends of the earth!
>
> Rudyard Kipling

Kipling's famous 'Ballad of East and West' was set in an area of South Asia that is now Pakistan. It points to a relationship in which 'the twain' do meet: in this case, two men from different worlds facing each other across the barrel of a gun. The romance of imperialism is dead, and the white man as colonial master has long departed the subcontinent. Yet, in an ironic twist, South Asia is the globe's only region where two strategic rivals remain locked in an ongoing hot–cold war spanning some six decades, a peculiar subcontinental relationship in which disputes could easily precipitate a major crisis with escalation potential. Meanwhile, from global Cold War to transnational 'war on terror', the military–industrial landscape of modern India and Pakistan has continued to be shaped by countless waves of cross-cultural interaction amid the shifting sands of international politics.

All this suggests that the history of globalization has a longer lineage than just a matter of decades, and its impact has been more profound. Growing interconnectedness between regions of the world – expressed as evolving networks of collaboration or escalating patterns of conflict – has been evident for centuries, and especially since the imperial and industrial expansions of the eighteenth and nineteenth centuries. Between the world crises of the eighteenth century and the cataclysm of the First World War, the forming and transforming of socio-economic, political and cultural relationships across porous borders and turbulent frontiers both fuelled and facilitated transfers of increasingly sophisticated military hardware and technology, resulting in an arming of the 'periphery' in South Asia.

In the dawn of Western great power rivalry and the twilight of Mughal rule on the subcontinent, regional elites and successor states competed for resources and products in the all-India military bazaar, while the English East India

Company found ways to harness the sinews of military-fiscal power to establish a British Raj over Western and indigenous opponents. From the mountain passes of Afghanistan and the Northwest Frontier, across the rivers, plains and cities of the subcontinent, into the jungles of Sri Lanka, the tentacles of colonial authority and commerce, capitalism and technological progress, meshed with the tangled realities of indigenous crisis to provoke anti-colonial protest and religious civil strife in an increasingly militarized zone.

In this sense, the 'globalized' character of military–industrial development and armed conflict in South Asia today has clear historical antecedents. Across a levelled and shell-shocked post-9/11 landscape, it has become even more important to apply this vital long-term perspective to our understanding of the present, so as to avoid the twin pitfalls of myopia and amnesia: viewing the 'modern' phenomenon of South Asia's militarization in deracinated form – severed from its roots in the historical past – and thereby failing to recall the broader connections and long-term patterns; or, at best, giving only cursory attention thereto. What is arguably new, on the other hand, is the raising of stakes in a world of nation-states having volatile nuclear capabilities and rapid internet communication; and, in the midst of pre-existing indigenous rivalries, the capacity of local warlords, resistance fighters or jihadists to re-export 'terror' as far afield as the core of the Western metropole.

This chapter examines the roots and ramifications of military–industrial globalization in South Asia, locating them firmly within the dynamic military cultural context of the subcontinent's history. In so doing, it strives to redress perceived imbalances in the contemporary emphasis of current debates about the nature and impact of globalizing supra-national forces. It also seeks to review possible implications of long-term trends and patterns for the future security of the region.[1]

Contemporary debates and definitions

Globalization is a contemporary 'umbrella' word used to describe the progressive increase in the scale of social processes from a local or regional to world level. Stemming from both national and international roots, it refers to a multiplicity of quantitative and qualitative transformations – variegated in nature, multi-dimensional in character – brought about by the augmentation and acceleration of social, political, economic and cultural relationships across the borders of countries, regions and continents, resulting in a more interconnected, interdependent world system.[2]

By this definition, the military-industrial configuration of South Asia is indeed the 'globalized' by-product of myriad cross-border interactions, emerging out of a complex interplay between the motive forces of a changing world order and the crises of indigenous societies. In military–strategic terms, transfers of military hardware and technology in South Asia have accelerated largely as a result of a world power having to maintain its hegemony and contain its rivals, or a South Asian power having to augment its military capabilities for purposes of resistance or conflict. In political–economic terms, the development of the South Asia defence industry has been driven by Western (and in the most recent case, American-led) global expansion, as well as by regional transformation and indigenous crisis in Asia. Shaped by these military–strategic and political–economic imperatives, the defence establishments of India and Pakistan were at first armed directly by foreign powers. But their pursuit of greater military-industrial self-reliance has led to a progressive 'global diversification' of companies and corporations, the 'internationalization' of supply networks, production systems, labour forces, management and financing. As this global military market unfolds across the subcontinent, however, the territorial boundaries of nation-states become more porous, and national sovereignty is diluted and reconfigured, allowing for the arming of groups and individuals beyond the interstices of state power, encompassing states in the wider South Asian 'periphery' such as Sri Lanka and Afghanistan.[3]

The arming of South Asia may be explained, in part, by military–strategic imperatives, generated according to shifts in global alliances and alienations over the past half-century or so. Witness the periodic arming of India by the United States. In the struggle against Japan and its Axis partners during the Second World War, the American-supported and funded defence production effort turned British India into a major arms producer and base for military operations in China, Southeast Asia, and the Persian Gulf. At the partitioning of the subcontinent in 1947, military assets were then divided roughly between India and Pakistan in the proportion 64:36, to reflect the communal balance. In terms of the balance of power in South Asia, this subsequently gave independent India enough firepower to fight Pakistan to a standstill in 1948, as well as overwhelm the Nizam of Hyderabad's forces that year, and overrun the Portuguese colonies of Goa, Daman and Diu in 1961.[4] Yet, with the fledgling nation's financial resources channelled into nation-building and only limited access to vital defence technologies, the Indian military machine proved inadequate for resisting the onslaught of Chinese forces during the India–China war of 1962, which ended in traumatic defeat for India.

During the 1950s and up until 1965, India obtained military assistance from the United States in their bid to contain communist China. In the late 1950s, this included substantial quantities of surplus Second World War American weapons, several advanced but largely defensive systems, air defence technology transfers, and $80 million in cash subsidies; and then, from 1963–65, substantial material and technical support to modernize India's ground and air forces.[5] Between the late 1960s and early 1990s, however, US–Indian relations cooled in the light of America's rapprochement with China and realignment with Pakistan; and transfers of military hardware and technology ceased. Only from the late 1990s has the US–Indian relationship revived, under the shadow of nuclear proliferation, with the need to develop India as a counterweight to Chinese ascendancy once again informing American strategic thinking.[6]

On the other hand, whilst pursuing a policy of official non-alignment through much of the Cold War era, India simultaneously maintained a military connection with the Soviet Union as part of a wider strategic alignment against China–US–Pakistan alliances. Around the time of the India–China war in 1962, the USSR began providing assistance to India's defence establishment in the form of high-altitude helicopters and a MiG-21 factory. Large quantities of Soviet-designed but Indian-manufactured weapons were produced thereafter. Soviet assistance reduced Indian dependence upon the West, and empowered New Delhi to counter the Chinese, who were assisting Pakistan by the 1960s. Fears of American encirclement following the arrival of nuclear-powered aircraft carrier *USS Enterprise* in Indian waters in 1971, and closer American ties with both China and Pakistan, further increased New Delhi's reliance on Moscow, prompting India to embark on the largest conventional arms-buying spree in the subcontinent's history. The Soviet Union, beset with *mujahidin* resistance soon after its invasion of Afghanistan in 1979, would in turn look to India as a quasi-ally who might open a 'second front' to Pakistan's southwest in order to divert military resources away from the Afghan frontier.[7]

For its part, Pakistan remains the only South Asian state capable of contesting India's regional dominance. Ironically, the arming of Pakistan has arisen from largely related military–strategic considerations: the United States and China seeking to expand their influence or contain rivals in the region, and Pakistan wanting to acquire weaponry in its contention against India. It was held that a stronger Pakistan could counter Soviet influence as well as resist Indian pressure in South Asia. However, the arming of both India and Pakistan enabled them to fight three wars with each other, the last of which culminated in the traumatic break-up of Pakistan itself and an open-ended arms race ever since.

Although Pakistan received around one-third of British India's military assets in 1947, it inherited few fixed installations and military–industrial facilities other than the obsolete defensive infrastructure of the Northwest Frontier and naval facilities at Karachi and Chittagong. After the first India–Pakistan war in 1948, Pakistan quickly became dependent on the United States for most of its military hardware and technology. Between 1954 and 1965, Islamabad received over $630 million in American cash subsidies and over $670 million in concessional sales and defence-support assistance.[8] But when American arms transfers were practically terminated in the mid-1960s, Pakistan attempted to build up an indigenous defence industry with mainly Chinese help.

China began rendering military assistance to Islamabad in the early 1960s and became Pakistan's principal arms supplier after 1965. Although this did not prevent Pakistan's defeat in the third of its wars with India, resulting in the loss of East Pakistan and emergence of independent Bangladesh in 1971, Pakistan had obtained by the late 1970s more than 1,000 Chinese T-59 tanks (constituting 75 per cent of its tank force) and 300 Chinese aircraft (perhaps 65 per cent of its air force). The Chinese also constructed a tank-rebuild factory and improved a light-arms plant and repair facility for the aircraft at Kamra near Taxila.[9] By the mid-1980s, Chinese nuclear and missile assistance to Islamabad further enabled Pakistan to keep pace with India's nuclear programme. By 1998, Pakistan was in a position to detonate six nuclear devices – equalling the combined achievement of Indian nuclear tests in 1974 and 1998 – and to continue highly publicized missile testing in competition with Pakistan.[10]

Meanwhile, in two major policy shifts, the United States resumed massive financial and military aid to Pakistan. Motivated by enhanced US interest in Gulf oil and the Soviet invasion of Afghanistan, America sought to sustain Pakistan's strategic co-operation and support Afghan *mujahidin* in the war against the Soviet Union. From the Carter administration, Pakistan obtained some ships and other equipment, but from the Reagan administration, Pakistan received over $3 billion worth of cash subsidies, F-16 aircraft, attack helicopters, tanks and howitzers. Following the 9/11 attacks in 2001, America once again enlisted Pakistan's help in a war in Afghanistan, this time as a support base and partner in tracking down Al-Qa'ida and Taliban leaders who had fled to Pakistan. By 2003, the Bush administration had written off $1 billion of Pakistani debt and offered a $3.2 billion five-year economic and military aid package, commencing in 2004.[11]

Against fluctuating trends in worldwide military expenditure, and fluid patterns of arms production and consumption in the international arms bazaar, the arms race between India and Pakistan continues apace with augmented military spending and accelerating weapons-procurement programmes. Despite an overall decline in global military expenditure between 1988 and 1998, reflecting the end of the Cold War, military spending in South Asia has kept well on track: between 1978, 1994 and 2004, it went from $3.45 billion to $7.5 billion to $19.6 billion in the case of India; and from $819 million to $3.5 billion to $3.33 billion in the case of Pakistan.[12] South Asia's share of world military expenditure more than doubled (from 0.8 to 2 per cent) over the last decade of the twentieth century, reflecting the military build-up between India and Pakistan. It saw the biggest increase in military spending for any region in 2004, largely because India boosted its defence budget by a staggering 19 per cent. In terms of both military spending and arms transfers during the 1990s, South Asia experienced the highest average annual growth rate of any region, with 5 per cent.[13]

Perhaps the most solid manifestation of this arming of South Asia has been the expansion and transformation of the military-industrial complex, at the very centre of state-sponsored arms transfers and production. As we have seen, independent India and Pakistan found it impossible to establish self-sufficiency in defence production without the necessary wealth and technology. Both states pursued instead a policy of 'self-reliance', which required the development of an indigenous military–industrial base for support, with varying degrees of dependence on reliable foreign sources for access to technologies, supply of components and complete systems. Over-reliance on licence production and direct procurement brought its own perils: import dependency, insufficient funding for critical and strategic technologies, and industrial underperformance. But more recent state-sponsored efforts have generated a new wave of 'joint-venture' military–industrial development, supplied by multi-national companies and international circuits of arms production, and served by global networks of information and finance. By enabling 'cross-fertilization' with technological innovation in the Western metropole, these hybrid efforts aim to eliminate technological gap and time lag in the South Asian periphery.

The Indian defence industry has relied on licence production and direct acquisitions as the principal form of supply for much of its existence. Between the 1960s and 1980s, the Soviet connection enabled a state with a sizeable trained workforce but slow-growing economy to maintain a fairly advanced defence establishment. India received preferential payment terms, in line with other socialist and developing countries, and could exchange Indian-manufactured goods for military equipment and components, MiGs, tanks and ships. But the oversupply of Soviet equipment reduced India's incentive to develop its own weapons or seek other sources, and alienated Western suppliers. India was prevented from selling its Soviet-originating but Indian-made arms on the international market, thus depriving India of a valuable source of military revenue. The arms themselves had a limited shelf life: Soviet reluctance to share technology and India's limited capacity for reverse-engineering Soviet products meant India ultimately lacked the capabilities to repair second-rate weapons or reconstruct the manufacturing process once the Soviet arms export establishment disintegrated. Although production patterns during the 1980s and 1990s show that India was able to initiate several projects for indigenous manufacture – including the Main Battle Tank Weapon 'Arjun' and the 5.56-mm INSAS assault rifle – Indian arms exports in the 1990s were neither of the kind nor quality that proved internationally competitive, even in the non-Western world.[14]

Then, from the mid-1990s, India's defence industry entered a new phase of self-reliance, emphasizing multi-national co-operation in areas of joint production, as well as indigenous private–public sector interaction and civil–military partnerships. In this respect, the Indian defence industry's transition from 'autarky' to 'going global' has been consonant with worldwide trends in the US-led global defence industry: consolidation and diversification following the end of the Cold War and emergence of new international security conditions; increased competition among manufacturers and progressive internationalization of defence production efforts; and, with growing cross-border interactions, a greater willingness of the state to countenance the participation of private enterprise in its strategic industries.[15]

By 2005, the Indian military–industrial complex would include an aircraft manufacturing conglomerate (Hindustan Aeronautics Limited); seven other large defence public sector units (DPSUs), for the production of electronics, ships, missiles, and other strategic materials; 40 ordnance factories; and a research organization dedicated to defence science and technology. The Indian Government has permitted foreign direct investment of up to 26 per cent in the defence industry, and private sector involvement of up to 100 per cent. New joint projects are already in the pipeline, to be developed in collaboration with India's DPSUs, possibly with a wider arms export strategy in mind: in the field of aerospace, involving two Russian design bureaus and American aviation giant Lockheed-Martin; in missile production, involving the Russians and European missile manufacturer MBDA; and in submarine manufacture, involving the

French. Meanwhile, over 15 licences have been issued domestically to private companies, for the production of military vehicles and weapons systems, while private enterprises like the Krasny Marine Services look well placed to revitalize India's naval–industrial complex.[16]

For the Pakistani defence industry, licence production and direct procurement have likewise proved to be the main mode of supply. While it could also draw upon a substantial skilled workforce, financial, technological and industrial limitations have circumscribed Pakistan's long-term aspiration to become the arsenal of the Islamic world. Pakistan is capable of supplying simpler arms to its Islamic neighbours, and some weapons systems have been bankrolled by Saudi Arabia and other Arab states. Yet Islamabad must still procure the most advanced military hardware and technology from the international arms market or its allies, under preferential payment terms.

From the mid-1960s, Pakistan developed the capability to manufacture virtually all its small arms – including a machine-gun and the G-3 rifle, both under West German licence, and the 106-mm recoilless rifle, an American design – as well as most ammunition, explosives, shells and mortars. During the 1980s, it acquired the means to completely reconstruct its Chinese-supplied tanks, as well as its Chinese and French-supplied aircraft. Over the past two decades, naval-industrial facilities have also been modernized, centring upon indigenous establishments (like the Karachi Naval Dockyard, and Karachi Shipyard and Engineering Works Limited) and indigenous shipbuilding (such as the *Larkhana*-class patrol and *Jalalat*-class missile boats). But Pakistan remains heavily dependent on Chinese and (US-led) Western sources for new tanks, military vehicles and aircraft of all kinds, artillery, missiles, electronics and other strategic materials. Apart from its technical capacity for the delivery of nuclear weapons the American F-16 has, in particular, become a political symbol of America's commitment to support the Pakistani nation-state against India and other opponents in the wider world.[17]

In this connection, the arming of South Asia has also manifested itself as a creeping militarization beyond the official jurisdiction of the state: the arming of 'non-state actors' such as local warlords, regional resistance groups and worldwide terror networks. If South Asia remains one of the world's most militarized zones, it is not simply on account of rivalries between global or regional powers in Asia. Modern India and Pakistan are nation-states constructed out of the myriad societies and often polarized communities of the subcontinent, whose growing sense of alienation, independent aspirations and volatile ambitions have required only weaponization in order to trigger fresh waves of violence.

D. K. Palit, a Sandhurst-trained Indian general, once characterized India–Pakistan wars as 'communal riots with armour'. The two major conflicts of 1948 and 1965 – and the Kargil crisis of 1999 – were collisions over the former princely state of Jammu and Kashmir; the conflict of 1971 was over divided territories and communities that became Bangladesh; and near-clashes in 1955, 1987, 1990 and 2002 were motivated by the same communal tensions.[18] Even as 'homegrown' terrorists and 'guest' militants continue to make rival areas of Kashmir their main theatre of operations, the fragile fabric of the nation-state has itself been exposed and fundamentally challenged by a host of powerful indigenous forces: a series of secessionist movements in the case of India; and militarism and Islamic revivalism, in addition to regionalism and separatism, in the case of Pakistan.[19]

Apart from ongoing political–military instability in Kashmir, India has faced challenges from other secessionist movements. With Pakistani support, the Sikhs have fought for 'Khalistan', an independent Sikh state in the Punjab. Separatist and autonomist movements have gained momentum among the Nagas, the Mizos and other tribal groups in India's northeast, along the border with Bangladesh. There has also been trouble with Tamil separatists in southern India, leading to wider entanglements with Tamil extremists in Sri Lanka's civil war. As a way of pressuring Colombo to negotiate a peace settlement with moderate Tamils, New Delhi allowed the southern Indian state of Tamil Nadu to provide sympathetic financial and military aid to extremist Tamil groups in northern Sri Lanka. The Liberation Tigers of Tamil Eelam were thus transformed into a world-class terrorist movement. But the policy backfired spectacularly in 1987, when India and Sri Lanka signed an agreement whereby Sri Lanka acknowledged India's security concerns and allowed India to move in to disarm the Tigers. Instead of surrendering their weapons to the Indian Peacekeeping Force, the Tigers turned them first on their Tamil rivals and then on the surprised Indian troops. Between 1987 and 1990, Indian forces were drawn into a bitter and futile conflict in the jungles of northern Sri Lanka.[20]

Pakistan's involvement in the dying stages of the Cold War conflict between America and Russia, fought out in neighbouring Afghanistan, would bring an equally bitter harvest and further militarization. Arms seeped from supply conduits established by the CIA and were channelled by the Pakistan military security agency (ISI) to select groups of Afghan *mujahidin*. Traditional arms bazaars in the Northwest Frontier (such as at Darra), along with new centres of production adjacent to the Afghan frontier, added to the flow of weapons by replicating machine-guns and rifles and even US-supplied stinger missiles. The birth of a 'Kalashnikov culture' in the mid-1980s made it possible to hire arms on the streets of Karachi for a small sum of money: criminal gangs and rival sectarian groups (such as the *muhajirs* in Karachi and Hyderabad) soon possessed firepower surpassing that of the police and security forces.[21]

Meanwhile, Afghan *mujahidin* financed their military operations with drug money. Local warlords became drug-lords as traditional opium fields in autonomous tribal areas of Baluchistan and Northwest Frontier Province boosted their production dramatically in the unsettled conditions created by the influx of three million Afghan refugees after 1979. Heroin followed the same clandestine routes out of the country as weapons found their way in, later to surface on the streets of the Western metropolis. As the West, China, and Arab states poured in money and military supplies for the militants, the jihad in Afghanistan assumed a life of its own and spawned a second generation of *mujahidin* who called themselves *Taliban*, the 'students of Islam'. With the Taliban's support of Osama Bin Laden, and the subsequent Al-Qa'ida attacks on America between

1998 and 2001, it was only a matter of time before the United States and Pakistan found themselves drawn into the dynamics of a more nebulous global conflict – the 'war on terror'.[22]

Military–industrial globalization in contemporary South Asia broadly suggests a scenario in which indigenous military developments have, up until recently, proved largely subordinate to the global and regional interests of others. Yet, as the volatile military cultural context of the subcontinent might indicate, there had been episodes in the earlier history of globalization when this was clearly not the case.

Historical roots and ramifications

Growing interconnection between regions of the world, manifested in evolving networks of collaboration as well as escalating patterns of conflict, has been evident for centuries. But the global forces of Western imperial and industrial expansion, gaining momentum from the mid-eighteenth century onwards, brought new motive forces and motors of change. Between the world crises of the late eighteenth century and the cataclysm of the First World War, the forming and transforming of social, commercial, political and cultural relationships across porous borders and turbulent frontiers both fuelled and facilitated transfers of increasingly advanced military hardware and technology.[23] This served to arm the periphery in South Asia long before the birth of modern India and Pakistan. As we shall see, however, the Western great power presence on the subcontinent was constrained by native powers whose indigenous military capabilities would – in addition to weapons and techniques acquired from the Europeans – create an almost 'revolutionary' impact on Indo-European relations, politics and society. Up until the mid-nineteenth century, a number of these indigenous military establishments would achieve technological near-parity with their Western counterparts.[24]

To begin with, it was 'industrious revolutions' and industrialization – occurring within the framework of a wider struggle for supremacy in Europe – which first enabled the modernization of the defence industry. From clusters of workshops to chains of factories, state-led initiatives spearheaded military innovation and industry across the West, pushing arms trade and technology by stages into higher gear. New technologies in metallurgy and steam power were applied to weapons and warfare, with devastating consequences. The progressive commercialization of war, military service, arms manufacture and supply would climax in the construction of a military–industrial complex, capable of producing anything from small arms to heavy armaments, ammunition and explosives to pontoon-bridges and warships.[25]

Just as it was an age of unprecedented industrial transformation, it was also an era of Western imperial expansion. While industrialization modernized the arms industry, imperialism 'globalized' it. In the early phases of Western expansion, European soldiers entered the services of Asian kingdoms and helped spread the knowledge of firearms. But the transfer of military hardware and technology between the European seaborne empires and the states of Asia was itself relatively sparing. Under the constraints of the prevailing mercantilist ethic, the English in coastal India were major importers of muskets yet reluctant arms dealers. What altered this cross-cultural relationship was the ebb and flow of great power rivalry, which gathered pace during the second half of the eighteenth century and fed into the mainstream of late nineteenth-century 'new imperialism'.[26] Imperial activity tended to destabilize frontiers: great power competition distorted judgments and encouraged pre-emptive strike; and the men on the spot, fired by personal ambition, fomented their own convenient crises. By augmenting and accelerating arms transfers from the Western metropole, the new industrial and imperial dynamic would eventually arm parts of the periphery with the most modern rather than the most obsolete of weapons.

Western great power rivalry was fought out in the South Asian periphery as far back as the mid-eighteenth century. The British and the French clashed on the subcontinent between 1740 and 1815 as part of a worldwide extension of their European conflict. Then, in a nineteenth-century version of the Cold War, Britain and Russia played the 'Great Game' in Afghanistan between 1828 and 1907, countering each other's expansion by diplomacy, subversion and other means of informal influence. Global military–strategic imperatives played their part in the arming of the region even then, although it is important to note here that the balance of military–industrial power favoured indigenous forces initially, before equalizing and finally tipping in favour of the West.

The Anglo-French duel for empire was fought with blazing intensity in southern India during the War of the Austrian Succession (1740–48), erupting again during the Seven Years' War (1756–63), and persisting as a security threat up until the French Revolutionary and Napoleonic Wars (1792–1815). In the early stages of the conflict, neither European power possessed sufficient manpower or military resources to achieve its objectives on its own. Instead, just as state-sponsored arms exports and cash subsidies comprised a major component of wartime diplomacy in Europe, massive arms shipments were supplied by the European trading companies to indigenous allies in South Asia: 'hardly a ship came' in the 1760s, 'that did not sell them cannon and small arms'.[27] In a rising crescendo of profit and violence, the East India Companies of both Britain and France now bartered weapons for commodities and concessions, or sold military services to Indian armies to further military–strategic ends.

By the 1760s, the British (in Madras, Bombay and Calcutta) had managed to turn the tide against the French (in Pondicherry). The breakthrough came in 1765, when the English East India Company acquired the vast land revenues of Bengal that enabled it to build and finance a huge native army, supplied from its own arsenals.[28] It was a pioneering demonstration in the 'global diversification' of a trading company. As one early commentator observed: 'A Company which carries a sword in one hand, and a ledger in the other, which maintains armies and retails tea, is a contradiction, and if it traded with success, would be a prodigy.'[29]

By the time of the Napoleonic Wars, this novel experiment in 'military-fiscalism' had paved the way for a British Raj in India. Even though the French were still arming indigenous opponents of the Raj, it was the British arms trade that had become the largest in the world, inundating South Asia not merely with swords but sophisticated muskets.[30]

And yet, however prodigious it proved to be, this British experiment in military-fiscalism can only be understood properly within the context of older patterns of governance in South Asia. The East India Company's experience of global diversification must likewise be viewed alongside indigenous examples of military–industrial globalization. Long before British global power dominated the subcontinent, the Mughals from Central Asia ruled India as a 'gunpowder empire', their authority resting as much on military hardware and technology as political organization and wealth.[31] Mughal small arms and heavy armaments, produced in state arsenals and foundries since the seventeenth century, served as instruments through which opponents could be overwhelmed and brought within the governance of Mughal military-fiscalism.

By the mid-eighteenth century, however, South Asia was convulsed by wider regional transformations and crises. Mughal India, like many of the old imperial centres of monsoon Asia, was hollowed-out to a mere shell of its former glory through the ascendancy of provincial elites, breakaway satrapies and successor states. It was further challenged by tribal breakouts in the resurgence of great warrior coalitions from Arabia and Central Asia, as well as the breaking-in of sustained European capital flows and commerce.[32] The waning of Mughal hegemony paved the way for greater autonomy among the lower ranks of India's 'hierarchy of kings' and other forms of indigenous capitalism: the revenue and military entrepreneurs, the big bankers, and the warrior peasant lords of the villages. All derived wealth from commodity trade, all speculated in money profit, and most needed cash to buy muskets, cannon, elephants and other symbols of power and status. The English East India Company was drawn into – and benefited greatly from – this turbulent scenario of war and opportunity: playing off one state against another, selling its own services and supplies in the 'all-India military bazaar'.[33]

Military–industrial globalization on the subcontinent proved to be a double-edged weapon. Arms and ammunition figured prominently among the stock-in-trade bartered to petty rajas for spices, but the stakes were raised when great princes like the Nizam of Hyderabad were drawn into this volatile military market. An internal arms race ensued, even as indigenous military production and technology began to assume a progressively 'modern' complexion. There was some reliance on European mercenary officers who served as military advisers, and some dependence on direct weapons procurement. But the bulk of firearms used by the armies of the regional magnates were, in fact, manufactured in local factories such as those at Lucknow, Pondicherry, Hyderabad, and Lahore. State arsenals and magazines sprang up in the former Mughal heartland around Delhi, producing cannon, muskets, gunpowder and shot equal to – if not exceeding – European standards. Three Indian armies, in particular, developed the capabilities to challenge British colonial authority on the subcontinent. They were the forces of the Maratha Confederation, the state of Mysore, and the Sikhs. With their foreign-assisted but largely homegrown military establishments, each had the capacity to deal a crippling blow to the Company's military machine before the great mutiny-rebellion of 1857 finally finished off Company rule.[34]

Soon after the Mughal emperor had submitted to his 'protection' in 1784, Mahadji Scindia, the greatest of the Maratha warlords, proceeded to establish his own 'military-industrial complex' near Agra. The Maratha ordnance factories emphasized adaptation rather than innovation, but incorporated relatively sophisticated indigenous technology and involved local manufacturers. These developments so alarmed the English East India Company that it forbade Britons to serve as gunners with the Marathas and sought to curtail the trade in muskets. But with the assistance of French and Portuguese military advisers, Scindia went on to create one of the finest armies in India – including the 27,000-strong brigade known as the 'Deccan Invincibles' – supplied from Scindia's arsenal at Agra. By combining these new weapons with new battlefield tactics, the Marathas came close to defeating the British on several occasions. During the Second Anglo-Maratha War (1803–05), Arthur Wellesley's success at Assaye owed more to a bayonet charge than any advantage in firepower conferred by Western arms, and the hero of Waterloo later called Assaye the hardest-fought battle of his entire career.[35]

Then, there was the military establishment of Mysore. The military foundations had been laid by the great warlord Haidar Ali, who was one of the first to appreciate the advantages of flintlock over against matchlock technology. In their wars against indigenous opponents, both Haidar Ali and his son Tipu Sultan obtained flintlock muskets from European, predominantly British, sources. European mercenaries, predominantly French, were also employed, and workshops and armouries were established for the maintenance and subsequent manufacture of firearms. But the 'Tiger of Mysore' would turn and bite one of the hands that fed it. In the wars of the 1780s, two-thirds of the arms used by Mysore against the East India Company were of British manufacture. By 1799, following the siege of Seringapatam in which Tipu Sultan was himself killed, the British recovered 52,000 flintlock muskets of British and French origin, as well as 47,000 flintlock guns of indigenous manufacture. Even more remarkable was the fact that there were only 320 matchlocks, all of which appeared unserviceable. This extremely small stock of what was then the Indian standard firearm attests to the modernity of Mysore's military establishment: small arms which generally continued to be used in other parts of India well into the nineteenth century were already being regarded as obsolescent by Mysore as early as the 1770s–80s. After Tipu's downfall, however, the French advisers and local manufacturers were removed, and nothing remains of the 'eleven armouries for making and finishing small arms'.[36]

But finally, in order to defeat their opponents in the Sikh Wars (1845–49), the British had to deploy armies equal in size and superior in artillery firepower.

This was no mean feat since, by the time of his death in 1839, the great 'Lion of the Punjab' Ranjit Singh had built up a 150,000-strong army, of whom about 65,000 were regulars 'trained by European soldiers of fortune and supported by ... guns of a type more modern than those used by the British'.[37] Like the Marathas and Mysore before them, the Sikhs relied on a combination of Western (mainly French) military advisers, direct weapons procurement, and indigenous arms production at the military-industrial establishment in Lahore.

In the wider South Asian periphery, a contest between Britain and Russia was being played out in Afghanistan, to the northwest of British India and to the south of an expanding Czarist presence in Central Asia. The 'Great Game' was a clandestine war of espionage and bribery, with occasional military–strategic pressure, as both European powers kept each other at bay by maintaining Afghanistan as a buffer state between them.[38] But even then, as now, the course and contours of the global conflict would be shaped by its indigenous military cultural context; and the arming of South Asia would manifest itself as a creeping militarization beyond the grasp of state authority.

The weakening of Mughal as well as Ottoman and Safavid authority had opened up these empires to attacks by powerful but unstable warrior coalitions of Afghan, Persian or Central Asian origin. As far back as the 1720s, Afghan tribal armies had eradicated Safavid influence from much of southeastern Afghanistan, and sacked many key cities in western Iran. Mughal India also suffered: Delhi capitulated to the armies of the Persian, Nadir Shah, in 1739. The untamed frontier of Northwest India remained in a state of perpetual flux: a new Afghan kingdom emerged to consolidate its hold over western Iran and Afghanistan, Sindh and the Punjab; northern India was invaded four times by the Afghans in 1747 and 1759–61, and menaced again in 1797; while the frontier and its society were progressively militarized and populated by warlike tribes such as the Afridis, Pathans and Baluchis.[39]

The British attempted to annex Afghanistan until they realized that the intractable Afghans could be bought more easily than fought. The British offered money, manipulated the tribal chiefs, and managed to turn Afghanistan periodically into a client state. Yet the instability persisted: it was a potent combination of deep mistrust of the British; perceived threat from Russia; fears of Ottoman or Persian aggression; Islamic revivalism and growing militancy among the frontier tribes; plus a further manifestation of forward policy. Britain's ploy of installing a puppet regime failed twice, leading to anti-colonial resistance and outright war in 1839–42 and 1878–80. From the British occupation of the Punjab in 1849 up until 1914, over 52 punitive military expeditions were mounted into tribal no-man's-land, as well as ongoing small-scale engagements along the shifting frontier line between British India and Afghanistan.[40]

Between the 1880s and 1900s, the British found themselves providing military equipment as well as financial assistance, leading to further militarization of the region. Initially, British subsidies and arms supplies were intended to centralize and strengthen the Afghan state. But the matter of 'open and unrestrained' arms transfers from British India to the Amir of Afghanistan grew more problematic over time. Afghan loyalties became questionable and security threats emerged out of the leakage of rifles from Kabul to the hostile frontier tribes.[41] Furthermore, despite the negotiation of the Durand Line (1893), which set an 'official' boundary for British Indian and Afghan influence over the tribes of the Northwest Frontier, it was apparent to agents on the spot that illicit arms shipments were finding their way from the Gulfs of Persia and Oman, along clandestine routes, across porous borders, into the hands of the tribesmen. Significantly, at least part of this arms trade was also financed by drug money – opium revenues and indigenous credit facilities – originating from within British India itself.[42] Large quantities of modern rifles from the West began to replace the indigenous *jezail* (tribal rifled musket) with which Afghan warriors had hitherto been armed.[43] The 'official' and 'unofficial' arming of nineteenth-century Afghanistan would lead to a third Anglo-Afghan war in 1919; 60 years before the onset of a costly Russian (Soviet) occupation; and 80 years before yet another world power was drawn into the tribal politics of the militarized zone, with its globalized networks of terror.[44]

Future impact and implications

Every age presents its unique set of circumstances and challenges, with new constellations of world powers, regional intermediaries and local forces dominating the political firmament. Yet the unfolding history of over two centuries of military–industrial globalization in South Asia reveals longer-term patterns of collaboration and conflict that continue to reverberate.

First, there is the perennial crisis of small arms proliferation in South Asia. Travelling through Bengal in the mid-1820s, Bishop Heber of Calcutta noted that 'country arms' were readily available in a supposedly de-militarized district of British India; a musket could be bought for 20 rupees, while a brace of pistols cost just 16 rupees.[45] Traversing the streets of Karachi in the mid-1980s, one could just as easily and cheaply acquire an assortment of semi-automatic weapons.[46] In the long shadows cast by the Anglo-Afghan wars, the ancient rifles of British regimental life and the Gulf arms trade survived – restored or modified – to be effective sniping weapons against Soviet forces in Afghanistan. Likewise, in the aftermath of the global Cold War conflict, at least one independent analyst has observed the ongoing repercussions of recycled military firearms in the South Asian periphery: emerging 'gun cultures' linked to organized crime and political movements, insurgencies and sectarian violence.[47] For regional gun control associations such as the South Asia Small Arms Network, the task is to progressively disarm the periphery: promoting collaborative efforts between governments and civil society aimed at curbing small arms proliferation.

Second, there is the potential crisis of arms escalation linked to interlocking crises across Asia. Just as an arms race developed among successor states in Mughal India, and this crisis was part of a more general crisis confronting the other Asian land empires, so the dynamics of military build-up between India and Pakistan are similarly connected to military developments around the rest of Asia. Military–strategic polarization and build-up along the lines of a global Iron Curtain, dividing communist East from capitalist West, has long given way to fears of a globalized Asian 'nuclear weapons chain': fully-interactive, multinational, extending from Israel and Iran in the West, and Pakistan and India in the South, to China and North Korea in the East. While they are not necessarily contiguous, all the 'links' in the chain may have missiles capable of reaching at least two other nuclear weapons states, or have access to missile technology of ever-increasing range. Moreover, the chain is inherently unstable; the 'weakest link' could precipitate nuclear catastrophe. Iran's efforts at uranium enrichment have not so far yielded nuclear armament, but this could just be a matter of time. Iraq as a rogue state has been removed from the equation, yet the danger of armed insurgency still poses a threat to regional security. Apart from possible crises arising from their own strategic rivalry or internal instability, India and Pakistan must ensure – in the complex web of relationships involving the United States, Russia, China, Israel, Iraq, Iran and Afghanistan – neither South Asian power becomes the object of a superior nuclear alliance, or the subject of third-party (and terrorist) machinations.[48]

Third, and finally, there remains the persisting conundrum of the worldwide 'war on terror'. In a further ironic twist to Kipling's 'Ballad of East and West', a more nebulous global confrontation has taken shape around the South Asian periphery, in which 'the fault lines between civilizations [have become] the battle lines of the future', while the 'two strong men' are neo-conservative America and a supposed monolith called militant Islam.[49] In fact, the West has intoned the language of crusade and civilizing mission for centuries, and their evangelical zeal has been echoed in indigenous society by a long discourse of Islamic revivalism, incorporating strands of both anti-colonial protest and jihad. Osama Bin Laden originated from the same part of the world as Muhammad Ibn Abdul Wahhab, founder of the ultra-fundamentalist Wahhabi movement. Just as the Wahhabis from Arabia had embodied a more extremist dimension of Islamic revivalism during the late eighteenth century, so an array of eclectic millenarian and jihadi movements would do the same across the rest of the Islamic world in the nineteenth and twentieth centuries.[50]

Islamic extremists who emerged from these movements would not only sanction the force of arms, but also involve themselves in the arms trade. A century before the Taliban, 'the fiery exhortations of the mullas' and 'the revived activity of the Hindustani fanatics' had proved crucial in galvanizing anti-colonial resistance and arms transfers across the Northwest Frontier where Kipling set his poem.[51] Decades before Osama and his terrorist training camps, a 'holy' Afghan named Khalifeh Khair Mahomed had developed 'a keen interest in gunrunning', emigrating to Persian Baluchistan where he supplied 'countrymen who made the annual pilgrimage to the Gulf for the purchase of arms'.[52] Long before American-made and supplied military equipment was turned on the Americans themselves, British-made weapons – transported to the Gulf by British shipping agencies, backed by British insurers and banks – were being acquired by Islamic warriors to be used against British colonial forces out in the periphery.[53] What has changed in the twenty-first century is the capacity of extremists in today's world to re-export their 'terror' to the urban frontiers of the Western metropole, suicide bombings and all.

As had been the case with the British and their collaborators a century ago, the main difficulty facing America and its allies in the 'war on terror' is that the porous frontier itself is part-problem and part-solution. Like the Northwest Frontier of British India, Pakistan as an ally in the war against terrorism remains a potential source of Islamic radicalism linked to terror, apart from also being a loose cannon in the nuclear weapons arena.[54] Like British attempts to transform Afghanistan into a client of the Raj via puppet regimes presiding over a centralized Afghan state, the path for America in contemporary Afghanistan (and Iraq) is similarly fraught amid the shifting alliances and alienations of tribes and warlords, where there is little distinction between religion and politics. Moreover, there is a danger that events flowing from the war against terrorism will produce a similar radicalism in the West: isolationism, Islamophobia, racism and religious revivalism that could echo – albeit in a very different form – the policies of the Taliban. In a world where the global village becomes the turbulent frontier, and moderates of East and West get caught in the crossfire, the ultimate reconciliation may only take place at 'God's great Judgment seat'.

Notes

1 I am grateful to Gyanesh Kudaisya and Dipankar Banerjee for their insights and comments on an earlier draft of this chapter.
2 D. Held, A. McGrew, D. Goldblatt and J. Perraton, *Global Transformations* (Oxford: Blackwell, 1999), pp. 1–2, 16; A. G. Hopkins (ed.), *Globalization in World History* (London: Pimlico, 2002), pp. 16–17, 48–49.
3 M. T. Berger, *The Battle for Asia: From Decolonization to Globalization* (London: RoutledgeCurzon, 2004), pp. 136–137.
4 S. P. Cohen, *India: Emerging Power* (Washington, DC: Brookings Institution, 2001), pp. 128–129; see also A. M. Wainwright, *Inheritance of Empire: Britain, India, and the Balance of Power in Asia, 1938–55* (Westport, CT: London: Praeger, 1994).
5 Cohen, *India: Emerging Power*, pp. 132–134. While the US concentrated on modernizing India's army and air force, Britain assumed responsibility for India's navy during that burst of military co-operation with the West in 1963–65.
6 Cohen, *India: Emerging Power*, pp. 136–137, 268–298; V. M. Gobarev, 'The US should treat India as an ally', in W. Dudley (ed.), *India and Pakistan: Opposing Viewpoints* (Farmington Hills, MI: Greenhaven, 2003), pp. 118–128; P. R. Chari, 'Implementing the Indo-US Nuclear Deal: A Pyrrhic Struggle', *India Defence* (7 January 2006); S. Devare, *India and Southeast Asia: Towards Security Convergence* (Singapore: Institute of Southeast Asian Studies, 2006), pp. 32–34. India has even been able to acquire a Falcon radar system from Israel, a close ally of the United States. On the other hand, concerns surrounding India's efforts to gain nuclear weapons and ballistic missile capabilities cloud the issue of helping India develop space launch and satellite capabilities that it claims are necessary to counter the growing security threat from China. Technologies used in commercial satellite and space launches could facilitate India's strategic missile programmes.
7 Cohen, *India: Emerging Power*, pp. 138–142, 147.

8 S. P. Cohen, 'U.S. Weapons and South Asia: A Policy Analysis', *Pacific Affairs*, 41:1 (Spring 1976), pp. 49–69; S. P. Cohen, *The Pakistan Army* (Berkeley: University of California Press, 1984), pp. 7, 138.

9 W. H. Wriggins, 'Pakistan's Foreign Policy after Afghanistan', in S. P. Cohen (ed.), *The Security of South Asia: American and Asian Perspectives* (Urbana: University of Illinois Press, 1987), pp. 70–71. Of the Chinese-supplied aircraft, 144 were MiG-19/-F-6s that, together with French Mirage IIIs and Mirage Vs, formed the backbone of Pakistan's air force.

10 Cohen, *India: Emerging Power*, pp. 184–185.

11 Wriggins, 'Pakistan's Foreign Policy after Afghanistan', in Cohen (ed.), *The Security of South Asia*, pp. 71–72; S. P. Cohen, *The Idea of Pakistan* (New Delhi: Oxford University Press, 2005), pp. 302–304.

12 The International Institute for Strategic Studies, *The Military Balance 1978–79, 1994–95* and *2004–5* (London: Oxford University Press, 1979, 1995 and 2005); A. Siddiqa, 'Pakistan: Political Economy of National Security', in V. Kukreja and M. P. Singh (eds), *Pakistan: Democracy, Development and Security Issues* (New Delhi and London: Sage, 2005), pp. 123–136. The present military regime in Pakistan is keen to embark upon socio-economic development, but recent reductions in defence budget have been marginal, denoting cosmetic changes rather than any substantive policy reversal.

13 US Department of State website, 'Military Expenditures and Arms Transfers 1999–2000', *Fact Sheet* (6 February 2003).

14 D. R. Mohanty, 'Changing Times? India's Defence Industry in the 21st Century', *Bonn International Center for Conversion, Paper 36* (Bonn, 2004); Cohen, *India: Emerging Power*, pp. 142–144; The International Institute for Strategic Studies, *The Military Balance 1999–2000* (London: Oxford University Press, 2000). Indian arms exports in the late 1990s were valued at only $5 million, compared to China's $600 million and Iran's $80 million.

15 R. A. Bitzinger, 'Globalization in the Post-Cold War Defence Industry: Challenges and Opportunities', in A. Markusen and S. Costigan (eds), *Arming the Future: A Defense Industry for the 21st Century* (New York: Council on Foreign Relations, 1999).

16 Ministry of Defence, Government of India, *Annual Report 2004–2005* (New Delhi, 2005); V. Sakhuja, 'Rejuvenating Indian Military Industrial Complex', *South Asia Analysis Group, Paper 1533* (New Delhi, 2005).

17 Cohen, *The Pakistan Army*, pp. 150–152; see also P. I. Cheema, 'Arms Procurement in Pakistan: Balancing the Needs for Quality, Self-Reliance and Diversity of Supply', in E. Arnett (ed.), *Military Capacity and the Risk of War: China, India, Pakistan and Iran* (Oxford: Oxford University Press, 1997); and A. Siddiqa-Agha, *Pakistan's Arms Procurement and Military Build-up, 1979–1999: In Search of a Policy* (Basingstoke and New York: Palgrave, 2001).

18 D. K. Palit, quoted in Cohen, *India: Emerging Power*, p. 224; P. Bidwai, 'Nuclear Weapons Decrease India's and Pakistan's Security', in Dudley (ed.), *India and Pakistan: Opposing Viewpoints*, p. 39; Cohen, *The Idea of Pakistan*, p. 12.

19 Cohen, *The Idea of Pakistan*, pp. 42, 51–56, 73–77; 97–130, 161–229; K. Sridharan, 'Grasping the Nettle: Indian Nationalism and Globalization', in L. Suryadinata (ed.), *Nationalism and Globalization: East and West* (Singapore: Institute of Southeast Asian Studies, 2000), pp. 294–316; Kukreja and Singh (eds), *Pakistan: Democracy, Development and Security Issues*, pp. 19–21, 25–30, 39–57.

20 K. M. de Silva, *Regional Powers and Small State Security: India and Sri Lanka, 1977–90* (Washington, DC: Woodrow Wilson Center Press, 1995), pp. 79–336; Cohen, *India: Emerging Power*, pp. 113, 147–149, 236–241.

21 I. Talbot, *India and Pakistan* (London: Arnold, 2000), pp. 231–234; L. Ziring, 'Pakistan: Terrorism in Historical Perspective', and R. Harshé, 'Cross-border Terrorism:

Roadblock to Peace Initiative', in Kukreja and Singh (eds), *Pakistan: Democracy, Development and Security Issues*, pp. 168–205 and 246–257, respectively.

22 M. Ewans, *Afghanistan: A New History* (Richmond: Curzon, 2001), pp. 149–209; A. Rashid, *Taliban: Militant Islam, Oil and Fundamentalism in Central Asia* (London: IB Tauris, 2000), pp. 13–30, 117–127; P. Marsden, *The Taliban: War and Religion in Afghanistan* (London: Zed Books, 2002), pp. 26–66, 146–156.

23 For a wide historical angle on globalization and its overall impact on the world before 1914, see C. A. Bayly, *The Birth of the Modern World 1780–1914: Global Connections and Comparisons* (Oxford: Blackwell, 2004).

24 See D. B. Ralston, *Importing the European Army: The Introduction of European Military Techniques and Institutions into the Extra-European World, 1600–1914* (Chicago and London: University of Chicago Press, 1990); and P. J. Marshall, 'Western Arms in Maritime Asia in the Early Phases of Expansion', *Modern Asian Studies*, 14:1 (1980). Historian Peter Marshall has argued that while the potential capacity for Europeans to wage war more effectively than Asians had perhaps existed since the 'military revolution' of the seventeenth century, only in the early nineteenth century could the full force of this potential be felt on Asian battlefields: it was only then that arms production in Europe was accelerating, shipping costs to the East were falling, European governments were displacing the trading companies and taking a direct interest in Asia, and territorial possessions in India were providing the British with new resources of men and money. Marshall's thesis warrants reconsideration in the light of the dynamics of military-industrial globalization advanced in this chapter, particularly given the vitality of indigenous military industries in South Asia between 1750 and 1850.

25 W. H. McNeill, *The Pursuit of Power: Technology, Armed Force, and Society since A.D. 1000* (Oxford: Blackwell, 1983), pp. 236–237, 262ff.; C. Trebilcock, *The Industrialization of the Continental Powers, 1780–1914* (London: Longman, 1981), pp. 26–29, 346–349.

26 See D. R. Headrick, *The Tentacles of Progress: Technology Transfer in the Age of Imperialism, 1850–1940* (New York and Oxford: Oxford University Press, 1988).

27 Col. H. Munro's evidence, *Reports from Committees of the House of Commons*, (London, 1803–06), vol. III, p. 169.

28 C. A. Bayly, *New Cambridge History of India*, 2.1: *Indian Society and the Making of the British Empire* (Cambridge: Cambridge University Press, 1988), pp. 50–53, 84–87; see also D. M. Peers, *Between Mars and Mammon: Colonial Armies and the Garrison State in India 1819–1835* (London: Tauris Academic Studies, 1995).

29 J. R. McCulloch, 'Indian Revenues', *Edinburgh Review*, 45 (1827), p. 365. For a modern treatment of the English East India Company's history, see H. V. Bowen, *The Business of Empire: The East India Company and Imperial Britain, 1756–1833* (Cambridge: Cambridge University Press, 2005). Of course, there was global diversification of trading activities as well as trade goods, and the British traded more than just tea and arms. The end of the American Revolutionary War (1782–83) and the passing of Pitt's Commutation Act (1784) consolidated British control of the wider 'country' trade, and encouraged the activities of powerful and capital-rich agency houses and agents adept at both the commodity trade – in tea, spices, opium, indigo, calicoes, cotton piece goods, raw silk, ceramics, and saltpetre – as well as the arms trade.

30 C. A. Bayly, *Imperial Meridian: The British Empire and the World 1780–1830* (London: Longman, 1989), p. 130; see also H. A. Young, *The East India Company's Arsenals and Manufactories* (Oxford: Clarendon Press, 1937); and D. Harding, *Small Arms of the East India Company 1600–1856* (London: Foresight Books, 1997), vol. 1: *Procurement and Design*. From the establishment of the first military depots, workshops and armouries on the subcontinent in the late 1760s, up until the end of Company rule in 1858, the arsenals of the English East India Company were capable

of producing their own gunpowder, brass ordnance, gun-carriages, percussion caps, bullets and other military stores. The only important articles of military equipment the Company did not manufacture in India itself were small arms. Although some were purchased in India and produced in several of the Indian states, the bulk were procured by the Company from its own network of workshops and factories in Birmingham and London, which supplied weapons of high standard for service not only in India, but elsewhere.

31 K. N. Chaudhuri, *Asia before Europe: Economy and Civilization of the Indian Ocean from the Rise of Islam to 1750* (Cambridge: Cambridge University Press, 1990), pp. 101–103.
32 Bayly, *Imperial Meridian*, pp. 16–74.
33 Bayly, *Indian Society and the Making of the British Empire*, pp. 47–48.
34 H. Compton, *A Particular Account of the European Military Adventurers of Hindustan from 1784–1803* (London, 1893), pp. 385–387; S. Bidwell, *Swords for Hire: European Mercenaries in Eighteenth-century India* (London: J. Murray, 1971), p. 55; P. Barua, 'Military Developments in India 1750–1850', *The Journal of Military History*, 58:4 (1994), pp. 607, 611.
35 Bayly, *Indian Society and the Making of the British Empire*, pp. 98–103; R. G. S. Cooper, *The Anglo-Maratha Campaigns and the Contest for India: The Struggle for Control of the South Asian Military Economy* (Cambridge: Cambridge University Press, 2003); Letter from A. Wellesley to Major Malcolm, Camp, 26 September 1803, in *Supply Despatches and Memoranda of Field Marshal Arthur Duke of Wellington, K. G.* (London, 1858), vol. 4, p. 180.
36 Bayly, *Indian Society and the Making of the British Empire*, pp. 95–98; R. Wigington, *The Firearms of Tipu Sultan 1783–1799* (Hatfield: John Taylor Book Ventures, 1992), pp. 7–8, 12, 32–33; Lieutenant E. Moor, *A Narrative of the Operations of Captain Little's Detachment … During the Late Confederacy in India, against the Nawab Tippoo Sultan Bahadur* (London, 1794), pp. 478–479; A. Beatson, *A View of the Origin and Conduct of the War with Tippoo Sultaun* (London, G. & W. Nicol, 1800), p. 158. See also I. Habib (ed.), *Confronting Colonialism: Resistance and Modernization under Haidar Ali and Tipu Sultan* (London: Anthem, 2002). In addition to small arms, Mysore developed the ability to deploy artillery with stunning effect, and also pioneered efforts to build a navy.
37 Barua, 'Military Developments in India', pp. 612–613; C. E. Carrington, *The British Overseas: Exploits of a Nation of Shopkeepers* (Cambridge: Cambridge University Press, 1950), p. 438; see also A. Singh Madra and P. Singh, *Warrior Saints: Three Centuries of the Sikh Military Tradition* (London: IB Tauris in association with The Sikh Foundation, 1999).
38 See K. E. Meyer and S. Brysac, *Tournament of Shadows: The Great Game and the Race for Empire in Asia* (London: Little, Brown & Company, 1999).
39 Bayly, *Imperial Meridian*, pp. 36–39.
40 T. R. Moreman, 'The British and Indian Armies and North West Frontier Warfare, 1849–1914', *Journal of Imperial and Commonwealth History*, 20:1 (1992), p. 36.
41 Armaments in Afghanistan', *Arms and Explosives*, July 1901, p. 100.
42 E. M. Chew, 'Arming the Periphery: The Arms Trade in the Indian Ocean during the Nineteenth Century' (PhD thesis, University of Cambridge, 2002), pp. 209–210; C. A. Trocki, *Opium, Empire and the Global Political Economy: A Study of the Asian Opium Trade 1750–1950* (London: Routledge, 1999), pp. 83–85.
43 British Foreign Office (FO) 539/79/1, India Office to Foreign Office, 7 May 1880; India Office (IO) L/P&S/18, Memorandum D 182, Appendix T, 'The Arms and Ammunition Traffic in the Gulfs of Persia and Oman'; A. Keppel, *Gun-running and the Indian North-West Frontier* (London: J. Murray, 1911), pp. 49–50; Moreman, 'The British and Indian Armies and North West Frontier Warfare', pp. 40, 46–47, 58. The locally-made *jezail* continued to outclass the small arms employed by British

Indian troops for years after the First Afghan War, enabling resisting Afridis, Mahsuds and Pathans to harass British forces from out of range, combining superior marksmanship with skirmishing tactics in guerrilla warfare. The progressive adoption of Snider, Martini-Henry and Lee-Metford rifles by British forces redressed the imbalance for a time, but by the early 1890s, substantial numbers of modern precision-arms were also beginning to reach the Afghans, Baluchis, and other hill tribes – via Muscat – thus offsetting any British superiority in firepower. The intractability of the region's terrain, in conjunction with the tactics and strategy of tribal warriors, and the influx of even more lethal weapons, would ultimately jolt the British into developing a specific training doctrine suited to military operations in the Northwest Frontier.

44 See E. O'Ballance, *Afghan Wars 1839–1992: What Britain Gave Up and the Soviet Union Lost* (London: Brassey's, 1993); W. Maley, *The Afghanistan Wars* (Basingstoke and New York: Palgrave, 2002).
45 R. Heber, *Narrative of a Journey Through the Upper Provinces of India from Calcutta to Bombay, 1824–1825* (London, 1828), vol. 1, p. 135.
46 Talbot, *India and Pakistan*, p. 231.
47 M. Tully, 'The Arms Trade and Political Instability in South Asia', *Churchill Review* (1995).
48 Cohen, *India: Emerging Power*, pp. 189–190; Cohen, *The Idea of Pakistan*, p. 305. Islamabad's nuclear programme is a further concern, especially following revelations about the movement of nuclear and missile technology to and from Pakistan. Leakage of its nuclear expertise is a potentially destabilizing factor in Northeast Asia (via ties to North Korea), the Persian Gulf region (via Saudi Arabia and Iran), and the Middle East (via Libya).
49 S. P. Huntington, 'The Clash of Civilizations?' *Foreign Affairs*, 72:3 (Summer 1993), p. 22.
50 Bayly, *Imperial Meridian*, pp. 179–184; see also P. Hardy, *The Muslims of British India* (Cambridge: Cambridge University Press, 1972); J. A. Clancy-Smith, *Rebel and Saint: Muslim Notables, Popular Protest, Colonial Encounters (Algeria and Tunisia, 1800–1904)* (Berkeley and London: University of California Press, 1994).
51 Keppel, *Gun-running and the Indian North-West Frontier*, pp. 56–57, 68–70, 72–75.
52 H. H. Austin, 'Gun-running in the Gulf', *Blackwood's Magazine*, 208 (1920), p. 324.
53 IO, L/P&S/18, Memorandum D 182, Appendix T, 'The Arms and Ammunition Traffic in the Gulfs of Persia and Oman'; FO 539/79/224 and 230, Lloyd's Bank to Foreign Office, 15 and 21 April 1898; 'The Persian Gulf Trade in Fire-Arms', *Arms and Explosives*, July 1898, p. 159; 'The Persian Trade in Fire-Arms', *Arms and Explosives*, August 1898, p. 179; IO, L/P&S/7, Letters from India, No. 257 of 1902, Curzon to Hamilton, 23 January 1902.
54 S. Kumar, 'Reassessing Pakistan as a Long-Term Security Threat', in Kukreja and Singh (eds), *Pakistan: Democracy, Development and Security Issues*, pp. 223–245.

5 Globalization's impact on threat perception and defence postures in Northeast Asia

Guibourg Delamotte

New threats – such as the fight against terrorism and nuclear threats, long-time concerns which globalization has remodelled – have added branches to the defence policies of Japan and South Korea. The impact of globalization on defence policies of East Asian states is therefore a direct one as far as new threats are concerned.

Globalization's effect on old threats, such as territorial disputes, is indirect. Globalization blurs the line between domestic and international factors. The intervention of the media alone, and access of foreign media to national information, introduces international elements into national debates and gives national debates international repercussions. Whilst creating a more unified world, globalization enhances nationalism worldwide and politicians contribute to, and take advantage of, this side effect of globalization. To this extent, policies concerning territorial disputes appear as a by-product of globalization. Globalization fuels nationalism and a need on the part of public opinions to revert to local identities, which politicians instrumentalize. National leaders sometimes use mutual threats to further their defence agendas, which may be based on global or domestic concerns. Therefore, domestic concerns retain a tremendous importance over defence policies, but are always in some degree of interaction with global factors.

In discussing globalization's impact on threat perception and defence postures in Northeast Asia, I shall focus on Japan, China and South Korea, and their mutual relations and reciprocal fears. My emphasis will tend to be on Japan. I take as a starting point Peter Van Ness's definition of globalization, as 'human activities that have a reshaping planetary impact'.[1] The issues that I shall address are the fight against terrorism and the fight for non-proliferation. The means deployed against those threats via the 'war on terror' are no less global. I thereby include in this analysis the impact of the US military's transformation and modernization on South Korea, Japan and China. I understand 'defence postures' to mean defence policies and policies regarding matters of interest to national safety, and shall consider threat perceptions at both government and public opinion levels.

How have Japan and South Korea adjusted their defence policies to new threats, and how are they taking part in the 'war on terror'? Tensions between

Japan and China result partly from the fact that both countries are becoming 'symmetrical powers' (economic, political, military): what impact do these tensions have on defence postures in East Asia? How do ensuing changes in defence policies modify threat perception in the region?

Global threats have a direct impact on national defence policies in East Asia and on the modernization of the armed forces in the region. Domestic agendas often drive political leaders to emphasize threats in order to influence public opinion. Beyond threats, globalization offers opportunities, which none of the regional powers are willing to compromise.[2]

Global threats and national defence policies

The fight against terrorism has reshaped Japan's defence policy. The attitudes of South Korea, Japan and China with respect to non-proliferation have been widely different. The three countries are modernizing their armed forces to address new threats in more specific and suitable ways.

The fight against terrorism and defence policies

For Japan, the significance of participating in the 'war on terror' went beyond the alliance with the United States and economic considerations, though such factors also weighed in. Japan engaged in the 'war on terror' immediately after 9/11.[3] The policy set up included diplomatic efforts against terrorism and international co-operation to combat terrorism via the freezing of assets, as well as the passing of an Anti-Terrorism Special Measures Law on 19 October 2001, which provided for the dispatch to the Indian Ocean of ships and aircraft. In comparison with the period of the Gulf War, when the Japanese government had found itself unable to obtain the swift passage of a law on co-operation with the United Nations, or the precautions inserted in the 1992 Peacekeeping Operations Law, the 2001 law is remarkable in two ways. It was adopted within a few weeks of the 9/11 attacks; it undertook to take Japanese troops as close to a country at war as they had been since the Second World War. It provided rear support to US (and allied troops) on the distant fringes of the geographical boundaries of the US–Japan alliance (the 'Far East' in the 1960 Security Treaty; 'areas surrounding Japan' in the 1997 Guidelines on Security), establishing a new legal framework that superseded previous security arrangements.

In parallel with this military response, Japan kept up the non-military and traditional aspects of its security policy. It contributed to the international effort for the reconstruction of Afghanistan, through refugee and general assistance to Afghanistan and neighbouring countries: in the conference held on 21–22 January 2002 in Tokyo, Japan pledged $500 million over 2.5 years for the reconstruction of Afghanistan.

Japan also supported the US endeavour to free Iraq, though initially on the grounds that there might be WMD in Iraq. At the Madrid conference on the reconstruction of Iraq, on 24 October 2003, Japan committed itself to a

$5 billion assistance package of $1.5 billion in grants and $3.5 billion in loans. It also sent 600 men to Iraq on a reconstruction and humanitarian mission in 'non-combat zones', sheltered by Dutch and later Australian troops. The Japanese government was extremely cautious in deploying troops, and effectively did so only after re-involvement of the UN in Iraq and the end of the war had been proclaimed. The deployment of the Self-Defence Forces (SDF) took place after the end of the war, which was launched on 20 March 2003 and ended on 1 May the same year. Resolution 1483 of the UN Security Council, approving the establishment of a US-led administration, was passed on 22 May 2003; Japan's law for the dispatch of the SDF to Iraq was adopted on 26 July 2003. On 16 October 2003, resolution 1511, mentioning the vital role of the UN in the reconstruction of Iraq, was passed. The plan organizing the dispatch was adopted on 9 December and the first deployment took place on 26 December. This was Japan's first intervention in a country, which though no longer technically at war, remained highly unstable. However cautious and moderate in scale, the dispatch represented a considerable effort, caused tremendous uproar in the Diet and was highly unpopular. Nonetheless, after the adoption of the bill authorizing the dispatch, and before the plan organizing it, M. Koizumi was re-elected in September 2003 as head of the Liberal–Democratic Party and as Prime Minister in September 2005: however unpopular, his Iraqi policy bore no electoral consequence.

Furthermore, new threats – and specifically terrorism – became important parameters of the National Defence Programme Outline upon its renewal in November 2004. The previous one dated from 1995 and was now considered outdated in view of the emergence of the 'new threats' in question. The aim of the new outline was to turn the SDF into an agile, flexible force, deployed so as to be able to counter unpredictable threats, such as commando raids, for instance. Furthermore, a 'Plan for the Prevention of International Terrorism' involving the police, not the SDF, was adopted in December 2004.

Domestically, Japan was first made aware of a terrorist threat by the sarin gas attack of March 1995, perpetrated by the religious group Aum Shinrikyô. This chemical attack appeared as a stepping-stone in the era of nuclear, chemical and biological (NCB) terrorism. However, it was only after 9/11 that Japan adopted a wide range of measures for the prevention of terrorism.

In 2003–4, the Diet also adopted a set of laws on emergency situations. Though plans for emergency legislation were made in 1963 as well as 1976, the government was never able to push them through the Diet. In spite of fierce opposition in June 2003 and 2004, the majority were convinced that Japan needed a decision-making process suitable for emergencies and determining the prerogatives of local councils, what the treatment of prospective prisoners should be (intended for Japan to be able to ratify the Additional Protocols to the 1949 Geneva Conventions on the Treatment of Prisoners of War), and to provide for co-operation with US armed forces based in Japan. Terrorism has thus achieved what the Communist threat never could: it increased threat perception in the Diet to the level needed for it to pass the 2001 and 2003 dispatch laws, which have expanded the SDF's scope for intervention, as well as pass a set of laws on emergency situations, which had been regarded as anti-democratic and militaristic in nature until then. The adoption of emergency legislation has marked an important step in Japan's entry into the post-Cold War era.

The 'war on terror' has not, however, had an impact of similar magnitude on South Korea's defence policy. According to a poll held in 2002 by the Pew Research Center, 72 per cent of South Koreans opposed the US-led war against terrorism and 24 per cent supported it; in Japan, the figures were almost reversed.[4] Nonetheless, South Korea was the third contributor in manpower to the war in Iraq, after the US and Britain: it sent 3,600 troops there, as well 660 engineers and medical personnel. It also allocated $60 million in Official Development Assistance (ODA) to Iraq. As in Japan, the National Assembly decision to dispatch troops on 21 March 2003 was very unpopular. The rationale for the dispatch of troops was to strengthen the alliance; to contribute to world peace and security; economic factors, such as energy resource security and participation in post-war reconstruction, were also brought up. Still, another global challenge that East Asia faces is the proliferation of Weapons of Mass Destruction (WMD) epitomized by the North Korean nuclear crisis, and it is to that issue which we now turn.

Nuclear threats and defence policies

China was responsible for much of the nuclear proliferation that occurred in Asia and the Middle East from the late 1970s. It sold nuclear technology to Pakistan and Iran; missile technology to Pakistan, Iran, North Korea and Libya; intermediate range missiles to Saudi Arabia; materials used to make chemical weapons to Iran; and advanced communications equipment to Iran, North Korea and the Taliban when they ruled Afghanistan.[5] Such transfers to Pakistan, Libya and Iran occurred in the late 1980s and early 1990s, even while China was acceding to the Non-Proliferation Treaty (NPT)(1992), signing and ratifying the Chemical Weapons Convention (CWC) (1993, 1997 respectively), signing the Comprehensive Test Ban Treaty (CTBT) (1996), and joining the Zangger Committee (1997). Since 1997, however, China has grown increasingly cautious in the area of arms exports. On 25 August 2002, it issued expanded missile export control regulations and revised the 1997 list (Regulations on Export Control of Military Items).[6] In 2004, it joined the Nuclear Suppliers Group. It is engaged in consultations with the other multilateral regimes regarding the control of arms exports, including the Missile Technology Control Regime, the Australia Group and the Wassenaar Agreement. That China has become aware of the necessity to abide by such regimes is one of the positive effects which globalization has had on its defence policy.

Today, the primary nuclear threat to East Asia's stability is North Korea and proliferation resulting from the past connections between North Korea and Pakistan, as evidenced by revelations about Pakistani scientist A.Q. Khan's activities. South Korea and Japan's positions with respect to North Korea differ substantially. To Japan, the North Korean threat dates back to the early 1990s and is therefore fairly recent. To South Korea, on the other hand, perception of North Korea as a threat dates back to the end of the Korean War, even if this has tended to recede over the past three years.

The North Korean threat has existed as the focus of South Korean defence policy throughout the post-war period as well as the basis for the South Korea–US alliance. When US–China relations improved from the beginning of the 1970s and the Carter administration began to withdraw some of America's Korean troops in 1978, South Korea feared abandonment and started a nuclear enrichment programme in 1978, which it officially stopped only under US pressure in 1981. It had completed the ratification of its accession to the NPT in 1975, but pursued some components of its programme until 2000.[7] The White Paper on Defence published in December 2000 continued to designate North Korea as South Korea's 'main enemy' regardless of the change brought to the two Koreas' relationship following the historic summit between Kim Dae-Jung and Kim Jong-Il in June 2000. Only since January 2003 has President Roh Moo-hyun been elected on a mandate to secure peace and prosperity for Korea, on the basis of the peaceful resolution of the North Korean nuclear issue and the establishment of an inter-Korean economic community. The President has been successful in downplaying the North Korean threat and easing dialogue with the North. The 2005 White Paper on Defence no longer refers to the Communist regime's conventional weapons and WMD, and forward-deployed troops have been downgraded from a 'military threat' to a 'direct threat'. Today, South Koreans resent the North less than the Japanese.

Japan's position with respect to nuclear weapons and non-proliferation has been as anti-nuclear as the US–Japan alliance allowed. Japan is deeply aware that it has been the only country to suffer from the use of nuclear weapons, and its pacifist constitution has led it to contribute to the strengthening and widening of disarmament and non-proliferation regimes throughout the world.[8] Japan has submitted nuclear disarmament resolutions every year to the UN General Assembly. It promoted the establishment of the International Atomic Energy Agency's Additional Protocol (1997), which provides for reinforced safeguards and verification measures, and contributed to the universalization of the non-proliferation regimes (the NPT, the CTBT) by assisting developing countries in their implementation. It also contributed to the launch of the Hague Code of Conduct against Ballistic Missile Proliferation (2002).

This non-nuclear stance has been a pillar of Japan's defence policy since 1968, when Prime Minister Satô articulated the 'three non-nuclear principles': Japan rejects the possession, the acquisition, and the introduction of nuclear weapons onto its territory. In practice, the third branch of the principle has been violated by the requirements of the alliance with the US, and the introduction of nuclear weapons into Japanese waters by US military vessels. For Japan to benefit from the protection of the US nuclear umbrella implied in itself some degree of tampering with the non-nuclear principles.

In spite of the protection thereby afforded, the Japanese have felt threatened by North Korean missiles ever since what the Japanese government considered to be a test launch in August 1998. Ronald Reagan, and George Bush after him, had sought Japan's involvement in a joint missile defence project. Four months after the test launch, in December 1998, Japan finally agreed to joint research with the US on a Missile Defence System (MDS). Between fiscal years 1999 and 2004, Japan allocated some ¥29.3 billion ($236 million) to the MDS.

The missile launch also accelerated the adoption of the 'Law Concerning Measures to Ensure the Peace of Japan and Security of Japan in Situations in Areas Surrounding Japan', in May 1999. Debates on this law started in April 1998, prior to the North Korean missile launch, and this law was required to ensure the entering into force of the new Japan–US Guidelines on Security of 1997. The missile launch did not influence substantially the pace of adoption or the content of the law. However it gave the Japanese people and their representatives a sense of increased urgency for an effective framework of co-operation with the US. The law allows Japan to provide rear support to the US in the event of an attack against Japan or in Japan's surrounding areas – a 'situational' rather than geographical concept – even though the Japanese government argued at the time that the wording referred to Asia.

New threats and military modernization

Globalization has also had an impact in terms of shaping the means deployed to fight new threats, and in this regard, the South Korean and Japanese governments are modernizing their armed forces.[9] The South Korean armed forces' modernization is being carried out with a view to enabling South Korea to play a greater role in regional defence. At present, it lacks the ability to do so effectively without US military backing, which is why the US has recently reaffirmed its commitment to South Korea's defence. Although the US would assume command during a conflict in the peninsula, South Korea has already exercised peacetime control of its troops since 1994, and the South Korean Minister for Defence and the US Secretary of Defense have now reached further agreement, in a joint statement issued in October 2005, to 'appropriately accelerate talks about granting South Korea wartime operational control'.[10] In the same statement, the two countries agreed to bring down the number of US forces deployed in South Korea from 33,000 to 29,500 (compared with a previous level of 37,000). This move represents a further compromise; in 2004, President Bush had announced the unilateral withdrawal of 12,500 troops, creating some uneasiness in Seoul.

South Korea's military modernization involves cutting 170,000 troops from the current 675,000 and adding more sophisticated weapons and missiles to its arsenal, including F15 jets and precision-guided tactical missiles. It is also in the process of converting its 'whole defence structure into one centring around knowledge and information, taking advantage of computers and information technology' so as to gain efficiency in war or peacetime; and this it aims to do by 2015.[11] Consequently, South Korean defence expenditure has been increasing steadily: spending was $20.7 billion in 2005, almost double from $11.9 billion in 2001.[12]

In Japan, the modernization of the defence forces is also taking place alongside a strengthening of the Japan–US Alliance. In October 2005, the Japanese Ministers for Defence and Foreign Affairs, together with the US Secretary of State and Secretary of Defense, published an intermediate report on changes to be brought to the alliance in order to ensure the gradual inter-operability of the two armies. Even more than South Korea, Japan is eager to appear as a trustworthy ally: its defence policy constraints imply greater dependency than South Korea's, and it hopes to gain greater autonomy within and through the alliance by playing along.

The majority of Japanese citizens support the alliance though they do not wish to see their troops sent around the world to act alongside the US.[13] Japan's defence policy was born in the context of the Korean War and on America's strong advice. As such, it has been limited historically to the exercise of self-defence, the three conditions of which are: an imminent and illegitimate act of aggression against Japan; the absence of alternative means to deal with the aggression; a use of arms confined to the necessary minimum. In seeking to become a 'symmetrical (economic, political, military) great power',[14] Japan encounters many restrictions derived from Article 9 of its constitution, which renounces belligerence as a right pertaining to nationhood. Japan is keen to alleviate the inconveniences of the US presence, and it hopes to gain weight within the alliance in order to become more influential in its operation, less subject to US pressure, and better able to express dissenting views.

The modernization of Japan's defence forces, undertaken at the end of 2004, has been both qualitative and operational in character. The missile defence system is an important aspect of its new defence posture, as is the improvement of inter-operability with the US armed forces. Yet, at $44.7 billion in 2005, Japan's defence budget has been increasing only marginally (up from $40.4 billion in 2001), and is comparable in scale to France's $41.6 billion budget and the UK's $51.1 billion budget in 2005.[15] With the new Mid-Term Defence Programme (2005–9), Japan has now entered a five-year period of decline in its defence spending.

The 'war on terror', the North Korean nuclear threat, and the modernization of defence forces as a prerequisite for responding to such 'new threats', altogether illustrate the extent to which global challenges have directly influenced national defence policies. In other instances, globalization's impact on defence policies may be indirect.

Global challenges, national agendas and threat perception

Domestic agendas retain tremendous relevance in the crafting of defence policies, though they often reveal some degree of interaction with, and concern for global challenges. Hence, the Taiwan issue is governed by domestic concerns, which are determined by the larger international context of China's relations with the US. Defence policies designed to secure energy resources similarly reveal the significance of domestic concerns in an area where globalization impacts heavily. Furthermore, national leaders sometimes use international threats to capitalize on threat perception in their country and to further their domestic agendas in the field of defence.

Old concerns, new times: the Taiwan issue

By some accounts, China's defence spending has increased by double-digit figures since 1989.[16] Defence expenditures in China were valued at $62.5 billion in 2004, up from $43.5 billion in 2001.[17] The publicly reported defence budget, at $29.5 billion for 2005 ($35 billion for 2006), does not include proceeds from defence sales, procurement, R&D and most pensions for retired personnel. The US believes China's effective budget to be three times its stated budget.[18] Since the end of the 1990s, China has acquired modern aircraft, which make up a growing percentage of its air force inventory, guided-missile destroyers and submarines (also fitted with advanced anti-ship cruise missiles) from Moscow. China has also considerably reduced the size of its army. One concern driving this modernization is the fear of a technological gap between US power and its own. In upgrading its armed forces, it seeks to uphold the credibility of its deterrence.

Chinese relations with Taiwan have soured with the adoption of the Anti-Secession Law in March 2005, which was symbolically significant as well as consistent with government doctrine expressed in the White Paper on Defence 2004, where Taiwan was called a 'top priority' for China's armed forces.[19] China's White Paper on Defence 2004 went on to stress:

> The separatist activities of the Taiwan independence forces have become the biggest immediate threat to China's sovereignty and territorial integrity as well as to peace and stability on both sides of the Taiwan Straits and the Asia-Pacific region as a whole.

The Taiwan issue is not dissimilar to the North Korean one to the extent that neither China nor North Korea would find advantage in launching attacks, though both countries derive advantage from upholding the plausibility of an attack. There would be little sense in North Korea launching a missile on Seoul or Tokyo, only to face immediate and massive retaliation; it would, however, make much more sense for North Korea to keep up the pressure on its neighbours and remain in control of the bargaining process when entering into negotiations with them. Similarly, invading Taiwan would make little sense for China: Taiwan is the biggest provider of foreign direct investment to the country, and third-party intervention would be immediate. Nonetheless, the threat of an attack allows the status quo to subsist. Furthermore, Taiwan appears as a justification for the Chinese military's modernization. To a certain extent, the Taiwan issue justifies the budgetary claims of the People's Liberation Army (PLA).

The global context of China–US relations is of paramount importance in the Taiwan issue. Furthermore, globalization's economic effects have a tremendous impact on cross-strait relations, and act in favour of mainland China's 'one country, two systems' policy for Taiwan. Air and sea links are gradually being established; businessmen from Taiwan put pressure on their government to ease restrictions on cross-strait trade and investment; and the integration of information industry manufacturing between Taiwan and the mainland is advancing rapidly. Taiwan's electronic and information technology industry is crucial for the economies and armed forces of Western countries; at the same time, the delocalization of production to China is allowing technology transfers to an extent that is not well known and is hardly controllable. The Taiwan issue is an instance where domestic and global concerns are highly intertwined in shaping China's defence policy. Another such instance is energy.

Energy and defence policies

Energy is an area where domestic concerns and globalization blend to produce nationalism and determine defence policies. Although oil and gas account for only a small portion of China's energy consumption, China became the second largest consumer of oil in 2003 and the second importer in 2005. Its energy consumption is likely to grow considerably in the near future: even though China ranks second globally to the US in installed electricity capacity, its use of electricity is just 38 per cent of the world's average.[20] Eighty per cent of Chinese oil imports reach China via the Strait of Malacca in the South China Sea (which stretches from the Strait of Taiwan to the Strait of Malacca). President Hu Jintao describes the need to ensure protection of this vital passage as 'China's dilemma': the South China Sea is relevant to China for its potential resources and for its strategic location.[21]

The US Geological Survey estimated oil potential for the region at 28 billion barrels, whilst optimistic Chinese estimations have suggested that total reserves could be as high as 213 billion barrels for the entire South China Sea.[22] And yet, the region could prove to be even more significant for its gas resources; most of the fields explored in the South China Sea's regions of Brunei, Malaysia, Indonesia, Thailand, Vietnam and the Philippines contain gas, not oil.

Most of the islands of the South China Sea are in the Paracel and Spratly Island chains. These are claimed concurrently by Malaysia, the Philippines, Vietnam, Taiwan and Brunei. The 'Declaration on the Conduct of Parties in the South China Sea', agreed to in 1999 and signed in 2002, has eased tensions over the Spratly Islands, though it constitutes no legally binding Code of Conduct. China also occupies some of the Paracel Islands, which are claimed by Vietnam and Taiwan, and no significant progress has been made as far as these islands go.

According to one report written for the US Defense Secretary's Office, 'China is building strategic relationships along the sea lanes from the Middle East to the South China Sea in ways that suggest defensive and offensive positioning to protect China's energy interests, but also to serve broad security objectives'. China is building up its military forces to be able to 'project air and sea power' in the region from the mainland and Hainan Island. China upgraded a military airstrip on Woody Island and increased its presence through oil drilling platforms and ocean survey ships.[23] According to the report,

> China ... is looking not only to build a blue-water navy to control the sea-lanes, but also to develop undersea mines and missile capabilities to deter the potential disruption of its energy supplies from potential threats, including the US Navy, especially in the case of a conflict with Taiwan.

Growing piracy and maritime terrorism have also contributed to this build-up.

Energy, combined with territorial claims (and accompanying fishing rights), is also a source of tension between China and Japan. Japan is yet more dependent than China for its energy resources. It imports 80 per cent of its energy supplies and remains the world's third biggest oil consumer. As a consequence, Japan and China find themselves in competition over nearby natural resources, notably in the East China Sea. In November 2004, officials from the National Defence Agency established three scenarios of possible attacks by China: (1) China might attack parts of Japan to prevent aid of US forces in Japan in the event of a clash between China and Taiwan; (2) China might take military action to seize the Senkaku islands; and (3) China might move to secure its interests in the East China Sea.

Japan's claim to the Senkaku (Daioyu) islands is rejected by both China and Taiwan, though more vocally by the former than the latter. The seabed around the Senkaku is likely to contain natural gas, possibly oil. China's claim in the East China Sea is based on the limits of the continental shelf, which it claims should be used even though they stretch Chinese territory to the vicinity of Okinawa. Japan has attempted to get China to agree to a median line, which it eventually adopted unilaterally in 2003. Further north from the Senkaku, the Chinese have suggested that they would start exploration on several locations situated close to the median line, raising concern on the Japanese side that it would pump from under the seabed what ought to be common resources. The two governments are attempting to reach an agreement for joint drilling in the area, which proves difficult owing to disagreement on the territorial boundary.

Another issue between the two countries is the tiny island of Okinotori, over which Japan claims sovereignty and from which it draws its Exclusive Economic Zone (EEZ), thereby expanding south. China cannot claim concurrent sovereignty over the islet, but denies that it should be considered an island for the purpose of the delimitation of Japan's EEZ. According to the UN Convention on the Law of the Sea, 'rocks which cannot sustain human habitation or economic life of their own shall have no EEZ' (Article 121). At high tide, only a patch of rock the size of a tennis court remains above water. The Japanese government therefore has plans to consolidate the rock; last year, the Japanese coastguards requested funds to build a lighthouse on it. The waters surrounding the rock are not only relevant for the fish, which they provide; they may also have oil.

Apart from commando raids, large-scale disasters and ballistic missile attacks, the new National Defence Programme Outline identifies invasions of Japan's remote islands and intrusions into Japanese waters by armed vessels as potential threats to Japan's security. Preserving Japan's territorial sovereignty and safety is one of the SDF's primary missions. But in practice, it is the Japanese coastguards, not the SDF, who are first to be confronted by intruding vessels. The coastguards were only lightly armed until 2001. In 1999, the MSDF had to be called in upon the incursion of an unidentified vessel. Incursions from Chinese vessels have been increasing, from five in 2002 to 22 in 2004.[24] The Maritime Security Agency Law was revised in 2001 to allow coastguards to pursue vessels and have weapons on board.

Defence policies designed to secure energy resources therefore answer for domestic concerns in a field where territorial claims exacerbated by globalization tend to fuel nationalism. Domestic concerns and global considerations also combine in mutual threat perceptions.

Capitalizing on mutual threat perceptions

In some instances, political leaders pursuing national goals attempt to make the most of threat perception to further these goals. However undeniable global or international threats may be, they are thereby given a further political dimension, which they might not have had if the national context been otherwise.

Japan's quest for 'normality' is interesting in this respect. The North Korean threat has been commonly acknowledged in Japan since 1998. Furthermore, since 2004, public officials have expressed some degree of concern over China's military build-up.

Japanese politicians have perceived the North Korean threat primarily via the nuclear and ballistic programmes, and incursions by North Korean vessels. Among the public, however, the kidnappings of Japanese citizens have had a tremendous emotional impact.[25] The normalization talks launched by Prime Minister Koizumi in September 2002 led North Korea into admitting the past abduction of Japanese citizens and some of them were reunited with their families. North Korea, however, agreed only to their visit to Japan, not to their repatriation. North Korea considered as a breach of trust the fact that the former abductees were not sent back, and the normalization talks stalled. The Japanese public, in turn, viewed the subsequent lack of progress on the issue – and false evidence submitted in the process – as a national affront. The attitude of the Japanese government hardened consequently. It has insisted that the issue be brought up in the Six-Party talks and has thereby succeeded in internationalizing what it considers as acts of terrorism. In the talks, its stance is now closer to that of the US than to that of South Korea.

China's military build-up has also come to be considered as a security concern in Japan. This was made explicit in the new National Programme Defence Outline adopted in November 2004. Japan fears that it might get caught up in an American intervention against China in the event of a Chinese military action against Taiwan. Furthermore, Chinese missiles pose a direct threat to Japan. Some Japanese leaders have emphasized that nuclear weapons are defensive in nature and would provide a better deterrent than the US umbrella, which may fault with time. This, however, is not the public's view on the issue.

Public opinion, and the fact that it remains fundamentally pacifist, is an important consideration in Japan's formulation of defence policy. The many changes that have occurred in Japan's defence policy since the beginning of the 1990s and the Gulf War – leading the SDF to intervene in peacekeeping operations, and to further changes from then on – and the efforts of the Liberal Democratic Party (LDP) to get the public accustomed to the idea of a revision of the constitution, have made the Japanese aware of the inconsistency between their constitution and the reality of their defence policy. Nonetheless, roughly 60 per cent of the Japanese are against a reform of Article 9 of their constitution. The LDP is therefore cautious of any move it makes. Its political agenda is to reinstate Japan as a full-fledged state, though what this might mean remains subject to debate.

There is, therefore, a tendency on the part of some Japanese leaders to magnify global threats in order to sensitize threat perception in the public.[26] By intervening overseas in such situations as the war in Iraq and by simultaneously stressing Japan's vulnerability, Japanese leaders reinforce the alliance, but they also let people know that, were it not for this dependency, they might actually have a choice as to whether or not to intervene side by side with the US. Consolidation of the Japan–US alliance is sought in the name of the fight against terrorism and nuclear threats, but for Japanese leaders, this strengthening also aims at granting Japan greater autonomy.

Global threats have led Japanese leaders to realize the vulnerability of their country and, on the whole, this has reinforced the strategic value of the alliance. However, such threats have also provided opportunities and arguments to press for changes in the field of defence. The intervention in Iraq was an instance where objective and opportunity converged. The first argument for the dispatch of troops put forth by Prime Minister Koizumi was Japan's safety. In later speeches, the Prime Minister sought to establish a link between the North Korean nuclear issue and Iraq – between terrorism and the proliferation of WMD. He also emphasized the need for Japan to take part in international co-operation activities and seek 'an honourable place' among nations.

China depicts Japan as

> [T]he junior partner in the US's attempt to contain China. … The anti-Japanese sentiment one encounters among the PLA at all levels is palpable. Distrust of Japan runs deep, transcends generations, and is virulent among the generation of the PLA officers in their forties and fifties.[27]

China fears containment, and Japan's greater involvement in international operations increases this fear. Hence, China's White Paper on Defence 2004 has referred to the nuclear developments on the Korean peninsula, Taiwan's rise, and Japan's proposed constitutional changes as 'security threats'.

Anti-Japanese demonstrations are both encouraged and contained by the Communist Party. The weakening ideological base of the Party has prompted it to resort to nationalism as a factor of social cohesion. The 'Japan threat' is instrumentalized in China much like the 'China threat' is in Japan. In December 2004, China's Foreign Ministry spokesperson Zhang Qiyue stated: 'We are deeply concerned with the great changes in Japan's military defence strategy and its possible impact'.[28] Escalating mutual threat perception between the two heavyweights of East Asia – virtual, distorted, real or imagined, as in a mirror game – leads to an upscale in regional tensions.

As in Japan, public opinion in South Korea is closely monitored and is highly sensitive to the Dokdo issue. Japan denies South Korea's sovereignty over the Takeshima (Dokdo) islands. Japan first declared Takeshima to be part of its territory on 22 February 1905, which South Korea considers as but a prelude to its further annexation. In February 2005, the Prefectural assembly of Shimane declared 22 February to be Takeshima day. The Japanese government argued that it could not interfere with local autonomy. This provoked outrage in South Korea, at a time when the Japanese Ministry for Education was reviewing textbooks. Historical issues – over which the Japanese media and public are very divided – receive great attention from the media in both countries, and fuel mutual resentment or discomfort. The January edition of the 2005 South Korean White Paper on Defence did not mention them and was highly criticized. A revised edition was published in March, which mentioned: 'South Korea is fully committed to the defence of its territories.... Our main mission is to build up a strong defence posture against any provocative military acts threatening our sovereignty'.

Like in Japan and China, threat perception in South Korea is to some extent instrumentalized. In an internal report leaked to the Korean press, the Japanese Ministry for Foreign Affairs suggested that President Roh was fostering anti-Japanese sentiment to strengthen its political power base.[29] In spite of the fact that Japan and South Korea are allies of the US, and thereby part of what is referred to as a 'virtual alliance', and though both countries emphasize the importance of their relationship, Japan–South Korean relations have deteriorated even as relations between the two Koreas improved.

A March 2005 poll conducted jointly in South Korea, China and Japan indicated that 63 per cent of South Koreans had a negative opinion of Japan, whilst a majority was unable to express a decisive opinion of the US, China or North Korea.[30] The country that they felt was most threatening to South Korea was North Korea (46 per cent), but the poll also showed that Japan is considered a threat by a substantial number of people (among 28 per cent of those surveyed). The Chinese military appeared as a threat to peace and stability in East Asia to only 6.7 per cent of South Koreans. A more recent poll conducted by the Korea Institute of Defence Analysis suggests the percentage of South Koreans who are concerned by China's military rise may have increased: 38 per cent thought China would be the biggest threat to South Korea's security in the next ten years, more so than either Japan (24 per cent) or North Korea (21 per cent).[31]

The same poll conducted in Japan revealed that the only country on which the Japanese had a distinctly strong and unfavourable opinion was North Korea (79 per cent). North Korea was also considered the biggest threat to Japan's security, according to 57 per cent of those surveyed; China, at approximately 13 per cent, was not far above the United States. Though the stability of the Korean peninsula was considered the major threat to East Asian stability (to 43 per cent of the people surveyed), the Chinese military (19 per cent) and tensions over the Taiwan Straits raised greater concern in Japan than in South Korea.

As for results on the Chinese side, the country that garnered the largest number of unfavourable opinions was Japan (64 per cent), followed by the US (less than 40 per cent). On the other hand, the US was considered a threat by 72 per cent, and Japan by just 20 per cent of those surveyed. China–Taiwan relations appeared as the major threat to East Asian security (67 per cent), more so than the presence of US troops (32 per cent).

Threat perceptions both validate and enable particular defence policy decisions. For this reason, political leaders seek to influence their degree of impact. Beyond threats, however, globalization also creates opportunities.

Beyond threats: globalization's opportunities

China is becoming more global; in gaining economic weight, it has become more active in international politics. Conversely, having lost some of its economic confidence in the 1990s, Japan came to realize that it ought to play a greater political role and has been very active diplomatically in the past few years: for instance, hosting peace conferences on Afghanistan (2002) and the peace processes of Aceh and Sri Lanka (2003). Unsurprisingly, the nationalisms of these two 'emerging powers' have come to clash.

The China–Japan rivalry manifests itself at both the international and regional levels, through old, new and post-modern tensions. Old tensions on energy issues affect their policies towards Russia and India. China and Japan are attempting to gain firm assurances on the part of Russia that the Siberian oil pipeline will follow the route that they favour (Daqing versus Nakhodka routes). Meanwhile, Japan has been eager to strengthen its ties with India and the two countries signed a Plan for Comprehensive Energy Co-operation in September 2005. New tensions appear between the two countries in the international arena. China perceives Japan's claim to a permanent seat on the UN Security Council as a challenge; its growth is enabling it to take part in international peacekeeping operations (in Liberia and the Democratic Republic of Congo in 2003; and in Haiti and Latin America in 2004) as well as launch an active aid policy towards Southeast Asia, Africa, and the South Pacific. Tensions that can be labelled 'post-modern' arise between the two countries in their competition to shape region building, as was apparent prior to and during the East Asian Community Summit of Kuala Lumpur in December 2005.

However, beyond threats, globalization provides ample opportunity for co-operation. No matter how prone East Asian governments are to viewing power considerations and nationalism as a path leading to power, they are also aware that globalization's opportunities should not be missed.[32]

Furthermore, new challenges call for increased co-operation: such is the case of diseases and region-wide natural disasters. In 2003, the South Korean government noted:

> The rapid advances of globalization coupled with the deepening of interdependence have diversified transnational or non-military threats such as terror, environmental pollution, natural disaster, and illegal refugees. Recently new forms of diseases, namely Acquired Immune Deficiency Syndrome (AIDS) and Severe Acute Respiratory Syndrome (SARS) have also emerged as new forms of threats.[33]

Such plagues require regional policies. Japan provided a $23 million assistance package to countries hit by SARS in 2003: either bilaterally, or via the Asian Development Bank and World Health Organization. During the East Asian Summit, it committed itself to supplying some financial assistance against avian influenza. It also provided $500 million to countries hit by the tsunami in December 2004 (compared to China's offer of $40 million). Japan is now providing information to Indian Ocean countries via its meteorological agency, in co-operation with the Pacific Tsunami Warning Center based in Honolulu, until the Indian Ocean early-warning system becomes operational.

Globalization has undoubtedly shaped defence postures and threat perceptions in East Asia. China, Japan and South Korea are modernizing their armies, adapting them to new threats and new wars. A great number of issues confronting states and guiding the development of their defence policies today have a global dimension as well. If threats have become global, so too have the remedies and solutions applied to them.

The significance of global threats lies not only in the actual threats, or the need to react and counteract them, but also in the leverage that they provide national elites to further political agendas in the field of defence. Global threats deliver a two-pronged impact on national security policies: first, via the need to adapt their contents; and second, in the resonance that political discourse grants them.

At present, national agendas in East Asia reflect a changing balance of power, with two claimants for political and economic leadership. In claiming new roles, China and Japan occasionally clash. They are, however, eager to appear constructive with respect to regional integration, and swift to take advantage of the opportunities for co-operation that globalization provides in many fields. Globalization may have the adverse effect of fuelling nationalism, but it also provides opportunities which even nationalists are not willing to miss out on.

Notes

1 Peter Van Ness, 'Globalization in and Security in East Asia', in Samuel Kim (ed.), *East Asia and Globalization* (Lanham: Rowman & Littlefield, 2000), p. 256.
2 For general reference, see John Baylis, Steve Smith and Patricia Owens (eds), *The Globalization of World Politics: An Introduction to International Relations Theory* (Oxford: Oxford University Press, 2004); G. John Ikenberry and Michael Mastanduno (eds), *International Relations Theory and the Asia-Pacific* (New York: Columbia University Press, 2003); Samuel Kim, *The International Relations of Northeast Asia* (Lanham: Rowman & Littlefield, 2003); and J.J. Suh, Peter Katzenstein and Allen Carlson (eds), *Rethinking Security In East Asia: Identity, Power, and Efficiency* (Stanford: Stanford University Press, 2004).
3 Source: Ministry of Foreign Affairs (MOFA), 2002 (Japan).
4 Tim Shorrock, 'Roh Win Underscores US–Korea Rift', *Asia Times*, 21 December 2002.
5 Source: Council on National Relations (US).
6 www.nti.org/db/china/conexcon.htm (on 1 February 2006).
7 Jungmin Kang, Peter Hayes, Li Bin, Tatsujiro Suzuki and Richard Tanter, 'South Korea's Nuclear Surprise', *Bulletin of the Atomic Scientists*, 61:1 (January–February 2005), pp. 40–49. South Korea admitted in the Fall of 2004 that 'it had conducted chemical uranium enrichment from 1979 to 1981, separated small quantities of plutonium in 1982, experimented with uranium enrichment in 2000, and manufactured depleted uranium munitions from 1983 to 1987'.
8 Source: MOFA, 2004 (Japan).
9 Modernization of the Chinese military will be addressed at a later point in this chapter.
10 Donna Miles, 'Leaders Meet on Future of US–South Korea Alliance', *American Forces Press Service*, 21 October 2005.
11 *Defence White Paper 2000* (ROK).
12 The International Institute for International Affairs (IISS), *The Military Balance 2005–6* (London: IISS, 2006).
13 According to a government poll of 2004, 71 per cent of the Japanese feel close (or relatively close) to the Americans.
14 David Shambaugh, 'China's Military Views of the World', *International Security*, 24:3 (Winter 1999–2000), p. 68.
15 *The Military Balance 2005–6*. Note, however, that pensions are not included in these figures.
16 'Chûgoku Kokubôhi 14.7% zô' ('China's Defence Budget up 14.7%'), *Yomiuri Shimbun*, 5 March 2006.
17 *The Military Balance 2005–6*.
18 US Secretary of Defense Donald Rumsfeld made this point in Singapore in June 2005, and again in Beijing in October 2005. See also 'The Military Power of the PRC', *Annual Report to Congress* (Washington DC: Office of the Secretary of Defense, 2005).
19 *Annual Report to Congress*, op. cit. This marked an intensification of rhetoric over the previous White Paper, published in 2002.
20 Jasper Becker, 'China in an Energy Quandary', *Asia Times*, 28 August 2003.
21 David Zweig, Bi Jianhai, 'China's Global Hunt for Energy', *Foreign Affairs* (September–October 2005).
22 www.eia.doe.gov/emeu/cabs/schina.html (Energy Information Administration, US Government).
23 Bill Gertz, 'China Builds-up Strategic Sea Lanes', *Washington Times*, 18 January 2005.
24 'Gensen Kôrokaitaku Mokutekika' ('Is the Aim to Open up Sea-lanes for Nuclear Submarines?'), *Yomiuri Shimbun*, 12 December 2004.

25 A poll on Japanese attitudes toward China and other nations (conducted jointly in Japan, South Korea and China), showed that close to 49 per cent of the Japanese consider the kidnapping of citizens as what best describes their first impression of North Korea, as opposed to the development of nuclear weapons (23 per cent) or other issues.

26 'Chûgokukyôiron, Koizumi Shushôga Hitei Yasukuni Sanpaideha Jironkyôchô' ('Koizumi Rejects China Threat Theory, Favoured Speech on Yasukuni'), *Asahi Shimbun*, 27 December 2005. One should note, however, that Prime Minister Koizumi has insisted that China should not be considered a threat to Japan.

27 David Shambaugh, op. cit., pp. 68–69.

28 'China Concerns Japan's Defence Overhaul', *China Daily* (Xinhua), 10 December 2004.

29 'Noh Seiken, Hannichiha Shiji Kakutokusaku', *Yomiuri*, 6 April 2006.

30 A poll conducted jointly by *Dong-A Ilbo* in South Korea, the *Asahi Shimbun* in Japan, and the Institute of Sociology, Chinese Academy of Social Sciences, in China, in March 2005 and released on 26 April 2005.

31 English edition of the *Chosun Ilbo*, 20 March 2006.

32 The theoretical perspective on the extent to which the economic links created by globalization reduces the likelihood of conflict between nations, and the correlation between economic relations and political demands have been considered by Brian Pollins earlier in this volume.

33 *Participatory Government Defence Policy 2003*, p. 21.

6 Globalization's impact on threat perceptions and defence postures in Southeast Asia

Two views

Rizal Sukma and K.S. Nathan

RIZAL SUKMA

Introduction

The effects of globalization on national, regional and international security have, in fact, been a favourite subject of debate among academic and policy circles.[1] One key question that forms the core of the debate has been whether globalization would produce security-enhancing or security-eroding effects on national, regional and international security. One view argues that globalization increases the level of economic interdependence, raises the costs of conflict or war, and therefore leads to more peaceful relations among states. Others, however, contend that "globalization can generate economic rivalry among states ... over scarce natural resources, which again often threatens to spill over into military conflict."[2] A recent study even finds that there is "no conclusive evidence to prove that states are abstaining from wars due to globalization."[3] As globalization itself is an ongoing process, this debate will undoubtedly continue.

In between these two opposing views, a third argument emphasizes that globalization produces both security-enhancing and security-eroding effects. Globalization often produces different security effects in different issue-areas and in different national and regional contexts. Indeed, the implications of globalization for security have been mixed. In some cases, globalization can reduce security concerns of states, promote deeper co-operation, and therefore reduce the risk of armed conflicts among states. In other cases, however, it generates and aggravates security problems and therefore heightens conflict. How globalization either improves security or heightens insecurity has also become more complex due to the ability of the process to generate new security problems, shape and alter national threat perceptions, and define national and regional responses.

This chapter addresses both the security-enhancing and security-eroding effects of globalization in Southeast Asia. It examines primarily the impact of *economic* globalization on the national security of five ASEAN states, in terms of threat perceptions, the multiplication of security problems, and policy responses, especially with reference to the defence policies of these states. The discussion is divided into three sections. The first section provides an overview of some characteristics of traditional threat perceptions of the five Southeast Asian states. The second section examines the extent to which globalization has (or has not) altered threat perceptions within the region, and explores new security challenges facing these countries as the results of globalization. The third section discusses the response by these states to the new security challenges brought about by globalization.

Southeast Asian threat perceptions: the predicaments of post-colonial states

Modern Southeast Asian states, with the exception of Thailand, are the product of colonialism. The path to independence took different forms in the region. Indonesia and Vietnam proclaimed their independence in 1945, but were forced to fight a bitter war of national liberation until independence was recognized by the Dutch in 1949 in the case of Indonesia, and by the French in 1954 in the case of Vietnam. But the unity of Vietnam was only achieved in April 1975 with the fall of Saigon. The remaining Southeast Asian states – the Philippines, Malaya, Laos and Cambodia – took a relatively peaceful path to independence. Britain was forced to accelerate the process of Burmese independence in 1948, in light of the growing popularity of the revolutionary nationalism of Aung San. Singapore became a sovereign state under different political circumstances after the city-state opted to leave the Federation of Malaysia in August 1965. The process of decolonialization in Southeast Asia was completed when Brunei became an independent state in January 1984.

Domestic security concerns

The circumstances under which these countries became sovereign states, and the ensuing post-independence experience in state-building and managing foreign relations, has had far-reaching effects on Southeast Asian threat perceptions. It has been noted that that "with the departure of the colonial powers from the region, the new government of Southeast Asia faced a serious challenge in ensuring domestic stability and regime legitimacy."[4] The more pressing task was the creation of a shared identity that binds and holds together different sets of people, often with distinct ethnic, racial and religious identities, within a united entity called the nation-state. Such an identity is also required in order to give distinct meaning to their new status as an independent and sovereign political entity, different but equal to their former colonial masters. Indeed, the process of state identity-creation occupies a central place in the internal political process of these countries. It has even become an important aspect of the broader, ongoing task of nation- and state-building.

Indeed, the challenges are daunting because "nation-building, so called, is not an exercise which comes within the compass of 5-year plans or indeed within the life span of any one generation of political leaders."[5] The success of this process is largely determined by the ability of the governments to overcome a set of problems that often engulf many post-colonial states. Indeed, the survival of the ruling regimes, and in some cases the states themselves, is contingent on the ability to address and manage problems such as internal economic weaknesses, political and ideological divisions, national identity, lack of modern political and legal institutions, the primacy of personal rule, unstable civil–military relations, regime (in)security, ethnic and religious differences, separatism, and external dependencies. Given these problems, most Southeast Asian states – especially the five founding members of ASEAN – attached greater priority to overcoming domestic problems, thus rendering internal security as an important dimension of national security.

Even though the preoccupation with internal security constitutes the most common aspect of Southeast Asian threat perceptions, they vary with regard to the relative salience of each aspect of internal problems that threatens national security the most. For example, Singapore is more concerned with the problem of racial harmony than economic weaknesses and separatism. Indonesia under the New Order was, and still is, the most obsessed with any form of internal threats to national security, and "defines a threat as anything that can negatively affect the attainment of the national objectives and survival."[6] The problem of economic weaknesses and political independence has been more pressing in Vietnam, Laos, Cambodia and Burma (Myanmar) than in any other regional states. The importance of each problem also changed as domestic and external circumstances underwent significant changes. The threat of communist insurgencies was a serious matter in Malaysia, Indonesia, the Philippines, and Thailand between the 1950s and 1970s, but it receded by the early 1980s.

Despite such differences, three common internal security priorities typical of post-colonial states can be delineated. First, all Southeast Asian states see the preservation of sovereignty and political independence as the most important core values of national security. Second, they also prioritize the importance of maintaining regime legitimacy and the central role of the state as the provider of both security and prosperity. Third, governments in Southeast Asia are determined to ensure domestic stability characterized by internal order and the absence of threats to regime survival. And, in order to address these concerns, the governments of Southeast Asian states believed in the merits of a strong state playing central role as the provider of both security and prosperity. This, in turn, was translated into a degree of authoritarian control and strong emphasis on economic development; a political trait that has characterized most Southeast Asian states even until today.

External security concerns

While internal threats have been the primary source of concern for most Southeast Asian states, they could not escape the dominating feature of international relations within the region. Although not always articulated in explicit terms, they are also concerned with security threats coming from the external environment. During the Cold War, Southeast Asia became a region where fierce ideological competition took place between the United States and the Soviet Union. The region was also the subject of the quest for influence among major powers, including China and Japan. It was also a region where two communist giants, China and the Soviet Union, vied for influence. Indeed, as Southeast Asia had continuously been subject to the influence of outside powers, the governments in the region were filled with a degree of suspicion regarding the intention of external powers. They differed, however, with respect to which major power posed a more serious threat to their respective national security.[7]

The more pressing external security concerns, however, generally take two forms. First, except for the states of Indochina during the late 1970s, the nature of external threats in Southeast Asia was rarely formulated in terms of direct military invasion from abroad. States were more concerned with possible external intervention in the domestic domain, either from extra-regional powers or from neighbouring states within the region. For example, the problems between some ASEAN countries and the People's Republic of China during the 1960s and 1970s fell into this category. Within the region, countries fighting insurgent groups (such as Thailand, Burma and the Philippines) worried that the rebels would find elements of support in neighbouring states. In other words, external factors entered Southeast Asian threat perceptions mostly through the fear that they might aggravate internal weaknesses and domestic vulnerability. Conceived in this way, the predominant security concern of Southeast Asian states remained internal in nature.

Second, external threat could also stem from the state of bilateral relations between Southeast Asian countries. This form of external security concern could be generated, for example, by traditional rivalry created by the legacy of historical animosity, competing organizing ideology of the state, and unresolved territorial dispute with one or a group of neighbouring countries. For example, Vietnam's invasion of Cambodia in December 1978, seen as a development that would vindicate the thesis of "domino effects" of communism in Southeast Asia, was seen as a threat to Thailand. There were also fears that the prospect of a communist-dominated Indochina under Vietnam would provide a new impetus for communist insurgency within their respective territories, thus undermining pro-West and pro-capitalist regimes in ASEAN states. Indonesia's policy of *konfrontasi* in the first half of the 1960s served as a stark reminder to Malaysia and Singapore that hostility from a neighbour cannot be discounted. Territorial disputes served to accentuate concerns over the national integrity of the state. Conceived in this light, the external security concerns of ASEAN states were closely linked to domestic security concerns of regime legitimacy and survival, national identity, and domestic stability.

Policy responses: regional co-operation and foreign policy orientation

Close linkage between internal and external sources of threats in Southeast Asia served as the basis for regional co-operation. As Acharya has argued, "domestic weaknesses would produce a convergence of political, economic and security predicaments among a group of Southeast Asian states, who would view regional co-operation as a necessary means of coping with internal as well as external vulnerabilities."[8] As one observer remarked, "the necessity to co-operate … is deemed a function of a 'hostile' environment"[9] both in a domestic and external context. Similar interests in economic development did not result in fierce inter-state competition. On the contrary, the governments of Southeast Asia saw the necessity to create a regional order which would permit member countries to pay more attention and devote their resources to the more pressing task of internal consolidation and development. Such an objective necessitated a friendly relationship among regional countries that was sought through the adherence to the principle of non-interference in domestic affairs.

This principle was then seen as a significant factor which made it possible for member countries to avoid conflicts, thus allowing their governments to concentrate on the primary task of "putting one's house in order" as the basis of regime legitimacy. This would serve as a necessary, but not sufficient, condition for national political stability. As Michael Leifer put it, ASEAN "represents, as highest common denominator, a modest endeavour between states of equal standing in the expectation that co-operation and an absence of conflict can only facilitate stability internally."[10] To that extent, the presence of a friendly external environment and solid internal stability served as two important contexts for rapid economic growth which ASEAN countries had enjoyed uninterruptedly until the outbreak of financial crisis in 1997.

Regional co-operation is, by no means, the only policy response carried out by Southeast Asian states. Individually, regional countries sought to ensure their national security through various foreign policy orientations. The Philippines and Thailand forged an alliance with the United States. While maintaining a degree of non-aligned spirit, Malaysia and Singapore maintained close security ties with Britain through the Five Power Defence Agreements (FPDA). Indonesia's foreign policy continued to be coloured by strong attachment to the principle of non-alignment. Vietnam and Laos, until the end of the Cold War, were part of a security system led by the former Soviet Union. Burma represented an extreme case when the military junta in Rangoon took the country into an isolationist mode in 1962. These differences have been noted as one factor that hindered efforts at forging region-wide co-operation within the single regional entity embodied by ASEAN. It was only after the end of the Cold War in 1989 that all Southeast Asian countries came to have a convergent view regarding the merits of regional co-operation, thus realizing the eventual incorporation of all ten regional states into ASEAN.

Rapid growth in Southeast Asia was possible not only due to the presence of satisfactorily stable security environment, but also because of a world economic system that promoted open markets and sound economic policies.[11] Most ASEAN countries, especially the original five founding members, realized that an open economy would best serve their respective pragmatic national economic strategies of promoting growth through attracting foreign investment and expanding their export share in the world market. They realized that resistance to the increasing power of global capitalism would be futile. It was acknowledged that the core of this global capitalist system – the West – served as an important source of capital, technology, goods and services. The primacy of these elements for the success of economic development was well recognized by members of ASEAN. Therefore, these countries have consciously integrated themselves into the global economic system, taking its benefits to advance the pragmatic national and regional objective of promoting economic development at both levels.[12] Indeed, primarily due to the exposure of their domestic economy to the international economy, ASEAN economies have been described as being "among the more open in the world."[13]

ASEAN has thus become increasingly entangled in the process of globalization. ASEAN's participation in globalization, as we shall see in the following section, proved to be problematic. On the one hand, it served to accelerate economic growth and development, a prerequisite to the effective management of internal problems and domestic security concerns discussed earlier. It has also validated the merits of regional co-operation among regional states. On the other hand, however, it is also these three aspects of Southeast Asian internal security concerns – sovereignty, regime legitimacy and the central role of the state, and domestic stability – and the resulting response at regional level in the form of regional co-operation, that have come under pressure with the ascent of globalization and ASEAN's participation in the process. The challenges become even more complex when globalization also creates new security problems. Indeed, the main impact of globalization in Southeast Asia has been the creation of security uncertainty, which requires regional states to devise multiple strategies to overcome it.

Implications of globalization for Southeast Asian security

When it was established in August 1967, ASEAN was an experiment in ensuring regional security through the agreement to create a regional order that permitted member countries to pay more attention and devote their resources to the more pressing task of internal consolidation and economic development. This approach to regional security had served member countries well for the first three decades of ASEAN's existence. Indeed, the preservation of regional stability and the attainment of internal order allowed ASEAN countries to demonstrate and sustain remarkable achievements in accelerating domestic economic development, which resulted in economic growth of approximately 6–7 per cent annually. For all its achievements and limitations, by the early 1980s, ASEAN had been dubbed a "success story" of regionalism in the developing world.[14] The ascent of globalization in the early 1990s has accelerated economic development even further, driving ASEAN states closer and making them more integrated within the global economy.

The security implications of globalization for Southeast Asian security have been mixed. On the one hand, globalization has pushed regional countries closer into the habit of co-operation and thereby reduced some security concerns or threats that had existed earlier. None of the ASEAN countries is now worried about the possibility of going to war with one another. On the other hand, however, globalization has also reinforced the previous concerns over internal security, especially due to the challenge that globalization poses to sovereignty, regime stability and the central role of the state, and domestic order. It has also generated and perpetuated non-traditional security problems that widen the scope of threats facing regional states. In other words, globalization has produced both security-enhancing and security-eroding effects in Southeast Asia.

Security-enhancing effects of globalization: greater interdependence and co-operation

The threat-eroding impact of globalization in the region has been generated mainly, though not exclusively, through economic means that exposed the attractiveness of the market economy to ASEAN states and integrated them into the world economy. Despite various security concerns in the domestic and regional contexts, regional states have generally responded positively to the process of globalization. There has been a common view, at least among core members of ASEAN, that globalization served to promote and accelerate economic development. ASEAN countries realized that an open economy would best serve their respective pragmatic national economic strategy of promoting growth through attracting foreign investment and expanding their export share in the world market. They also realized that resistance to the increasing power of global capitalism would be futile. It was also acknowledged that the core of this global capitalist system – the West – served as an important source of capital, technology, goods and services.

The result of three decades of such outward-looking development strategy is evident on two fronts. On the regional front, it elevated the level of economic interdependence among ASEAN countries to an unprecedented scale. Even though intra-ASEAN economic exchanges and co-operation had been slow at the beginning of the Association's life, changes attendant from the end of the Cold War forced ASEAN leaders to realize that their economies were rapidly involved in market-driven processes towards regional and international economic integration. Rather than each country going its own way, they thought that by joining forces they could enhance their collective position and increase the gains from integration in the world economy. In addition, they believed that governments could facilitate this market-driven integration. As demonstrated by the agreement to form an ASEAN Free Trade Area (AFTA), ASEAN governments realized that improving and strengthening intra-ASEAN economic co-operation have become imperative for the viability and relevance of ASEAN for its members. This reflects ASEAN's judgement, though rarely stated, that the only way to survive in the world economy was to promote greater economic co-operation and integration in ASEAN. Growing interdependence among ASEAN countries then became a logical consequence of the deepening of regional economic co-operation.

The implication of such interdependence for regional security has been well noted. Hadi Soesastro, for example, maintains that economic interdependence and integration "contribute to economic growth and development of the region as a whole. As people's well-being in the region increases the region becomes more stable; this in turn improves regional security."[15] Steven Chan writes that "the deepening and widening networks of interests that characterize increasing interdependence should moderate international tension."[16] Scalapino argues that "given ... the growth of economic interdependence, the destructiveness of a major war to all parties, victor and vanquished alike, would be enormous."[17] In a similar vein, Harris points out that the pattern of behaviour for most of the Asia-Pacific powers seems to follow the proposition that "the growing economic interdependence of nations ... provides strong incentive for countries, even the major powers, to adopt trading (and investment) strategies for the development and maintenance of relationship in international society."[18] All in all, there was a widely held belief that economic interdependence has been conducive to regional co-operation and stability.

Indeed, the primary contribution of economic interdependence to security in Southeast Asia has been to contain or prevent actual and potential conflict from arising to the extent that could damage intra-ASEAN relations. Growing interdependence does increase the cost of the use of force as a means to solve differences. The acknowledgement of this logic, primarily due to the imperative of a stable external environment for national development, has been central in the policy of ASEAN member states towards each other. Consequently, ASEAN no longer sees the outbreak of war or a military confrontation among member states as an immediate security concern. Seen in this context, growing interdependence can be regarded as a factor that explains why Southeast Asia has enjoyed a relatively long period of stability.[19] To that effect, it can be argued that globalization has increased interdependence among Southeast Asian countries, and therefore reduced the likelihood of war among them.

However, economic interdependence alone, while necessary, is not a sufficient condition for peace. Keohane and Nye, for example, warn that "we are not suggesting that international conflict disappears when interdependence prevails. On the contrary, conflict will take new forms and may even increase..."[20] Indeed, there has been no convincing evidence that growing economic interdependence in ASEAN has successfully removed the sources or potential of conflict among its members. This is also partly due to the nature of Southeast Asian security being characterized by the more salient dimensions of internal security. Nor does interdependence remove any possibility for new conflicts to arise. In fact, globalization has brought with it more than just integrating forces that drive economic interdependence among states. Globalization has also brought threat-intensifying effects, which blend old and new threats to national and regional security.

Security-eroding effects of globalization: the blending of old and new threats

There are three dimensions of security-eroding effects of globalization in Southeast Asia. First, globalization has perpetuated some old security concerns. Second, it has forced states to respond to new non-traditional threats. Third, it has increased the security burdens of regional states. While this latest dimension of security-eroding effects of globalization does not necessarily represent a threat as such, it could nevertheless contribute to the erosion of security in the region.

As for the old security concerns, globalization has served the function of reinforcing the internal security concerns of Southeast Asian states. It has been mentioned earlier that the primary threat to national security for Southeast Asian states has been internal in nature. They were worried about anything that would erode state sovereignty, challenge regime legitimacy and the central role of the state, and undermine domestic stability. The forces of globalization did just that, and will continue to do so.

First, the source of challenges to state sovereignty brought about by globalization can be found in the process of opening up a national economy and integrating it into the global economy. Indeed, one of the crucial aspects of globalization has been its implication for the central role of the state as the dominant actor, not only in international relations but also in domestic politics. This, in turn, puts the state in a rather problematic situation. On the one hand, it has been argued that globalization poses a challenge to the sovereignty of state and limits state power.[21] The state no longer serves primarily as a buffer, or shield, against the world economy. The scope for state autonomy is then reduced in the context of economic globalization. On the other hand, the state may attempt to preserve its central role by seeking material gains from globalization. The state may increasingly facilitate globalization, acting as an agent in the process.[22]

Within the Southeast Asian context, the attempt to seek material gains from globalization during the 1990s may have helped the state to retain its role as a principal agent of development. This role is indeed crucial for the state since it serves as a primary factor that sustains the security of the regime. It is also imperative for the government to welcome the positive impact of globalization on economic development since it encourages growth and brings about new economic opportunities. Both of these serve as important sources of regime legitimacy. On the other hand, economic growth driven by states' integration into the economic globalization process may also bring about political consequences, primarily through the free flow of information, made possible by the revolution in information technology that carries with it new ideas and cultural values. Such political consequences have manifested themselves, among other things, in the rise of new groups in society that demand greater participation in policy process and politics, and the absorption of new ideas and demands (such as democracy, human rights, and social justice). Under such circumstances, the governments of Southeast Asia undoubtedly feel the autonomy-eroding impact of globalization. Indeed, there has been a rise in challenges to regime legitimacy and changing state–society relations as two attendant effects of globalization, in countries like Indonesia, Thailand, the Philippines, and (to a lesser degree) Malaysia.

The second security concern has been the effect of globalization on the permeability of the state to foreign penetration. A state's participation in the globalization process, which requires greater and deeper integration into the global economy, makes it more exposed to external influences. States with such outward-looking development strategy are confronted with growing economic interdependence as an inevitable consequence of globalization. In such circumstances, globalization then erodes the autonomy of governments in formulating and implementing national economy strategies and policies. For most developing countries in Southeast Asia, which view independency and autonomy as two significant political values, the autonomy-eroding effect of globalization clearly serves as one source of insecurity feeling. The suspicion that there will always be foreign forces trying to exploit the vulnerability and weakness of developing countries for their own benefits has been prevalent among regional countries. The growing permeability of states due to the revolution in information and communication technology (ICT), which intensifies the internationalization and globalization process of values, strengthens the sensitivity of regional states to a growing threat posed by the penetration of foreign values into their domestic domain. There are worries among Southeast Asian leaders that the globalization process may threaten social and cultural values in the society.

The third security concern is the impact of globalization on social structure and relations. Again, concerns over this issue are closely linked to the paramount importance of internal order for Southeast Asian countries. For example, it has been argued that a special challenge for Southeast Asia in assuring "domestic tranquillity is that of ethnic and religious relations."[23] Indonesia's government, owing to the fragile nature of ethnic and religious relations in the country, has been the most sensitive on this issue. On more than one occasion, government officials have warned that "globalization can strengthen the influence of liberalism which foster individualism, and deteriorate our nationalism, which, in turn, can encourage ethnic separatism to the effect of undermining the authority of the government."[24] The problems of ethnic divisions are also present in Thailand, the Philippines, and (to a lesser extent) Malaysia and Singapore. Ethnic tension in the region has been exacerbated not only by uneven distribution of the positive results of the economic globalization process, but also by the gap existing among different ethnic groups in tapping those advantages.

The fourth security concern is the impact of globalization on national unity and territorial integrity. The globalization process has not produced the same positive effects on every group in the society. Since globalization fosters competition, there will be winners and losers. Those who feel that they are left behind in the process might harbour separatist tendencies, such as the case in Indonesia, Thailand, the Philippines and Myanmar. As Southeast Asian states see territorial integrity as the basis for their existence and identity as an independent and sovereign nation-state, separatist tendencies are seen as a grave danger to the maintenance of that core value. Given the growing permeability of states, concerns over the spillover of domestic problems into the regional stage have been heightened. Indeed, given the surge of insurgencies in the region, Southeast Asian states are once again faced with the twin challenges of preventing internal conflicts from undermining regional security, on the one hand, and avoiding external factors from complicating domestic problems, on the other.

While globalization has perpetuated the existing internal security concerns, the nature of threats to the national security of Southeast Asian states has also become more complex due to the emergence of new threats. Security problems such as piracy, disputes over fishing ground, drug trafficking, arms smuggling, environmental degradation, terrorism, ethnic and communal violence, and transnational organized crimes have become a cause of common concern. There has also been a growing concern among Southeast Asian states over threats to human security such as poverty, hunger, human rights abuses, and infectious diseases. Even though these problems have been common in Southeast Asia for many decades, the growing frequency of their occurrences and the magnitude of the threat to the security of both the state and the people can be attributed to globalization. The growing threat of terrorism since 11 September 2001, the health crisis triggered by the problem of Severe Acute Respiratory Syndrome (SARS) in 2003, and now Avian flu, clearly demonstrate how security threats in Southeast Asia have become increasingly transnational, and therefore blurred the distinction between internal and external security. These problems serve as the latest reminder to all regional states that security interdependence has become an undeniable reality in Southeast Asia. What happens in one country certainly has an impact on others.

The transnational nature of security threat in Southeast Asia has been exemplified by the problem of terrorism. The current threat posed by terrorist network such as the *Jamaah Islamiyah* has been far too lethal compared to the previous terrorist acts perpetrated by communist insurgencies in the 1950s–1960s (Malaysia, Singapore, Thailand, the Philippines, and Indonesia) and religious extremists in the early 1980s (Indonesia). Previous terrorist attacks in some ASEAN states were motivated purely by domestic grievances and perpetrated by disgruntled domestic groups. The *Jamaah Islamiyah* constitutes a completely different form of terrorist threat. It is, first and foremost, a network whose activities encompass almost all Southeast Asian states. It also has global links with global terrorist networks elsewhere, even though the exact nature and extent of those links are still not well defined. Globalization has facilitated the creation of such networking through the skilful use of internet and other forms of modern communication technology by the terrorists. The network has also been forged by ease of travel in the era of globalization.

In between the internal and transnational security concerns, Southeast Asian states are also concerned with traditional security issues. Regional security concerns as a consequence of globalization have not been confined to non-conventional security issues alone. In a traditional sense, globalization facilitates changes in international and regional power structure. It provides opportunity for aspiring powers to acquire new status and exercise greater influence within an existing regional and international political structure. In Southeast Asia, the rise of China constitutes the most salient aspect of traditional security concerns. China has demonstrated well how a state's participation in the process of globalization has led to a dramatic improvement in national strength and capability. Over the last ten years or so, China has consistently demonstrated its ability to sustain economic growth at an impressive rate higher than that of its Southeast Asian neighbours. Along with its economic development, China's military capability has also improved significantly vis-à-vis Southeast Asian countries. In other words, China's participation, taking advantage of the process of economic globalization, has increased significantly the stature and standing of this country in the region. The concern with China relates, first and foremost, to the question of how China is going to use its new stature and influence in achieving its national interests and objectives in the region. Moreover, in economic terms, it is not yet clear whether China would become a competitor or a partner to ASEAN states. However, it is important to note that China has repeatedly assured regional states that its rise would be peaceful and China would continue to play a positive role in the stability and security of the region.

The third aspect of security-eroding effects of globalization in Southeast Asia has been the increase in the security burdens of regional states. Globalization clearly increases the need for new resources required for sustaining economic development of those states participating in the process of globalization. Here, three interrelated problems could arise. First, there has been an increase in the demand for gas and oil. Second, for littoral Southeast Asian states, the 200 nautical mile Exclusive Economic Zones (EEZs) serve as the most important sources of gas and oil, and also of marine resources such as rich fish stocks, and therefore "policing these Zones is becoming increasingly important for ASEAN economies."[25] As a consequence of the first two, the third problem stems from the overlapping territorial claims, especially over areas rich in such natural resources, which have become more difficult to resolve.

In other words, these three problems have increased the security burdens of Southeast Asian states, which calls for not only the need to protect owned resources, but also to reinforce claims over disputed territories. Indeed, globalization could also exacerbate these traditional security concerns that have already existed in the region even before the economies of regional states became more integrated with the global economy. Southeast Asia remains a region fraught with unresolved territorial disputes and border problems among the regional states. Malaysia, for example, has territorial disputes with Indonesia, Singapore, and the Philippines. Indonesia and Singapore also have an unresolved problem of boundary demarcation. The problem of borders security is evident in the case of Thailand–Myanmar and Thailand–Cambodia relations. The security-eroding effects of this particular problem have been demonstrated in the case of Malaysia–Indonesia disputes, first over Sipadan–Ligatan Islands, and now over the jurisdiction of Ambalat in the Sulawesi Sea. In addition to unresolved territorial disputes and maritime boundary issues, the water issue and Singapore's growing need for space through land reclamation have often disrupted Malaysia–Singapore relations.

The above discussion clearly reveals that globalization has presented the governments of Southeast Asia with an array of threats, old and new, to national security. In this context, however, it is important to note that there are differences among regional states with regard to which threat they perceive as more pressing to national and regional security, depending on the degree of their success in managing globalization. Of all the Southeast Asian countries, Singapore, Malaysia, Thailand, the Philippines and Indonesia have been the ones most exposed to globalization. However, the ability of these countries to manage the process of globalization differs. Malaysia and Singapore, for example, "have managed to take advantage of most of the globalization components that they consider beneficial, but still avoid those (boundary breakdown/penetration and enlargement) that threaten to overthrow their respective internal orders."[26] Meanwhile, despite also benefiting from globalization, Indonesia, and to a lesser extent Thailand and the Philippines, could not escape some negative effects of globalization that they sought to avoid, especially on the internal order of these countries.

This reality has resulted in two different sets of globalization-induced security concerns between the two groups of states. On the one hand, owing to their success in managing the negative impacts of globalization on internal order, Singapore and Malaysia are more worried about terrorism, piracy and environmental problems. Indonesia, Thailand and the Philippines, while sharing those same worries with Malaysia and Singapore, are also faced with those challenges that intensify their internal security concerns, such as threats to territorial integrity posed by armed separatist movements, communal violence, and internal instability. While these differences lead to the same response at regional level, regional states differ with regard to responses at national level, especially in defence policy.

Responding to the new threats: collective response and defence policy

Has globalization changed the way ASEAN states respond to threat perceptions? In general, the approach of Southeast Asian states to the management of security problems has not undergone any significant change. All Southeast Asian states believe in the merits of multilateralism in overcoming security threats brought about by globalization. As mentioned earlier, globalization has reinforced the intensity and scope of non-traditional security threats such as terrorism, insurgency, communal violence, and environmental problems. Even though these problems originate from the domestic domain of a state, globalization has made them transnational. It is this transnational character of security threat that forces regional states to co-operate in dealing with it. Even though these issues occasionally create bilateral friction among ASEAN member states, they continue to recognize the importance of regional co-operation to overcome the threats. In fact, the need, determination and urgency to co-operate among ASEAN states have become stronger over the last five years. However, the willingness to engage in collective action does not mean the absence of individual response to the problem.

Collective response: ASEAN's multilateralism

The growing confidence in collective response by ASEAN member states to threats has been reflected in a series of decisions to strengthen the mechanism for regional security co-operation. This has been carried out by (1) adopting security issues into the agenda of ASEAN co-operation since 1992; (2) taking the initiative to set up a multilateral security institution in the wider Asia-Pacific region in 1993; and (3) taking steps to bring ASEAN security co-operation to a higher plane through the agreement to transform the Association into a security community in October 2003. These significant steps reflect the awareness among regional states that the complex nature of security challenges facing Southeast Asia in the age of globalization can no longer be dealt with unilaterally by any single state. Globalization, therefore, has reinforced regional states' conviction about the merits of participating in multilateral institutions as a way to address problems and avoid conflicts.

ASEAN's initiative to establish the ASEAN Regional Forum (ARF) and the agreement to create an ASEAN Security Community (ASC) constitute two significant testimonies to that conviction. The ARF, which includes non-ASEAN states and all major powers, represents an experiment at a new security arrangement meant to "develop a more predictable and constructive pattern of relationships for the Asia-Pacific region" and "to foster the habit of constructive dialogue and consultation on political and security issues of common interest and concern."[27] It also serves as a venue for ASEAN and other extra-regional powers to co-operate in tackling security challenges brought about by globalization, especially on non-traditional security areas. Indeed, ARF member states acknowledge that "there were uncertainties and challenges which would increasingly require the attention of the ARF, particularly those posed by globalization" and therefore "in addressing regional security issues, the ARF should give due consideration to economic, social and human components of security, and the need to promote regional co-operation."[28]

The agreement on ASC represents the clearest, and most comprehensive, response by ASEAN states to the need for a deeper regional co-operation in dealing with security problems in the era of globalization. The Declaration of ASEAN Concord II confirms that the ASC

[S]hall fully utilize the existing institutions and mechanisms within ASEAN with a view to strengthening national and regional capacities to counter terrorism, drug trafficking, trafficking in persons and other transnational crimes; and shall work to ensure that the Southeast Asian Region remains free of all weapons of mass destruction.[29]

Such recognition clearly demonstrates ASEAN's awareness about the salience of non-traditional security threats to member states and regional security.

Indeed, the growing salience of non-traditional security threats perpetuated by globalization has forced member states to strengthen intra-ASEAN co-operation in overcoming such problems. Before 1990, for example, ASEAN tended to leave the task of resolving non-traditional security problems to individual member states, especially through development and nation-building measures. In the face of globalization, this approach has become inadequate. The transnational nature of threats requires transnational responses. In the context of war on terror, for example, it has been pointed out that

> [C]ombating international terrorism at the regional level calls not only for coordination of policies, but also for the abandonment of some sovereignty in favour of trans-regional co-operation. The principle of non-intervention needs to be dealt with, as it creates immense problems for regional co-operation over terrorist conflicts.[30]

ASEAN states have not abandoned even some of their sovereignty. However, the pace of regional co-operation in combating terrorism began to accelerate after the Bali Bombing in October 2002. Meeting during the Eight ASEAN Summit in November 2002, ASEAN leaders condemned "the heinous terrorist attacks in Bali..." and declared that they were "determined to carry out and build on the specific measures outlined in the ASEAN Declaration on Joint Action to Counter Terrorism..." They also promised "to intensify our efforts, collectively and individually, to prevent, counter, and suppress the activities of terrorist groups in the region." And, much has been accomplished by ASEAN states through security co-operation in this area. For example, intelligence exchange has led to the arrest of Mas Selamat Kastari, the head of the *Jamaah Islamiyah* (JI) network in Singapore, by Indonesian police. In terms of training, a number of courses run by Singapore in 2003 (on aviation security, intelligence analysis, post-blast investigation, and bombs and explosive identification) will certainly improve the capacity of law enforcement agencies in conducting their work.[31] While some see the issuance of various declarations by ASEAN as nothing more than rhetoric, within the ASEAN context it has significance as a way of registering political commitment to one another. More importantly, the place of terrorism in ASEAN agenda has shifted from merely a domestic issue to a common regional problem.

These developments demonstrate that Southeast Asia constitutes a region that has invalidated the thesis that globalization will always increase inter-state competition, and lead to intra-state conflict. On the contrary, globalization that increases the level of interdependence has strengthened the need to co-operate within a multilateral setting. This has, in fact, been consistent with ASEAN's approach to security all along, which sees co-operative efforts as the basis for dealing with threats. In other words, globalization has so far demonstrated the value of ASEAN's approach to the management of inter-state relations in the era of globalization.

National response: defence policy and non-traditional threats

While ASEAN member states share the conviction that security is best attained through multilateral co-operation, they also recognize the importance of national strategy to counter national security threats at national level. Such national strategy is, among other things, reflected in the national defence policy and posture of individual member states. However, it is not easy to determine the various influences on the defence policy of ASEAN states, because "any assessment of the importance of particular influences in a chosen ASEAN member is bound to be rather impressionistic."[32] Similarly, it is not easy to assess the extent to which national defence policy and posture has been a direct response to, or directly influenced by, globalization. What we can say here is that the defence policy and posture of an individual ASEAN member state would reflect, and be influenced by, the threat perceptions of the individual state, even though "threats have not been the most important influences on the development of these countries' armed forces: long-term, non-threat factors have generally been far more significant."[33] As mentioned earlier, regional states vary with regard to which threat they perceive as more pressing and vital to national security. These differences are then reflected in the national defence policies of individual states.

For Indonesia, the Philippines and Thailand, threats to internal security from armed rebellion remain the main preoccupation of armed forces in these countries.[34] Until the signing of a peace deal in August 2005, Indonesia's military had been fighting the armed separatist insurgency of the Free Aceh Movement (*Gerakan Aceh Merdeka*, GAM) in Aceh province, while continuing to face (to a lesser degree) a similar challenge from the Free Papua Organization (*Organisasi Papua Merdeka*, OPM) in Papua province. Communal violence, as demonstrated in bloody conflicts in Kalimantan, Maluku, and Poso, remains a formidable threat to internal security and stability. More importantly, terrorism has now come to occupy an important place in Indonesia's perceptions of national security threats. In the Philippines, national security continues to be disturbed by the resurgence of threats posed by communist insurgents, the Abu Sayaf Group (ASG), and the Moro Islamic Liberation Front (MILF). The surge of insurgency in Muslim provinces in southern Thailand has now brought the country into the same league as Indonesia and the Philippines. Like Indonesia, terrorism also poses a serious threat to the national security of the Philippines and Thailand.

In such circumstances, it is hardly surprising that the maintenance of internal security has been a major task for the military in these countries. Defence policies and posture would reflect such priority of internal security concerns. Indonesia's defence policy, for example, continues to focus on improving the capability to fight low-intensity war, especially counter-insurgency capability. Indonesia also plans to improve its defence posture so that the armed forces would have the capability "to uphold the Unitary Republic of Indonesia" (reflecting the concern over separatist threats) and "to undertake military operation other than war," especially to overcome the threats of terrorism and separatism.[35] Moreover, Indonesia's armed forces, especially the Army, have also emphasized the need to strengthen "rapid deployment forces" that could be deployed against any internal security threats. In Thailand, it has been noted that "much of what remains in a downsized Thai military budget must go for army-based internal security, leaving air and maritime forces with reduced resources even for routine operations."[36] Facing similar threats in the South, the Armed Forces of the Philippines (AFP) also has the same priorities. It has been noted, for example, that in light of the resurgent communist insurgency and a renewed Muslim secessionist rebellion, "the AFP's priority shifted from external defence and arms modernization to internal security concerns and the mere refurbishing of its old counter-insurgency equipment."[37]

Singapore and Malaysia do not face any threats from armed insurgency, and the risk of communal violence is far lower, if not non-existent. Both countries therefore place more emphasis on other problems as being more threatening to their national security. Terrorism, the possible spillover of internal instability from neighbouring countries (especially Indonesia),[38] infectious disease, and environmental problems are far more pressing and immediate security concerns for Singapore and Malaysia. Coupled with traditional security concerns, especially in its relations with Malaysia, and to a lesser degree Indonesia, Singapore adopts "a more comprehensive approach combining defence and security"[39] in its defence policy, geared to develop a defence posture capable of meeting the challenges of the unexpected. Nevertheless, in the face of terrorist threat, Singapore has renewed its interest in internal security capabilities.[40] Malaysia has also put more emphasis on the need to deal with non-traditional threats. In responding to the threat of terrorism, for example, Malaysian Defence Minister Najib Abdul Razak has called upon the Malaysian military to be prepared for low-intensity conflict and urban warfare.[41]

The need to overcome non-traditional security threats has also been incorporated into the defence policies and priorities of Indonesia and Thailand. Indonesia acknowledges there is a need to improve Indonesia's defence capability "to overcome non-traditional security threats that have become more pressing and immediate," especially maritime-based security threats, communal violence, and natural disaster.[42] In Thailand, as the possibility of armed conflicts between states has become increasingly unlikely, it has been acknowledged also that "non-traditional and transnational issues such as drugs and human trafficking now replace traditional military threats."[43] As these issues are closely linked with the problem of border security with Myanmar, "border security has always been in the realm of responsibility of the Armed Forces" because "the spread of drugs is still regarded as the most serious threat to the Thai national security – and likely to remain so for the foreseeable future."[44]

Despite the differences regarding the most pressing threats to internal security, all five Southeast Asian countries agree on the salience of maritime security threats to both national and regional security. To a varying degree, they have all paid attention to the development of naval capability. Singapore and Malaysia have been the most advanced in this regard. Indonesia, Thailand and the Philippines have undertaken more limited measures, for the lack of funds, to improve the capabilities of their respective navies, with the emphasis being the safeguarding of vital sea-lanes – principally the Straits of Malacca, Sunda, and Lombok, and the South China Sea – due to the longstanding problem of piracy and the possibility of a terrorist attack.[45] However, it is not immediately clear whether the improvement in naval capability in these states has been motivated only by the need to cope with maritime-based non-traditional security threats such as piracy, illegal fishing, smuggling or arms trafficking. Unresolved territorial disputes and the need to protect EEZs might have also contributed to the decisions by these countries to develop their naval capability.

Concluding remarks

Globalization has reinforced the characteristics of threat perceptions in most ASEAN states. Concerns over internal insecurity and fear of external intervention (both from within and outside the region) remain visible. Fortunately, long before ASEAN economies became progressively transformed by globalization, they had devised a common platform to manage the existing problems, namely regional co-operation through ASEAN. Globalization has not sharpened inter-state competition to the point that it increases threat perceptions, but it has, on the contrary, strengthened awareness of the growing interdependence among ASEAN states which, in turn, encourages them to deepen multilateral co-operation. Globalization, however, generates a different set of problems that helps to form a common threat perception among ASEAN states regarding the salience of non-traditional threats to national and regional security. While these new security threats have resulted in a common regional strategy of co-operative security, Southeast Asian states differ with regard to the most pressing threats to their own national security. Consequently, the effects of globalization on the defence policies of these countries have also been influenced by differences in threat perceptions.

Looking forward to the next ten years from now, the security challenges brought about by globalization would continue to shape and affect the security environment in Southeast Asia. In fact, as the revolution in IT continues, and the world becomes more integrated, the challenges might become more complex than they already are. Consequently, ASEAN member states would continue to improve their capability to overcome these threats. Some would embark upon a comprehensive defence development. Others would concentrate on the use of limited resources to address what are perceived to be pressing and immediate security threats within their internal context. Across Southeast Asia, however, globalization should continue to be accompanied by the growing commitment among regional states to manage its security implications through co-operative efforts.

K.S. NATHAN

Introduction: globalization, international and regional security

Globalization – as a universal, integrative process in terms of the pace and volume of political, economic, military, social, intellectual, technological and cultural transactions and exchanges – invariably produces an uneven impact on global community as this very society, divided politically into 194 nation-states, is extremely heterogeneous, with tremendous diversity in all the indices stated above. Cultural globalism is necessarily modified by local conditions, which in turn stem from geography, history, ideology, and capability of humans to transact their needs and address challenges at various levels. In this regard, one could even evaluate this phenomenon in terms of the "subjects" or initiators and "objects" or recipients of global processes. Individuals, communities, and states that are more adapt at coping with, and benefiting from globalization would welcome it as a factor conducing to the upliftment of their material condition, while those that lack these skills would not only fear its impact, but also react negatively to its manifestations. An NGO activist from Thailand has even claimed that "globalization is endangering every part of society, and perhaps economic globalization is the most powerful cause of many social illnesses...."[46] Evidently, the threat perception here relates to globalization's impact on human security – a concern, which falls within the broader ambit of non-traditional security.

To be sure, the cultural and economic dimensions of globalization are linked to the political and security dimensions of this multi-faceted phenomenon. This chapter is developed from the assumption that in the conduct of international relations, state security is still being prioritized over "human security" – hence the focus on threat perceptions by state actors and their responses, which in turn feed into policy inputs and outputs reflected in national and regional security formulation. This second part of the chapter therefore focuses on the strategic impact of globalization in, and security implications for, Southeast Asia.

Impact of globalization on threat perceptions and arms buildup in Southeast Asia

How do we assess threats and perceptions of threat to regional security in Southeast Asia? What are the sources of these threats? Are they of a traditional or non-traditional nature, or a combination of both? If the threat perceptions portray a traditional as well as non-traditional character, how are priorities assigned by policy makers to address them, especially in the context of the post-1997 Asian Financial Crisis reflecting the economic impact of globalization, and the post-9/11 context reflecting the impact of a globalized, asymmetric, non-traditional security threat to the region. These are some of the issues dealt with in this chapter.

Perceptions of globalization and its likely impact on domestic political and economic stability as well as the regional security scenario can, and do affect military modernization and security policies of regional states. The uncertainties surrounding the end of the Cold war since the early 1990s were marked by regional tendencies to modernize and strengthen military capabilities with the apparent objective of protecting national, especially territorial sovereignty.

China's rise and military modernization has invariably influenced the military and security policies of the ASEAN states. Although certain countries like Malaysia in particular have openly welcomed the rise of China, stating that Beijing does not pose any significant threat to regional security, the trend towards arms modernization in the ASEAN region has not abated.

Beijing lays claim to the entire South China Sea as part of its sovereign territory. China also passed a law on 25 February 1992 to this effect, wherein Article 2 of the controversial territorial law converted the South China sea into China's internal waters, while Articles 8, 10 and 14 endorse military action to defend Chinese sovereignty and interests in the contested waters.[47] Additionally, China's phenomenal annual growth rate at 8–10 per cent in recent years increases the pressure on energy resources to fuel its economic dynamism – and Beijing's natural tilt to the South China Sea to meet the PRC's growing energy demands could well spark tension with neighbouring regional states that have overlapping territorial claims: Malaysia, Vietnam, Philippines, Brunei, and Taiwan. China and the other claimants have evidently beefed up their defence postures in the South China Sea by acquiring more modern equipment to boost maritime surveillance. The strengthening of defence postures vis-à-vis the overlapping claims is clearly an indication of the salience of mutual threat perceptions in the maritime domain of national security. Competition for energy resources by the regional claimants could well intensify in the absence of effective conflict-management and resolution channels, given that the South China Sea region has proven oil reserves of about seven billion barrels, of which 70 per cent would be natural gas. The Declaration on Conduct signed in November 2002 between ASEAN and China obliges all claimants to renounce the use of force in pursuing their individual claims, and to conduct their behaviour according to the norms of international law. However, as Busyznski correctly argues, China's restraint will be more forthcoming – and potential conflict more manageable – if the dispute is situated in a balance of power context in which the interests and involvement of extra-regional powers are factored into the whole equation.[48] Indeed, mutual threat perceptions vis-à-vis the South China Sea are better managed if both institutional means as well as *realpolitik* are employed.

The globalization of terror: addressing threats through institutions

ASEAN's response to 9/11 terror was predictable in the sense that a regional or collective response could not in any way be contradictory to the global condemnation of terror at the level of international organization vis-à-vis the United Nations. ASEAN collectively condemned the terrorist attacks, and pledged to work very closely with the United Nations and also the United States in organizing a Global Coalition Against Terror. All ten ASEAN members (Brunei, Cambodia, Indonesia, Laos, Malaysia, Myanmar, Philippines, Singapore, Thailand, and Vietnam) endorsed various anti-terror measures at the Seventh ASEAN Summit (Brunei, 2001), and the Eighth ASEAN Summit (Phnom Penh, 2002). The Brunei Summit issued a strong statement that the September 11 attack on the United States "was a direct challenge to the attainment of peace, progress and prosperity of ASEAN and the realization of ASEAN Vision 2020."[49] Besides, the APEC Forum was another platform for ASEAN members to join forces with major global players like the United States, China, and Japan to condemn terror. The members of both fora attempted to implement UNSC Resolution 1373 which was unanimously adopted on 28 September, 2001.

Pursuant to UNSC Resolution 1373, the regional grouping held the ASEAN Ad Hoc Experts Group meeting in Bali, Indonesia in January 2002 to implement the ASEAN Plan of Action to Combat Transnational Crime. Eight task forces were established aimed at combating: (1) terrorism, (2) trafficking in persons, (3) arms smuggling, (4) sea piracy, (5) money laundering, (6) illicit drug trafficking, (7) international economic crime, and (8) cyber crime. This action plan was formally adopted in May 2002 to cover six strategic areas: information exchange, cooperation in legal matters, cooperation in law enforcement measures, institutional capacity building, training, and extra-regional cooperation. Significantly, each ASEAN member has agreed to establish a national anti-terrorism task force to facilitate cooperation with other members in the event of a terrorist attack, including apprehending suspects and searching and seizing of evidence.[50] And at the tenth ASEAN Summit in Vientiane in November 2004, both ASEAN and APEC members endorsed the Philippines as head of the APEC counter-terrorism task force. The leaders also approved the role of Japan and Indonesia in the ASEAN Security Community Plan of Action on Counter-Terrorism.[51]

At another institutional level, i.e. the ASEAN Regional Forum (ARF), the 23-member regional security consultative group held a workshop in April 2002 under the auspices of the Thai and Australian Governments. Malaysia took a further step in hosting the Special ASEAN Ministerial Meeting on Transnational Crime in May 2002, in furtherance of Resolution 1373.

Three ASEAN members – Indonesia, the Philippines and Malaysia – underscored their determination to fight terror in the region by signing an Anti-Terrorism Pact on 7 May 2002 in Putra Jaya, Malaysia's new Federal Administrative Capital (replacing Kuala Lumpur since June 1999, although Kuala Lumpur remains the capital of Malaysia). The above measures could be interpreted as state-level responses to threats of a transnational character linked to militants wanting to set up a single Islamic state comprising these three nations. The tripartite pact is aimed at (a) targeting potential terrorist threats, and (b) devising measures to tackle money-laundering, smuggling, drug-trafficking, hijacking, illegal trafficking of women and children, and piracy.[52] Significantly, the three ASEAN states are demonstrating their serious commitment to ensuring that terrorists would not make the region their operational base in view of the fact that they have been flushed out of Afghanistan. The eleventh ASEAN Summit in Kuala Lumpur (12–14 December 2005) reiterated the regional entity's commitment to combat terrorism and transnational crimes using traditional (state-level military cooperation) and non-traditional measures such as inter-faith dialogue to underscore ASEAN's position that it "rejects any attempt to associate terrorism with any race, religion, nationality or ethnic group."[53]

The emergence over the past two years of new flashpoints in southern Thailand adds a new dimension to the war on terror, as they also have the potential of straining bilateral relations between Bangkok and Kuala Lumpur as suspected Islamic militants, pursued by Thai security forces, seek refuge in Malaysian territory. Although the two countries are not expected to go to war over this issue, the persistence of Islamic militancy and violence in southern Thailand, southern Philippines, and Indonesia underscores the still prevailing weakness if not absence of ASEAN-led security multilateralism in Southeast Asia – a process that could oblige members to subdue national sovereignty in favour of enhanced regional security. ASEAN still prefers to uphold the age-old non-interference principle despite changing strategic dynamics in which non-traditional security issues cannot be effectively addressed using traditional security approaches grounded in national sovereignty.

Globalization and the arms race phenomenon in Southeast Asia

As Southeast Asian economies develop and modernize due to the expanded availability of financial and trained manpower resources, so too will their military power be shaped to address real as well as perceived threats and challenges to national security. While it is arguable that the military strengths of most Southeast Asian countries in the 1970s were at a rather rudimentary stage of development (with the possible exception of Thailand and Vietnam due to external inputs into the Vietnam War), this trend has certainly been reversed upwards through a conscious and consistent programme of military modernization. Southeast Asian leaders, like their counterparts elsewhere, are fully cognizant of the various elements that cumulatively combine to produce national power and security. Among these elements, military modernization to boost national capability and deterrence vis-à-vis neighbours is currently a key element in national security thinking and formulation in rapidly industrializing economies of the Association of Southeast Asian Nations (ASEAN).

Rather than get involved in a debate as to whether or not Globalization has fuelled an arms race in Southeast Asia, it would be more appropriate to focus on the factors contributing to military modernization and accelerated arms purchases by the ASEAN states, especially in the post-Cold War era of the 1990s and beyond. First, the existence and persistence of bilateral tensions between any two regional states provides a sufficient rationale to decision makers that maintaining adequate military capability to boost deterrence would in fact help secure rather than endanger peace. This scenario is played out in the Malaysia–Singapore relationship where Singapore in particular is concerned about the possibility, even if remote, of its larger northern neighbour entertaining predatory territorial ambitions arising from historical circumstances and colonial baggage. The republic's arms build-up, characterized by the purchase of state-of-the-art weaponry, hardly goes unnoticed in Kuala Lumpur. Singapore probably has the most powerful air force in ASEAN – a fact which affords some degree of counter-balancing via possession of superiority in other military assets. As stipulated by Colin Gray in his seminal study of the arms race phenomenon, four conditions must be met to conclusively establish the occurrence of an arms race: (1) there must be two or more parties conscious of their antagonism; (2) they must structure their armed forces relative to those of other participants, with a view to deterrence; (3) they must compete in terms of quantity (men, weapons) and/or quality (men, weapons, organization, doctrine, deployment); and (4) there must be rapid increases in quality and/or improvements in quantity.[54] In analyzing force modernization trends in Southeast Asia with a view to determining the existence or absence thereof of a regional arms race, Andrew Tan concludes that the phenomenon of "arms racing" rather than a full-fledged arms race in Southeast Asia seems to be the order of the day.[55]

Second, it is beyond question now that changes – perceived as well as actual – in the global and regional balance of power also drive arms acquisitions and military modernization. For Malaysia, the end of the Communist armed struggle and the demise of the Cold War necessitated a reformulation of military doctrine from counter-insurgency warfare to an emphasis on building conventional forces particularly vis-à-vis maritime threats to national security. This scenario of military development applies equally to other ASEAN countries with extended coastlines and maritime interests, such as Indonesia, Philippines, Thailand and Vietnam. Nevertheless, the capacity to develop, expand, and modernize military capabilities has undoubtedly varied according to the availability of budgetary resources to undertake force modernization. The Philippines, Indonesia, Vietnam and Myanmar have all been hamstrung by limited resources, while more impressive economic growth and better governmental capacity has enabled Singapore, Malaysia and Thailand to purchase high-tech weapons.

Third, the maritime zone encompassing the littoral states of ASEAN furnishes an area of concord as well as discord. Cooperation for joint exploitation of the natural and living resources of the South China Sea in which several states have overlapping claims – Malaysia, Vietnam, Philippines, Brunei, and also China and Taiwan – would necessarily entail the benign use of their respective military capabilities to address common threats such as piracy, smuggling, drug trafficking, environmental pollution, and terrorism. Yet, the reality of a conflict of national interests cannot be overlooked so that each country has found it increasingly necessary to define as well as defend its maritime interests. Additionally, as the realists would argue, a state's military power and prowess contribute towards enhancing national prestige in the community of nations. Through the possession of deterrent power, states as described by Morgenthau, feel that they promote dialogue and negotiation to ensure desired outcomes. In adopting this approach they might very well be encouraging an interactive arms build-up in the region, but from their perspective, this is not an intended but consequential development.

Fourth, all states as actors in the international system, are affected by technological progress, and in the military sphere, what we now call RMA or Revolution in Military Affairs. The RMA factor could well be generated by the major arms producers, but as technology is borderless in the era of globalization, technological innovation can either be bought from outside or be generated from inside a nation-state. In the post-Cold War era, the breakdown of old supplier networks means that the supply side control of recipients through arms transfers has become less feasible.[56] The corollary to this development is the creation of new supply networks for both hi-tech and medium grade weaponry at relatively low cost, thus facilitating the process of regional arms modernization. The RMA factor in enabling the acquisition by Southeast Asian armed forces of new air and naval systems has been visibly operative in the 1990s, and these systems have been crucial force multipliers in the upgrading of regional armed forces. These include: advanced command, control and communications systems, sometimes using satellites; technical intelligence systems, including signals intelligence and high-resolution satellite imaging; electronic warfare systems; and precision-guided munitions.[57]

While RMA or elements of it can deepen existing military disparities, Huxley and Willett pointedly remark that "RMA-based armed forces are not necessarily panaceas for East Asia, particularly Southeast Asia where low intensity security problems prevail."[58] This line of argument affords further proof that the character of security issues in Southeast Asia does not conduce towards a full-blown arms race in which the struggle for military superiority becomes an end in itself.

Several ASEAN states can produce varying levels of armaments to supply their own needs and also those of their neighbours. However, for state-of-the art weaponry, these countries can source them from the world's major industrial nations and other medium-sized powers at costs that have become affordable. Stiff competition on the supply side – deepened by certain external factors such as the collapse of the Soviet Union as well as the rise of China and India – means that a buyer's market now characterizes the global armaments industry. From the psychological dimension of national power, additional impetus for arms acquisitions in times of peace and low intensity conflict is invariably provided by the need to "keep up with the Joneses" with respect to strengthening fortifications in disputed territorial waters, and combating non-traditional security threats such as piracy, illegal migration, and terrorism.[59] Minor disputes over control of territory and resources in the Straits of Malacca and South China Sea at different points in recent times have involved the principal actors of ASEAN – Malaysia, Singapore, Indonesia, the Philippines, Thailand and Vietnam. Previous clashes involving at least two ASEAN states (Vietnam and the Philippines) with an external power (China) which asserts sovereignty over the entire South China Sea suggest at the very least that the ASEAN states would not neglect the

Table 6.1 Defence expenditures of ASEAN countries as a percentage of GDP

	1985	2001	2003
Indonesia	2.8	3.8	3.7
Malaysia	3.8	3.8	3.6
Singapore	6.0	5.1	5.2
Thailand	4.0	1.7	1.5
Philippines	1.4	1.6	2.1
Vietnam	19.4	7.2	7.1
Myanmar	5.0	5.0	5.0
Laos	7.1	0.9	0.8
Cambodia	n.a.	2.5	2.5
Brunei	8.0	5.5	5.2

Source: *The Military Balance 2003–2004*, London: Oxford University Press for International Institute for Strategic Studies (IISS), October 2003, p. 337.

military dimension of their national preparedness in dealing with Beijing's growing military power.

All the above factors notwithstanding, the nature and pattern of arms acquisitions exemplified by the ten-member ASEAN do not invariably point in the direction of an arms race due primarily to the availability of non-violent conflict resolution mechanisms which the regional body has cherished and developed since the 1976 Bali Treaty. Table 6.1 is quite instructive in that ASEAN countries' expenditure on defence relative to GDP is very low, and with the exception of Singapore, higher ratios relate more to internal security considerations than preparations against conventional threats from neighbours. Brunei's high defence expenditure in 1985 was directly related to gaining independence from Britain in 1984, while Vietnam's disproportionately high expenditure ratio can be explained by its military occupation of Cambodia (1978–1990). While the key ASEAN members are in the process of acquiring high-tech defence equipment from Western and Asian suppliers, the emerging picture is not one of a deliberate attempt to upstage neighbours in the battle for deterrence. The revitalization of ASEAN via three major projects: the ASEAN Security Community, ASEAN Economic Community, and the ASEAN Socio-Cultural Community is fairly indicative of the future goals and direction of this 38-year-old organization, i.e. away from conflict and towards cooperation.

It can be argued in the language of constructivism that habits of consultation have now been sufficiently developed to negate war as an instrument of national policy. As argued by Caballero-Anthony, ASEAN's conflict resolution mechanisms are more inclined towards norm-building and community-building through socialization and networking, assurance rather than deterrence, and informal third-party mediations rather than formal dispute settlement mechanisms requiring a more legalistic approach.[60] While the need for deterrence is an inevitable concomitant of national defence policy, that same need is not guided by the tendency to resort to force when national interests are perceived to be infringed in an intra-ASEAN context. Nevertheless, as Acharya aptly observes, the death of bipolarity followed by the absence of any credible multilateral mechanism in the Asia-Pacific region to manage peace and security problems "are powerful factors in the enhanced quest for military security by regional actors."[61]

Conclusion: the security challenges of globalization in Southeast Asia

Any objective evaluation of the progress, success or failure to date of ASEAN's anti-terror strategies must be premised on the consideration that terrorism alone does not inform the entire agenda, perspective and priorities of regional security approaches adopted by members of the regional grouping. In addition to the increased threat of global terrorism, Southeast Asia faces many other security challenges as well, many of which are unrelated to the September 11 episode. These challenges are the offshoot of expanding globalization and economic integration. Globalization has sharpened the cultural dimension of international relations in the sense that it has compelled state actors to decide on the correct mix of values needed to uphold the integrity of their own societies in terms of certain values pertaining to governance, democracy, and human rights. It is obvious that the end of the Cold War has left in its wake an ideological power vacuum which the superpower, the United States, has been obliged to fill through its doctrines of globalization and, now, after September 11, counter-terrorism. To be sure, Southeast Asian security approaches, strategies, policies and responses are invariably intertwined with the pressures and options emanating from unipolarity.

Second, other non-traditional security threats would also occupy the minds and energies of regional statesmen – such as piracy, illegal migration, drugs, religious militancy, environmental pollution etc. – accentuated as these are by globalization, and reflect problems beyond the problem-solving capacity of any single state. As noted by Andrew Tan and Kenneth Boutin, "globalization has resulted in new security threats to communities and individuals that are transnational in character and are increasingly defined in social and economic terms."[62] Indeed, globalization on the negative side, increases human vulnerability and insecurity although on the positive side, it enables countries, particularly smaller and developing countries, to achieve economic progress beyond the limits imposed by domestic resources and markets.[63]

Third, in the era of Globalization, international terrorists would exploit the ease of travel and communication to penetrate "failed states" or "failing states" in Asia – like Afghanistan and Pakistan in Central Asia, and Indonesia and the Philippines in Southeast Asia, and more recently, the newly independent East Timor which achieved independence on 20 May 2002. States with "receptive" Islamic populations such as Malaysia would also provide targets of penetration by religious militants unable to satisfy their aspirations and needs within the existing nation-state system, which they consider un-Islamic, and therefore evil and corrupt. Yet, it is equally noteworthy in the context of the post-September 11 regional security scenario that governmental capacity and legitimacy have not been seriously undermined in the ASEAN countries, i.e. terrorism has not been able to topple the existing governments in Southeast Asia or to significantly alter the political, economic and territorial status quo.

Fourth, the arms race phenomenon in Southeast Asia will be muted by the emergence of a growing sense of regional consciousness and empowerment, and the preference to resolve bilateral and multilateral disputes within the framework of the Treaty of Amity and Cooperation (TAC) principles, or ASEAN Concord I, endorsed at Bali in 1976. ASEAN Concord II in 2003 symbolized further progress in the goal of creating a "security community,"[64] while the inauguration of the First East Asia Summit in Kuala Lumpur in December 2005 can prove to be a community building exercise with the potential of mitigating mutual threat perceptions of a traditional nature thereby mitigating to some degree regional threat perceptions. Regional arms modernization programmes will, however, proceed apace based on resource availability, technological momentum triggered by RMA, and the inevitable need to address the "security dilemma" arising from the constraints of the nation-state system. In terms of external inputs, the regional security scenario in the first decade of the twenty-first century will still be characterized by American strategic preponderance. The US will still be a dominant force in shaping the future security architecture of Southeast Asia and Pacific Asia more by default than by design – as other regional and global actors are relatively weak vis-à-vis the United States. The rise of China, in balance of power terms, will most certainly be matched by countervailing power from the USA, Russia, Japan, Australia and India. In any event, Southeast Asia and ASEAN would attempt to benefit from the economic spin offs of a rising China and India through bilateral and multilateral economic arrangements. The Chiang Mai Initiative of May 2000 represents one such bold effort to enact measures that could avert another Asian financial crisis by linking the foreign exchange reserves of the 13 countries (ASEAN plus 3, i.e. China, Japan and South Korea), which amount to almost US$1 trillion.[65] The Asian Financial Crisis of 1997–1998 proved how economic collapse can trigger political instability and chaos, and expand the conditions that enable local and international terrorists to thrive and advance their agendas.

Fifth, ASEAN as a regional institution, and the ARF as a broader security process would continue to face major constraints in their ability to respond swiftly to acts of terrorism in Southeast Asia due to at least four factors that characterize the regional security environment: (1) porous borders and generally weak immigration controls, with administrative requirements being surmounted through corruption; (2) long-standing economic and trade links between Southeast Asia and Middle Eastern and South Asian countries, many of which operate outside normal financial channels not readily monitored by governments, and which in turn have facilitated funds transfers from the Middle East and South Asia to radical groups in the region; (3) widespread criminal activity including drug trafficking in the region which in turn can facilitate the movement of resources by terrorists; and (4) the availability of large supplies of indigenously produced and imported weapons in Southeast Asia.[66]

All these factors tend to dilute the effectiveness of multilateral security cooperation against terror so that regional security institutions such as the ASEAN Regional Forum(ARF) would function only at a moderate level, i.e. the ARF process would characterize security dialogues and discussions and remain at the first stage: confidence building. In the meantime, more concrete and performance-related bilateral and multilateral security arrangements underwritten largely by the United States, including anti-terror coalitions, would continue to define, energize, and underpin the security architecture of Southeast Asia well into the New Millennium.

Finally, the impact of globalization on threat perception and defence posture in Southeast Asia will continue to be reflected by: (a) the adoption of traditionally-based state-level security measures to enhance national security via military modernization and security cooperation with regional states and extra-regional powers especially the United States; (b) deepening and broadening regionalism to promote community formation via the ASEAN Community (ASC, AEC, and ASCC), and the newly established forum of East Asia Summit; and (c) unilateral, bilateral and multilateral measures to mitigate threats to regional security from non-traditional security issues especially transnational terrorism and the catastrophic effects of natural disasters since the December 2004 tsunami. Globalization most certainly has increased political awareness and urged the formulation of strategic policies to address both traditional and non-traditional sources of regional security in Southeast Asia.

Notes

1 In this chapter, the discussion of the impacts of globalization on national security in Southeast Asia is limited to the original five members of the Association of Southeast Asian Nations (ASEAN), namely Indonesia, Malaysia, the Philippines, Singapore and Thailand.
2 Christopher W. Hughes, "Conceptualizing the Globalization–Security Nexus in the Asia-Pacific," *Security Dialogue*, 32:4 (December 2001), p. 415.
3 See T.V. Pail and Norrin M. Ripsman, "Under Pressure? Globalization and the National Security State," *Millennium: Journal of International Studies*, 33:2 (2004), p. 376.
4 Amitav Acharya, *The Quest for Identity: International Relations of Southeast Asia* (Oxford and Singapore: Oxford University Press, 2000), p. 51.
5 Michael Leifer, *Dilemmas of Statehood in Southeast Asia* (Singapore: Asia Pacific Press, 1972), p. 1.
6 Dewi Fortuna Anwar, "Indonesia: Domestic Priorities Define National Security," in Muthiah Alagappa (ed.), *Asian Security Practice: Material and Ideational Influences* (Stanford: Stanford University Press, 1998), p. 489.
7 For a discussion on threat perceptions of individual Southeast Asian countries towards major powers, see Robert O. Tilman, *Southeast Asia And The Enemy Beyond: ASEAN Perceptions of External Threats* (Boulder and London: Westview Press, 1987).
8 Acharya, *The Quest for Identity*, p. 55.
9 Zakaria Haji Ahmad, "The World of ASEAN Decision-Makers: A Study of Bureaucratic Elite Perceptions in Malaysia, the Philippines, and Singapore," *Contemporary Southeast Asia*, 8:3 (December 1986), p. 204.

10 Michael Leifer, *Dilemmas of Statehood in Southeast Asia* (Singapore: Asia Pacific Press, 1972), p. 148.
11 Robert B. Zoellick, "Economic and Security in the Changing Asia-Pacific," *Survival*, 39:4 (Winter 1997–1998), pp. 30–31.
12 For a comprehensive explanation of rapid economic growth in ASEAN, see Hall Hill, "Towards A Political Economy Explanation of Rapid Growth in Southeast Asia," in Hadi Soesastro (ed.), *One Southeast Asia in A New Regional and International Setting* (Jakarta: Centre for Strategic and International Studies, 1997), pp. 93–149.
13 Ibid., p. 105.
14 See, for example, Linda G. Martin (ed.), *The ASEAN Success Story: Social, Economic, and Political Dimension* (Honolulu: East–West Centre, 1987); and Hussin Mutalib, "At Thirty, ASEAN Looks to Challenges in the New Millennium," *Contemporary Southeast Asia*, 19:1 (June 1997).
15 Hadi Soesastro, "Economic Development and Security in the Asia-Pacific Context," In Mohamed Jawhar Hassan and Sheikh Ahmad Raffie (eds), *Bringing Peace to the Pacific* (Kuala Lumpur: ISIS, 1997), p. 253.
16 Steve Chan, "Regime Transition in the Asia-Pacific Region: Democratization as a Double-Edged Sword," *The Journal of Strategic Studies*, 18:3 (September 1995), p. 64.
17 Robert Scalapino, "Asia – The Past 50 Years and the Next 50 Years," in Soesastro, *One Southeast Asia*, p. 12.
18 Stuart Harris, "The Economic Aspects of Security in the Asia/Pacific Region," *The Journal of Strategic Studies*, 18:3 (September 1995), p. 36.
19 See, for example, Sukma, "Security Interdependence in Asia-Pacific: View From Jakarta" *Strategi: Journal of Strategic Studies and International Relations*, vol. 7 (August 1999), pp. 37–59.
20 Robert Keohane and Joseph Nye, *Power and Interdependence: World Politics in Transition* (Boston: Little Brown, 1977), pp. 7–8.
21 James H. Mittelman, "The Globalization Challenge: Surviving at the Margin," *Third World Quarterly*, 15:3 (September 1994), p. 432.
22 Ibid., p. 431.
23 Robert A. Scalapino, "Southeast Asian Politics in the Age of Globalization," paper presented at ISEAS 30th Anniversary Conference on *Southeast Asia in the 21st Century: Challenges of Globalization* (Singapore, 30 July – 1 August 1998), p. 14.
24 *Angkatan Bersenjata* (Jakarta), 25 September 1992.
25 Malcolm Chalmers, *Confidence-Building in South-East Asia* (Bradford: University of Bradford, 1996), p. 63.
26 Thomas W. Robinson, "Asia-Pacific Security Relations: Changes Ahead," in Richard L. Kugler and Ellen L. Frost (eds), *The Global Century: Globalization and National Security* (Washington DC: NDU Press, June 2001), p. 1011.
27 Chairman's Statement, the First ASEAN Regional Forum, Bangkok, 25 July 1994, in *ASEAN Regional Forum: Documents Series 1994–1998* (Jakarta: ASEAN Secretariat, 1999), pp. 1–3.
28 Chairman's Statement, the Seventh Meeting of ASEAN Regional Forum, Bangkok, 27 July 2000.
29 Declaration of ASEAN Concord II, Bali, Indonesia, 7 October 2003.
30 Niklas Swanstrom, "Southeast Asia's War on Terror: Who Is Cooperating Across Borders?" *Harvard Asia Quarterly*, 9:1 and 2 (Winter/Spring 2005), p. 9.
31 Daljit Singh, "ASEAN Counter-Terror Strategies and Co-operation: How Effective?" in Kumar Ramakrishna and See Seng Tan (eds), *After Bali: The Threat of Terrorism in Southeast Asia* (Singapore: World Scientific and IDSS, 2003), pp. 214–215.
32 Tim Huxley, "The ASEAN States' Defence Policies: Influences and Outcomes," in Colin McInnes and Mark G. Rolls (eds), *Post-Cold War Security Issues in the Asia-Pacific Region* (Essex: Frank Cass, 1994), p. 136.

33 Ibid.
34 For a recent study on armed rebellion in Southeast Asia, see Andrew Tan, *Armed Rebellion in the ASEAN States* (Canberra: ANU, 2000).
35 Indonesia's Defence White Paper, *Mempertahankan Tanah Air Memasuki Abad 21* [Defending the Nation in the 21st Century] (Jakarta: Ministry of Defence, 2003), p. 83.
36 Sheldon W. Simon, "The Economic Crisis and ASEAN States' Security." Pennsylvania, US: US Army War College Strategic Studies Institute, 23 October 1998. Online, available at www.strategicstudiesinstitute.army/mil/pdffiles/00075.PDF.
37 Renato Cruz De Castro, "Societal Forces as Sources of Military Doctrine and Posture: The Case of the AFP Modernisation Programme, 1991–2003," in Amitav Acharya and Lee Lai To (eds), *Asia in the New Millennium*, APISA First Congress Proceedings, 27–30 November 2003 (Singapore: Marshall Cavendish, 2004), p. 213.
38 Malaysia, for example, closed its borders with Indonesia in Kalimantan in 1997 for fear of the spillover of ethnic conflict in Indonesia's East Kalimantan province.
39 Yeo Lay Hwee, "Singapore," in Charles E. Morrison (ed.), *Asia Pacific Security Outlook 2004* (Tokyo: JCIE, 2004), p. 172.
40 Andrew Tan, *Force Modernisation Trends in Southeast Asia*, Working Paper No. 59 (Singapore: IDSS, January 2004), p. 31.
41 Ibid.
42 Indonesia's Defence White Paper, pp. 50, and 81–82.
43 General (Ret) Teerawat Putamanonda, "Thailand's Security Environment," online, available at www.ndu.edu/inss/symposia/Pacific2002/putamanondapaper.htm.
44 Ibid.
45 Robert Hartfiel and Brian Job, *Raising the Risk of War: Defence Spending Trends and Competitive Arms Processes in East Asia*, Working Paper No. 44, Institute of International Relations, the University of British Columbia (March 2005), pp. 16–17.
46 Pipob Udomittipong, "Rethinking Education on the Verge of Globalization," in N.N. Vohra and J.N. Dixit (eds), *Religion, Politics and Society in South and Southeast Asia*, (Delhi: Konark Publishers Pvt. Ltd., 1998), p. 178.
47 For details, see Leszek Busyznski, "ASEAN, the Declaration on Conduct, and the South China Sea," *Contemporary Southeast Asia*, vol. 25, no. 3 (December 2003), pp. 343–362.
48 Busyznski, ibid., p. 343.
49 See "ASEAN Way of Fighting Terrorism," issued by the ASEAN Secretariat, Jakarta, 2002. Online, available at www.aseansec.org/12776.htm.
50 "ASEAN Efforts to Counter Terrorism." Paper prepared for the UN Counter-Terrorism Committee. Online, available at www.aseansec.org/14396.htm.
51 See, "Tenth ASEAN Summit Ensures Economic Growth in a Secure and Humane Environment." Statement of Hon. Alberto G. Romulo, Philippine Secretary of Foreign Affairs, 9 December 2004. Online, available at www.dfa.gov.ph/archive/speech/romulo/10thasean.htm.
52 *Straits Times*, 8 May 2002, p. 1.
53 *Chairman's Statement of the 11th ASEAN Summit: One Vision, One Identity, One Community*, Kuala Lumpur, 12 December 2005. Online, available at www.aseansec.org/18039.htm.
54 Colin S. Gray, "The Arms Race Phenomenon," *World Politics*, vol. 24, no. 1, October 1971, pp. 39–79.
55 Andrew Tan, *Force Modernisation Trends in Southeast Asia*, IDSS Working Paper No. 59 (Singapore: Institute of Strategic and Defense Studies, Nanyang Technological University, January 2004), p. 37.
56 David Mussington, *Understanding Contemporary International Arms Transfers*, Adelphi Paper No. 291 (London: International Institute for Strategic Studies, September 1994), p. 36.

57 Tim Huxley and Susan Willett, *Arming East Asia*, Adelphi Paper No. 329, (London: International Institute for Strategic Studies, 1999), p. 66.
58 Ibid.
59 For a more complete account of the arms modernization dynamics in Southeast Asia, see Andrew Tan, *Force Modernisation Trends in Southeast Asia*, January 2004.
60 Mely Caballero-Anthony, *Regional Security in Southeast Asia: Beyond the ASEAN Way*, (Singapore: Institute of Southeast Asian Studies, 2005), p. 258.
61 Amitav Acharya, *An Arms Race in Post-Cold War Southeast Asia?: Control*. Pacific Strategic Papers, No. 8. (Singapore: Institute of Southeast Asian Studies, 1994), p. 48.
62 Andrew T.H. Tan and Kenneth Boutin (eds), *Non-Traditional Security Issues in Southeast Asia*, (Singapore: Select Publishing for Institute of Defense and Strategic Studies, 2001), p. 5.
63 Chia Siow Yue, "ASEAN in the Age of Globalization and Information," in Simon S.C. Tay, Jesus P. Estanislao and Hadi Soesastro (eds), *Reinventing ASEAN*, (Singapore: Institute of Southeast Asian Studies, 2001), pp. 121–147.
64 Indeed, the most recent example of how bilateral territorial and resource disputes can be settled by negotiation and compromise, and not by force, is afforded by the agreement by Malaysia and Singapore to resolve the two-year problem over land reclamation works undertaken by Singapore in the Johor Straits, which Malaysia claims has affected shipping, navigation, the economic livelihood of fishermen and causes damage to the marine environment. *The Straits Times*, 27 April 2005, p. 1 and p. H2.
65 Joseph Y.S. Cheng, "Sino–ASEAN Relations in the Early Twenty-first Century," *Contemporary Southeast Asia*, vol. 23, no. 3 (December 2001), pp. 420–451.
66 See article by Frank Frost, Ann Rann and Andrew Chin, "Terrorism in Southeast Asia," Department of the Parliamentary Library, Parliament of Australia, Canberra, 7 January 2003. Online, available at www.aph.gov.au/library/intguide/FAD/sea.htm.

7 Globalization's impact on threat perceptions and defence posture in South Asia

B. Raman

General

For the purpose of this chapter, South Asia has been taken to cover India, Afghanistan, Pakistan, Bangladesh, Sri Lanka, Nepal, Bhutan and the Maldives. Even though China is not considered a part of South Asia, it has common borders with some of the countries of the region and their threat perceptions are influenced by the China factor. There cannot, therefore, be any meaningful discussion on this subject without a reference to this factor.

South Asia, as defined above, covers only about 10 per cent of the total land area of the Asian continent, but about 40 per cent of Asia's total population and between 45 and 50 per cent of Asia's Muslim population live in this area. Many analysts in India, including this writer, make a distinction between the Indian sub-continent and South Asia. When they talk of the Indian sub-continent, they have in mind India, Pakistan, Bangladesh, Nepal and Bhutan. Of these, India, Pakistan and Bangladesh constituted one political entity before the British left the sub-continent in 1947. Pakistan was born in 1947 through the partition of the British India, and Bangladesh was born in 1971 through the partition of Pakistan after a war of liberation waged by the Bengalis of the then East Pakistan, with Indian assistance.

Indian analysts, who talk of the Indian sub-continent, wish to keep in mind, in their analyses, the common historical, political, religious, and cultural heritage of these three countries. The term sub-continent is used less and less in Pakistan and Bangladesh. The political leadership and the policy-makers in these two countries do not wish to be reminded of this common heritage. Any highlighting of this common heritage by Indian analysts is viewed by them with suspicion – as indicating a hidden desire to reverse history and undo the 1947 partition. They, therefore, talk only of South Asia and have, for all practical purposes, banished any reference to the sub-continent from their strategic discourse. This has to be kept in mind since complexes arising from sub-continental memories tend to influence their mind-set and threat perceptions and have stood in the way of the progress of globalization in this area. They view any Indian enthusiasm for globalization as a concealed attempt towards political and economic re-subcontinentalization.

The threat perceptions of the countries of South Asia are influenced and will continue to be influenced in the short and medium terms by four factors:

- the India factor
- the China factor
- the Pakistan factor
- the non-state actors factor

The India factor

The India factor has had an impact on the threat perceptions of all the countries of this region except Afghanistan and the Maldives. This arises due to the following reasons:

- Asymmetry in size, human and material resources and economic and military potential.
- Perceived Indian willingness/tendency to assert its national interests even if they are detrimental to those of the neighbours. Examples: India's role in the creation of Bangladesh, alleged Indian support to the Tamils of Sri Lanka.
- Perceived Indian encouragement of its political favourites in the countries of the region. Examples: India's alleged soft corner for the opposition Awami League in Bangladesh and for the democratic forces in Nepal.
- Continuing differences relating to territory (Kashmir with Pakistan) and utilization of water resources (Pakistan and Bangladesh).

The other countries, except Afghanistan and the Maldives, tend to guard themselves against these factors by avoiding too close economic linkages with India, which comes in the way of the region as a whole benefiting from the fruits of globalization, by developing economic and military linkages with China and by supporting Chinese aspirations for a role in regional organizations such as the SAARC as an observer.

Pakistan and Bangladesh embarked on a policy of liberalization of their economies before India. Despite this, their economic development has not been as satisfactory as they would have liked it to be. Amongst the reasons, one could cite the bad internal security situation, which keeps foreign investors away despite a favourable policy framework; political instability due to periodic interventions by the Army in politics; inadequate investment in a modern education system due to the diversion of the limited resources to meet military and strategic needs; and failure to diversify the economy. Pakistan's economy continues to be largely a three-commodity (cotton and cotton textiles, leather goods and sports articles) and one-port (Karachi) economy. Bangladesh's economy continues to be largely textiles, jute and raw materials dependent.

Though India embarked on the liberalization of its economy only from 1991 onwards, its economy has made impressive progress freeing it from its past dependence on traditional goods such as textiles, tea, etc. India's rapid diversification and development of its economy have been facilitated by the fact that democracy has taken firm root in the country; that its internal security problems, though serious, are confined to areas in which the foreign investors are presently not interested; and that its founding fathers had shown foresight in investing heavily in a modern education system, including institutes of excellence in technology, which have significantly contributed to its emergence as a leading Information Technology (IT) power.

Complexes and concerns arising from the India factor continue to come in the way of the normalization of trade relations between Pakistan and India, the improvement in the trade relations between India and Bangladesh and progress towards the integration of the economies of the region through appropriate institutional and policy frameworks. Political factors continue to receive priority over economic and prejudices and fears continue to rule out pragmatism.

However, economic realities ultimately have a way of asserting themselves. One could already see a beginning of it in Pakistan. Its rulers and policy-makers have realized that a favourable policy framework and wide-ranging reforms alone will not attract foreign investors. They also need a market and consumers large enough to make their investments adequately profitable. Pakistan does not provide such a market and such a reservoir of consumers. Unless the foreign investors perceive the sub-continent as a whole as a single economic entity and market and are able to sell their products anywhere within this entity, they are reluctant to invest in Pakistan or Bangladesh alone, without guarantees of access to the Indian market.

The realization of this ground reality has already brought about a significant change in Pakistan's policy since General Pervez Musharraf came to power in October 1999. While continuing to oppose the normalization of economic relations with India till the differences over Jammu and Kashmir are settled, he has made an exception in respect of energy supplies. He is prepared now to allow the foreign investors investing heavily in the construction of oil and gas pipelines to Pakistan from Iran or Turkmenistan to cater to the requirements of the Indian market too, in order to make their investments adequately profitable. Significantly, even the religious fundamentalist parties, who continue to insist on a policy of "Kashmir first and the rest later", have not objected to what Gen. Musharraf describes as the stand-alone exception. If this exception materializes and if the benefits of it are felt by the Pakistani people, this will become more and more a rule than a mere exception.

Such a realization has yet to come about in Bangladesh. The trade relations between India and Bangladesh are not as restricted as those between India and Pakistan. There is a much, much freer flow of trade between the two countries. While encouraging a greater flow of trade with China, Bangladesh continues to prevent pragmatism, profitability and mutual benefits from having a free play to contribute to a rapid expansion of the bilateral economic relations with India.

Four examples could be cited as illustrations of the Bangladesh attitude:

- It refuses to sell its surplus gas to India on the ostensible ground that it wants to conserve it for its own future use. At the same time, it has reportedly entered into negotiations with China for selling it through a pipeline to China via Myanmar.
- It refuses to grant transit rights to India to facilitate the movement of Indian goods to India's northeast.
- It has been reluctant to permit a pipeline to bring gas from the Arakan area of Myanmar to India to pass through Bangladesh territory.
- During the period from July to December 2005, the value of Chinese exports to Bangladesh amounted to US$1.03 billion and Chinese imports from Bangladesh only US$27.9 million. During the same period, the value of Indian exports to Bangladesh amounted to US$820 million and imports from Bangladesh to US$105 million. India's imports from Bangladesh are still small, but they are four times the value of Chinese imports from Bangladesh. Chinese exports to Bangladesh are nearly 25 per cent more than those of India. And yet, while Bangladesh nurses a grudge against India on the grounds that it has allegedly been dumping its goods in Bangladesh and has not been buying enough from there, it does not voice a similar grievance against China.

Feelings of insecurity, an aggressive inferiority complex, and a me-too syndrome continue to influence policy-making in Pakistan. What India does, it must do too. What India gets, it must get too. One saw an example of this syndrome in action during the recent visit of President George Bush to India and Pakistan, when, during Mr Bush's talks in Islamabad, Gen. Musharraf reportedly pleaded with him to reach an agreement with Pakistan on co-operation in the development of civilian nuclear energy similar to the agreement offered to India. Mr. Bush had to point out to him that the needs and circumstances of the two countries are different.

These factors – feelings of insecurity, the inferiority complex and the me-too syndrome – will continue to influence the Pakistani mind-set and policy-making in the short and medium terms. Though there has been progress in the identification and implementation of confidence-building measures and in the promotion of people-to-people contacts, the relationship between the two countries will continue to be fragile and the exploitation of the opportunities for beneficial co-operation provided by globalization will be slow.

While Pakistan's longing for the acquisition of Jammu and Kashmir and its painful memories of 1971 could explain its attitude to India, no convincing explanation is possible for the behaviour of Bangladesh. While there are differences between India and Bangladesh over the utilization of river waters, there are no major differences over territory compared to the Kashmir issue with Pakistan, and Bangladesh has no negative memories of India's military might in action against it. The anti-Indian reflexes in Bangladesh are largely confined to the present ruling formation headed by Begum Khalida Zia and are not shared by the opposition headed by the Awami League, which was in the forefront of its independence struggle.

India–Bangladesh relations will continue to zig-zag – improving when the Awami League is in power and stagnating, if not declining, when the Bangladesh National Party comes to power. Globalization has not made any significant difference to this zig-zag and is unlikely to do so in the short and medium terms.

The China factor

China is not a South Asian power, but it has acquired a significant South Asian presence, by skilfully exploiting the complexes and reflexes of the countries of the region vis-à-vis India. Amongst the steps it has taken to make its presence felt in this region are:

- The clandestine supply of nuclear and missile technologies to Pakistan, which might one day fall into the hands of Al Qaeda and other jihadi terrorist organizations should the jihadis capture power in Pakistan.
- Strengthening Pakistan's military capability in the Army, the Air Force and the Navy in order to reduce its feeling of insecurity vis-à-vis India.
- Strengthening Pakistan's strategic infrastructure through projects such as the construction of the Gwadar port on the Baloch coast and the Mekran Highway connecting Gwadar with Karachi.
- Strengthening Pakistan's IT capability.
- Strengthening Bangladesh's military capability.
- Helping Bangladesh in the development of its energy resources.
- The reported offer of assistance to Bangladesh for setting up facilities for research into the peaceful uses of nuclear energy.
- Reported military supplies to the royal regime in Nepal at a time when India has cut down its military supplies in view of the suppression of democracy by the King.
- Reported assistance to Sri Lanka for the development of the Hambantota port.

These developments are viewed by many analysts, including this writer, as an attempt to strengthen China's strategic presence and influence in the South Asian region. However, these perceptions, not invalid, have not been allowed to resurrect feelings of animosity between India and China. The border dispute between the two countries continues to remain under negotiations without any visible forward movement. At the same time, there have been significant gestures – such as the Chinese recognition of Sikkim as a part of India and the bilateral agreement to resume border trade through the Sikkim sector.

The presence of the Dalai Lama and a large number of Tibetan refugees in the Indian territory and their activities – perceived by Beijing as political behind a religious facade – continue to be a matter of concern to China, but these concerns are no longer articulated in strong language.

China has shown signs of being comfortable with the idea of India emerging as an important power, but it does not seem to be comfortable with the prospect of India emerging as a power on par with China. This was evident from its strong opposition to India's aspirations of becoming a permanent member of the UN Security Council and its reticence on the question of the Nuclear Suppliers' Group (NSG) relaxing restrictions on the sale of civilian nuclear technology to India, despite India's initiative for separating its civilian nuclear establishments from its military and placing the former under international safeguards. It seems to be opposed to any unilateral concessions to India until such time when such concessions could be made applicable to Pakistan too.

Despite these factors, the trust deficit between India and China has steadily declined. India has been noting with not-openly-articulated concern the steady modernization of the Chinese Armed Forces and the growing Chinese military and economic linkages with the countries of South Asia, but it has not allowed this to come in the way of the steady improvement in the bilateral relations. At the same time, one has also noted the moderating role played by China during the military conflict in 1999 between India and Pakistan following Pakistani military intrusions in the Kargil sector of India's Jammu and Kashmir.

The leaderships of India and China have shown great political maturity in not allowing the continuing differences over the border come in the way of economic and other linkages. Bilateral trade has boomed during the last ten years – increasing from a total of about US$2 billion to US$13 billion. However, it needs to be underlined that this boom has been considerably due to the requirements of raw materials for the rapidly expanding Chinese industries, particularly its steel industry.

Globalization and the consequent networking and interactions between the policy-makers and the business classes of the two countries have contributed to a remarkable resurgence of interest in each other and to a dilution of the mutual threat perceptions. Nobody in India, any longer, talks – at least openly – of China as a threat. In the past, China was viewed mainly as a worrisome power. Now its image is more positive. The remarkable change for the better in Indian threat perceptions of China is evident from the fact that the Indian intelligence and security establishment no longer opposes, as strongly as it used to do in the past, the presence of Chinese companies even in cities such as Bangalore, India's Silicon Valley, where many of India's sensitive defence and other strategic establishments are located.

The steady forward movement of India and China towards a common shared future of prosperity and mutual confidence can be endangered if the leaderships of the two countries do not skilfully manage the misgivings in China over the implications of the growing strategic partnership between the US and India to its aspired pre-eminence in Asia and the world; and the likely tensions in Tibet, when the Dalai Lama ceases to be and the Chinese attempt to have their say, as they are bound to, in the selection of his successor. The continuously developing military, nuclear and other strategic linkages between China and Pakistan would remain a source of worry to Indian policy-makers and could stand in the way of the bilateral relations developing to their fullest potential.

The Pakistan factor

A reference has already been made to the Pakistan factor while discussing India–Pakistan relations. Two other aspects, which have not been touched upon earlier, need to be highlighted. The first relates to Pakistan's use of terrorism as a covert weapon to achieve its strategic objective of forcing a change in the status quo in Jammu and Kashmir. The second relates to its long-nourished objective of acquiring a strategic depth vis-à-vis India by bringing Afghanistan under its control and by establishing military and strategic linkages with Iran.

It was these objectives, which led Pakistan to set up a clandestine infrastructure not only in its territory, but also in Afghan territory for training and arming terrorists for use against India. It was this infrastructure that Al Qaeda, the Taliban and the various terrorist organizations, which are members of the International Islamic Front (IIF) of Bin Laden, came from. This infrastructure continues to function undisturbed, creating national security problems not only for India and Afghanistan, but also for other countries.

Pakistan's strategic relationship with Iran, the foundations for which were laid by the late Zulfiquar Ali Bhutto and the Shah of Iran, led to the flow of funds from Iran to Pakistan's military nuclear programme to produce what was described as the world's first Islamic atomic bomb. The recent enquiries by the International Atomic Energy Agency (IAEA) of Vienna into Iran's clandestine nuclear programme have brought out the covert role of Dr A.Q. Khan, the so-called father of Pakistan's Islamic bomb, in assisting Iran to become the world's second Islamic military nuclear power.

Will the so-called Islamic bomb developed by Pakistan with funds not only from Iran, but also from Saudi Arabia and Libya and any similar bomb developed by Iran with Pakistani complicity fall into the hands of Al Qaeda, the IIF and organizations such as the Lashkar-e-Toiba (LET) and become the world's first jihadi atomic bomb? It is fears caused by the spectre of a jihadi bomb in the hands of the terrorists that should explain India's vote in the IAEA in favour of a continued role by the Agency to pre-empt this danger.

Afghanistan, a pre-2001 failed State, has yet to start benefiting from the fruits of globalization. India's efforts to develop trade links with Afghanistan and bring it into the global economic mainstream continue to be thwarted by Pakistan's refusal to grant Indian businessmen transit rights to Afghanistan through Pakistani territory.

The non-state actors

The US-orchestrated covert war against the Soviet troops in Afghanistan in the 1980s turned the region into a playground for non-state actors of various hues, persuasions and motives – jihadi and sectarian terrorists, transnational crime mafia groups, narcotics producers and smugglers and money-laundering gangs. These non-state actors turned Afghanistan into a failed state and almost caused the collapse of the Pakistani economy before 2001.

The anti-communist jihadi terrorism of the 1980s gave place to the anti-modernization terrorism of the 1990s personified by the Taliban, which, in turn, has given way to the revanchist terrorism of the present decade personified by Al Qaeda and the International Islamic Front (IIF). The Al Qaeda and the IIF organizations are revanchist in character, medieval in their objectives and frighteningly modern in their methods of operation.

Even after more than four years of the so-called war on international terrorism was launched on 7 October 2001, the international community is not yet able to get the better of a determined, well-motivated and elusive enemy. Two of the four epicentres of international jihadi terrorism are located in this area. The first is in the Waziristan area of Pakistan, from where Al Qaeda, the Taliban, the Islamic Movement of Uzbekistan (IMU), the Jundullah (Army of Allah) and the other components of the IIF are making a determined bid to stage a comeback in Afghanistan. This is also the epicentre from which the continuing use of terrorism against India is fuelled.

The second epicentre is located in Bangladesh, which has become an alternate command and control for jihadi terrorists from the Harkat-ul-Jihad-al-Islami (HUJI) and the LET operating in Indian territory. The epicentre in Bangladesh has also serious implications for the future security and stability of Myanmar and southern Thailand.

Narcotics production in Afghanistan has again increased significantly and the resulting cash flow has nullified any benefits to the war on terrorism from the campaign against terrorism funding mounted after 9/11 under the UN Security Council Resolution No. 1373.

There is no trust deficit coming in the way of networking and co-operation among the non-state actors. As a result, the non-state actors have benefited more than the state actors of the region from the fruits of networking, freer flow of human beings, the communications revolution and the innovations in science and technology. Al Qaeda and the IIF are making better use of the Internet than the state actors.

Globalization has given rise to two parallel trends towards a radicalization of sections of the youth of South Asia. The first trend is a radicalization of sections of the youth of all communities due to continuing economic and social disparities despite the growing economic prosperity.

Uneven distribution of the newly created wealth and opportunities is a major cause of this trend. There are more haves than in the past, but the number of have-nots is still very high and is more than the total population of many countries of the world. For example, in India, about 260 million people are still below the poverty line.

There has been an aggravation of the divide between the privileged and the under-privileged and of the feelings of relative deprivation among different layers of the society. The result: ideology, which, according to conventional wisdom, should have become increasingly irrelevant in pragmatism-driven economies, has assumed a new relevance. One sees this in the resurgence and aggravation of ideological terrorism. Examples include the Maoists of India and Nepal.

The second trend is the growing radicalization of sections of the Muslim youth, more due to religious than economic reasons. Anger against the non-Muslims, who are projected as the enemies of Islam for allegedly committing various wrongs against the Muslims, has given rise to a new kind of terrorism personified by Al Qaeda and the International Islamic Front (IIF). Innovations in science and technology, knowledge of Information Technology and modern means of communication are sought to be used by the revanchist terrorist elements not as forces of creation, but of destruction, not to integrate, but to disintegrate.

The tensions caused by the old divide between the developed and the developing or the underdeveloped have been reduced, but the attempts by these elements to create a new divide between Islam and the rest have brought in new threats to peace, security and prosperity.

As a result of these trends, dealing with threats to internal security has become an over-riding preoccupation of the states of the region, consuming a considerable proportion of their resources, time and attention. Linkages between sources of internal and external threats to security are stronger in the South Asian region than in any other region of Asia. Exploitation of internal tensions by external actors – state as well as non-state – for strategic reasons has come in the way of the region reaping the full benefits of the process of integration and globalization.

The result of this is that there is greater progress towards integration with the societies and economies of countries outside the region than of countries in the region. For example, the countries of the region are moving closer to those of Southeast Asia, bilaterally as well as multilaterally, than to each other.

There has been a positive change in the relations of the countries of the region with countries outside the region such as the US, China, Japan, etc., but there has been little change in their relations with each other. Countries outside the region such as the US, China and Japan are viewed with decreasing suspicion and increasing comfort. There is, consequently, a greater comfort level in the relations of the countries of this region with such powers outside the region.

However, there are incipient positive trends, which are having an impact on inter- as well as intra-regional relationships, despite continuing inter-regional sources of discord. For example, energy requirements driving India and Pakistan on the one side, and India and China on the other, towards solutions based on co-operation rather than competition in their energy quest.

The likelihood of threats to regional and global trade has been driving the countries of Asia towards a search for co-operative counter-terrorism and maritime security initiatives and mechanisms. However, the persistence of traditional distrustful mindsets in the South Asian region makes the search for such co-operative security mechanisms fractional rather than well integrated. An example is Pakistan's attempts to keep India out of the co-operative mechanisms in the Gulf area despite India's support for the association of Pakistan with the ASEAN Regional Forum.

The trust deficit, which is a defining characteristic of the threat perceptions in the South Asian region, will continue to make the progress towards inter-regional integration slow and halting in the short and medium terms, but it is bound to acquire the needed momentum as the compulsions of economics acquire predominance over traditional sources of mistrust and discord.

Part III

Globalization and the defence economy in the Asia-Pacific

8 Defence and the economy

An introduction*

Ron Matthews

Introduction

Globalization is not a new phenomenon, but this time around its impact has propelled the world economy into uncharted territory. The global economy is now more open and interdependent than ever before. The WTO and its predecessor body, the GATT, has facilitated an explosive growth in world trade and development. The process began in the late 1970s and was subsequently reinforced by the implosion of the Soviet Union (1991), leading to the disappearance of the bipolar international military balance of power and the redundancy of Communism as a viable and sustainable political ideology. Capitalism lay behind these events, establishing itself as the dominant economic model. Nowhere, is the impact of re-ordered political–economic priorities more evident than in Northeast Asia, where 25 per cent of global output is generated. The region's three strongest economies have all gained from economic liberalization. Japan, still the world's second biggest economy, has benefited from a series of institutional and corporate liberalization reforms as a direct response to the economic difficulties faced during the 'lost' decade. Japan's economy is now growing again, enjoying huge trading surpluses, and becoming increasingly global through (real and potential) integration into the world's security and diplomatic frameworks. Similarly, South Korea's economy has grown dramatically over the last two decades, buoyed by inward foreign investment into emerging high technology sectors, such as defence, aerospace and electronics. The process has been assisted by Seoul's policy-emphasis on raising research and development (R&D) expenditure in local science and technology endeavours, and its capacity to develop high quality technologies to penetrate foreign markets. Finally, China's dynamic entry onto the world's economic stage has begun to change the tide of economic history. Dispensing with the economic dead-hand of Karl Marx has transformed China into a land of serial entrepreneurs, catapulting its economy from nowhere into becoming the world's fourth biggest in 2006. Significantly, China, as with the other two principal economies of Northeast Asia, is a member of the WTO, subscribing to the capitalist ethic of profit-maximization and possessing the intangible but critically important ingredients of cohesiveness and commitment, vital for the creation of a national identity.

Classical economics is the seed-germ of the globalization process. Adam Smith's paradigm of 'perfect' competition denotes open and unlimited access to markets, subscription to free trade, a diminution in the role of government, and a reduction in barriers to the efficient working of sectoral, national and international markets. These were the characteristics of globalization in the nineteenth century, and, indeed, in more recent times. Globalization, however, is not a concept isolated to commercial firms producing civil products, such as cars, cameras and refrigerators. It also has relevance and applicability to the production of fighters, warships and main battle tanks. In fact, progressive liberalization of public sector activity, including competitive tendering, lean logistics, performance management and financial management, has meant that the commercial imperatives of efficiency and cost-reduction now permeate the broad spectrum of defence resourcing policies. This tighter fusion of civil–military management processes has coincidentally led to the recognition that a focus on security rather than defence is the way forward. Asian governments are ahead of their time in this respect, but Western policymakers are catching up fast, introducing polices designed to leverage defence capability through the strengthening of national capacity in 'dual-use' R&D, project management, systems integration and high technology manufacturing areas. Thus, globalization is signified not only by increased commercial integration between countries but also by heightened economic integration between the civil and defence communities. Under this interpretation, Northeast Asia is strongly positioned to benefit from globalization because the industrial and technological strategy of the region's mega-economies is one that exploits the integration synergies of both these interconnected trade and civil–military industrial dimensions

The thrust of this chapter is therefore to explore these issues, with particular reference to Northeast Asia. The chapter's structure has three parts:

- Definitional discussion of globalization and the development of a methodological framework for examining the impact of globalization on the defence economy.
- Development and critical evaluation of the concept of a 'defence ecosystem', representing a mosaic of stakeholder interests rather than the traditional focus based solely on the defence aspect.
- Critical evaluation of globalization's impact on the Northeast Asian economy.

Contemporary nature of the defence economy

Before evaluating the nature of globalization's impact on the defence economy of Northeast Asia it is helpful to begin by probing the powerful but subtle relationship between defence and the broader economy. This is perhaps best tackled by defining the nature and bases of defence economics. In this context, a typical definition would be that employed by Michael Intriligator, who argued that...

Defense Economics is concerned with that part of the overall economy involving defense-related issues, including the level of defense spending, both in total and as a fraction of the overall economy; the impacts of defense expenditure, both domestically for output and employment and internationally for impacts on other nationals; the reasons for the existence and size of the defense sector; the relation of defense spending to technical change; and the implications of defense spending and the defense sector for international stability or instability.[1]

Whilst Intriligator's definition is comprehensive, embracing all essential ingredients of the subject-matter, its 'catch-all' quality is also its weakness. The policy-orientated nature of defence economics demands a structured focus on resource management, influenced by internal defence community efficiencies, an awareness of the trade-offs between defence and the broader commercial economy, and, increasingly, recognition of the integrative benefits between regional and global defence relationships.

The generic economics of Adam Smith are grounded in the classical theories of choice, opportunity–cost and optimal resource allocation theory. By contrast, the thrust of defence economics is more refined, focusing on the management of scarce resources applied to the defence context. The 'new' twenty-first century interpretation of defence economics is multi-layered, carrying three levels of analysis: first, a focus on the critical policies, plans and resourcing decisions linked to the 'balance' of investment options across the defence spectrum; second, greater understanding of the nature of the relationship between defence expenditure and economic growth; and, third, the need to evaluate the impact of globalization on sovereign national defence economies. Each of these levels of analysis will now be examined in turn.

Defence resource management

The defence economy comprises a complex web of governmental, industrial–commercial and military stakeholders. This relational structure has been formally characterized as the 'iron triangle', with each leg of the triangular structure comprising myriad relationships both within and between the three defence economic elements.[2] At the core of these relationships is government, particularly, though not exclusively, the Ministry of Defence (MoD), influencing through its policies all aspects of the triangle. Take, for instance, the case of the UK: in the post-Cold War era, and more so in the new millennium, defence resourcing decisions are increasingly being taken in partnership. Right from the start-point of threat assessment, scenario analysis is employed to identify future threats through Delphi techniques. The process involves futurologists, seasoned defence civil servants, specialized academics and military personnel; the resource base widening as the breadth of threats expands. More tellingly, at the operational level, Armed Forces (AF) are being pushed to work together: jointery at the national level, through tri-service operations, and coalition at the international level, through different national AFs working together. Equally, in formulating weapons and equipment responses to assessments of future emerging threats, UK industry is now actively encouraged to engage at the concept stage, the earliest and least visible of all six phases of the defence acquisition (CADMID) cycle.[3] Indeed, throughout the military equipment life-cycle, the iron-triangle of government–industry–military is now meant to be partnership-based, reflected by the Anglo-Saxon policy emphasis on relational management and Integrated Project Teams (IPTs). 'Trust', a major feature of Asian management culture, is now being promulgated amongst stakeholders in defence acquisition and linked project management activities. The introduction of partnering policies is, in part, driven by the need to eradicate hitherto confrontational practices, but this is no easy task, given the inherent frictions and compromises involved in balancing stakeholder objectives: the Ministry of Defence's primary aim being to achieve value-for-money, often a euphemism for reducing the taxpayers' burden through cost-reduction policy initiatives; industry, by contrast, seeks the commercial imperative of profit maximization; and, last but not least, the military's overarching goal is to procure the most effective (and thus often the most expensive) battle-winning military capability. The inherent tensions in seeking to achieve all these goals simultaneously are self-evident.

Balancing act: defence expenditure versus economic growth

The putative view of the defence economy is that it carries a welfare cost; that is, defence, in all its operational, logistical and industrial forms, represents a burden on society. At the core of this trade-off is opportunity–cost. In the defence context, the greater a nation's scarce resources allocated to defence the less there will be available for the more productive commercial sector. Whilst even the production of bombs can contribute to the economy in the short-run, through, for instance, income creation, export promotion and employment generation, in the longer-run there is a danger that an economy's scarce resources will be 'crowded-out' from the commercial sector. The negative effects of this crowding-out will likely impact on the economy in two ways:

- Outweighing short-run economic multipliers from increases in defence expenditure, and thus dampening the rate of economic growth.
- Raising output redundancy, as increased defence production adds nothing to the volume or variety of goods available for personal consumption, and only minimal expansion of the means of production, thus contributing little to wealth creation through rising levels of capital goods production.

The intellectual catalyst for this 'defence-development' dilemma was Emile Benoit's 1973 thesis on the relationship between defence expenditure and economic growth.[4] Heroically, though perversely, Benoit argued that there was a positive relationship between defence spending and the expansion of national income. Based on data reflecting the economic impact of the 1963 Sino-India war, Benoit made the huge intellectual leap that India's raised level of defence expenditure had somehow 'caused' the subsequent increase in the country's economic growth. His thesis led to a veritable explosion in studies examining the nature of the defence–development nexus. After decades of intensive research and debate, the generalized view today is one that has reverted to the conventional judgement, positing an inverse relationship between defence expenditure and economic growth.

It would be wrong to believe, however, that the debate has now run its course; the 'trade-off' controversy remaining a hot topic in both intellectual and policy-making circles. An important recent factor fuelling the debate has had regard to the increased contemporary opportunities for exploiting civil–military integration. The development benefits of such exploitation derive from the increased value-added of commercial inputs into modern weapons systems and their associated infrastructure and services. Hence, this new defence economic model suggests that perhaps Benoit's thesis has finally come of age, and that growth in defence expenditure is calibrated with increased productivity, enhanced innovation and also income creation in the commercial sector, thus connoting a positive relationship between defence and development. There is limited scholarship on the nature and causal flow of this relationship, but at a time of intense defence resource scrutiny, the issue has never been more important. Greater civil–military integration reduces the cost of defence, whether it is through:

- Defence research and production linkages to the commercial sector, such as by encouraging technology spin-offs, e.g. the UK Qinetiq experiment.
- Defence production, through technology spin-ons from raised levels of COTS (commercial-off-the-shelf) investment into defence systems.
- Infrastructure/services investment via, for instance, Private Finance Initiatives (PFIs), outsourcing and contractorization programmes.[5]

It would be helpful if an optimal civil:military expenditure relation could be identified, but unsurprisingly, there exists no MILEX/GDP level having generic applicability. Rather, a country's defence burden is influenced by a basket of geo-strategic, cultural and historical considerations. One thing for sure, though, civil–military integration can work both ways, not only is it now feasible to consider that defence spending contributes to income generation, but, equally, rising levels of national income may accommodate enhanced defence expenditure without any change in a country's defence burden. The fundamental issue remains, however: how much is enough? In other words, what is the appropriate proportion of a country's resource-base that should be devoted to defence?

Globalization and the tension between competition and protectionism

In the defence domain, the search for more efficient processes of resource allocation has now become a global imperative. Just as in the commercial environment, the 1990's confluence of national liberalization policies and inter-national free trade has obliged governments and defence contractors alike to recognize the threats and opportunities of enhanced global competitiveness. Yet, the business of defence has traditionally been immune from competition and free trade because of protected markets. In the US, for instance, 'Buy America' legislation dating back to the 1930s has ensured almost total defence–industrial sovereignty. In Russia (and before that, the Soviet Union), defence industry has always been regarded as 'strategic', and hence protected from foreign invest-ment. Also, the multitude of national defence industries within the European Union are protected from competition under Article 296 of the Treaty of Ams-terdam, and across the globe the vast array of emerging nations' defence sectors, including those of China, India, Pakistan, Malaysia, Singapore, and most of those in Africa and Latin America, remain in protective public sector hands. However, whilst protectionism persists, it progressively co-exists with the process of global competitive tendering, impacting deeper into the defence value chain as well as at the prime contractor level. Due to the high cost of developing modern sophisticated weapon systems, the need is to suppress cost escalation pressures. Competitiveness, however, is more than just low-cost procurement, it is also concerned with the evolvement of specialization to secure differential comparative advantage. Protectionist measures may well nurture local techno-logy suppliers at the systems level, but the search for defence industrial sover-eignty may well be circumvented by global competition at the sub-systems level.[6]

Defence globalization, then, is a fact of life. Indeed, given policy-emphasis on the pursuance of a Revolution in Military Affairs, the pressures to manage costs efficiently have never been greater.[7] As a result, defence corporatization, outsourcing, contractorization, public–private partnerships, regional collabora-tive relationships and global development/acquisition consortiums have become an international phenomenon, transcending national boundaries. Technology offsets have facilitated the movement of manufacturing outside the traditional centres of excellence in the advanced countries, but beyond this the trend now is for strategic industries to relocate high value-added research investment into overseas knowledge communities. Rolls Royce's growing partnership with Sin-gapore's Nanyang Technological University is a good example of this trend. The process of defence globalization is entrenched and unlikely to be transient, particularly because of the blurred divide between what constitutes defence and civil technologies. It is difficult to exaggerate the importance of the forces at work: the irrevocable change to the nature of weapon systems and the doctrine of their use; the transformation of production processes, with the associated search for through-life capability management; and, at the core of conventional defence industrial policy, a questioning of the validity of contemporary sustain-ability of sovereign defence industrial capacity. These, and other issues, are explored in greater detail in the next section.

Defence globalization: threats and responses

Weapon systems are no longer mechanical, but electronic. They are 'smart' rather than dumb, with payloads released from stand-off locations. The modern battlefield has come to be dominated by systems. The imperative of C4ISTAR through a system-of-systems approach defines transformational warfare. This broad term encapsulates a wide array of RMA-type capabilities, from stealthy (low signature) technology to aspects impacting on doctrinal change. It is this definitional breadth that allows transformational technologies to have relevance not only in conventional battlefield scenarios but also in those asymmetrical ones. Thus, whilst the headline-catching events of both Gulf conflicts have focused on the surgical accuracy and devastating effects of precision-guided munitions, there has in parallel been a huge amount of US and European invest-ment into intelligence, reconnaissance and surveillance technologies, to thwart and defeat the omnipresent terrorism treat.

Unmanned Aerial Vehicles (UAVs) are a product of such investment, with numerous countries (including Singapore, Israel, China, South Korea and Japan) eager to emulate the success of US and other Western defence contractors. Most notably, in this respect, is the success of Boeing, and more recently, the UK company, BAES; the latter having worked closely with Rolls Royce to develop bespoke UAV propulsion systems. UAVs have been increasingly successful in loitering, reconnoitring, and then 'taking-out' terrorists in both Iraq and Afghanistan. It can also be surmised, with confidence, that much research and development work is currently being undertaken into the development of smart sensors to detect the presence of suicide bombers, at a distance, as well as the presence of 'dirty' nuclear, biological and chemical devices in heavily populated urban areas. Ubiquitous twenty-first century threats, ranging from conventional 'hot wars' to terrorist aggression, can therefore all appropriately fall under the purview of RMA-technology responses. The technology-gap enjoyed by the advanced countries, vis-à-vis those in the developing world, suggests US and European dominance in the development of transformational technologies. The question, however, is whether this is an immutable international division of labour or whether there is a case for believing that Northeast Asian States, as well as other regions and countries, can close this technology gap? The answer to the question lies in the nature of defence globalization and its impact on the sourcing of RMA technologies.

Access to high technology is the major challenge of all countries, rich and poor. Even the US seeks access to foreign technology, because it is difficult, if not impossible, for any country to be a specialist supplier of all technologies. Thus, US defence companies are working with, for instance, Japanese contrac-tors to develop ducted rocket motors and British companies for the development and production of ejector seats from Martin Baker and specialized vertical lift aero-engine fan technology from Rolls Royce for the global F-35 Joint Strike Fighter.[8] Therefore, in theory, and increasingly, in practice, defence globaliza-tion is facilitating the transfer of defence-related technology. This then begs the further question as to the nature of defence globalization and the associated processes of technology transfer.

First and foremost, the global economic environment is characterized by a high degree of competitiveness. Accordingly, in the search for cost-reduction, defence procurement agencies will often invite international bids, as a means of circumventing national monopoly–monopsony market structures. Open defence competition is normal practice for developing economies with rudimentary defence industrial bases, driven more by the need for technology acquisition than cost-reduction, but is only a recent development for the advanced countries. The UK, in particular, throughout the 1990s, has increasingly procured military equipment from the US; the latter being a high-quality, 'low-cost' (due to the relatively higher scales of production, e.g. the F-16 fighter and potentially the F-35 Lightning combat aircraft). Moreover, acquisition of US weapon systems means that UK armaments are compatible with those of the US military when pursuing coalition warfare. Invariably, off-the-shelf acquisition from offshore vendors requires local licensed production, and, inevitably, this eats into the cost savings achieved through competition, negating at least partially the point of the exercise.

Aside from conventional international trade, defence firms seek to transfer technology through the development of manufacturing bases in customer countries. Transfer mechanisms include acquisition, merger, and strategic alliances. Examples of such mechanisms would include BAES' acquisition of the US defence companies, United Defense Industries and Armor Holdings, as well as the strategic alliance between the Italian company, Agusta, and Britain's Westland helicopter company, leading eventually to the purchase of the British concern by Agusta's Italian holding company, Finmeccanica. Other forms of technology transfer might include outsourcing and offsets; the latter concept being viewed as a mechanism for facilitating significant work-placement and technology transfer from the advanced country vendor to the arms purchasing nation. Licensed production is the principal conduit for offsets-related technology transfer, whereby the purchasing country is allowed to locally produce a foreign weapons system. The problem, however, is that the value-added from local production tends initially to be low, with much of the sophisticated systems and sub-assemblies imported from the foreign defence contractor. As a means of overcoming this problem, 'buy-backs' have been sought by the arms purchasing government. Buy-backs require overseas vendors to purchase an agreed volume of local licensed production, which would then be integrated into the vendor's home-country output. Often, if the buy-back work reaches a high and consistent quality level, then a global supplier network may materialize through long-term contractual relationships extending beyond the timeframe of the formal offsets agreement. This is, indeed, what happened following Westland's 1980s sale of Lynx Helicopters to South Korea. The subsequent licensed production and buy-back provisions led to South Korean aerospace manufacturers becoming firmly embedded into what is now AgustaWestland's value chain.

Defence globalization, then, is concerned with international industrial integration; that is, countries and companies being drawn together in a global network of defence-related vertical processes of production, embracing R&D, manufacturing, sales and marketing, and, finally, the provision of through-life support. These industrial, technological, and business networks are complex. For emerging nations, the challenge is to penetrate such networks and gain access to technology through contractual and collaborative arrangements. Some countries have been successful in this regard, but the real objective of gaining high-technology, high value-added work, may still elude them. It thus remains a truism, that whilst defence industrial latecomers seek access to advanced techno-logy, the advanced country defence contractors will be intent on maintaining, if not extending, technology gaps.

Defence globalization can work, however, but only if all players agree to play the game. If only a handful of countries engage in open defence trade, inviting offshore defence vendors to bid for domestic defence contracts, then, inevitably, this will lead to a loss of local defence industrial sovereignty. The UK, for example, has recognized belatedly that continued off-the-shelf acquisition of US weapon systems will lead progressively to erosion of indigenous defence indus-trial capability. This recognition is symbolized by the publication in December 2005 of the UK MOD Defence Industrial Strategy (DIS).[9] The DIS was trig-gered by anxieties over the negative impact of open defence trade, not only in terms of the loss of domestic production capacity but also the lack of technology access and 'ownership', particularly intellectual property rights. The catalyst for this latter anxiety was the US refusal in the Summer of 2005 to accede to the UK MOD request for access to source codes and other proprietary knowledge following Britain's decision to purchase 150 Joint Strike Fighter (JSF) aircraft.[10] Britain's concern was that it had paid $2 billion to become a full member of this global defence consortium and yet was denied access to the technology enabling independent local capability for through-life maintenance.

A further more broadly based frustration, if not irritation, is that while the UK had opened its defence market to foreign competition, the US, by contrast, was beginning to wind-back on its globalization credentials, reverting instead to increased reliance on its protectionist 'Buy America' legislation. Yet, the US was not alone in pursuing de-globalization policies; this being reflected by a similar emerging European trend. For instance, France, has long been promoting polices of economic patriotism (for civil industry) and competitive autonomy (for defence industry).[11] Germany had begun to introduce legislation to forestall foreign ownership of its defence companies;[12] and other European countries were similarly pursuing protectionist defence policies, subscribing religiously to Article 296 of the Amsterdam Treaty that limits competition in member coun-tries' defence industries.[13] To the British, the DIS represents an admission that open defence trade is perhaps a misnomer, and thus the strategy signals protec-tionist measures for UK production capacity of selected critical technologies.[14] BAES, in particular, is likely to benefit from this policy démarche, through a MOD provision of long-term partnering agreements that guarantee production contracts and profitability. Such measures were intended deliberately to assuage

BAES' threat of closing dockyards and production facilities in the UK, and relocating capacity instead to the more profitable US defence market. The conceptual framework for the DIS rests on the notion of 'appropriate sovereignty', defined in terms of its three key components.[15]

- *Strategic assurance*: capabilities retained onshore because they provide those technologies or equipment important for the *safeguarding of the State*.
- *Defence capability*: retention of equipment and technologies within the UK industrial base, necessary for Britain's Armed Forces to enjoy particular assurance of continued and consistent equipment performance; thus a specific need to assure security and sustainability of supply.
- *Strategic influence*: an indigenous industrial capability requiring specific capabilities to give the UK an important strategic influence in military, diplomatic or industrial terms. A key priority in this regard is to ensure access to high technology international collaborative projects, necessary to strengthen political, diplomatic and military relationships between the UK and other countries.

Arguably, for most countries, protectionist sentiment and policy for national defence industry is as important as ever, with government intervening to safeguard jobs and capability in sectors of vital national interest, and therefore too important to be left to businesses with differing commercial objectives. Certainly, in the Asia-Pacific, government has in nearly all cases ensured that the defence economy remains the preserve of the State. However the cultural mindset of Asia-Pacific countries has deliberately woven defence into a broader tapestry of security relationships, and, as detailed in the next section, this has had significant implications on the nature of the region's defence economy as well the associated impact of defence globalization.

Asia-Pacific's defence 'eco-system'

The concept of national security has long been a preoccupation of Asia-Pacific States, deriving, most likely, from their history of vulnerability to invasion and often colonialization. However, the post-Second World War coming-of-age of these States provided them with the dual-impulse for non-dependent economic growth and defence industrial self-reliance. Lofty goals, maybe, but Asia-Pacific states have been prepared to pay the cost-premium required for public sector control of defence establishments. Defence output is the ultimate 'public good', too important to be left to the commercial diktat of commercial enterprise. This 'model' applies to most Asia-Pacific states, save for Japan, possessing a commercial defence industrial complex. Moreover, the emphasis on defence, as but one element of a broad security framework, is a model applicable to several nations across the Asia-Pacific region. Singapore, for instance, has developed its well-known 'total defence' concept, and of relevance to Northeast Asia, the States of China, South Korea and Japan, all also interpret security from a broad-based perspective, incorporating not just defence, but also economic growth, development, technological capability, political stability, international diplomacy, and even foreign aid. This multi-disciplinary approach makes the goal of self-reliance that much more feasible. The Chinese refer to this goal as *zi li geng sheng*, the Japanese as *kokusanka*, and the (North) Koreans as *Ju'che*. The thrust of these policy approaches is to maximize security outcomes by cross-threading and synergizing the interrelated elements of national security.

Northeast Asia's security frameworks are dynamic and evolving, as evidenced below by Figure 8.1 which seeks to conceptualize Japan's contemporary comprehensive security framework. Japan's policy position is to expand the defence element to encompass emerging twenty-first century threats. This new 'Integrated Security Strategy' seeks to develop a multifunctional flexible defence response to existing and evolving regional conventional threats, including China's growing naval capability and North Korea's nuclear and missile threats. Simultaneously, through international cooperation, the Integrated Security Strategy seeks to tackle the emergence of asymmetrical threats to homeland security. These threats cover: terrorism, including nuclear, biological and chemical threats; cyber warfare; the health dangers of SARS/H5N1; and natural disasters, such as earthquakes and tsunamis.[16]

Although Japan's security framework is multi-dimensional, as is also the case with its counterparts in South Korea and China, arguably the core relation in the framework is between defence and the economy. Today, this might aptly be described as the defence 'eco-system', where 'eco' has both an economic and an 'ecological' derivation; the latter, in the sense of a complex and 'living' organism. Thus, in the twenty-first century, a defence eco-system refers to a complex organism, comprising the Armed Forces, MOD, defence industry, the Treasury, Ministries of Trade and Industry, commercial high-technology contractors, transnational and local subcontractors, universities and specialist R&D

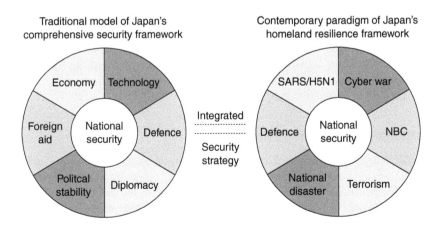

Figure 8.1 Japan's integrated security strategy.

institutes. To make sense of this complexity, Northeast Asian States have sought to closely manage their defence economies so as to secure high and positive degrees of integration. National unity, and the Asian consensual approach, has supported the robust pursuit of strong civil–military integration. The process has facilitated technological spin-offs from the commercial economy to support defence industrialization. In post-war Japan, for instance, MITI has played a critical role in orchestrating Japan's development of what might be termed strategic industries, representing the economic growth poles of the country's industrialization push. Similarly, for South Korea, the government has promoted industries through sponsorship of high technology products in the *Chaebol* industries. Moreover, China, as the contemporary latecomer to industrialization is adopting the same model; that is, institutional fostering of what the Chinese call 'pillar' industries. Across all three Northeast Asian states the development characteristics are the same: promotion of high value-added, knowledge-intensive, innovative, and most of all, dual-use industries. Over recent times, China has introduced a technology transfer strategy aimed at the promotion of high-technology inward FDI into the commercial sector. This has the potential through technological 'spin-on' to support not only defence industrialization, but also the more advanced RMA-type technology breakthroughs. Development through the process of civil–military integration demands a re-think on the conventional negative trade-off between defence expenditure and economic growth, in the sense that defence contracting is now in large measure indistinguishable from high-technology commercial work. This 'integration' benefit is not related to the platforms but rather the high-technology commercial inputs that presently capture the majority of value-added in defence programmes. Thus, in the twenty-first century, defence production, if not a positive influence on economic growth, is arguably no longer a crowding-out depressant. Caution, however, is required in the interpretation of China's dual-use growth performance. Whilst most observers would accept that China has successfully engineered the transformation of its economy, achieving sustained growth in its pillar industries, the underlying expansion in local value-added has only just begun. For instance, in China's strategically important, civil–military, semiconductor industry, value-added only averages 16 per cent of product value.[17] Globalization may therefore facilitate technology transfer, but real development, and, indeed, self-reliance, will remain elusive, without the creation of local value chains and a supporting sub-structure of innovative indigenous suppliers.

Evaluating globalization's impact

Globalization has highlighted and honed Northeast Asia's defence industrial model. It is a model that reflects the importance of techno-nationalism, bridging the divide between commercial and defence elements of the local economy. The push for frontier technological capability is recognition of the critical role technology plays in ensuring national security. Techno-globalization pressures have forced a broadening in the scope of national security, as illustrated in

Figure 8.1, to incorporate RMA-type technologies in addressing terrorism, insurgency and other twenty-first century asymmetrical threats. Globalization has thus impacted on Northeast Asia in several ways as detailed, below:

- Enhancing the policy-emphasis given to technology access, particularly through foreign direct investment, targeted on the development of high technology strategic industries.
- Reinforcing the relevance of the long-standing cultural and institutional importance attached to exploitation of high value-added, critical dual-use, technologies applicable to the technological development of both the commercial and defence sectors of host economies.
- Recognizing the growing imperative of adopting national security frameworks encapsulating the interests and contributions of a disparate stakeholder base; this defence eco-system model more sensibly mirroring the reality of today's diverse and complex 'security' relationships, rather than the traditional focus solely on defence.
- Pressuring elevated levels of competitiveness and productivity, with the policy objective of securing dynamic high technology comparative advantages and thus closing technology-gaps with advanced country competitors.
- Continuously searching for viable and sustainable innovative, high-technology, knowledge-intensive industries, enhancing national security through progressive contributions of locally generated value-added output.
- Promoting sustainable indigenous defence-related industrial capability for achieving the ultimate policy-goal of self-reliance.

However, perhaps the most striking impact of globalization on Northeast Asia is the revealed relevance of the region's various national security frameworks as a policy benchmark for other States. This is evidenced, for instance, either directly or indirectly, by the belated introduction of the United Kingdom's December 2005 Defence–Industrial Strategy, heralding a prescriptive policy that seeks self-reliance in identified key sectors of the national defence economy. Again, reflecting the UK case, in late 2007 the Joint Doctrine and Concepts Centre published a revised British Defence Doctrine that included the development of a new, but certainly not novel, comprehensive security framework.

There is, of course, a cost premium associated with protectionism, but the real lesson of Northeast Asia's national security planning regimes and approaches towards comprehensive and integrated security is that the cost premium can be minimized through prudent and proactive management of the globalization process.

References and notes

* I am indebted to Professor Trevor Taylor for his helpful comments on an earlier draft of this chapter.
1 M. Intriligator, 'On the Nature and Scope of Defense Economics', *Journal of Defense Economics*, 1/1 (1990) p. 3.

2 See, the classic publication in this area, G. Adams, *The Politics of Defense Contracting – The Iron Triangle*, New York: Council on Economic Priorities (1982).

3 *The Acquisition Handbook*, London: MOD Edition 6 (October 2005).

4 See, E. Benoit, *Defense and Economic Growth in Developing Countries*, Lexington MA: Lexington Books (1973).

5 In policy circles, enhanced civil-military integration is of growing importance. Such integration may take several forms: the UK Qinetiq project is an extreme example of defence privatization (albeit with a high level of government ownership), where a principal policy plank has been to encourage commercial exploitation of UK Defence Research and Technology capability; there is also the trend of big defence prime contractors progressively focusing on what they see as their core competence, often project management and systems integration, and outsourcing all other activities to both commercial and defence companies; and, finally, there is the emergence of public–private partnerships, transcending geographical boundaries, where the MOD exploits the capital, expertise and efficiencies of a broad array of commercial undertakings.

6 For the US and UK, the re-supply challenges experienced in the Afghanistan and Iraq conflicts, has led to greater support for national defence industrial self-reliance rather than blind commitment to cost reduction policies and globalization of the supply network.

7 See, R. Matthews and J. Treddenick, *Managing the Revolution in Military Affairs*, Basingstoke: Palgrave (2001).

8 The US is willing to secure defence-related components and sub-assemblies from overseas suppliers as long as a domestic systems integration capability is maintained. The development of the F-35 Joint Strike Fighter is evidence of this approach. A useful document outlining the US defence globalizing strategy is the *Final Report of the Defense Science Board Task Force on Globalization and Security*, Washington DC: Office of the Under Secretary of Defense for Acquisition and Technology (December 1999).

9 *Defence Industrial Strategy*, Defence White Paper (December 2005) CM 6697.

10 See, D. Serastopulo, 'US Told *Not* to Block Expertise on F-35', *Financial Times* (15 March, 2005) p. 4.

11 See, P. Tran, 'Economic Patriotism Worries French Execs', *Defense News* (17 October, 2005) P4.

12 The German government can veto transactions that would involve a foreign company buying 25 per cent or more of any domestic defence business on the grounds of national security; See, J. Boxell, 'BAE Forced into Cut-price Sale', *Financial Times* (31 December, 2005).

13 Amongst other things, Article 296 of the Treaty of Amsterdam (1997) states:

> [A]ny member state may take such measures as it considers necessary for the protection of the essential interests of its security which are connected with the production of or trade in arms, munitions and war material; such measures shall not adversely affect the conditions of competition in the common market regarding products which are not intended for specifically military purposes.

14 The British OD has a three-tiered acquisition policy position: first, that the systems are of such critical importance that they must be procured from domestic sources; second, of lesser importance, are those that can be procured collaboratively with allies; and, third, the lower-order items that can be procured from any source.

15 *Defence Industrial Strategy*, op. cit., p. 22.

16 The methodology that lies behind Figure 8.1 has its basis in a 2004 report by Japan's Council on Security and Defense Capabilities (a private advisory panel to the prime minister more commonly referred to as the Araki Commission). The Araki Commission proposed an 'Integrated Security Strategy', arguing that in the current era the

need is for a two-pronged defence strategy that puts international peace cooperation activities on an equal footing with the defence of Japan; the latter including homeland security – encompassing non-traditional security threats, many of which require to be addressed through international cooperation. The report argues that in the current era, a self-reliant, conventional threat-based strategy is not a practical possibility for many, if not most countries. The Araki Commission's Integrated Security Strategy therefore adopts a threefold approach that includes: a) Japan's own efforts; b) cooperation with an alliance partner; and c) cooperation with the international community in a way that both protects the homeland and contributes to improving the international community as a whole. See, D. Fouse, 'Japan's FY 2005 National Defense Program Outline: New Concepts, Old Compromises', *Asia-Pacific Security Studies*, vol. 4, no. 3 (March 2005).

17 Interview, Professor Linda Sprague, China–Europe International Business School, Shanghai (26 September, 2005).

9 Globalization and defence industry in East Asia

Seeking self-sufficiency and teaming up for dual-use technology

Arthur S. Ding

New mode of globalization[1]

Globalization has become a piece of fashionable jargon in the post-Cold War era. In the economic sense, it indicates a global flow of capital, investment, production, technology and manpower in the form of international trade, and various types of collaboration through which national economies are integrated with the international economy. However, globalization is not a new phenomenon. It has existed for as long as there has been division of labour, comparative advantage and international trade. In this sense, globalization is a continuing process, and every nation's economy is integrated with the international economy to different degrees and in various modes.

Nevertheless, the mode and pace of globalization might vary depending on the particular industry it impacts. For the defence industry, there has been a sharp contrast in the mode of globalization before and after the end of the Cold War, and the key factor contributing to the emergence of this new mode of globalization was the shrinking global defence need.

Before the collapse of the Soviet Union, the globalization of the defence industry largely took the form of arms trade and licensed production. Arms trade occurred mostly in the form of delivering complete systems and platforms. In the case of licensed production, final assembly was the most common form, with importing nations striving to move up the production ladder through manufacturing spare parts, components and sub-systems. As pointed out by Richard Bitzinger, globalization at this stage was politics-driven. In order to strengthen the defence capabilities of its allies against possible invasion by the Soviet Union, the United States (US) supplied complete systems or platforms to allied nations, or improved the defence industrial capability of its allies through licensed production.[2]

The Soviet Union's collapse has had a heavy impact on the defence industry. It made a large defence industry difficult to maintain, because there was no legitimate reason to keep a huge defence budget in which voluminous amounts were spent on procurement and research and development (R&D), as had been the case during the Cold War era. Demand was soon shrinking and the market was downsized. On the other hand, the cost of R&D increased substantially.

Shrinking market demand has made any single nation unable to afford the rising R&D cost. The consequence has been that, in the past decade, many major defence contractors from Western countries have chosen to exit from the industry by selling production lines, along with R&D units, or to undertake merger and acquisition on a survival basis if choosing to stay in the industry.[3] However, reconsolidation of this kind in the post-Cold War era has not been enough to cope with the shrinking market, and further measures have had to be adopted.

Another mode of globalization emerged subsequently. This took the form of the marketing agreement, team, joint venture or strategic alliance co-production, and parent/subsidiary relationship, across the territorial borders of nations.[4] This mode of globalization has brought into being new relationships of transnational cross-border collaboration between defence industries. These relationships serve multiple purposes despite the fact that there are potential negative consequences of arms proliferation.[5] First, the rising cost of R&D can be shared by joint member nations. Second, market access can be maintained to meet the needs of the production economy. Third, lower costs of assembly can be achieved. But finally, this mode of globalization is industry-driven.[6] In order to cope better with the drastically shrinking market and rising R&D cost, defence contractors have taken the initiative to further consolidate their own position. This mode of globalization is qualitatively different from what was happening during the Cold War era.

Common characteristics across nations in Northeast Asia

As stated above, the old mode of globalization was driven by political considerations throughout the period of the Cold War. Nations in Northeast Asia were on the receiving end of finished systems and sub-systems from major Western suppliers during the Cold War era. For various reasons, including national security, anticipated spin-off effect and prestige, nations in this region attempted to build up their own indigenous defence industry. The scale of production varied but these "second-tier"[7] arms-producing countries were able to accomplish goals with a certain degree of success.[8]

There are some common characteristics shared by the defence industries of the "second-tier" arms-producing countries in this region. The core characteristic is that they did not have an indigenous capability for R&D and manufacturing. Second, all these countries started to develop their defence industry through final assembly: manufacturing components and spare parts, and manufacturing sub-systems, which were licensed by the "first-tier" countries. In other words, a dependency relationship developed among nations in this region that had the ambition to develop an indigenous defence industry through the ladder up. They depended on Western countries to release technology, along with components, spare parts and sub-systems to meet their particular needs.

China and Japan were two of these nations. Despite the fact that China could be proud of its comprehensive capability to produce a wide range of arms that met the need of its three services, China still lacked the indigenous capability for manufacturing truly advanced weapons. Despite its highly developed manufacturing capability in the civilian sector, Japan had to import advanced arms from the US for decades.

Generally, however, the end of the Cold War has not had as much of a negative impact on defence industries in Northeast Asia as it has in other regions. The end of the Cold War created a huge surplus capacity in the defence industries of Western countries, and the defence market became a buyer's market. But these new market conditions have not shattered Northeast Asia's defence industries, even though domestic end users could more easily switch to Western arms exporters.

Rising arms demand in Northeast Asia[9]

Contrary to the shrinking arms demand in other regions, the demand for arms in Northeast Asia has not shrunk in the post-Cold War era. Furthermore, the defence industries of this region have not suffered unduly from the lowered prices of arms. Several factors account for this opposite trend. Taiwan–China relations have been the most prominent factor, and this was particularly the case following the Taiwan Strait crisis of 1995–96. After the crisis, China learned one lesson: it was that the US would definitely get involved in a future Taiwan Strait conflict, and Beijing would have to be prepared as early as possible in such a scenario of different contingencies.[10] Military build-up was one of the necessary measures that China has had to undertake since then.

The Kosovo campaign reinforced China's threat perception of the US and its allies in the West. In 1999, while intervening to stop Yugoslavia's policy of genocide and launching military operations without United Nations authorization, the US and its NATO allies dropped bombs on China's embassy. This was a shock to the Chinese government, and created a perception that the US might somehow intervene in China's "internal affairs" based on the premise of upholding the universal value of human rights.[11]

The 2003 Iraq War was a further reminder to China of US military capabilities. Despite the fact that the US was stuck with post-war reconstruction, the flexibility of the US military operation impressed the Chinese military. After the 1991 Gulf War, many Chinese military analysts had forecast that no more progress would be made for the US military because the US military would be content with what had been accomplished. The 2003 Iraqi War disproved this forecast.

China has also been concerned with Japan's role in a Taiwan Strait conflict. Following a meeting of defence and foreign affairs ministers of America and Japan, a joint communiqué was released in February 2005, in which both countries included Taiwan as their common strategic objective,[12] and indicated that both countries hoped to settle the Taiwan Strait issue peacefully.[13]

Finally, the security of sea-lanes of communication has become critically important for China, as China is increasingly dependent on imported energy for economic development. China has become the second largest oil importer in the world; total imports in 2005 have exceeded the 100-million barrel mark, and the figure is expected to grow rapidly. Shipping security has become the biggest issue, since this issue involves China's energy demand, economic development and political legitimacy. The shipping line for energy supply stretches from the Middle East, across the Indian Ocean, to China's east coast. Eighty per cent of imported crude oil has to pass through the Malacca Strait. China's current military capability cannot be projected to safeguard the entire shipping line, and China's energy supply can be easily cut off.[14]

Since the Taiwan Strait crisis, China has stepped up its arms procurement programme. Russia has been the main source for this extensive procurement, and what China has procured from Russia focuses on military hardware and technology for the navy, air force, early warning systems, and various sub-systems, areas in which China's technological weakness has been the most obvious. China's goal is apparent. Politically, China has attempted to send a clear-cut signal to Taiwan and the US that China is very serious about the Taiwan issue. Militarily, through this short-term foreign procurement, China has attempted to build up a capability to withstand and deny rather than defeat a US intervention force.

Furthermore, there is a rising need for China to protect its sea-lines of communication as China's energy imports have rapidly increased. In fact, the Chinese navy has increased its defence procurement over the past few years, most notably in the procurement of advanced warships. The *Washington Post* reported on 20 March 2004 that all of China's naval shipyards had been in full production since 2000; and, including landing ships, about 70 warships of different types were built between 2002 and 2004, and this figure did not include those extra missile destroyers and submarines procured from Russia.[15]

The delivery of jet fighters to the Chinese air force inventory also increased in 2005. According to the Chinese media, Shenyang Aircraft Corporation – China's premier producer of jet fighters (including the J-8II and Russian SU-27 converted J-10) – delivered more jet fighters to the air force than at any time in the past, and its production and capacity were in full operation.[16]

Finally, China's defence budget has also been rising. Entering the post-Cold War era in the 1990s, China's annual defence budget recorded two-digit increases in yearly spending, and this trend has persisted since 2000. Between 1994 and 2004, China's defence budget rose from RMB$5.5 billion (roughly equivalent to US$633 million) to RMB$21 billion (US$2.5 billion), a four-fold increase.[17]

Rising demand for capable indigenous defence industry

For China, the long-term goal of building up a strong autarkic defence industrial capability remains unchanged. Actually, three events have heavily reinforced its determination in this regard. The first of these occurred in 1960. In response to a request from Beijing, Moscow started to supply finished systems and technologies to China in the late 1950s, including technology to manufacture the atomic bomb. However, the Soviets cut off aid and withdrew all personnel and programmes in 1960 amid deteriorating Sino–Soviet relations.

China suffered the second blow in 1989. After China established diplomatic relations with the US, arms technology transfers started between the two countries upon China's request, and one of the major programmes – the "Peace Pearl" programme – was intended to provide technological assistance to upgrade the capability of China's J-8 fighter. However, the US cancelled the assistance programme after China launched the 1989 Tiananmen crackdown.

The third blow came in 2003–04. Beijing had requested the European Union (EU) to lift the prohibition of arms transfers to China, a sanction that was imposed by the EU after the 1989 Tiananmen crackdown, and the EU responded positively. In fact, some dual-use systems had been exported to China even before China made this request. However, pressured by the US, which was concerned that EU-manufactured arms could be used by the Chinese military to confront US soldiers in the Taiwan Strait, the EU has postponed the lift decision for more than two years, and the timing remains uncertain.[18]

All three cases have had a cumulative effect. China firmly believes that it is completely impossible for the US to export arms and technology to China in the wake of perceived competing US–China relations. The likelihood that the EU will lift the sanction decision remains uncertain under the US pressure. Although Russia agreed to export finished systems, sub-systems, and technologies to China, it has limited what could be exported to China, and Russian arms exports to India have been more sophisticated than those sold to China.

China's study of relevant World Trade Organization (WTO) rules has also reinforced this belief.[19] The WTO, which is representative of globalization trends, does not have regulations on arms R&D, production and trade because this is a matter involving the national security of each nation. While the civilian products of the defence industry are regulated by relevant WTO rules, it is up to other international and domestic regulations to control the production and trade of military goods. This exception in the WTO rules implies that China cannot rely upon arms imports from other countries for defence modernization.

Under these circumstances, China has had to make the development of indigenous defence industrial capability its top priority. Although some imports of military and dual-use systems and sub-systems should not be excluded, imports can only serve as supplementary and secondary products. In the newly released guideline for the development of national defence science and technology for the eleventh 5-Year Planning period, the Chinese government points out that China has to strive to upgrade indigenous innovation capability and to construct an innovative system for national defence science, technology and industry.[20]

All these factors have made China realize that it can only rely on itself to build up comprehensive defence industrial capability without resorting to illusive "globalization." The US government will definitely not permit American defence contractors to form joint venture businesses or team up with Chinese counterparts, and judging from the experience of the postponed lift decision, it seems the US will not tolerate the EU reaching similar arrangements with China.

China's perception of globalization

Globalization has become a fashionable research topic in China. Chinese scholars perceive that globalization is a phenomenon that cannot be averted. There is no other way but to actively participate in the process. For them, it is not a matter of whether China needs to respond to the challenge of globalization, but of how to respond. They argue that if China cannot handle this challenge well, China will run the risk of being expelled from "the globe."[21]

Furthermore, many Chinese analysts regard globalization as a double-edged sword that can cut in both directions. In the positive sense, participating in the globalization process can bring development opportunities and benefits to China; globalization has brought investment, capital and production to China and benefited China's economic development. Conversely, globalization can bring deprivation and exploitation to some groups or nations, and further widen inequality and injustice.[22] It is up to each country to find appropriate ways of taking advantage of positive aspects of globalization and to avoid negative ones, along with other alternatives.[23]

Despite the argument that China should participate actively in the globalization process, Chinese scholars are still concerned that globalization may bring more negative consequences to the technological development of developing countries, of which China is one. For these scholars, two problems are particularly conspicuous.[24] The first is the problem of dependency. Chinese analysts argue that technologically weak nations will become increasingly dependent upon technology provided by advanced countries, while advanced countries will set more barriers for technology transfer. The second is the brain drain problem. Globalization facilitates a brain drain in developing countries because talented people tend to be attracted to (and remain in) developed countries, further consolidating the leading status of the latter. Meanwhile, developed countries try hard to block developing countries' efforts at upgrading their technological capabilities.[25]

This concern applies to China's defence industry. China is concerned that after entering the WTO, competition over manpower among different sectors or industries will become more intense, leading to a potential brain drain in China's defence industrial sector, thus affecting R&D and production of arms.[26] China is also concerned that the manufacture of both civilian and military products will be affected, either directly or indirectly, since many spare parts and components are of dual-use, and a further opening of production market to foreign companies will directly affect the basis for arms research and production.

Despite China's concern with the potential negative consequences of globalization, and realization that it has to develop its own indigenous defence industrial capability under no illusion of collaboration with Western countries, it seems that China still has high hopes for joint development projects with other nations. These joint projects have been part of China's new era of reform and open door policy, because the Chinese leadership understands that exchanges with the foreign scientific and technological community will be conducive to China's own development of science and technology.

Furthermore, China places high value on civilian, particularly dual-use, technology. While China does not have any illusions about the benefits of globalization for its own defence industry, China has some expectations of the positive implications of globalization for potential civilian technology. Globalization has made civilian and dual-use technology flow internationally, and China can take advantage of this opportunity to further transfer and transform that technology for military purposes.

Adjustment of defence industry's civilian production

As mentioned previously, China remains seriously concerned about the bearing that entering the WTO might have on the civilian production line of its defence industry. But China has made a commitment to open its domestic market to many products and services within a certain period of time after joining the WTO. This would include the opening of the production market to civilian products manufactured by its defence industry.

Unlike the defence contractors of many Western countries who started to undergo defence conversion and produce civilian products after the end of the Cold War, the Chinese defence industry underwent across-the-board defence industry conversion much earlier. In fact, the process of conversion started as far back as the late 1970s, after economic reforms had begun.[27]

A major reason for this early start was to solve the over-capacity problem of the defence industry. Deng Xiaoping put defence modernization last among the "Four Modernizations," which included modernization in agriculture, industry, science as well as defence. The low priority implied that no extra money would be poured into the defence budget, and the impoverished defence industry would have to find its own way to survive. The capacity of the industry prior to conversion was also excessively large. There were actually five traditional defence industries, and each hired about 500,000 employees. The five industries were ordnance, shipbuilding, aviation, nuclear, and aerospace. They were highly compartmentalized, characterized by "stovepipe-like" integration without any horizontal linkage, and were full of redundancy in terms of production capability. Furthermore, like any other state-owned enterprise in China, these five industries ran everything from kindergartens and schools of various levels to many social and welfare systems.

The goal of the Chinese leadership in implementing the conversion was straightforward. They expected the defence industries to diversify production into the civilian field, so that the defence industrial enterprises could themselves survive and the state could be relieved of a heavy burden, while limited resources could be channelled into developing state-of-the-art projects. Moreover, with the potential spin-off effect, it was hoped that investment returns could be obtained from heavy investment in defence industry over the previous four decades, and further help to alleviate demands on the state purse.

In fact, the Chinese leadership was disappointed with the performance of these defence industries. Although the leadership had hoped for industrial spin-off, to transform and turn "advanced" military technology into civilian products, the defence industries ended up importing various kinds of machinery or technology from Western countries to manufacture civilian products. In other words, no spin-off effect could be realized. Military technology was not turned successfully to manufacture civilian products, and civilian products turned out by the defence industrial enterprises had nothing to do with the defence industry's main mission. For instance, aviation enterprises produced small cars, the tank factory produced washing machines, and the artillery factory produced motorcycles. All these civilian products were not spin-off products, and the machinery used for their manufacture was imported from the West.

Several types of defence industry conversion were made in order to manufacture these civilian products. The first was to form joint ventures with foreign enterprises and to have foreign enterprises provide machinery as capital. In these cases, foreign enterprises imported outdated production lines from other countries into China. A typical case was Jianshe Group, which was the largest motorcycle producer in China.[28] Jianshe co-operated with Japan's premier motorcycle producer, Yamaha Motor Company, and later formed a joint venture with Yamaha to produce motorcycles in 1982 and 1991, respectively.[29]

The second was the turn-key project, importing a whole production line from foreign countries without any recourse to their own expertise. Many of the television (TV) factories, which were part of defence electronics enterprises in China, adopted this type, despite the fact that they were able to produce military electronic equipment. Two examples can be given to illustrate this. The China Panda (formerly Nanjing Radio) Factory embarked on a mission to produce military radio-related products, and introduced Japanese technology in 1985 to manufacture an 18-inch colour TV.[30] The Sichuan-based Changhong Machinery Factory, which was transformed into Changhong Electric Appliance Company in June 1988, also introduced a colour TV production line from Matsushita of Japan in 1986.[31]

The third type was to participate in the worldwide division of labour and become a sub-contractor of Western defence industry contractors. A typical case of this started in the early 1980s, when China's aviation industry began to assemble whole passenger aircraft and produce some sub-systems for American aircraft manufacturers. Their expectation was to eventually develop and manufacture their own 180-seat passenger aircraft, on a fully indigenous basis, by 2010.

Between 1986 and 1994, China assembled 35 MD-82/83 aircraft for MacDonnell Douglas (MD). Five of the 35 were shipped to the US, while 30 were purchased by China's airline companies. Later, both sides decided to co-operate on the MD-90 passenger aircraft, with the content rate set at 70 per cent. In addition, China manufactured three further sub-systems for MD.[32]

China has also attempted co-operation with Europe's Airbus. The agreement was to form a new company involving Airbus, China and Singapore, to manufacture 1,000 100-seat AE-100 regional jets. The Chinese aviation system would be responsible for manufacturing wing and frame and final assembly, and the first jet was expected to roll out from the production line in 2003.[33]

Chinese analysts have been concerned that China's accession to the WTO would have a negative impact on those civilian production lines of the defence industry sector.[34] On the one hand, in terms of efficiency, the defence industry's civilian production line has been worse than that of ordinary state-owned enterprises.[35] On the other hand, after entering the WTO, foreign producers would be accorded national treatment; the import tariff would be lowered, and the foreign partners would export their own products to China directly rather than continuing the joint venture with Chinese counterparts.

Analysts are worried that some "strategic industries" might lose their competitiveness after being admitted into the WTO.[36] The automobile industry is one these, in which the forecast is that the domestic market for sedan and truck vehicles would be lost to Western competitors. Motorcycles, home electrical appliances, civil aircraft and steel would also suffer from reduced competitiveness.

Despite this kind of potential negative impact, the Chinese government's policy has been to continue the conversion in the context of further reform of state-owned enterprises in the late 1990s.[37] The focus of late 1990's reform was to address the property rights system, establishing a clear definition of rights and responsibilities. Once this property rights issue had been addressed, acquisition, merger and investment could then be undertaken among both state-owned and private enterprises.[38]

There were basically two new modes for China to continue the conversion process. The first one was to sell the factory-in-deficit; for instance, to sell off Jiangxi Radio Factory to Tsinghua University's business organization, Tsinghua TongFang Company Limited. The second was to restructure poorly performing enterprises and list them in the stock market; for instance, the AviChina Industry and Technology Company Limited, which was listed in the Hong Kong stock market on 30 October 2003.

It should be emphasized that there were some exceptions amid the generally poor performance of the conversion. A good example was the Chinese aerospace industry's international business development.[39] Since the 1980s, China's aerospace industry provided two types of services. The first service was the payload business: to install a customer's facility in China's satellite; and after the satellite returned to the globe, to send back the facility to the customer for experimental analysis. The second service was the launch business. Since the 1990s, China has participated actively in the international satellite launch business by using the indigenously developed series of Chang Zheng (Long March) Rockets. China has been aware of its own comparative advantage, the low launch cost and the benefit of demand over supply for the launcher over the past decade or so. Both types of services have been successful, and China has built up a good reputation in this field.

China's joint venture on dual-use technology

The Chinese government has been highly interested in co-operation with foreign countries – particularly European countries – in the area of dual-use technology. The reason is not difficult to imagine: it is completely impossible to import arms and military technology from the US and EU, while Russia has imposed limitations on what military hardware and technology may be exported to China. Under these circumstances, the development and acquisition of dual-use technology has been the only feasible approach. Furthermore, in the era of information warfare, the distinction between military and civilian use has been largely blurred. Globalization has made dual-use technology more easily accessible than before, and dual-use technology can be transformed and applied to arms for military purposes.

The dual-use technology from EU member nations is more accessible than that of the US. In a world moving towards a multi-polar system, the EU has tried hard to develop its own capabilities across the board, independently of the US. The EU has approached China independently, and this has given China access to EU dual-use technology that it needs. Co-operating with the EU has thus enabled China to obtain better and more sophisticated technology than it has at present.

Space-related technology is another major area in which China has a particular interest in seeking co-operation with foreign countries. This involves manufacturing advanced satellites for navigation, survey and surveillance, and communication, functions that have defence applications and serve as operations multipliers. With these functions, China can project its operations much further away from its shores.

Since the late 1990s, China has formed a wide range of co-operation arrangements with EU counterparts. The first instance of that took place between Tsinghua University and Surrey University (in Britain) over the micro-satellite project. Surrey University was world-renowned for developing various micro-satellites and remains one of the leading institutes in this field. Surrey was also well known for jointly manufacturing micro-satellites with various institutes and universities around the world. It was reported that Tsinghua University set up an aerospace research centre in 1998, and dispatched several engineers to Surrey in October 1998 to learn relevant technology. Beginning in July 1999, both universities started to jointly manufacture micro-satellites, and the first 50-kg experimental micro-satellite with a 40-m resolution capability was completed in 2000. The jointly manufactured micro-satellite was successfully launched into space in June 2000 for a communication and remote sensor test.

The overseas learning experience has enabled China to develop a more advanced indigenous micro-satellite. Tsinghua University learned the whole process of developing a micro-satellite, which included mission analysis, comprehensive design, manufacturing, assembly, test and evaluation, and operation. On their own, Tsinghua developed a smaller 25-kg micro-satellite, and this micro-satellite was successfully launched into space on 18 April 2004.[40] With the cumulative experience of overseas study and indigenous satellite production, it has been reported that Tsinghua is developing another much smaller satellite. The so-called micro-electric mechanic satellite (MEMS) will be less than 5-kg, with micro GPS receivers, camera and micro-propellant. It is intended to be a pilot project, the purpose of which is to test the critical technology contained in the MEMS.

Another joint venture that has attracted worldwide attention is the Galileo project. Run by the EU, the Galileo project is composed of 30 navigation satellites to build up an accurate navigational system in space with an expected total budget of €4 billion. Once fully operational in 2008, the Galileo project is expected to have a margin of error of only 1-m, a figure which is much more accurate than the 10-m of the US GPS system.[41] Giove-A satellite, which serves a test function for the whole Galileo programme, has been launched in December 2005 by a Russian rocket; and the following one, Giove-B, will be launched in March 2006.[42]

The EU had decided to develop its own Global Positioning System in the early 1990s, and the final decision to develop the project was made in February 1999. In order to resist pressure from the US, which tried to block the EU from developing the project, non-EU countries were approached to jointly develop the project and share the cost.

Under these considerations, China was approached in June 2001. After more than two years of discussion and negotiation, an agreement between the EU and China was reached in October 2003, and a further agreement to delineate scope and concrete items for co-operation was signed on 9 October 2004. Under the agreements, China – the first non-EU participant nation – agreed to invest €200 million. Of this amount, €70 million will be used for the period of development, while the remainder will be used for the period of deployment.[43] China has also set up a new enterprise as EU Galileo Industries' counterpart in China. The new company, China Galileo Navigation Satellite Company Limited, has four shareholders from four defence-related institutes: China Aerospace Science and Industry Corporation; China Electronics Technology Group Corporation; China Satellite Communications Corporation; and China Academy of Space Electronics Technology that comes under China Aerospace Science and Technology Corporation.

China will definitely benefit from the Galileo project. As a formal non-EU member, China is to participate in the decision-making of the Galileo project, R&D and management. This will, in turn, enable China to improve R&D, manufacturing, management, and commercial and military applications of its own budding navigation satellite system.[44]

The Galileo project can also generate tremendous business opportunities for China. As a full member of the project, which will allow China to obtain earlier receiver specification data for end users, China can both manufacture positioning-related products as well as sell positioning-related services in China and the wider world. This is particularly the case for the receiver, because the Galileo receiver would be compatible with those of the US GPS and Russia

GLONASS systems. It is estimated that by 2025, the navigation system could generate €205 billion from selling receiver-related products and a further revenue of €168 billion worth of value-added opportunity.[45]

The military applications of the Galileo project have, however, generated concern among countries in the Asia-Pacific region. The system can ensure a margin of error of less than 1-m, and with such accuracy in navigation, China's military platforms and munitions will be provided with precision strike, positioning, and navigation, as well as command, control, and comprehensive battle management capabilities.

Spin-on effect and cost-down

As we have observed, the distinction between military and civilian use has largely blurred in the era of global communications and information. Globalization has made dual-use technology more easily accessible than ever before, and this technology can be transformed and applied to arms for defence purposes.

On the other hand, the "civilian sector" in China is growing and has become more capable than before after 20 years of reform policy in China. This is particularly the case in the field of information and communications related industries, industries that have attracted more and more talented people by offering a more promising future.

Furthermore, this civilian sector has probably benefited from globalization more than the military sector. Unlike the traditional defence industry, which has been constrained by bureaucratic red tape and institutional rigidity as well as national security restrictions, the civilian sector can exchange freely with overseas counterparts with far fewer limiting factors. The most important of these factors involves innovation. China's defence industry has not been innovative enough over the past two decades to provide the Chinese military with the expected advanced weapons systems. The reason for this apparent lack of innovation probably lay with the institutional rigidity and lack of flexibility so characteristic of the state-owned enterprise system. The civilian sector, however, is not constrained by this problem.

Against this background, China launched a new programme in 2000 that does have the potential to implement the ideas of its paramount leader and chief architect Deng Xiaoping: *jun min jie he* (civil–military integration). The Chinese government plans to involve the civilian sector in the state's arms production and defence services. A remark made by Yu Zonglin, a vice-chairman of the Commission of Science, Technology and Industry for National Defence (COSTIND), has confirmed this trend:

> Allowing civilian technological and industrial resources to participate in defence construction, as well as encouraging and promoting civilian enterprises' superior technology to produce military items ... will create substantial significance for further breaking through the closeness of the traditional defence industry community; reducing redundancy, facilitating mechanism

reform in the management and operation of R&D and production, stepping up orderly competition in the armaments market, and pushing for the institutionalization of integrating military and civilian sectors.[46]

As part of the package facilitating this integration, the Chinese government has gradually built up a licence system. Another vice-chairman of COSTIND, Zhang Huazhu, made the comment:

> Because of the special needs of the defence industry, rigorous reviewing and confidential mechanisms are required since private enterprises are engaging in defence production. Beginning in 2000, we have gradually undertaken licence-reviewing measures for all enterprises interested in engaging in the production of military items. Those passing the reviewing process have three types of licences: the permit for undertaking R&D and production; confidential clearance; and quality control licence.[47]

The Chinese media reported that some civilian enterprises have sold their products to the Chinese military. In 1999, Chengdu-based private enterprise, Guoteng (also known as Goldtel) Group – along with Chengdu's University of Electronic Science and Technology of China, and China Electronic Technology Corporation's 30th Institute – won a defence contract over bids from many state-owned defence industrial enterprises. After winning the contract, the three jointly organized Guoxingnet Corporation – controlled by the Guoteng Group – to produce a navigation satellite receiver.[48] According to the Chinese media, this was the first case of a private high-tech enterprise entering into defence production. In July 2001, Guoxingnet won another contract, over 12 other competitors, to produce a satellite navigation positioning system. Then, on 8 January 2002, Sichuan University's Zhisheng Company and Sichuan's Jiuzhou Enterprise Group jointly won a military contract worth RMB$190 million.[49]

Laboratory facilities are also included in the spin-on category of the integration of military and civilian production. As of 31 December 2005, it was reported that 121 laboratories had been approved for licences, out of a total of around 200 applications. Among those approved were laboratories run by the traditional defence industries (including shipbuilding, aviation, aerospace, ordnance and nuclear production), as well as other industries (chemical, mechanical, electronic and metallurgical). The civilian sector, too, had its share of the 121 labs.[50]

Conclusion

There are two trends of development in Northeast Asia in the field of international relations. One trend supports further globalization in the context of China's accession into the WTO, along with the development of regionalization in East Asia. China's accession into the WTO has attracted more investment, human resource and capital, further integrating China into the global economy.

The regionalization illustrated by "ASEAN Plus 3" – in which the ASEAN member nations along with China, Japan and South Korea are to form the largest free trade zone in the world – will integrate China with neighbouring countries.

However, it seems that another trend is moving in the opposite direction. There are growing tensions in Northeast Asia. The US regards China as a major power standing at a strategic crossroads, as the latest Quadrennial Defense Review Report released in February 2006 indicates, and military deployment by US forces has continued to be strengthened although the US has urged China to play a responsible stakeholder role in the region. Sino–Japanese relations have deteriorated because of different interpretations of history and shrine issues, along with energy and maritime territorial disputes, regional power competition, the US–Japan security alliance and the Taiwan factor. Taiwan–China relations have also declined because of political differences.

Faced with uncertain political development, China is likely to see the need to continue its current military modernization to prepare for a worst-case scenario. China is likely to perceive that continued military modernization could send a strong enough signal to the US of China's determination to uphold the established One-China principle, and thus have the US pressure Taiwan not to deviate from the commitment made by the Taiwanese government.

China fully understands that it cannot rely on foreign countries to support its military modernization in the long term, and self-sufficiency remains the only lasting option. The US will definitely not export military-related technology to China, and under US pressure there is no timetable for the EU to lift the sanction imposed after the Tiananmen crackdown of 1989. Neither is there any possibility of importing technology from Israel because of US pressure. There is little likelihood of China forming a regional defence consortium with neighbouring countries. Political tension and regional power competition, along with restrictions under the Japanese constitution, will make Japan reluctant to share technology with China. South Korea might be more inclined to form such a consortium with North Korea on the grounds of strong nationalist sentiments.

However, the team and joint venture approach – part of a new mode of globalization – remains highly feasible for China to adopt. China's space industry is highly developed and, in the case of the EU's Galileo Project, has been invited to form a team or joint venture business. China's participation has enabled it to learn how to manufacture a navigation satellite of its own for future military use. It is likely that China will further develop its defence industry through this approach.

Globalization has made dual-use technology more accessible than before, and this still offers China the best long-term prospects for developing its own defence industrial capability. This is particularly the case in the field of information and communications, and wherever the defence industry will be required to provide advanced hardware to the Chinese military. On the other hand, continuing diversification into civilian production will remain China's policy, along with possible spin-on and cost-down measures. The end objective is to relieve the state of its military-fiscal burden, while limited resources can be channelled into developing state-of-the-art military technology, and the civilian sector can provide sufficient and innovative input to arms development.

Notes

1 The author would like to thank Dr Nan Li and conference colleagues for providing revision suggestions and comments, and Richard Bitzinger and Masako Ikegami for sharing their articles with him.
2 Richard Bitzinger, "Globalization in the post-Cold War Defense Industry: Challenges and Opportunities," in Ann R. Markusen and Sean S. Costigan (eds), *Arming the Future: A Defense Industry for the 21st Century* (New York: Council on Foreign Relations, 1999), pp. 305–333.
3 Ibid.
4 For a definition of these types, see Mark A. Lorell, Julia F. Lowell, Richard M. Moore, Victoria A. Greenfield and Katia Vlachos, *Going Global? US Government Policy and the Defense Aerospace Industry* (Santa Monica, CA: Rand, 2002), pp. 28–30. According to Lorell, a "team" is described as when "two or more companies agree to work together as approximately equal partners to pursue a specific project or a large market segment ... government or industry initiated." A "joint venture" denotes "two or more companies [forming] a separate legal entity in order to pursue a particular program or a larger market segment ... industry initiated."
5 For an analysis of the negative consequences, see Richard Bitzinger, *Toward a Brave New Arms Industry? The Decline of the Second-Tier Arms-Producing Countries and the Emerging International Division of Labor in the Defense Industry*, Adelphi Paper 356 (London: IISS, June 2003).
6 Bitzinger, 1999, op. cit.
7 This term is borrowed from Bitzinger, 2003, op. cit.
8 It should be noted that these countries' aspirations fell apart in the immediate aftermath of the Cold War, because the major Western suppliers now sought to provide arms at lower prices in order to secure the market, and a buyer's market emerged.
9 In view of its dominant position in East Asia, the author will focus mainly on China's perception and defence industry arrangement in the context of globalization.
10 Arthur S. Ding, "The Lesson of the 1995–96 Taiwan Strait Crisis: Developing a New Strategy toward the US and Taiwan," in Laurie Burkitt, Andrew Scobell, and Larry M. Wortzel (eds), *The Lessons of History: The Chinese People's Liberation Army at 75* (Carlisle, PA: US Army War College Strategic Studies Institute, July 2003), pp. 379–402. For a comprehensive analysis of the process and calculation of US involvement and implications, see Robert S. Ross, "The 1995–96 Taiwan Strait Confrontation: Coercion, Credibility, and the Use of Force," *International Security*, 25:2 (Fall 2000), pp. 87–123.
11 Arthur C. Waldron, "The Kosovo War: Implications for Taiwan," in Susan Puska (ed.), *People's Liberation Army after Next* (Carlisle, PA: US Army War College Strategic Studies Institute, August 2000), pp. 255–277.
12 For statement and related explanation, see "Joint Statement of the U.S.-Japan Security Consultative Committee," online, available at www.state.gov/r/pa/prs/ps/2005/42490.htm, and "Remarks With Defense Secretary Rumsfeld and Japan's Foreign Minister Machimura and Defense Minister Ohno," online, available at www.state.gov/secretary/rm/2005/42492.htm respectively.
13 It should be noted that neither the US or Japan regard China as a threat. However, they are concerned about China's rising military capability and its implications for the Asia-Pacific order. "Japanese Cabinet Decides China Is Not a Threat," AFP, 31 January 2006, online, available at www.jpn.co.jp/reports/Japanese_Cabinet_Decides_China_Is_Not_A_Threat.html.

14 The author is grateful to Dr Nan Li for pointing out this factor. It is argued that security of the sea-lane of communication has become the most urgent issue for China's security policy at the present time, and it has dominated military procurement and deployment policy. For a comprehensive analysis of China's maritime security and energy demand, see *China and Eurasia Forum*, November 2005, online, available at www.silkroadstudies.org/new/inside/publications/CEF_archive.htm#November2005.

15 "Zhongguo zhengquanli fazhen haijun pinmin zaojian [China is doing its utmost to develop navy and spares no time in building new warships]," *Washington Post*, 20 March 2004, online, available at big5.china.com/gate/big5/military.china.com/zh_cn/news/568/20040322/11649389.html.

16 "Gangmei: zhongguo zhanji daodan qunian chaoe shengchan [Hong Kong media: China overproduced jet fighters and missiles last year]," Central News Agency, 6 January 2006, cited in *United Daily News*, 6 January 2006.

17 *National Defense Report 2004* (Taipei: Ministry of National Defense, 2004), cited from http://report.mnd.gov.tw/eng/e1–3.htm.

18 For a comprehensive analysis of issues pertaining to the rise of China, including US–EU differences on the sanction lift, see Bates Gill and Gudrun and Wacker (eds.), *China's Rise: Diverging US–EU Perceptions and Approaches* (Berlin, Germany: Stiftung Wissenchaft und Politik, August 2005), online, available at www.swp-berlin.org/forscher/forscherprofil.php?id=75&PHPSESSID=ad594f0715c72e537f9fa b2efce97185, and Seth G. Jones and F. Stephen Larrabee, "Let's Avoid Another Trans-Atlantic Feud," *International Herald Tribune*, 13 January 2006.

19 Dong Baotong, "Guanyu WTO gueize yu zhongguo guofang keji gongye fazhan ruogan zhongyao zhangce wenti [About WTO Rules and Important Issues on the Development of China's Defence Science and Industry]," *Guofang Keji Gongye* [Science and Industry for National Defence], 3 June 2003, online, available at www.costind.gov.cn/n435777/n435789/n439727/4733.html.

20 "Guofang kegongwei shiyiwu qixiang zhongdian 2006 juezhan raoyue tance gongcheng [Seven Major Project for the COSTIND's Eleventh Five-Year Plan, Survey Engineering Project for Spacecraft Flying around the Moon a Decisive Battle in 2006]," China Net, 5 January 2006, online, available at big5.china.com.cn/chinese/TEC-c/1083926.htm.

21 Szu-chien Hsu, "Quanqiuhua: dalu xuezhe de guandian [Globalization: Mainland Chinese Scholars' Viewpoints]," *Zhongguo dalu yanjiu* [Mainland China Studies], 43:4 (April 2000), pp. 1–26. It seems that the Chinese government endorsed the view of actively participating in the process in order to address domestic resistance for economic reform. For an excellent analysis, see Margaret Pearson, "The Case of China's Accession to GATT/WTO," in David M. Lampton (ed.) *The Making of Chinese Foreign and Security Policy in the Era of Reform* (Stanford: Stanford University Press, 2001), pp. 337–370.

22 Hsu, op. cit.

23 Ma Weiye (ed.), *Quanqiuhua shidai de guojia anquan* [National Security in the Age of Globalization] (Hubei: Jiaoyu Chubanshe, October 2003), p. 12.

24 Ma Weiye (ed.), ibid., pp. 268–269.

25 Ma Weiye (ed.), ibid. However, it should be pointed out that brain drain problem has been lessened somewhat for China, because more and more Chinese students who were trained in Western countries chose to return to China after completing school, in the light of China's growing economy.

26 Dong Baotong, op. cit. China's defence industry did have a brain drain problem right after the reform started, and this was particularly the case for defence industry factories located in the interior provinces. This problem should be relieved progressively as more college graduates have entered the job market over the past two or three years.

27 For a comprehensive analysis of China's defence conversion, see Paul H. Folta, *From*

Swords to Plowshares? Defense Industry Reform in the PRC (Boulder, CO: Westview, 1992), and Joern Broemmelhoerster and John Frankenstein (eds), *Mixed Motives, Uncertain Outcomes, Defense Conversion in China* (Boulder, CO: Lynne Rienner, 1997).

28 For Jianshe Group's profile, see www.jianshe.com.cn/groupinfor/groupinfor.asp.
29 For a brief history of the cooperation between Jianshe and Yahama, see www.jianshe.com.cn/groupinfor/groupinfor13.asp.
30 For a brief history of China Panda, see China Panda Chronology, online, available at www.chinapanda.com.cn/about_panda/gongsijieshao/dashiji1980.htm.
31 For a brief history of Changhong, see Changhong Chronology, online, available at cn.changhong.com/catalogglobal/9.jsp.
32 For related analysis on China's aviation industry by Chinese analysts, see Wang Xiaoqiang, "Zhongguo hangkong gongye hequ hecong [Whither China's Aviation Industry?]," online, available at www.usc.cuhk.edu.hk/wk_wzdetails.asp?id=1161. For an analysis of organizational differences between these two cases in China, see Gao Liang, "Zhongguo minhang gongye de xiankuang ji qi wenti – yi MD90 ganxian feiji xiangmu weili [Current Situation and Problem of China's Civil Aviation Industry – A Case of MD90 Jet]," *Zhanlue yu guanli*, 2000, no. 4, online, available at www.usc.cuhk.edu.hk/wk_wzdetails.asp?id=105.
33 Wang Xiaoqiang, op. cit. It should be emphasized that the acquisition of MD by Boeing shattered China's dream of manufacturing civilian passenger jets on an indigenous basis. After having acquired MD, Boeing announced in April 1997 that beginning mid-1999, Boeing would no longer continue production of the MD-90, and this would make China's investment in the aviation industry almost completely redundant. Another blow came from Airbus. Right after Boeing had announced its intention to discontinue the purchasing order of the MD-90, Airbus cancelled its co-operation with China to produce regional jets on the grounds that there was no need for the 100-seat passenger aircraft.
34 Ye Weiping, "Rushi shiyexia de zhongguo jungong chanye yanjiu [A Study of China's Defence Industry in the Wake of Entering the WTO]," *Zhanlue yu guanli* [Strategy and Management], 2000, no. 3, online, available at www.usc.cuhk.edu.hk/wk_wzdetails.asp?id=1052, and Yang Fan, "Jiaru WTO dui zhongguo jingji de yingxiang [Impacts on China's Economy after Entering the WTO]," *Dandai Zhongguo Yanjiu* [Contemporary China Studies], 2000, no. 4, online, available at www.usc.cuhk.edu.hk/wk_wzdetails.asp?id=1016.
35 Feng-cheng Fu and Chi-keung Li, "An Economic Analysis," in Broemmelhoerster and Frankenstein, op. cit., pp. 47–64.
36 Ye Weiping and Yang Fan, op. cit.
37 This section is drawn from Arthur Ding, "Civil–Military Relationship and Reform in the Defence Industry," IDSS Working Paper No. 82 (Singapore: Institute of Defence and Strategic Studies, June 2005).
38 It seems that the Chinese government has attempted industrial restructuring through domestic and international merger and acquisition. This view is aired in a book foreword written by a former deputy minister of the Ministry of Foreign Trade and Economic Cooperation, Long Yongtu, who was also chief representative of China's WTO negotiation team. Liu Li, *Jingji quanqiuhua – Zhongguo de chulu hezai* [Economic Globalization – Whither China's Direction?] (Beijing: Zhongguo shehui chubanshe, 1999), pp. 186–217.
39 This section is drawn from Wang Xiuqing, Luo Ge, and He Shaoqing, "Zhongguo hangtian guoji hezuo de chenggong fazhan [Successful Development for China Aerospace Industry's International Co-operation]," *Zhongguo Hangtian* [China Aerospace], 2000, no. 6, online, available at www.space.cetin.net.cn/docs/ht0006/ht000601.htm, and Zhang Zhiqian, "Zhongguo huojian jinru guoji shichang de qianqian houhou – jinian zhongguo duiwai shangye weixing fashe fuwu shizhounian

[Story about China's Rocket into International Market – 10-Year Anniversary for China's Commercial Launch Business]," *Zhongguo Hangtian*, 2000, no. 4 online, available at www.space.cetin.net.cn/docs/ht0004/ht000406.htm.

40 Ying Tianxing, "Zhonggong zhongdian daxue jiji yanfa xiaoweixing weixing zhi yanxi [Study on China's Top University actively developing small and micro satellites]," *Zhonggog yanjiu* [Studies on Chinese communism] (Taipei), 39:3 (March 2005), pp. 107–117.

41 For an analysis on the security implication of the Galileo project, see Gustav Lindstrom, *The Galileo Satellite System and Its Security Implications*, Institute for Security Studies of the European Union Occasional Paper No. 44, April 2003.

42 "GALILEO On Track: Successful Launch of the GIOVE-A Satellite," 28 December 2005, online, available at europa.eu.int/rapid/pressReleasesAction.do?reference=IP/05/1712&format=HTML&aged=0&language=EN&guiLanguage=fr.

43 China–Europe GNSS Technology Training and Co-operation Centre, online, available at www.cenc.org.cn/news/news2005091701.htm.

44 For an analysis of the capability of China's navigation satellite system, see Geoffrey Forden, "Beidou weixing dingwei xitong dui zhongguo heliliang de yingxiang [Impact of China's Beidou Positioning System on China's Nuclear Force] (Chinese translation)," online, available at www.surveyor.com.cn/Article/Meander/200601/Article_168.htm.

45 Liu Huanran, "Ouzhou qielilue weixing daohang jihua de yingyong ji xiaoyi fenxi" [Benefit Analysis on the Navigation Application of the EU Galileo Satellite], *Zhongguo Hangtian* [Aerospace China], 2000, No. 5, online, available at www.space.cetin.net.cn/docs/ht0005/ht000507.htm.

46 "Zhongguo jiang jiakuai shishi wuqi zhuangbei keyan shengchan xukezheng zhidu [China will speed up the pace for the establishment of licence system for R&D and production of weapons and equipment]," China.com, 2 April 2004, online, available at big5.china.com/gate/big5/military.china.com/zh_cn/head/83/20040402/11658110.html.

47 "Junpin shichang kaifang, minqi hui qiang junqi de fanwan? [If defence products market opens to all, will private enterprise win over defence industrial enterprises?]," Xinhuanet, 8 May 2004, online, available at www.sc.xinhuanet.com/content/2004–05/08/content_2090797_1.htm.

48 For the story of Guoxingnet, see "Minqi Guoxing chuangru weixing daohang dingwei xitong [Private enterprise Guoxingnet makes inroads into navigation satellite position system]," *Eshiyi shiji jingji baodao* [Economic Report in the Twenty-first Century], 26 August 2003, in business.sohu.com/22/89/article212498922.shtml.

49 "Junpin shichang kaifang, minqi hui qiang junqi de fanwan?" op. cit.

50 "Zhongguo 121jia jungong han minqi shiyanshi huo guofang kegongwei renke [In China, 121 defence industry and civilian laboratories were approved by COSTIND for licence]," China.com, 31 December 2005, online, available at military.china.com/zh_cn/news/568/20051231/12995785.html.

10 Exploring Southeast Asia's twenty-first century defence economies

Opportunities and challenges in the era of globalization, 1993–2005

Renato Cruz De Castro

Since the emergence of the modern international system, states have considered it imperative to finance their defence establishment by depending primarily on domestic factors such as the relative strength of the bureaucracy vis-à-vis the society, the popularity of the regime, and the natural resources of the state. States find it necessary, as well, to take into account the overall performance of the economy, the impact of defence spending, and production patterns in terms of total output and price levels in the defence sector. Although the international economy has always been an important source of funds and technology for the national defence sector, most states' security objectives are generally based on the Colbertist doctrine of defence self-sufficiency within a state's frontiers.[1] The accepted international pattern is the nationalization of military power. States recruit soldiers from their own national populations, bargain for access to indigenous communities to enable them to control local resources, develop industrial infrastructures for the production of weapons, use tariffs and customs as instruments of (national) economic policy, and propagate an ideology aimed at mobilizing the population around a claim to political independence and autonomy.[2]

The states' quest for the development of their autonomous defence capability, however, is seemingly thwarted by globalization. Globalization is the process whereby many social relations become relatively de-linked from (national) territorial geography, so that human lives are increasingly played out in the world as a single place.[3] Within this general social process, national economies are subsumed and rearticulated into the global system by international process and transaction.[4] The national economy is permeated and transformed by international forces. Thus, domestic national policies, whether involving public officials or private corporations, always factor in the predominant determinants of international production and distribution.

Despite the rhetoric of globalization, however, the nation-state is still the supreme territorial, administrative, political and military unit that defines "the good and most basic human community." National sovereignty, territorial integrity, and the development of an autonomous and powerful military capability are still guarded and valued by most nation-states, especially those in

Southeast Asia where the struggle for independence from colonial masters is still fresh in the collective consciousness. In decades past, the economies of most of Southeast Asia have increasingly been integrated into this emerging global economy. While globalization is taking place and economic integration is becoming more important to the region, war (and the preparedness for it) remains a preponderant concern among a number of Southeast Asian states. While promoting economic globalization strategies such as currency devaluation, tariff reduction, lifting of restrictions on foreign direct investments and fostering an export-oriented-industrialization, the possibility of war or military confrontation – and the need to assert national pride – have prompted some Southeast Asian states to develop and modernize their defence economies.

This chapter explores how four of these states – Singapore, Malaysia, Thailand and Indonesia – are managing their globalizing national economies, while simultaneously maintaining viable and relatively autonomous defence economies.[5] The study pays particular attention to the problem of how these Southeast Asian states are coping with globalization relative to their national defence economies. It attempts to address pertinent questions such as: (1) how these Southeast Asian countries are harnessing globalization to effect economic growth and development; (2) the origin and status of these countries' defence economies; and (3) how these states are managing their autonomous defence industries in the face of globalization. These four original member countries of the Association of Southeast Asian Nations (ASEAN) were selected on the basis of four criteria: the size of their national economy; the relative exposure of their local economy to the global economy; the size of their armed forces and amount of defence spending; and the existence of a viable and functional defence economy.

Defence economy refers to the relations or linkages between the commercial, financial and industrial capabilities of a state, on the one hand, and its politico-military capabilities on the other.[6] It encompasses the role of the state in all aspects of defence preparation, such as defence financing and logistics, weapons production, and research and development. It involves the organic connection between the states' accumulation and manipulation of capital (the realm of exploitation) in order to create the organization of coercion (the realm of domination).[7] The nature of a defence economy depends on the various combinations of capital and coercion formulated by different kinds of states in the past. Over time, states adopted different ways of accumulating and generating capital even as the influence of coercion in international affairs expanded during the modern era.[8] This chapter will therefore focus on the macro-economics of the defence economy, which includes the overall performance impact of defence spending on the economy and selected government spending, as well as the existence of a viable, functioning and autonomous defence industry.

Harnessing globalization for war preparation

During the nineteenth century, the states' concern with their national security made industrialization a military and an economic imperative. Strategic industries became central to the national industrial strategies and import-substitution programmes of many states. Subsidies to industries and trade barriers were rationalized on the grounds of national defence needs. These policies were justified on the basis of parity with those of other states; otherwise national independence might be compromised or even lost.[9]

The development of an autonomous defence capability is thus considered the optimum or preferred choice states must aim for. It is assumed that the key actors in seeking power and security in international relations are the states, which seek to assure and enhance their own security and prosperity within the limits of scarce limited national resources. At the level of the states themselves, security policy can be seen as the process by which national (state) interests are independently pursued within an insecure world.[10] Autonomy in defence matters embodies the freedom from external control, and is defined as the decisive exercise of sovereignty by the nation-state. Autonomy in defence affairs also enables states to exercise as much freedom as possible in order to avoid being drawn into events that have harmful consequences, and to fend off restrictions on their actions, particularly with respect to ensuring their security and exercise of sovereignty. For most self-respecting states, the major security objective is the development of a capable and autonomous military capability that will enable them to deal with external threats. The extreme form of this notion is epitomized by the economic philosophy of mercantilism which advocates that the power of the state becomes an end in itself, and all considerations of the national economy and individual welfare must be subordinated to the single purpose of developing the potentialities of a nation to prepare for war, or to wage war.[11]

Since the late twentieth century, however, some analysts and academics have maintained that states exist in a world where the greater part of their political and economic functions are determined by globalization, a process by which national cultures, economies and borders are being subsumed into a larger (and more macro) global unit. They contend that the process of globalization fosters the formation of a truly global economy which assimilates national economies and renders domestic strategies of economic management increasingly irrelevant.[12] Proponents of globalization argue that the state is in the process of transformation towards weakness: the authority (and security) of the state "leaking," "moving up," or "evaporating" toward forces, agents, and entities beyond it, including international organizations, transnational organizations, transnational associations, the global market, or the global civil society.[13]

More significantly, certain scholars see globalization as a challenge to the traditional concepts of sovereignty, national security, and exclusive territorial jurisdiction. Politically, globalization implies that political activities and processes, embracing the exercise of power, authority and security, are no longer primarily defined by national, legal and territorial boundaries.[14] This process might, in turn, undermine the states' ability to develop and manage their autonomous national defence capabilities. A globally structured and de-contextualized national economy means that states have no other choice but to tap the global market as sources of capital, defence-related technology and raw materials. Increasing globalization of civil industrial sectors involved in defence production makes acquisition and production of a weapons system subject to the decisions of other authorities and corporations beyond the scope of national jurisdictions.[15] As a result, the state is forced to accommodate the forces of globalization to the detriment of its own policy-making autonomy in economic and security domains. Consequently, autarky may no longer be a viable national strategy as states become increasingly dependent on the global economy for goods, services, and defence-related technology.

An American academic clarifies the current tension between the states' needs to adjust to economic globalization and to maintain an autonomous defence sector:

> While states are increasingly adopting the logic of economic liberalism and the global division of labour in their pursuit of wealth, public officials charged with defence policy remain preoccupied with achieving autonomy in foreign affairs and military superiority over all possible rivals. There is thus an underlying tension between nationalistic conceptions of security and the globalization of economic activity.[16]

The collapse of the Soviet Union in 1991 showed to the world the cost of maintaining a "fortress strategy" in managing a national defence economy. High-ranking officials tasked with national security planning are now required to rethink their economic strategy in terms of globalizing their wealth-creation capabilities while maintaining a viable defence-related economic sector. Since economic growth and technological know-how are important prerequisites for developing their military prowess, states are caught in a dilemma of ensuring the survival and autonomy of their defence capabilities while at the same time maintaining a national economy that is open to the global flow of capital, technology and raw materials.

Some nation-states are more successful than others at securing advantageous positions in the globalizing world economy while at same time developing and managing their defence economies. Most of the successful examples are in Northeast and Southeast Asia.[17] Four Southeast Asian states stand out: Singapore, Malaysia, Thailand, and Indonesia. Compared with most developing states in other regions of the world, these four states maintain an open economy (especially in trade), thus generating economic growth to finance their defence economies.[18] Singapore exhibits the strongest structural adjustment in the shift toward more capital and skill-intensive manufacturing activities for the global market. Malaysia has long established a low protection and outward orientation since it became independent. Thailand has always maintained a fairly open economy and has liberalized further. Indonesia has simplified its protectionist regime, and lowered the general rate of protection for local manufactures. The openness and international orientation of these Southeast Asian countries are apparent in terms of their share in the world's exports, their engagement in foreign trade, and their share in the world's foreign direct investment (FDI) inflows, which reveal another route for the emerging globalization of the region's economies.[19]

These four national economies moved roughly in the same general economic direction, achieving economic growth primarily through changing from import-substitution industrialization to export-oriented industrialization. While these countries have not totally abandoned the import-substitution strategy, the switch to export-oriented industrialization marked the beginning of rapid economic growth in each of these economies.[20] Transfers of Japanese and South Korean industrial plants to Southeast Asia, owing to rising labour costs at home, hastened this adoption of export-oriented industrialization. The move triggered an increase in regional trade in components and machinery, and facilitated absorption of the experience and knowledge needed to access the world market. The four second-tier East Asian newly industrialized countries (NICs) also managed to expand manufactured exports sharply on account of their attractive domestic environments, which favoured the relocation of foreign low value-added manufacturing and promoted the development of local resource-based activities, especially after 1986.[21] Basically, these countries participated in a "multiple catch-up" process through which Japan led the Asian NICs (South Korea, Taiwan, and Hong Kong), while they went through stages of comparative advantage. As the NICs followed Japan into capital-and-knowledge intensive production, the four ASEAN countries moved into exports from light industries and simpler electronics.[22] These countries also developed an export-oriented strategy while diversifying the markets for their ever-expanding exports. Their main markets included the US, Japan and the neighbouring Asian industrializing states, and Europe.[23]

As a component of their export-oriented industrial development, these states encouraged the flow of foreign direct investments into their manufacturing sector by providing special services and facilities, offering special tax concessions, and extending financial assistance or subsidies to foreign investors.[24] Generally, they also have no exchange controls or restrictions on the repatriation of capital, and remittance of profits, dividends and interests. These incentives encouraged the entry of multinational corporations (MNCs) into their economies, leading to their rapid industrial development and technological advancement.[25] Moreover, they actively promoted and managed FDI inflows and combined export promotion with more traditional infant-industry policies in specific sectors, and attempted to foster production linkages and technology transfer from foreign-dominated export sectors to local supporting industries.[26]

On closer inspection, the policies adopted by these countries vary and reflect different development objectives, options and perceptions of foreign investors. Generally, Singapore's policies are more liberal, with the absence of conditions restricting the operation of foreign enterprises, whereas the policies of the three other states are relatively more restrictive.[27] The countries also differ in the consistency of their policies vis-à-vis foreign investments over time, but all states have become more selective in their approach.[28] These investments have brought to the host countries not only employment but also "managerial ability, technical personnel, technological knowledge, administrative organization, innovations in products and production," and additional capital outlays.[29] Besides, the entry of MNCs hastens the pace of technological changes in the countries, thus boosting their export-oriented industrialization.[30] Finally, the influx of foreign investments has enabled these countries to pursue vigorously their export-oriented industrialization. American, Japanese, and Taiwanese investments comprise a significant portion of the capital needed to propel these Southeast Asian states to a full-blown export-led economic development strategy.[31]

Another important factor enabling these four ASEAN states to effect rapid economic growth is their adoption and implementation of neo-classical macro-economic policies. The general policy of these four ASEAN states could be characterized as neo-liberal, which involves the policy of rolling back the state and making the private sector the engine of growth.[32] It involves "getting the prices right" by letting free market-based price signals determine the most efficient allocation of resources for national economic growth.[33] These states also allegedly promote relatively open economies, avoid the provision of more incentives to some industries than to others, and generally limit the state's role in the economy.[34] Such a thrust entails moderate growth in money supply, fiscal deficits that have been generally modest, external indebtedness that has never threatened to impair international creditworthiness, and a sizeable public sector that supplies badly needed public goods such as physical infrastructure and education.[35] Malaysia, Singapore and Thailand have been quite exemplary in adhering to this macro-economic policy, while Indonesia was able to enact reasonably successful neo-liberal macro-economic reforms only in the 1980s.[36] These states also pursue relatively predictable macro-economic policies that provide an important foundation for future growth, and attract foreign investments even in the face of political instability.[37]

Macro-economic predictability, along with low inflation, enhances investors' confidence and stimulates the state to plan ahead. With the implementation of stable and consistent macro-economic and neo-mercantilist exported-oriented policies, these Southeast Asian states aim to create the necessary institutions that enable them to build their war-fighting capacity or defence economies.[38] Unlike their counterparts in Northeast Asia, they would implement defence industrialization strategies that are driven less by geo-strategic influences, but more by the pursuit of national prestige, growing state assertiveness and expanding economic base.[39]

The emergence of Southeast Asia's defence economies

Southeast Asia's defence economies are relatively new phenomena, which became apparent only in the early 1980s. The end of the Second World War saw most Southeast Asian states reeling from the physical and social devastation. Their post-war societies were racked by radical guerrilla movements. The fledgling states of Malaya, Singapore and Thailand found themselves mounting counter-insurgency campaigns against various communist-led armed movements in the region. These states' defence capacity grew rapidly because of the need to mobilize and coordinate financial, manpower and other resources to confront the revolutionary threat posed by communist neighbours and insurgents. These newly independent states relied on foreign military assistance for a large proportion of their military equipment. Malaysia and Singapore received the bulk of their military hardware from their former colonial master, the United Kingdom. In the early 1970s, however, foreign military assistance declined, forcing these states to buy the necessary military hardware, either secondhand or brand new.[40]

Most of the major weapons systems acquired in the early 1970s were secondhand and acquired from the frontline service of their original owners, such as Britain, France, Israel, or the United States. This acquisition of low-cost weapons systems, in turn, led to the rapid expansion of regional armed forces in Indonesia, Malaysia, Singapore and Thailand: the establishment of multi-squadron air forces, division-sized armoured units, and navies equipped with capital ships.[41] This pattern of improving their military hardware continued well into the 1980s as Southeast Asian states purchased new and advanced weapons systems from arms manufacturers in the West. Southeast Asian force modernization during this period involved a radical shift from internal security concerns – from COIN (counter-insurgency) and coastal protection – to more balanced conventional warfare force structures.[42] This development begs the question of how these Southeast Asian states were able to afford the investment of vast resources to meet their defence requirements?

The answer is really simple. Despite unexpected strategic developments, most Southeast Asian economies experienced rapid economic growth well above the world average in the 1970s. Resilience was the common feature of the economic growth recorded in the region, which validated the popular perception of the emergence and dynamism of the region's economic performance as a "miracle." Indonesia, Malaysia, Singapore and Thailand experienced strong economic growth marked by structural changes. From 1970 to 1980, Singapore recorded an average growth rate of 9 per cent per annum, followed closely by Thailand 6.9 per cent, Malaysia 7.9 per cent, and Indonesia 7.9 per cent.[43] The World Bank observed that from 1965 to 1990, the growth rate in these four countries was about double that of its "middle income" group of countries, while Singapore's rate was triple.[44] These countries grew more than twice as fast as the rest of East Asia, roughly three times as fast as Latin America and South Asia, and five times faster than sub-Saharan Africa.[45] They have also outperformed the industrial economies and the oil-rich Middle East–North Africa region.[46] Singapore led the pack when it posted rapid growth rates during two periods, 1960–69 and 1970–85, while Indonesia, Malaysia and Thailand showed accelerating growth, with higher growth rates in the second period rather than in the first.[47] Although these high-growth economies experienced slumps in the early 1980s due to the fall in commodity prices or compounding domestic policy mistakes, they exhibited reliance and flexibility that enabled them to contain economic slowdown and effect economic recovery.

These four ASEAN economies had considerable success in rapidly increasing their production and changing the structures of their economies. In Indonesia, Malaysia, Singapore and Thailand, the share of the industrial sector in the Gross Domestic Product (GDP) increased while the share of the agricultural sector declined. The rapid growth and transformation of these countries' economies coincided with the major strategic developments in East Asia, such as the Vietnamese invasion of Kampuchea, the expansion of Soviet military power in the region via Vietnam, the simmering territorial dispute over the South China Sea islands, these states' lingering historical rivalries, and the decline of regional insurgencies. This convergence of domestic economic thrust and geo-strategic trends colluded to pressure these states into increasing their levels of military spending, formulate aggressive arms import policies, and develop their incipient defence industries.

The geo-strategic trends and sizeable economic growth ensured a steady supply of capital necessary for these four successful Southeast Asian countries to enhance their defensive capacities. Their economic success validated the findings of several studies positing that there is a close and positive correlation between defence expenditures and economic growth. Having the highest GNPs, both Singapore and Malaysia registered the highest rates of increase in defence spending and arms acquisition.

Singapore began establishing its reputation for being the "most heavily armed country on earth," with the creation of sizeable armed forces, crowded into its small territory, fully equipped for conventional warfare by the 1970s. In the mid-1970s, Singapore purchased relatively a large amount of light tanks, M-111 APCs, A-4 Skyhawks, and F-5 fighters. Then in the mid-1980s, Singapore acquired eight US-made F-16 fighter-bombers worth US$280 million, symbolic of its intention to maintain armed forces that are second to none in the region. Such defence procurement enabled Singapore to modify its essentially defensive and defeatist "poisoned shrimp" strategy to a more forward defence posture that coincided with rapid economic growth, increasing economic power, and the resultant increase in defence spending and military capability that the country experienced in 1980s.[48] Rapid economic growth enabled the government to make the Singapore Armed Forces (SAF) stand out – at least in maritime Southeast Asia – as the most modern, well-equipped and technically-proficient armed forces, with a mature conventional operations capability in its land forces and a nascent joint warfare capability across all three services.[49]

As its economy grew in the mid-1970s, Malaysia took some tentative measures to strengthen its air force and navy. It acquired one squadron of US-made F-5s in 1972, and expanded its air force a decade later by ordering 88 second-hand US A-4 Skyhawks. It also bought patrol boats from South Korea and low-cost frigates from West Germany, as well as missile-armed fast attack craft from France and Sweden.[50] In the mid-1980s, the Malaysian economy grew rapidly and this enabled the government to effect a force modernization aimed at developing the capabilities of the Royal Malaysian Air Force (RMAF) and Royal Malaysian Navy (RMN), in order to protect the country's national resources and reinforce Kuala Lumpur's territorial claims in the South China Sea. The RMAF ordered 18 MIG-29 and eight McDonnell Douglas F/A-18Ds from Russia and the United States, respectively.[51] It also acquired four King Air B200Ts to enable it to have maritime patrol functions. The RMN, on the other hand, was able to acquire two UK-built Yarrow frigates and 16 former Royal Navy Wasp helicopters, with a view to developing its naval aviation capability. The country's economic growth enabled the RMAF to focus on developing its maritime and conventional functions, which in turn enabled Kuala Lumpur to acquire a degree of regional power-projection capability.[52]

Thailand announced a 9-year modernization programme in 1986, commencing development of its local manufacturing capacity and indigenous shipbuilding facilities. It also formed several armour divisions with the offensive capacity to respond to any possible conventional military threats from its neighbours. Thus, in the early 1990s, the Thai military shifted its focus from counter-insurgency to a conventional warfare capability. The topmost priority then was to develop an effective and more compact armed forces with modern military equipment, ranging from M-60 main battle tanks and F/A-18 fighter-bombers to a light helicopter carrier (*Chakkrimreubet*).[53]

Indonesia, for its part, acquired 31 light frigates from the former East Germany and two squadrons of Hawk fighters from the United Kingdom in the 1990s. Despite its efforts to project a modest increase in defence spending, Indonesia also acquired a number of weapons systems aimed at strengthening the navy as a response to the fluidity and uncertainty of the wider regional order in the post-Cold War era. Like the three other ASEAN states, Indonesia's goal is to develop its naval and air capabilities to effect "a shift from coastal defence and law enforcement to long-range patrol, escort and strike capabilities way beyond the outer limits of its maritime exclusive economic zone (EEZ)."[54] All these examples prove that extraordinary economic growth can provide a country with the necessary largesse to sustain a substantive weapons acquisition programme.

Robust economic growth also enabled these countries to lighten the military burden, as the proportion of GNP allocated to defence declined vis-à-vis total government expenditures. Malaysia, Singapore, Thailand and Indonesia all reduced the proportion of GNP directed to military spending, thus lightening their military burden from 1977–87.[55] Furthermore, as the agricultural sectors of the economy decreased their share of the GDP, the industrial and service sectors became increasingly dominant.[56] The four states were able to adapt well to the economic and technological realities that accompanied the acquisition of new and advanced weapon systems: for example, Indonesia's procurement of A-4 Skyhawk fighter-bombers, or Singapore's and Thailand's purchase of state-of-the-art F-16 Falcons.[57] These acquisitions materialized because the growth rates of these countries' defence spending was generally less than the rate of growth of their GNPs. The growth of these Southeast Asian states, averaging almost 7–8 per cent per annum over a 10-year period, meant that defence spending has been increasing substantially without incurring the opportunity costs to economic development traditionally associated with unrestricted defence spending in many developing countries.[58] As one Australian defence analyst points out:

The rates of economic growth provide the single best indicator of increase in defence expenditures. In the 1960s to late 1980s ASEAN showed a consistent and close positive correlation between economic growth and defence expenditures. Those countries with the highest rates of growth of GNP had the highest rates of increase in defence expenditures. Singapore and Malaysia are the prime examples. Those countries with slower growth rates, such as the Philippines and Indonesia, also had the slowest increases in defence spending.... ASEAN states increased their defence spending through the last decade because their increased economic capacity provided the opportunity to address increasing security concern.[59]

Southeast Asia's defence industries

Globalization has made the economies of Singapore, Malaysia, Thailand and Indonesia open, vibrant, productive and expansive, enabling them to focus on building up their war-fighting capacity. Perhaps the most concrete proof of these four countries' political independence and economic transformation is their defence industries. Defence industry is defined as the aggregate ability to provide the manufacturing, production, technology, research and development, and resources necessary to produce the materials for common or national defence.[60] The defence-industrial base is made up of a myriad of industrial activities, from shipbuilding to semi-conductor production. It provides a vital connection between the defence budget, the national defence programmes, and the required economic inputs of labour, equipment, capital, technology and raw material to implement these programmes. This industrial base is embedded in the larger economic technological and political capabilities of a state. Government officials managing these defence industries often get caught between two opposing forces: the need to formulate appropriate responses to meet their national security objectives, on the one hand, and the goal to achieve economic viability for these industrial enterprises, on the other. Following the general pattern in East Asia, these four countries have developed domestic defence industries to manufacture basic military hardware (small arms, light artillery, patrol boats), while reserving procurement funds for the acquisition of sophisticated items not easily produced at home.[61] However, in Southeast Asia, the development of these national defence industries has generally been driven less by strategic influences, and more by economic development plans, prestige factors, and, in some cases, the ambition of political leaders.[62]

Among these four states, Singapore is ahead in developing and sustaining a small but modern, forward-looking defence industry that is the most advanced and broad-based of its kind in Southeast Asia.[63] Stemming from the country's lack of strategic depth and relatively limited defence resources, but also its economic and technological advantages, Singapore's defence industry is geared primarily to provide locally assembled equipment for the Singaporean Defence Forces, and to update systems that are already in place. It is capable of final assembly or co-production, or complete license production of less sophisticated weapons, as well as limited research and development improvements to local license-produced arms.[64] It has manufactured equipment or updated systems for the Air-Force's A-4 and F-5; the Army's AMX-13 and M-113A1 armoured vehicles, and M-71 Howitzers; and the Navy's Victory-class missile corvettes, Fearless-class patrol vessels, Endurance-class landing ships and (possibly in the future) La Fayette-type frigates.[65] Singapore's defence industry is currently involved in Revolution in Military Affairs (RMA)-related areas such as advanced electronics and signal processing, information system security, advanced guidance system, communications, electronic warfare, sensors, and unmanned vehicles.[66] Confident of its advanced defence industry, the Singapore government has signed up to participate in the development of the US-originating Joint Strike Fighter (JSF) programme, which could replace the F-16 in the near future.[67] Singapore is also fully committed to developing export-oriented arms industries, having formed an array of military enterprises and trading firms.

Next to Singapore in terms of developing and maintaining an advanced defence industry is Indonesia. Former President Suharto supported the defence-related industrial programmes of then Research and Technology Minister B. J. Habibie. Since the 1970s, the government has funded civil–military strategic industries that include aerospace, shipbuilding and electronics. Like Singapore, Indonesia has developed the capability to engage in the final assembly of small arms, ammunition, and artillery systems, as well as co-produced or complete license production of weapon platforms such as helicopters and transport air-craft. Indonesia's defence industry has successfully designed and manufactured medium-sized transport aircraft, fast patrol craft and warships (up to corvette size), and have maintained and repaired naval vessels including submarines.[68] The Indonesian defence industry was intended to promote self-reliance in arms production and to stimulate the development of export-oriented civilian indus-tries. Most production was concentrated in a handful of state-owned enterprises, including *PT Industri Pesawat Terban Nusantara* (IPTN), which makes aircraft and helicopters. In the mid-1990s, these firms were able to expand their capacity to produce modern weapons; the goal was to make Indonesia self-sufficient in the manufacture of all but the most advanced weapons by the early decades of the twenty-first century.[69] However, with resource limitations, Indonesia has moved at a somewhat slower pace than expected.[70] The Asian financial crisis has taken its toll on the country's defence industry. In 1999, the International Mone-tary Fund (IMF) pressured the government to cut its support for the domestic aerospace industry. Indonesia's defence industry is also under threat, as senior military officers have doubted the reliability of domestically produced equip-ment, often preferring "off-the-shelf" purchases from Western suppliers.[71] Observing the impact of the Asian financial crisis on Indonesia's defence indus-try, a specialist on Southeast Asian defence industry notes: "Indonesian [defence] industry faces the dual challenge of having an armed forces that cannot afford to buy its equipment and a government that does not provide the massive direct support of the past."[72]

Malaysia and Thailand are still in the process of establishing a solid foundation for domestic arms production. Malaysia's defence industry is part of former Prime Minister Mohammad Mahathir's Vision 2020 plan to transform the country into a fully industrialized state by the year 2020. Compared to its counterparts in Singapore and Indonesia, it has limited defence-production facilities but is aspiring to expand its indigenous defence industrial bases. It aims to provide logistical support to the Malaysian Armed Forces and to contribute to the broader economy by reducing the importation of foreign parts and increasing local employment. The Malaysian defence industry is focused on the maintenance, repair and modernization of the armed forces' existing equipment. Beyond these functions, it has assembled light aircraft, upgraded the country's fleet of Lockheed C-130H Hercules transport planes, and has constructed and assembled naval vessels such as offshore patrol vessels, and fast patrol craft.[73] Thailand has the smallest and least-developed defence industry among the four Southeast Asian states, focusing mainly on simple licensed production and overall maintenance of its armed forces inventory. It has produced components for track vehicles, performed in-house overhaul of equipment, and manufactured small weapon systems such as anti-tank rockets. Like Malaysia, Thailand has adopted aggressive offset policies recently in an attempt to expand its embryonic defence industry.

A cursory review of these countries' defence industries reveals that an economy that is open and globalized is the one that has the most modern and advanced war-preparations capabilities. By opening its national economy and implementing a rapid industrialization policy based on export growth, Singapore has generated the necessary resources and developed the required economic and technological advantages (particularly a highly-educated workforce and strong information technology) to build relatively sophisticated defence-industrial capabilities. Not only can Singapore provide for the needs of its armed forces, its defence industry is now exporting arms to other countries. As a German defence analyst notes:

> Singapore has been a small arms and ammunition supplier to Asian and other developing nations but its emerging industrial capabilities are extending much further than that.... The government encourages export of arms. ST Engg is trying to improve its collaboration with international defence firms, an example of which is the partnership with Vickers Defence Systems (UK) and Teledyne Brown Engineering (US). The recent purchase by ST Engg of a significant stake in Timoney of Ireland is also to be seen in the framework of this general trend ... Singapore holds the promise of having a growing and successful defence industry that delivers technologically advanced products.[74]

Managing Southeast Asia's defence economies, 1993–2003

Historically, the most significant economic activity of the states has been the provision of national security and the preparation for war.[75] The development of war-fighting capabilities and the conduct of war are considered to be not only political, but also economic choices. The decision to prepare for conflict or wage a war is often dependent on several economic factors, including the capability of the state to finance troops and weapons; the ability of the state to tax its society; the availability of other sources of revenue to defray the cost of the war; and the natural resources and industrial infrastructure available for such an undertaking. The undertaking is often influenced by two views of the relationship between war preparation and the state of the economy.

The first view asserts that there is always a trade-off between guns and butter, military spending and capital investments. If a state increases the resources it devotes to military activities without increasing the GNP, then the civilian sector or even the overall health of the economy suffers.[76] While this concept attributes the economic success of post-war Japan and West Germany to their ability to make the US bear the cost of their domestic security and defence at the end of the Second World War, it also highlights the fact that military expenditures have opportunity costs in terms of economic growth, consumption, investment and social services since huge military spending spells fewer resources for capital outlay and other government expenditures. In other words, defence spending diverts scarce resources to essentially non-productive assets and investments. A government falls into a rut where it continuously pours amounts of money into defence because the defence industrial base must be maintained despite its cost to the wider economy.[77]

The second view holds that war preparation and war become the driving force for business and economic growth. Preparation for war or wartime conditions fuel a cycle of demand that leads to increase in economic output and overall industrial output.[78] Under certain conditions, an increase in military expenditures may have little or no opportunity costs to a given state, assuming that the economy can afford this form of government spending. This perspective questions the guns versus butter trade-off and suggests the ability of modern industrial states to finance their defence spending without jeopardizing either economic growth or development.[79] For instance, East Asian countries like South Korea and Taiwan achieved some of the highest rates of economic growth despite "a heavy defence burden in both dollars and manpower."[80] Other North and Southeast Asian countries have maintained impressive economic growth rates and viable social welfare systems despite continued external threats and heavy defence spending, thus negating the theory of any absolute trade-off between guns and butter. Significantly, some defence spending constitutes productive investment, including financial support for military research and development, procurement, and construction projects, all of which have positive spin-offs and spillover effects on civilian economy.[81] As a form of Keynesian economics, military Keynesianism holds that war preparation is a set stimulant for the civilian economy.[82] Renowned British economist John Maynard Keynes opined that military spending has a salutary effect on the civilian economy. He argued that defence preparation produces more than weapons; it generates fuller civilian employment, stimulates private consumption, nurtures innovators by assuring demand for products, and, in general, enhances competitive forces in the economy. Military Keynesianism provides a straightforward formula for economic growth – the intrinsic effect of military spending is to stimulate demand for capital goods, promote regional development, and enhance the skills of the labour force.[83]

An examination of the management of four ASEAN states' defence economies from 1993 to 2003 follows. It analyses the effects of defence spending on the overall GDP and fiscal policy of these countries. Maintaining a defence economy is a function of both economic growth and government spending. Defence spending is one of the few components of government expenditures that can be controlled or substantially altered in the annual budget. For example, spending on a weapons system can be accelerated or restricted, depending on the overall objectives of the government and its fiscal policy. This is more closely linked with annual shifts in economic policy than any other government programme.[84]

The statistical test attempts to determine how defence spending has affected the four states' economic growth, overall government spending, and other government expenditures. Proper maintenance and management of the defence economy is predicated on the absence of a guns versus butter dilemma in the economy. This means that the national economy is large enough to sustain a defence economy, and there is no need to divert resources away from investments and other government services. The test has three possible results:

1   Significant negative correlation A: increasing defence spending/declining GDP, government spending, and selected government expenditures ($p < -0.05000$). This suggests that a trade-off is indeed occurring in the economy. Increasing defence spending is causing a decline in GDP growth, diverting resources away from the civilian economy, and affecting other government expenditures.
2   Significant negative correlation B: decreasing defence spending/increasing GDP, government spending, and selected government expenditures ($p < -0.05000$). This suggests that there is no guns versus butter effect in the economy. Defence spending might be stimulating the economy, or defence spending has simply no effect on the economy.
3   Significant positive correlation: increasing defence spending/increasing GDP, government expenditures ($p < 0.05000$). There is no evidence that a guns-versus-butter-trade-off is occurring in the economy. It indicates that the economy can afford to grow and provide more resources to other sectors of the society despite increasing defence outlay. It also suggests that a military Keynesian effect is occurring, in which defence preparation is triggering fuller employment, economic development, and increase in government expenditures in other sectors of the society.

Result of the test (Indonesia): The test results indicate a significant positive correlation between defence spending and GDP growth (0.94), and overall and selected government expenditures (0.83 and 0.81 respectively). They suggest the absence of any gun versus butter-trade-off in Indonesia's economy. This implies that the Indonesian economy can afford to increase its defence spending without affecting overall economic growth and government expenditure. This may also signify the occurrence of a military Keynesian effect within the economy.

Result of the test (Malaysia): Like Indonesia, Malaysia shows no indication that there is a guns versus butter trade-off occurring in the economy. There are no significant negative correlations between defence spending and GDP growth (–0.20); between defence expenditures and overall government spending (0.88); and defence spending and selected government spending (0.89). The data suggests that the Malaysian economy can afford to pay its war-preparation cost without affecting its GDP growth and other government expenditures.

Result of the test (Singapore): The Singaporean case illustrates significant positive correlations between defence spending and net (0.94) and selected government spending (0.88). Surprisingly, there is a significant negative correlation between defence spending and GDP growth. This indicates a case of a guns versus butter trade-off (–0.77). The significant inverse relationship between Singapore's arms spending and GDP growth could be attributed to the fact that the 1997 Asian financial crisis caused the Singaporean government to increase its defence spending in an effort to show the world just how prepared it was to commit resources to defence "in good times and bad" in order to maintain the confidence of its citizens, and that of foreign investors.[85] Consequently, this increase was reflected not only in terms of local currency and dollars but also, according to official figures, as a proportion of GDP.[86] By the time its GDP growth had slowed down, Singapore kept its defence budget at 6 per cent of its GDP as it bought three additional submarines from Sweden and 12 F-16 C/Ds armed with beyond visual range precision-guided munitions with global positioning.[87] This might have triggered a guns versus butter trade-off, in which a radical increase in defence spending adversely affected the GDP growth rate. However, this was a temporary phenomenon resulting from an assertion of national pride and prestige at a time of general economic slowdown and wider regional financial crisis.

Result of the test (Thailand): Among the four countries, the Thai case presents insignificant negative correlations in all three sets of variables: defence spending and GDP (0.25); defence spending and net (–0.18) and selected (–0.22) government expenditures. However, the data does not necessarily indicate a guns versus butter trade-off since the inverse relationships are very weak. A feasible explanation might be how the Asian financial crisis tilted Thailand's domestic balance against the military, in favour of civilian politicians. This may have placed greater constraints on the free-spending Thai military.[88] The Asian financial crisis also made the government overly concerned with the increasing current-account deficit that forced Bangkok to freeze its spending at the 1995 levels, and to postpone the procurement of submarines and a communication satellite. In the midst of the Asian financial crisis, the IMF required the Thai government to reduce overall government budget, including defence. This

Table 10.1 Indonesia (rupiah, millions)

Year	Defence spending	Net gross domestic product (overall national expenditures – defence spending)	Net overall government expenditure (defence spending)	Selected government expenditures (education, health, economic and social development)
1993	2,390	327,386	27,480	29,035
1994	2,151	380,069	27,552	29,067
1995	2,682	451,886	30,080	31,488
1996	8,747	523,821	73,474	67,264
1997	8,199	619,496	101,103	94,730
1998	11,065	944,689	161,604	154,194
1999	9,984	1,089,748	219,862	210,694
2000	11,449	1,253,470	208,486	200,862
2001	16,416	1,451,239	255,762	247,055
2002	19,291	1,591,274	226,749	214,044
2003	27,446	1,759,245	230,488	210,175

Sources: Asian Development Bank, *Key Indicators 2002* (Pasig City, the Philippines: The Asian Development Bank, 2002), pp. 172 and 177; *Key Indicators 2004* (Pasig City, the Philippines: Asian Development Bank, 2004), pp. 155 and 159.

Table 10.2 Malaysia (Malaysian ringgit, millions)

Year	Defence spending	Net gross domestic product (overall national expenditures – defence spending)	Net overall government expenditure (defence spending)	Selected government expenditures (education, health, economic and social development)
1993	7,388	164,806	34,953	20,152
1994	7,858	187,603	38,483	23,508
1995	8,892	213,581	41,732	24,314
1996	9,060	244,672	49,433	30,459
1997	8,921	272,874	51,494	31,596
1998	7,276	275,967	55,411	34,174
1999	9,230	291,110	60,083	36,730
2000	9,291	331,415	75,197	48,137
2001	11,597	321,054	87,396	55,016
2002	13,363	347,295	91,313	61,291
2003	16,433	375,579	98,144	66,376

Sources: Ibid., pp. 232–3, 236–7; and ibid., pp. 192 and 195.

Table 10.3 Singapore (Singapore dollars, millions)

Year	Defence spending	Net gross domestic product (overall national expenditures – defence spending)	Net overall government expenditure (defence spending)	Selected government expenditures (education, health, economic and social development)
1993	4,049	92,744.0	12,305	6,795
1994	4,347	102,305.8	10,712	7,278
1995	4,592	113,176.4	14,641	9,596
1996	5,878	122,365.4	21,557	14,540
1997	6,865	133,414.3	16,892	12,719
1998	7,678	129,940.3	19,802	15,800
1999	7,595	132,475.4	18,659	14,342
2000	7,701	152,187.2	22,420	21,305
2001	8,141	145,314.2	25,689	NA
2002	NA	NA	NA	NA
2003	NA	NA	NA	NA

Sources: Ibid. pp. 334–5, 338–9; and ibid., p. 260.

Table 10.4 Thailand (Thai baht, millions)

Year	Defence spending	Net gross domestic product (overall national expenditures – defence spending)	Net overall government expenditure (defence spending)	Selected government expenditures (education, health, economic and social development)
1993	75,631	2,395,277	445,375	NA
1994	86,230	2,606,743	492,986	NA
1995	94,681	2,847,055	548,043	432,356
1996	100,220	3,015,118	718,863	572,082
1997	98,172	2,974,484	833,533	676,140
1998	86,133	2,663,551	755,728	594,315
1999	74,809	212,343	758,255	570,579
2000	71,268	2,933,391	781,925	573,798
2001	75,394	2,983,678	833,219	610,487
2002	76,724	3,162,306	878,780	636,457
2003	77,027	3,380,357	919,171	669,425

Source: ibid.

austerity programme, along with the rapid depreciation of the baht, prevented any new arms procurement except parts. Bangkok cancelled its order for eight F/A-18 fighter-bombers, airborne early warning (AEW) aircraft, armoured personnel vehicles, transport and air-defence radar, and in-flight refuelling tankers.[89] This could not be considered a classic example of a guns versus butter trade-off since the Asian financial crisis merely created the opportunity and rationale for the civilian government to impose certain restrictions on the free-spending habits of the Thai armed forces.

Pearson correlation test: defence spending and its general macro-economic impact

The statistical test reveals no significant negative correlations between defence spending and GDP growth in all four cases. Although Singapore has recorded a significant negative correlation of (–0.74), this cannot be considered a case of a long-term guns versus butter trade-off but rather a short-term result of the island-state's political decision to increase defence spending during an economic slow-down for the sake of national prestige. Indonesia and Malaysia show positive correlations in almost all the variables, while Thailand exhibits an insignificant positive correlation between defence spending and GDP (0.25), with insignificant negative correlations in defence spending and net government (–0.18), and defence spending and net and selected government expenditures (–0.22) respectively. These insignificant correlations reflect the civilian government's determined efforts to clip the wings of the Thai military. Overall, there is no quantitative evidence that the four ASEAN economies are experiencing any guns versus butter trade-off in financing their respective defence economies. This absence is traceable to two factors: (1) rapidly growing economies that can afford to finance a relatively high level of defence spending without incurring the opportunity costs to economic development and other government spending; and (2) independent states that want status symbols to project the image of a sovereign, modern, affluent, and industrialized nation.[90]

Rich nation, strong army: is this enough?

Less than a decade after the 1997 Asian financial crisis, these four Southeast Asian countries have reactivated their long-term plans for military modernization, aimed at three key areas: military organization, arms purchases, and military industrialization. Their defence acquisition programmes, put momentarily on hold, have resumed with the purchase of new military hardware for their well-equipped air and naval forces; these have developed a significant capacity for "power projection."[91] Singapore and Malaysia are both eyeing the acquisition of submarines.[92] Thailand is also looking at the possibility of acquiring Holly-class frigates, while Indonesia is waiting for six CN-235 maritime patrol aircraft.[93] Indeed, the economic recovery of the region has enabled these states to strive again for the capacity to deploy their military forces in their maritime

Table 10.5 Summary table for correlations between defence expenditure and selected variables of four ASEAN states

Countries	r	p	Interpretation	r	p	Interpretation
Indonesia						
Net GDP defence spending	0.94	0.000	Significant	0.97	0.000	Significant
Net government defence spending	0.83	0.000	Significant	0.97	0.000	Significant
Selected government defence spending	0.81	0.002	Significant	0.87	0.000	Significant
Malaysia						
Net GDP defence spending	−0.20	0.003	Significant	0.84	0.001	Significant
Net government defence spending	0.88	0.002	Significant	0.85	0.000	Significant
Selected government defence spending	0.89	0.000	Significant	0.85	0.000	Significant
Singapore						
Net GDP defence spending	−0.74	0.141	Significant	−0.32	0.406	Not significant
Net government defence spending	0.85	0.000	Significant	0.97	0.000	Significant
Selected government defence spending	0.85	0.004	Significant	0.93	0.000	Significant
Thailand						
Net GDP defence spending	0.25	0.242	Not significant	−0.04	0.894	Not significant
Net government defence spending	−0.18	0.729	Not significant	−0.14	0.669	Not significant
Selected government defence spending	−0.18	0.571	Not significant	−0.08	0.831	Not significant

territories and to distant locations. Force modernization is transforming these states' militaries along the lines of the RMA, leveraging on quality rather than quantity, and allowing them to develop a powerful deterrent that delivers more "bang for the buck."[94] However, is this "bang" capable of deterring the new security challenges of the twenty-first century?

The 9/11 terrorist attacks in the US unveiled to the world a new global security challenge for the twenty-first century: the qualitative transformation of the low-intensity conflict. A low-intensity conflict is a form of political violence waged by organizations other than the state against state actors.[95] Mostly occurring in developing countries, this type of warfare is waged either between a state and some other organization, or between two such organizations.[96] Instead of the state's politico-bureaucratic war-making institutions, sub-state social groups formed and led along personal and charismatic lines conduct wars against each other or against the state.[97] The belligerents do not field armies that are clearly distinct from the people; the organizations in question thrive precisely because their combatants cannot be easily distinguished from the non-combatants who surround them.[98] Thus, this type of strife involves adversaries that are asymmetric in capabilities; and the weaker side, the sub-state actor, attempts to bring about political change by organizing and fighting more effectively than its stronger adversary, the state.[99]

In recent times, the security of Singapore, Malaysia, Thailand and Indonesia has been threatened not by states with conventional forces, but by an amalgam of transnational terrorist movements. These range from insurgent groups fighting for autonomy or secession in Muslim-dominated regions, to radical Islamist paramilitary groups that are bent on waging low-intensity conflicts against their governments. From the late 1990s, Southeast Asia saw the emergence of a terrorist threat that has since assumed an essentially transnational or stateless form.[100] On the heels of 9/11, the region was profoundly shaken by the discovery of terrorist cells operating in Malaysia and Singapore. These cells were reportedly planning to attack American targets in Singapore and the Malacca Straits. In Indonesia and Thailand, there are insurgents who currently engage in political activism and military operations, and hence enjoy widespread support, pursue genuine political agendas, and often rely on guerrilla warfare to advance their secessionist objectives. Malaysia, Indonesia and Thailand are also beset by various Islamic paramilitary groups that operate as militias or even common criminal gangs, involved in extortion, kidnapping and racketeering. These various Islamic fundamentalist groups pose a danger to the health of these four ASEAN economies. As a case in point, the discovery of international terrorist cells in Malaysia and Singapore in 2001, followed by terrorist bombings in Bali (October 2002) and Jakarta (August 2003), had a depressing and adverse effect.[101]

The emergence of radical Islamic movements in Southeast Asia in the 1990s resulted from the convergence of several international phenomena.[102] These included the reaction to the onslaught of globalization particularly associated with the United States, frustrations with the repression and corruption in secularist states, the desire to create a pan-Islamic Southeast Asia, and the return of terrorist veterans from the fighting in Afghanistan.[103] Unfortunately, despite their well-equipped air and naval power projection capabilities, modern military establishments can hardly address these diverse, amorphous and systemic security challenges. States will have to wage a long, protracted, and low-intensity campaign against these groups without relying on the expensive high-technology weaponry that is the pride and joy of their modern armed forces.[104]

Another latent security challenge to these four Southeast Asian states is the emergence of China and India as possible economic rivals. China, now the third largest manufacturer of goods, receives a huge amount of foreign direct investment. India lags behind China in terms of economic growth but will probably sustain a high level of economic growth in the coming years. Like China, India will also be an economic magnet for trade and foreign direct investments. A combination of sustained economic growth, active absorption of advanced technologies, huge market, and export-oriented industrialization will enable both countries to shape the regional political economy. Their cheap domestic labour and huge markets give them a competitive edge against these Southeast Asian states. In view of these developments, Indonesia, Malaysia, Singapore and Thailand will need to rethink their export-oriented strategy and make functional again the import facet of their defence economies.[105] As economic behemoths, China and India can be daring and daunting in their increasing competitiveness. For example, they could flood the world market with cheaper manufactured goods that would simply overwhelm any country's export-oriented industries. This could, in turn, lower economic growth, limit resources for defence, and cause a general slow-down in these four states' arms-modernization programmes. How China and India choose to exercise their growing economic clout in the region, and whether they relate co-operatively or competitively with smaller Asian states, are key security concerns facing these four Southeast Asian states.

Conclusion

Based on the experiences of Singapore, Malaysia, Thailand and Indonesia, it can be concluded that globalization does not adversely affect the ability of states to develop and maintain a viable defence economy. Adopting the general economic strategy of an open and globalized economy, and creating and managing a viable and functioning defence economy do not necessarily place these states in a dilemma. They have not experienced any tension arising from their nationalistic conceptions of security as they build an autonomous defence economy, while ensuring the globalization of their national economies. These states have found that economic liberalization and the global division of labour in the generation of national wealth complement their preoccupation with developing and managing an autonomous and functional defence economy. These clear-cut thrusts help them in their pursuit of two very important goals in a globalizing world: ensuring economic development and prosperity; and enhancing national security in an anarchic international environment.

By opening their economies to the global market, Singapore, Malaysia, Thailand and Indonesia are able to generate the necessary wealth to finance their war preparation. Implementing a strategy of export-oriented industrialization and neo-liberal economic policies has helped them modernize their conventional armed forces that could be sustained by their existing defence economies. Thus, these states have become skilled and seasoned practitioners of a new form of modern statecraft – neo-mercantilism. Analytically, Singapore, which has the most open economy in Southeast Asia, can best afford to develop and manage the most advanced defence industry in the region. All in all, the statistical test shows that these four countries can afford their defence economy without ever triggering a long-term guns versus butter dilemma.

These countries are, however, confronted by new security risks – low-intensity conflicts, and the emergence of China and India – that cannot be addressed by their modern defence capabilities. These challenges could, in the long run, undermine the basis of their vibrant and modern defence economies – export-oriented industrialization. This raises the question of whether the ways and means of eighteenth-century statecraft – a rich nation bankrolling modern and strong conventional armed forces – are still the most appropriate instruments for addressing the security challenges of the twenty-first century.

Notes

1 Ethan Barnaby Kapstein, *The Political Economy of National Security: A Global Perspective* (Columbia, SC: University of South Carolina Press, 1992), p. 21.
2 Charles Tilly, *Coercion, Capital, and European States, AD 990* (Oxford: Blackwell, 1997), pp. 96–126.
3 Jan Aart Scholte, "The Globalization of World Politics," in John Baylis and Steven Smith (eds.), *The Globalization of World Politics: An Introduction to International Relations* (Bath: Bath Press, 2001), p. 15.
4 Paul Hirst and Grahame Thompson, *Globalization in Question: The International Economy and the Possibilities of Governance* (Cambridge: Polity, 1996), p. 10.
5 Another possible candidate to this list is Vietnam. In 1986, the Vietnamese Communist Party (VCP) adopted the strategy of *doi moi* or economic renovation. This economic strategy involves market-oriented economic development policies and an aggressive foreign investment strategy, all aimed at globalizing the Vietnamese economy. This led to the growth of the Vietnamese economy and an increase in its defence expenditure by almost 100 per cent. By the mid-1990s, Vietnam turned to Russia for the acquisition of six Su-27s and two missile corvettes. Clearly, by the end of the 1990s, Vietnam was in the process of upgrading its air force and navy to protect its 3,000-km coastline, as well as its claim in the South China Sea. However, Vietnam has followed a different path from the four other Southeast Asian states in terms of economic development and force modernization. Prior to the 1980s, Vietnam was able to build an advanced conventional military force due to Soviet economic assistance while most Southeast Asian military forces were focused on counter-insurgency. Vietnam embarked on a policy of economic globalization only in the mid-1980s and allowed its conventional military force to stagnate. Vietnam only began reviving its external defence capabilities in the mid-1990s and is presently embarking on an extremely modest modernization programme that places priority on refurbishing and upgrading existing weapons systems. Vietnam is still operating from a very low level of defence expenditures. Hanoi is also highly

selective in its arms acquisition. And as a consequence of its external dependency on the Soviet Union, Vietnam's defence industry is now moribund. Vietnam is embarking on a programme designed to modernize its forces in order to catch up with its more affluent and advanced Southeast Asian neighbours. See Carlyle A. Thayer, "Force Modernization: The Case of the Vietnam People's Army," *Contemporary Southeast Asia*, 19:1 (June 1997), pp. 1–27; Carlyle A. Thayer, "Defence Relations and Force Modernization," *Southeast Asian Affairs* (Singapore: Institute of Southeast Asian Studies, 1999), p. 2. Online, available at http://proquest.umi.com/ pqdweb?did=972496001&sid=Fmt=3&clientld=47883&VName=PQD.

6 See Kapstein, op. cit., pp. 14–21, and Lee D. Olvey, James R. Golden, and Robert C. Kelly, *The Economics of National Security* (Wayne, NJ: Avery, 1984), p. 2.

7 See Charles Tilly, *Coercion, Capital, and European States AD 990–1992* (Oxford: Blackwell, 1997), pp. 16–20.

8 Ibid., pp. 125–91.

9 Stephen Gill and David Law, "Military-Industrial Rivalry in the Global Political Economy," in Kendall W. Stiles and Tsuneo Akaha (eds), *International Political Economy: A Reader* (New York: HarperCollins, 1991), p. 368.

10 Richard Little and Michael Smith (eds.), *Perspectives on World Politics* (New York: Routledge, 2006), p. 4.

11 For a comprehensive discussion of the relations between economic development and military prowess, see Edward Mead Earle, "Adam Smith, Alexander Hamilton, Frederich List: The Economic Foundation of Military Power," in Peter Paret (ed.), *Makers of Modern Strategy: from Machiavelli to the Nuclear Age* (Princeton, NJ: Princeton University Press, 1986), pp. 217–61.

12 Hirst and Thompson, op. cit., p. 1.

13 K. J. Holsti, "States and Statehood," in Richard Little and Michael Smith, op. cit., pp. 25–6.

14 Anthony G. McGrew and Paul G. Lewis (eds), *Global Politics: Globalization and the Nation-State* (Cambridge: Polity, 1992), p. 3.

15 For an incisive and thorough discussion of the impact of globalization on the defence economy, see Graham Allison, "The Impact of Globalization on National and International Security," in Joseph Nye and John D. Donahue (eds), *Governance in a Globalizing World* (Washington, DC: Brookings Institute, 2000), pp. 72–85.

16 Kapstein, op. cit., p. xiii.

17 Richard Stubbs, "War and Economic Development: Export-Oriented Industrialization in East and Southeast Asia," *Comparative Politics*, 31:3 (April 1999), pp. 337–55.

18 Hal Hill, "ASEAN Economic Development: An Analytical Survey – the State of Field," *The Journal of Asian Studies*, 53:3 (August 1994), p. 839.

19 See Moha Asri Abdullah and Raymond K. H. Chan, "Emergence of a Global Economy in Southeast Asia: 1990s and Beyond," in Raymond K. H. Chan, Kwan Kwok Leung and Raymond M. H. Ngan (eds), *Development in Southeast Asia: Review and Prospects* (Aldershot: Ashgate, 2002), pp. 94–5.

20 Stubbs, op. cit., p. 338.

21 Rajah Rasiah, "Manufacturing Export Growth in Indonesia, Malaysia and Thailand," in K. S. Jomo (ed.), *Southeast Asian Paper Tigers? From Miracle to Debacle and Beyond* (London and New York: RoutledgeCurzon, 2003), p. 60.

22 Richard F. Doner, "Approaches to the Politics of Economic Growth in Southeast Asia," *The Journal of Asia Studies* 50, 4 (November 1991), p. 826.

23 Ibid., p. 349.

24 Lim Chong Yah, *Southeast Asia: The Long Road Ahead* (Singapore: World Scientific, 2004), p. 139.

25 Doner, op. cit., pp. 840–2. Also see Abdullah and Chan, op. cit., p. 93.

26 Greg Felkner and K. S. Jomo "New Approaches to Investment Policy in the ASEAN 4," in K. S. Jomo op. cit., p. 81.
27 Lim, op. cit., p. 137.
28 Ibid., p. 137.
29 Ibid., pp. 138–9.
30 Hill, op. cit., p. 841.
31 See Stubbs, op. cit., pp. 345–7.
32 See G. Sivalingam, *Competition Policy in ASEAN Countries* (Singapore: Thomson Learning, 2005), pp. 5–6.
33 A group of scholars in the late 1980s and early 1990s argued that these states were not really neo-liberal states but developmental states. According to the scholars, these states owed their development to the central role played by the state itself in economic development. This chapter, however, does not intend to engage in this neo-liberal versus development state debate. For more on this debate, see Robert Gilpin, *The Global Political Economy* (Princeton, NJ: Princeton University Press, 2001), pp. 305–40. Also see Doner, op. cit., pp. 830–1.
34 Hill, op. cit., p. 818.
35 Ibid., p. 845.
36 Ibid., pp. 845–7.
37 Bowie and Unger, op. cit., p. 188.
38 Stubbs, op. cit., p. 350.
39 Susan Willett, "East Asia's Changing Defence Industry," *Survival*, 39:3 (Autumn 1997), p. 4. Online, available at proquest.umi.com/pqdweb?did=13625740&sid=7& Fmt=4&clientld=47883&RQT=309&VName=PQD.
40 Anil R. Pustam, "Southeast Asian Defence Industry: Quo Vadis?" *Military Technology*, 26:3/4 (March/April 2002), p. 1. Online, available at proquest.umi.com/ pqdweb?did=120660951&sid=Fmt=4&clientld=47883&RQT=309&VName=PQD.
41 Aaron Karp, "Military Procurement and Regional Security in Southeast Asia," *Contemporary Southeast Asia*, 11:4 (March 1990), p. 336.
42 Carlyle A. Thayer, *"Regional Military Modernization Strategies and Trends"* (Unpublished paper, presented at a conference on Security and Societal Trends in Southeast Asia, White-Meyer House, Meridian International Center Washington, DC, 6–7 September 2000), p. 3.
43 Lim Chong Yah, *Southeast Asia: The Long Road Ahead* (Singapore: World Scientific, 2004), p. 43; and figures from World Bank, World Development Indicators Online, 2003. Online, available at publications.Worldbank.org/WDI.
44 Hill, op. cit., p. 833.
45 World Bank Policy Research Report, *The East Asian Miracle: Economic Growth and Public Policy* (Washington, DC: Oxford University Press, 1993), p. 2.
46 Ibid., p. 2.
47 Ibid., p. 28.
48 See Bernard Loo, "Explaining Changes in Singapore's Military Doctrine: Material and Ideational Perspectives," in Amitav Acharya and Lee Lai To (eds), *Asia in the New Millennium* (Singapore: Marshall Cavendish, 2004), p. 368.
49 Ibid., p. 367.
50 Karp, op. cit., p. 348.
51 See J. N. Mak, "The Modernization of the Malaysian Armed Forces," *Contemporary Southeast Asia*, 19:1 (June 1997), p. 41.
52 Ibid., p. 49.
53 Panitan Wattanayagorn, "Thailand: The Elite's Shifting Conceptions of Security," in Muthiah Alagappa (ed.), *Asian Security Practice: Material and Ideational Influences* (Stanford: Stanford University Press, 1998), pp. 440–1.
54 Dewi Fortuna Anwar, "Indonesia: Domestic Priorities Define National Security," in Alagappa, op. cit., pp. 506–7.

55 Andrew L. Ross, "Growth, Debt, and Military Spending in Southeast Asia," *Contemporary Southeast Asia*, 11:4 (March 1990), p. 249.
56 Abdullah and Chan, op. cit., p. 89.
57 Karp, op. cit., pp. 346–51.
58 Willet, op. cit., p. 2.
59 Thayer, op. cit., p. 7.
60 Kapstein, op. cit., p. 92.
61 Michael Klare, "East Asia's Militaries Muscle Up," *Bulletin of the Atomic Scientists*, 53:1 (January/February 1997). Online, available at proquest.umi.com/pqdweb?did-10683008&sid=7&Fmt=4&clientld=47883&RQT=309&VName=PQD.
62 Tim Huxley and Susan Willett, *Arming East Asia* (New York: Oxford University Press, 1999), p. 50.
63 Pustam, op. cit., p. 4.
64 Willet, op. cit., p. 7.
65 Pustam, op. cit., pp. 4–5.
66 Richard A. Bitzinger, "Come the Revolution: Transforming the Asia-Pacific's Militaries," *Naval War College Review*, 58:4 (Autumn 2005), p. 48.
67 John F. Brindley, "A Pause between Defence Spending Sprees?" *Interavia*, 57:660 (January/February 2002), p. 3. Online, available at proquest.umi.com/pqdweb?did=110353604sid=1&Fmy=4&clientld=47883&RQT=309&VName=PQD.
68 Pustam, op. cit., p. 6.
69 Klare, op. cit., p. 3.
70 Ibid., p. 6.
71 Huxley and Willet, op. cit., p. 50.
72 Philip Finnegan, "Defence and Aerospace in SE Asia: The Way Forward," *Military Technology*, 26:9 (September 2002), p. 2. Online, available at proquest.umi.com/pqdweb?did=222231871&sid=Fmt=4&clientld=47883&RQT=309&VName=PQD.
73 Pustam, op. cit., p. 6.
74 Ibid., p. 5.
75 Kapstein, op. cit., p. 15. See Tilly, op. cit.; and Brian M. Downing, *The Military Revolution and Political Change* (Princeton, NJ: Princeton University Press, 1992).
76 Bruce Russett, "Defence Expenditures and National Well-Being," in Kendall and Tsuneo Akaha (eds), *International Political Economy: A Reader* (New York: HarperCollins, 1991), p. 333.
77 Kapstein, op. cit., p. 49.
78 Ibid., p. 20; and Russett, op. cit., p. 334.
79 Ibid., p. 44.
80 Kapstein, op. cit., p. 44.
81 Ibid., p. 50.
82 See Richard J. Samuels, *Rich Nation, Strong Army: National Security and Technological Transformation of Japan* (Ithaca, NY: Cornell University Press, 1994), p. 11.
83 Olvey, Golden, Kelly, op. cit., p. 53.
84 Ibid., p. 53.
85 See Huxley and Willett, op. cit., p. 22.
86 Ibid., p. 22.
87 Thayer, op. cit., p. 9.
88 Thayer, op. cit., p. 8.
89 Huxley and Willet, op. cit., pp. 16–17.
90 Willet, op. cit. p. 4; and Huxley and Willet, op. cit., p. 51.
91 John F. Brindley, "A Pause between Defence Spending Sprees?" Interavia 57:660 (January/February 2002), p. 1. Online, available at proquest.umi.com/pqdweb?did=110353604&sid=1&Fmt=4clientld=47883&RQT=309&VName=PQD.
92 Jan Wiedemann, "Increasing Demand for New Builds in the Asia-Pacific Region,"

Naval Forces, 26:3 (2005), p. 2. Online, available at proquest.umi.com/pqdweb?did=869399231&sid=8&Fmt=clientId=47883&RQT=309&VName=PQD.

93 Ibid., p. 2; and Brindley, op. cit., p. 2.

94 See Bernard Loo, "Transforming the Strategic Landscape of Southeast Asia," *Contemporary Southeast Asia*, 27:3 (December 2005), p. 401.

95 Martin Van Creveld, The *Transformation of War* (New York: The Free Press, 1991), p. 198.

96 See Martin Van Creveld, "What is Wrong with Clausewitz," in Gert de Nooy (ed.), *The Clausewitzian Dictum and the Future of Western Military Strategy* (The Hague: Kluwer Law International, 1997), pp. 7–23.

97 Ibid., p. 200.

98 Van Creveld, op. cit. 1997, p. 11.

99 James D. Kiras, "Terrorism and Irregular Warfare," in John Baylis, James Wirtz, Eliot Cohen, and Colin S. Gray (eds), *Strategy in the Contemporary World: An Introduction to Strategic Studies* (New York: Oxford University Press, 2002), p. 211.

100 See Zachary Abuza, "Learning by Doing: Al Qaeda's Allies in Southeast Asia," *Current History* (April 2004), p. 171.

101 See Carlyle A. Thayer, "Southeast Asia Marred Miracle," *Current History*, 103:672 (April 2004), p. 178.

102 See Zachary Abuza, "Funding Terrorism in Southeast Asia: The Financial Network of Al Qaeda and Jemaah Islamiyah," *NBR Analysis*, 14:5 (December 2003).

103 Abuza, op. cit., p. 172.

104 For more discussion on this type of war, see Van Creveld, op. cit., pp. 18–25.

105 Ibid., p. 178.

11 Globalization's impact on defence industry in Southeast Asia*

Rommel C. Banlaoi

Introduction

Although some countries in Southeast Asia have already published their defence white papers to express their views on defence and security issues confronting the region (as observed in Table 11.1), there is still very little discussion on national defence industries. In some cases, there is a total absence of information. With the exception of Singapore and Thailand, members of the Association of Southeast Asian Nations (ASEAN) do not contribute regularly to the Annual Security Outlook of the ASEAN Regional Forum (ARF) (Table 11.3), which aims to promote greater understanding, confidence, and transparency among participants through the yearly publication of their perspectives on global and national security situations. This indicates the reluctance of many countries in Southeast Asia to really pursue "openness" in the area of defence and security. Globalization, which has increased transactions and the interconnectedness of states, has not yet really enhanced defence transparency in Southeast Asia.

Table 11.1 Publication of defence white papers in Southeast Asia

ASEAN countries	Year of publication
Brunei	2004
Cambodia	2000
Indonesia	2003
Laos	–
Malaysia	–
Myanmar	–
Philippines	1998
Singapore	2000, 2004
Thailand	1994, 1996
Vietnam	1998, 2004

Source: Rommel C. Banlaoi, *Defence Policies in Southeast Asia: A Comparative Study* (Research Funded by the National Defence College of the Philippines, 2005).

Table 11.2 ASEAN regional forum annual security outlook, 2000–2005

ASEAN countries	2000	2001	2003	2004	2005
Brunei	–	–	X	–	–
Cambodia	–	X	X	–	–
Indonesia	–	–	–	X	X
Laos	–	–	–	–	–
Malaysia	–	X	–	–	–
Myanmar	–	–	–	–	–
Philippines	–	–	–	–	–
Singapore	X	X	X	X	X
Thailand	X	X	X	X	X
Vietnam	–	X	–	–	–

Source: ASEAN Secretariat, ASEAN Regional Forum Annual Security Outlook. Online, available at www.aseansec.org/

As a result of this limited transparency, the examination of defence industry in Southeast Asia becomes rather more difficult. Despite a strong clamour for defence transparency in the midst of globalization, many governments are still generally hesitant when it comes to disclosing substantive information about the size and scope of their defence industries because of various national security considerations.[1] The situation is more problematic in Southeast Asia because defence industry is associated inevitably with the issue of military build-up or force modernization that touches deeply the national sensitivities of states. While the globalization of defence industry has provided both challenges and opportunities in the region, it has failed thus far to promote greater transparency in this area, notwithstanding the fact that with the possible exception of Singapore, the region's defence industries have hardly been "secret."[2]

Most of the "globalization" issues in the defence industry are actually issues about "internationalization," "transnationalization" and "civilianization."[3] This chapter seeks to examine the impact of globalization on the current state of defence industry in Southeast Asia, and its impact on intra-ASEAN relations as well as ASEAN members' relations with major powers.

The state of defence industry in Southeast Asia

The concept of defence industry is used interchangeably with arms industry, military industry, and arms production. This chapter uses the concept of defence industry to refer to the "industry that is involved in the production of weapons, equipment, military devices and machinery, as well as raw materials that are needed for producing military products."[4] From the existing scholarly literature, there are two major theoretical traditions that inform the development of national defence industry: mercantilism and liberalism.[5]

Mercantilism conforms to the realist theory of international relations asserting that each state is responsible for its own defence in the midst of international anarchy. Force build-up is considered imperative to pursue autonomous defence. Mercantilism upholds the principle of autarchy, or self-sufficiency, in defence. It also asserts the interventionist role of state in the defence sector.

Liberalism, on the other hand, limits state intervention. Because defence is viewed as a non-excludable public good, it is considered prone to market failure. The role of the state is to correct the infirmities of the market by being the monopoly supplier of defence goods.[6] Liberalism also upholds the principle of free markets and comparative advantage. It asserts that "states abandon inefficient industries to move factors of production to their most productive uses."[7] It is therefore "uneconomic" to venture into defence-related production. Investing in defence industry is presumed to be a political rather than an economic decision.

In a study conducted by the Bureau of Industry and Security of the US Department of Commerce, defence industry in Southeast Asia is considered to be generally undeveloped.[8] The region's defence industrial base (DIB) remains generally weak and is considered to be in its lower stages of industrial development. The DIB refers to "the sectors of the economy that produce goods, services and technology for the defence establishment."[9] According to Keith Krause, there are 11 stages for the development of DIB. These are:

1   Capability to perform simple maintenance.
2   Overhaul, refurbishment, and rudimentary modification capabilities.
3   Assembly of imported components, simple licensed production.
4   Local production of components or raw materials.
5   Final assembly of less sophisticated weapons, some local component production.
6   Co-production or complete licensed production of less sophisticated weapons.
7   Limited research and development (R&D) improvements to local license-produced arms.
8   Limited independent production of less sophisticated weapons, limited production of more advanced weapons.
9   Independent R&D and production of less sophisticated weapons.
10 Independent R&D and production of advanced arms with foreign components.
11 Completely independent R&D and production.[10]

With the exception of Singapore, and to a certain extent Indonesia and Malaysia, ASEAN states still have embryonic national defence industries (Table 11.3). To use Krause's linear stages of defence industrial development, the defence industries of most countries in Southeast Asia may be located within stages 1–5 of defence industrialization. Malaysia was considered to have already reached stage 6, and Indonesia stage 7. Singapore has the most developed DIB, having reached stages 8–10.

In order to provide their armed forces with small arms, ammunition, light aircraft and small naval vessels, all founding members of ASEAN embarked on

Table 11.3 Defence industrial development in ASEAN countries

ASEAN countries	Defence industrial environment
Brunei	Undeveloped. It buys weapons primarily from UK and France.
Cambodia	Undeveloped. It buys arms primarily from China.
Indonesia	Developing. But it continues to rely on the procurement of weapons from US, Holland, Russia, Israel and France.
Laos	Undeveloped. It buys weapons from China, France and Russia.
Malaysia	Developing. Though it produces small arms and 105-mm artillery shells, it continues to rely on foreign sources, primarily from the United Kingdom. It also buys weapons from Russia and France.
Myanmar	Undeveloped. It even has a limited capability to purchase weapons. It buys weapons from Russia and barters some from North Korea. But China is its major sources of cheap weapons.
Philippines	Undeveloped. Though it has the Government Arsenal, it continues to import weapons primarily from the United States.
Singapore	Developed. It is considered as the role model of developing countries in the area of defence industry. It has a strong arms industry that caters to domestic and export needs. The Singapore Technologies (ST) is the holding company for most of its arms industry.
Thailand	Undeveloped. Although it produces some ammunition, it relies heavily on foreign sources for virtually all defence-related equipments. It buys weapons from the US, China and UK.
Vietnam	Undeveloped. It buys weapons from, France North Korea and Russia.

defence industrialization programmes in the 1970s.[11] With the exception of Brunei, the original ASEAN member states invested their scarce economic and political resources in such a way as to bolster their defence industries. Table 11.4 shows how major weapons production by the original ASEAN member states, from the early 1950s to mid-1980s, reflects that allocation of resources.

There were various reasons why these original ASEAN states decided to pursue national defence industrialization in the past. The general motivation was political, which was anchored in the mercantilist assumption that a state must increase self-reliance and reduce dependence on foreign arms suppliers. National defence industries were viewed as "political industries."[12] Though investing in a national defence industry might not be efficient from an economic perspective, having a strong national DIB was considered to be an important source of national pride and a vital symbol of national sovereignty.[13]

But, there was also an economic motivation. Local arms production was thought to be a major source of savings on meagre foreign exchange. Investing in national defence industry was viewed as an integral part of import-substitution industrialization that aimed to trigger local economic production and mitigate brain drain common to developing countries. It was also believed that national defence industrialization could lead to the cheaper unit cost of weapons, thus reducing defence expenditure outlay.[14] It was assumed that technological advances in national defence industry could spill over to civilian industry, which could, in turn, improve the country's long-term economic growth.[15] National defence industry was perceived as the fertile ground from which the seeds of a country's overall economic industrialization might then grow and flourish.

With the exception of Singapore, all national defence industrialization efforts in Southeast Asia in the 1970s failed to really take off because most countries in the region found it very expensive and economically inefficient to actually maintain a national defence industry.[16] ASEAN states had small national defence markets that could hardly sustain ambitious national defence industrialization. As Andrew Ross once observed, "Long-term domestic demand will prove inadequate to sustain national arms industries."[17]

Though there was a proposal to create a regional market for defence industries in ASEAN to reduce reliance on arms imports from foreign suppliers, ASEAN states had a problem of effectively harmonizing their respective defence policies to propel regional cooperation.[18] Issues associated with defence were also considered hard, sensitive political issues that ASEAN states were not very ready to discuss at that particular juncture. Even on the soft issue of a regional car industry, ASEAN states had a problem in really pooling their domestic resources.

ASEAN states were also constrained enormously by the imperatives of overall national economic development. Maintaining a national defence industry in the midst of a weak national economic industrial environment was very burdensome. The national economic industrial environment of many ASEAN states was not conducive for the establishment of a national defence industry. As stressed by Susan Willet, the production of "complex weapons platforms are well beyond the capacity of smaller Southeast Asian economies, whose industrial capacity infrastructure and skills base are insufficiently developed."[19] Though the region experienced remarkable economic growth in the 1980s as a result of foreign direct investment in local industries and export-oriented economic policies, the 1997 Asian financial crisis halted all economic momentum, which resulted in the failure to sustain the growth of the region. The financial crisis caused the disarray of Southeast Asian economies. The dire economic situation unleashed by the 1997 financial crisis had a tremendous impact on the region's quest for national defence industrialization. The economic crisis also affected the region's force modernization programmes.

Another reason why defence industrialization in Southeast Asia did not prosper was, essentially, the nature of their security threats. Security threats facing most ASEAN countries were predominantly internal rather than external.[20] Though ASEAN states have bilateral security tensions with one another,[21] they have formed the habit of managing inter-state conflict through peaceful means,[22] prompting experts to describe ASEAN as a nascent security community.[23]

Table 11.4 Major weapons production in the ASEAN countries (early 1950s to mid 1980s)

Country	Types of weapons	Country of origin	Years in production	Stage of production
Indonesia	NU-90 Belalang trainer	US	1959–1966	4
	PZL-104 Wilga (Gelatik) trainer	Poland	1964–1975	3
	LT-200 trainer	US	1974–1976	4
	CN-212 Aviocar transport	Spain	1976–1984	3
	BO-105 helicopter	West Germany	1976–1984	1
	SA-330 Puma helicopter	France	1981–1983	1
	AS-332 Super Puma helicopter	France	1983	1
	BK-117 helicopter	West Germany	1984	1
	CN-235 Transport	Spain	1984	2
	Bell Model 412 helicopter	US	1986	1
	Lapan XT-400 STOL transport	Indigenous	–	Prototype
	ST-200 trainer	Indigenous	–	Prototype
	NB-109 helicopter	West Germany	–	1 Planned
	Mawar class patrol craft	Indigenous	1966–1970	5
	LCM type landing craft	Indigenous	1976–1979	5
	Kupung class landing craft	US	1978–1980	4
	PB-57 type patrol craft	West Germany	1984	1
	Banai class patrol craft	Indigenous	1984	5
	60 ton patrol craft	West Germany	–	3 Planned
	60 ton patrol craft	West Germany	–	3 Planned
	Boeing jetfoil	US	–	3 Planned
Malaysia	RCP type landing craft	West Germany	Early 1970s	?
	Jerong class patrol craft	West Germany	1976–1977	?
	Jernih class landing craft	Indigenous	1977–1978	5
	Mutiara survey ship	West Germany	1978	?
	PZ class patrol craft	West Germany	1981–1983	?
	Vosper type 32 m patrol craft	Singapore	1982–1983	?
	Offshore patrol craft	South Korea	1985	?
Philippines	SF-260 MP COIN trainer	Italy	1973–1974	1
	BO-105 helicopter	West Germany	1974	1
	BN-2A Islander transport	Britain	1974	1
	XT-001 trainer	Italy	–	4 Prototype
	T-610 Cali jet trainer	US	–	4 Prototype
	28 ft speedboats	Indigenous	1971–1972	5
	Abra class patrol craft	Singapore	early 1970s	?
	Type 9209 patrol craft	Australia	1975–1976	3?
	46 ft patrol craft	Indigenous	1978–1979	5
	Mayon type patrol craft	Indigenous	1982	5
Singapore	S-211 jet trainer	Italy	?	1
	AS-332 Super Puma Helicopter	France	1985	1
	Ayer class patrol craft	Britain	1968–1969	?
	Type A/B patrol craft	Britain	1971	?
	Type 27M landing craft	Britain	1971–1975	?
	TNC-45 fast attack craft	West Germany	1974–1977	4?
	Bataan class patrol craft	Indigenous	1975	5
	Waspada class fact-attack craft	Britain	1978–1979	?

Table 11.4 Continued

Country	Types of weapons	Country of origin	Years in production	Stage of production
	Type 32 M landing craft	Britain	1979	?
	Swift class patrol craft	Australia	1980–1981	?
	Saba al Bahr landing craft	Indigenous	1981–1983	5
	PB-46 type patrol craft	Indigenous	1984	?
	PB 57 type patrol craft	West Germany	1984	?
Thailand	River patrol craft	?	1978–1979	?
	Suriya class support ship	Indigenous	1979	5
	Thalang type support ship	West Germany	1980	?
	Patrol craft	?	1980–1982	?
	Suk class support ship	Indigenous	1982	5
	Thong Kaeo class landing craft	Indigenous	1982–1983	5
	Sattahip class patrol craft	Indigenous	1984	5
	PS-700 class landing ship	France	–	? Planned
	PSMM-5 fast attack craft	South Korea	?	3?

Source: Andrew L. Ross, "The International Arms Trade, Arms Imports, and Local Defence Production in ASEAN," in Chandran Jeshurun (ed.), *Arms and Defence in Southeast Asia* (Singapore: Institute of Southeast Asian Studies, 1989), pp. 30–33.

The absence of "actual" external threats, however, did not spare ASEAN states from gargantuan internal security concerns like domestic political stability, economic development and social cohesion.[24] The national regime's quest for "security" encouraged some ASEAN states to pursue autonomous defence industrialization. The perceived security uncertainties associated with the rise of China in the twenty-first century[25] and the myriad of non-traditional security issues[26] confronting the region have encouraged ASEAN states to invest in national defence industry development. But investing in national defence industry in Southeast Asia was domestically unpopular because of the lack of national consensus on what really constitutes national security in individual ASEAN states.[27] This has prompted ASEAN states to exercise self-restraint in national defence industrialization and rely more on foreign procurement rather than the domestic production of heavy military weapons and equipment. Tim Huxley has explained candidly that Southeast Asia failed to develop a strong national defence industry because many regional states did not actually favour domestic defence production, arguing that "they viewed acquisition from abroad as opportunities for making commissions on defence contracts."[28]

Singapore

Among the countries of Southeast Asia, only Singapore has made it to the top 20 countries with the largest arms industries in the world (Table 11.5). Singapore Technologies (ST) is the country's pre-eminent defence firm, which has developed capabilities not only to produce arms for domestic but also for global market.[29]

Table 11.5 Top 20 countries with the largest arms industries in the World, 2002

Rank	Country	Source
1	USA	Government
2	France	Government
3	United Kingdom	Government
4	Germany	–
5	Japan	Government
6	Russia	Government
7	Canada	Private Industry
8	China	–
9	Israel	–
10	Italy	Government
11	South Korea	Government
12	Australia	Government
13	India	Government
14	Netherlands	Government
15	Singapore	–
16	South Africa	Government
17	Spain	Government
18	Sweden	Government/Private
19	Taiwan	Government
20	Ukraine	–

Source: Eamon Surry, "Transparency in the Arms Industry," *SIPRI Policy Paper*, no. 2 (Stockholm: Stockholm International Peace Research Institute, January 2006), p. 4.

Many factors led to the remarkable defence industrialization of Singapore. Its traumatic separation from Malaysia and the "survival crisis" of the government under the aegis of the People's Action Party (PAP) "implanted the seeds of the local defence industry."[30] Lee Kuan Yew's conscious determination to achieve self-sufficiency in arms for strategic and political reasons was a major driving force behind the rapid development of Singapore's defence industry. British withdrawal in the 1960s also left a very good infrastructure for the development of a national defence industry in Singapore.[31]

For Singapore, developing a strong domestic defence industry was a strong expression of national sovereignty. Developing a self-reliant defence industry was viewed as an important means to strengthen national political independence[32] and as an integral part of a country's defence capability.[33] Singapore's former Defence Minister Tony Tan even stressed that a strong national defence industry was the cutting edge of its armed forces.[34] Singapore, which invests an average of 4 per cent of its annual defence budget in research and development, "has gone beyond upgrading military hardware into designing and building its own armaments" through its national defence industry.[35] Though Minister Tan asserted that the primary aim of the defence industry was to provide for the domestic needs of its armed forces, he also stressed that if Singapore found buyers overseas, "then it is a bonus."[36]

But the primordial reason why Singapore vigorously pursued defence industrialization was strategic. With its vulnerable size and location, Singapore intentionally developed its national defence industry to shore up its deterrent capability. Singapore's notion of security is very much in the realist tradition that the idea of autonomous defence and the principle of balance-of-power are critical factors in its security calculations.[37]

Brunei, Indonesia, Malaysia, the Philippines and Thailand also decided to boost their national defence industries through indigenous production. But these countries were motivated largely by their pursuit of national prestige and domestic economic development. Limited financial capability even obstructs the implementation of their national defence industrialization programmes. In Indochina, Vietnam has the potential of developing its national defence industry because of the recent opening of its economy. But the rest of the Indochinese countries (Cambodia, Laos and Myanmar) do not show any clear signs of defence industrialization because of political and economic challenges.

Brunei

Brunei has expressed its intention to develop and sustain "a highly competitive defence industry."[38] It has adopted a "flexible defence industrial policy" towards that end. But it continues to rely on foreign defence procurement rather than domestic production. The Royal Brunei Technical Services Sdn Bhd is the government's main procurement arm. The United Kingdom is its main supplier of military weapons and equipment. Its failure to develop indigenous defence industry may be attributed to the fact that Brunei faces no internal security threat or actual external security threat that warrants a strong national defence industry. It also currently enjoys warm ties with its closest neighbours, Indonesia and Malaysia. As an oil exporting country, Brunei finds it economically more efficient to buy, rather than produce, for its weapons needs.

Indonesia

To lessen its dependence on foreign manufacturers and to reduce the use of scarce foreign currency reserves on weaponry, the Indonesian Parliament urged in 1978 the development of domestic defence industry.[39] Former President B.J. Habibie, who was then the Minister for Research and Technology, even proposed in the mid-1990s the modernization of Indonesian economy through defence industrialization.[40] Former Indonesian President Abdurrahman Wahid also proposed the breaking of his country's reliance on the United States for military equipment and urged instead the strengthening of domestic defence industry by expanding its network with international suppliers of military weapons and equipment. To sustain its national defence industrialization initiative, Indonesia hosted the Indo Defence Expo and Forum in 2004 and again in November 2006. The Indonesian Defence Industry has embraced the concept of cooperation and joint ventures in promoting the growth of the national defence industry sector.[41] Currently, Indonesia has the PT IPT Nusantura or Indonesia

Aerospace (IAe), PT PAL shipyard, PT Pindan ammunition firm and Perum Dahana explosive firm, which are all state-owned defence industries run by the Council of Ministers on Strategic Industries. But Indonesia's current economic situation is making it hard to really pursue indigenous defence industrialization. Despite these difficulties, Indonesia announced the commissioning of four locally built craft in October 2006: three PC-40 class patrol boats and a transport vessel.[42] In general, Indonesia continues to be dependent on external arms suppliers. In fact, Indonesia's domestic defence industry facilities are still inadequate for the repair of certain complex weapons systems.[43]

Malaysia

Malaysia's defence industry programme, on the other hand, aims to support materially its armed forces and to contribute to economic growth by reducing import dependency and increasing local employment.[44] The country's leading company in the defence industry is SME Group, which is under the Ministry of Finance. SME Aerospace assembles light aircraft while SME Aviation manufactures aircraft components. SME Ordnance produces small arms ammunitions. Private defence firms like the PSC Naval Dockyard Sdn Bhd constructs and assembles naval vessels. Interestingly, SME Aviation has produced Malaysia's first locally produced aircraft, the Swiss-designed MD3–160 trainer.[45] To transform Malaysia into a developed nation by 2020, former Malaysian Prime Minister Mahathir Mohamed launched his "2020 Vision" programme. Part of this programme is to build a strong DIB. In 1999, Malaysia formed the Malaysian Defence Industry Council (MDIC) for this purpose. Chaired by the Ministry of Defence, the MDIC aims to perform the following functions:

*   Assist in the promotion of the products and services of local defence industry companies.
*   Disseminate information to defence companies regarding offsets and transfer of technology.
*   Facilitate the dissemination of information relating to export opportunities and assist defence companies in accessing foreign markets.
*   Assist and coordinate representation of defence companies at relevant overseas trade shows, promotions and marketing activities.
*   To act as a clearinghouse for the exchange of information and to organize seminars on defence industry related issues.
*   Develop and build upon working relationships with appropriate foreign defence industry organizations.[46]

The Philippines

In the Philippines, the government has the Self-Reliance Defence Posture (SRDP) Programme to promote national defence industrialization under the aegis of the Government Arsenal (GA) of the Department of National Defence

(DND).[47] The SRDP encouraged the GA to enter into partnership with local manufacturers in the domestic production of small arms, radios, and assorted ammunition. One of the major accomplishments of the SRDP was the manufacture of the M-16A1 rifle under license from Colt Industries, an American company.[48] The implementation of SRDP "not only increased Philippine self-reliance, but also cut costs, provided jobs, and saved much-needed foreign-exchange funds."[49] But the country's unstable fiscal situation obstructs the successful implementation of this programme. Even its force modernization has been affected by the country's budgetary situation.[50] The Philippines is currently pursuing a defence reform programme called the Philippine Defence Reform (PDR), which aims to adopt a strategy-driven, multi-year defence planning system for purposes of upgrading its capability to respond to various security threats.[51] But the PDR does not cover the development of a national defence industry. In fact, the PDR even justified the continuing procurement of military weapons from the United States, which is the Philippine's main source of Excess Defence Articles (EDA), Foreign Military Sales (FMS), and International Military Education and Training (IMET). In December 2004, the DND released the Defence Planning Guidance (DPG) for 2006–2011.[52] The DPG urges the GA to continue its mandate "to design, manufacture, provide, and repair small arms, other weapons, ammunition for these weapons, and other munitions" for the Armed Forces of the Philippines (AFP) and the Philippine National Police (PNP). But limited national budget prevents GA from effectively fulfilling its mandated missions. As such, the Philippines must continue the importation of military weapons and equipment from the US.

Thailand

Thailand has a very small DIB. Some of its private industries have produced small defence items such as uniforms, storage batteries, glassware, preserved foods, some electronic devices, and certain pharmaceutical and chemical products.[53] But production of armaments only began in the late 1960s. The Thai armed forces have performed an in-house overhaul of military equipment and weapons. In the past, the Thai Air Force Directorate of Aeronautical Engineering has produced aircraft while the Royal Thai Army Research and Development Division built an anti-tank rocket.[54] With aid from the United States, Italy, and Japan, Thailand also attempted to strengthen its naval repair facilities in the 1980s, resulting in the production of a variety of naval vessels, including six fast coastal patrol boats.[55] But Thailand finds it very difficult to develop a strong national defence industry because it finds it cheaper to buy weapons and military equipment than to produce them.[56] Though Thailand is able to produce small arms ammunition, it relies heavily on external sources of military weapons, accessories, transportation and communication. The United States was Thailand's main source of defence equipment. But recently, Thailand has diversified its defence suppliers to include China, France, Germany, Italy, Spain, Israel, South Korea, and Austria.

Indochina

There is little available information on the state of defence industry in Cambodia, Laos and Myanmar. Only Vietnam has provided some general information on its defence industry but detailed information is still difficult to obtain. Vietnam has expressed its serious intention to develop a self-reliant defence industry. It regards national defence industrialization as an important component of overall economic industrialization.[57] It continues to rely, however, on foreign acquired advanced military technologies. Thus, "cooperative relations with foreign countries are being broadened so as to acquire advanced technologies with a view of bringing the Vietnamese defence industry to a higher level of development."[58] France, Russia, and North Korea are Vietnam's main sources of military weapons.

The globalization of defence production: impacts on Southeast Asia

With the exception of Singapore, which is motivated by strategic reasons in its defence industrialization, all countries in Southeast Asia have regarded defence industrialization as part of the overall scheme to industrialize their economies.[59] Their quest for national defence industrialization, however, has something of a "chicken and egg problem" since it also depends heavily on the overall state of the industrialization of their economies. The globalization of defence industry makes national defence industrialization in Southeast Asia an even more difficult venture because of the myriad factors that this chapter intends to discuss.

It has been observed that defence industry is "belatedly doing what its commercial counterparts have done for decades – gone global."[60] But the advent of globalization leads to the internationalization, transnationalization and civilianization of defence markets and corporate structures.[61] Globalization facilitates international, transnational and civilian collaboration in defence production.[62] The globalization of defence industry refers to a movement from autarky to an internationally oriented market in terms of research, production, management and sales of military technologies. The globalization of defence industry not only means exporting arms but also establishing design, production and marketing operations of military products in foreign locales.[63]

Some scholars identify three ways in which the globalization of defence industry exhibits itself:

1   Procurement of weapons from other countries and taking part in the production of these weapons (including granting of special permits, joint cooperation and development ventures, and compensation trade). Example: Joint production of F-16 fighter jets by the United States, Holland, Denmark and Norway.
2   Military cooperation packages covering weapons trade, production and maintenance, and joint military exercises between different countries. Example: India–Russia 10-year military cooperation agreement package.

3   Cross-border joint ventures, and joint research and development projects between and/or among nations. Example: Joint venture for the production of Eurofighter-2000 by Britain, Germany, Italy and Spain.[64]

According to Jurgen Brauer, there is a need to differentiate between internationalization and transnationalization when talking about globalization of defence production. Internationalization refers to a process where a defence firm "operates production facilities in a variety of countries that are relatively independent of one another."[65] Transnationalization, on the other hand, means "production and production facilities across countries [that] are interdependent with one another."[66] The globalization of defence industry exhibits both the processes of internationalization and transnationalization. But there is another process defining the globalization of defence industry – the process of civilianization. It means that the civilian sector becomes increasingly involved in the global defence production.

Impact on Southeast Asia's defence spending and procurement

The globalization of the defence industry coincided with the dramatic fall in world defence spending by about one-third in real terms from 1989 to 1996 – from around US$1,300 billion to US$800 billion.[67] Out of 100 of the world's largest defence companies in 1990, only 24 companies remained in existence by 1998 and those that remained "grew larger through a series of consolidating mergers."[68] But by 2005, there was a rise in world defence spending as countries readjusted their security policies in the context of the global war on terrorism.

Prior to the 1997 Asian financial crisis, ASEAN countries (particularly Indonesia, Malaysia, Philippines, Singapore and Thailand) were involved in major upgrades of their armed forces, which warranted increased defence spending. Asian countries spent US$165 billion on their armed forces each year before the crisis occurred, nearly double their 1990 outlays and some 20 per cent of global defence spending.[69] In 1996, Asians accounted for almost 50 per cent of all worldwide purchases of large conventional weapons like combat aircraft, armour, ships, and submarines.[70]

But this increased defence spending prior to the 1997 crisis did not result in the development of a strong national defence industry. Defence spending only aimed at arms acquisition, rather than indigenous defence industrialization. Arms acquisition even before the financial crisis was built on a fairly small base.[71] The 1997 Asian financial crisis would bring arms acquisition by ASEAN states to a grinding halt.

Though defence spending in Southeast Asia has bounced back from massive defence cuts following the regional financial crisis,[72] there is no increased funding for the development of domestic industry in the region. Domestic defence industry facilities in ASEAN countries remain inadequate to pursue self-sufficiency in arms production. The renewed interests in defence spending are not really meant to develop national defence industry but primarily to

purchase weapons from international sources, which would be cheaper than producing them domestically. With a stronger purchasing power, the globalization
of defence industry has given some ASEAN states wider windows to shop for
arms rather than to produce them. In other words, global defence production has
served to discourage indigenous defence production in Southeast Asia.

Table 11.6 shows percentage changes in ASEAN defence spending from year
to year, while Table 11.7 shows ASEAN defence spending as a percentage of
Gross Domestic Product (GDP) after the 1997 Asian financial crisis. Tables 11.6
and 11.7 show that defence spending in ASEAN has increased, especially after
the 9/11 terrorist attacks on the United States in 2001.

After 9/11, most ASEAN countries have justified the increase in their defence
spending to enhance their capabilities to fight terrorism. Strangely, some of the
weapon systems being procured by ASEAN are externally oriented, which
according to one analyst "have no other role than in interstate warfare."[73]
Among these weapons are fighter aircraft, naval combatant vessels and submarines.[74] Despite that, none of these weapons are considered destabilizing.

Because defence spending has increased in Southeast Asia, particularly in the
aftermath of 9/11, the major impact of the globalization of defence industry has
been to turn the region into one of the prime markets for defence exports of
developed countries. As shown in Table 11.8, two of the top ten leading recipients of arms deliveries to developing nations are ASEAN countries (Malaysia
and Indonesia).

It was projected that defence exports to Asia would rise to $70 billion
between 2002 and 2006.[75] Even Singapore, the only ASEAN country with a very
strong DIB, now prefers to procure rather than to produce what it needs for its
defence. As a result of the globalization of defence industries, existing domestic
defence industries in Southeast Asia, particularly in Singapore, are opening their
firms to foreign investors in order to build equity and market links with
developed nations for capital, technology, and markets.[76]

Table 11.6 Annual percentage changes in ASEAN defence spending, 1998–2003

Countries	1998	1999	2000	2001	2002	2003
Brunei	10.6	−18.1	−25.1	3.6	−5.5	−
Cambodia	−6.5	−5.4	−3.3	−11.0	−5.8	−1.8
Indonesia	−21.3	−17.6	30.1	5.1	5.5	−
Laos	−34.3	47.7	−1.1	8.5	−	−
Malaysia	−26.5	35.3	−9.2	24.5	13.7	6.6
Myanmar	−17.7	−0.8	34.9	−	−	−
Philippines	−1.7	−2.0	5.3	−6.3	13.2	1.5
Singapore	13.2	1.9	−3.3	2.4	5.5	1.2
Thailand	−11.7	−12.7	−12.6	−3.8	1.9	1.2
Vietnam	−	−	−	−	−	−

Source: Robert Hartfiel and Brian Job, "Raising the Risks of War; Defence Spending Trends and
Competitive Arms Processes in East Asia," *Working Paper*, no. 44 (March 2005).

Table 11.7 Defence spending in ASEAN countries as a percentage of GDP, 1998–2002

Countries	1998	1999	2000	2001	2002
Brunei	9.4	−7.3	−6.5	−7.6	7.0
Cambodia	4.2	3.8	3.5	3.0	−2.7
Indonesia	1.1	0.9	1.1	1.1	1.2
Laos	1.6	2.2	2.0	2.1	–
Malaysia	1.6	2.1	1.7	2.2	2.4
Myanmar	2.3	2.0	2.1	–	–
Philippines	1.2	1.1	1.1	1.0	1.0
Singapore	5.5	5.5	4.7	5.1	5.2
Thailand	2.1	1.8	1.5	1.4	1.4
Vietnam	–	–	–	–	7.7

Source: Robert Hartfiel and Brian Job, "Raising the Risks of War; Defence Spending Trends and Competitive Arms Processes in East Asia," *Working Paper*, no. 44 (March 2005).

In short, the globalization of defence industry challenges the indigenization of defence industry in Southeast Asia. The globalization of defence industry makes the indigenization of defence production less motivating, and the rise of defence industry globalization has, in many instances, brought about the rapid decline of defence industry indigenization. As Richard Bitzinger has pointed out, the current trend towards the globalization of defence industry is increasingly replacing previous trends toward the indigenization of defence industry.[77] Susan Willet has also underscored the fact that globalized arms production "is increasingly supplementing or even replacing wholly indigenous weapons production and more traditional forms of weapon-systems transfers."[78] As a result of globalization, Southeast Asian countries have become more reliant on foreign suppliers to meet the military equipment needs of their defence establishments.[79]

Table 11.8 Arms deliveries to developing nations in 2003: the leading recipients (in millions of current US dollars)

Rank	Recipient	Deliveries value (2003)
1	Saudi Arabia	5,800
2	Egypt	2,100
3	India	2,000
4	Israel	1,900
5	China	1,000
6	South Korea	700
7	Malaysia	600
8	Taiwan	500
9	Kuwait	300
10	Indonesia	300

Source: Richard F. Grimmett, "Conventional Arms Transfers to Developing Nations: 1996–2003." *CRS Report for Congress* (Washington DC: Congressional Research Service, 26 August 2004).

Impact on intra-ASEAN relations

As a result of the globalization of defence production, ASEAN states have also explored the possibility of regional defence industrial collaboration.[80] Malaysia and Singapore had even made formal agreements for this purpose. However, this kind of initiative failed to really materialize because of mutual suspicions on matters impinging upon national defence and security issues in the region.[81] Thus, defence industrial cooperation in Southeast Asia "remained a no-go area for reasons of security as well as national prestige."[82]

But one important consequence of the globalization of defence industries is that it has allowed ASEAN states to "shift away from traditional, single-country patterns of weapons production towards a more transnational pattern of research, development, production and marketing of military equipment."[83] It has also allowed ASEAN states to shop abroad for, rather than produce, their own conventional weapons. This trend has security implications for intra-ASEAN relations, since more prosperous states will have a broader range of international sources from which to acquire foreign weapons that could, in turn, heighten the insecurities of less prosperous states in the region.

Though the primary motivation behind defence acquisition in most Southeast Asian countries has been internal security, there has been an external dimension as well. In the wake of the Asian financial crisis, arms build-ups have been renewed by some states in order to address perceived threats emanating from their immediate neighbours,[84] particularly in the context of bilateral tensions in post-Cold War ASEAN.[85] Thailand's aborted plan to acquire F/A-18 Hornets from the US was a reaction to Malaysia's decision to purchase the same aircraft together with Russian MiG-29 Fulcrums.[86] Myanmar's interest in acquiring F-7M Airguard fighter-bomber from China raised some concerns in Thailand.[87] Myanmar's purchase of a squadron of ten MiG-29 jetfighters from Russia aimed to counter Thailand's F-16 jet fighters.[88] The acquisition of F-16 combat aircraft by Singapore, Indonesia and Thailand reflected a determination not to be left behind their neighbours in Southeast Asia.[89] The plan of the Philippines to acquire 24 fighter jets, particularly F/A-18 Hornet and F-16 from the US as well as the Mirage 200 and MiG-29 from Russia has caused some security concerns in the region, especially in Malaysia and Vietnam. Thus, defence procurement and weapons acquisition in ASEAN have tended to exacerbate the region's security dilemma. Military acquisitions in one ASEAN state have triggered counter-acquisitions in other ASEAN states, which according to Alan Collins, "provide a tangible manifestation of security dilemma" in Southeast Asia.[90]

To overcome intra-ASEAN security dilemmas and to improve the management of inter-state conflicts in Southeast Asia, ASEAN leaders met in Bali, Indonesia on 7–8 October 2006 where they signed the ASEAN Concord II adopting the concept of ASEAN Security Community (ASC) to bring security cooperation in the region to a higher plane. The ASC affirms the ASEAN way of the peaceful settlement of disputes and non-interference in the domestic affairs of member states. In other words, the ASC upholds the ASEAN principle of renouncing the threat or use of force to settle differences and to manage disputes.

Impact on ASEAN relations with major powers

The globalization of defence industry gives major powers greater competitive advantage in the global production of military weapons and equipment. In fact, major powers continue to dominate the top 20 countries with the largest arms industries in the world. Developing countries that ventured into national defence industrialization still had to import defence materials from major powers and this truly affects the attainment of self-reliant defence industrialization. Though some countries in Southeast Asia attempted to produce small arms to meet their domestic needs, arms production had long been the monopoly of great powers.[91] ASEAN countries' strong orientation towards their former colonial powers even prevented the development of a truly self-reliant domestic defence industry. As Andrew Ross puts it:

> The ASEAN countries tended to acquire arms primarily from their former colonial powers during the 1950s and 1960s. Long accustomed to being commanded, trained, financed, and equipped by Western colonial powers, ASEAN militaries, as most militaries in the developing world, were apparently reluctant to sever the close corporate, and even personal, ties that had bound core and peripheral militaries under colonialism. They, therefore, turned to the former colonial powers for arms....[92]

Despite the colonial baggage, the globalization of defence industry has encouraged some ASEAN states to establish partnership with some major powers in this area. Indonesia, Malaysia, and Singapore began making deals with major powers in defence industrial production, particularly in the shipbuilding and aviation industries. The Philippines has also offered its shipbuilding facilities for American defence contractors.

Among the major powers, the US continues to be the main source of military technology transfers to Southeast Asia. The US has been leading in arms transfer agreements worldwide. In 2004 alone, the US ranked first in the value of all arms deliveries worldwide, making nearly $18.6 billion in such deliveries and representing 54.4 per cent of total arms deliveries worldwide.[93] It is important to note that as a result of the globalization of defence industry, ASEAN countries are exploring the prospect of diversifying their sources of military technologies from other major powers like Russia and China.

During the Cold War, Russian arms exports, through the former Soviet Union, were only concentrated in "likeminded" Southeast Asian states such as Cambodia, Laos, Myanmar and Vietnam. After the Cold War, Russia began exporting arms to other states like Indonesia, Malaysia and Thailand. Studies show that, from 2001–2004, Russia ranked second among all arms suppliers to developing countries, making $21.7 billion in agreements.[94]

Prior to the East Timor Crisis, the US was main supplier of military weapons and equipment to Indonesia. With the US arms embargo, Indonesia negotiated for the delivery of Russian arms in 1997. Indonesia ordered 12 Su-30 fighters from Russia. But the 1997 Asian financial crisis thwarted the transaction. In 2003, Russia and Indonesia renewed their arms transaction, which resulted in the signing of a contract for the delivery of two Su-27SK fighters, two Su-30MK aircrafts and two Mi-35 combat helicopters.[95] In 2004, Indonesia expressed an interest in purchasing eight more Russian fighters, but the tsunami disaster later that year curtailed the purchase.

In 1994, Russia delivered 18 MiG–29SE/UB fighters to Malaysia, whose major arms supplier was the United Kingdom.[96] In 2003, Malaysia bought 18 Su-30MKM multipurpose aircraft from Russia. Vietnam has also renewed its longstanding role as a market for Russian arms exports. Vietnam has taken delivery of six SU-27 fighter aircraft from Russia. Vietnam is also completing the structure of its Naval Forces with Russian military equipment.[97] In 1999, Russia delivered two (Tarantul-2 class) missile boats. In 2003, Vietnam purchased two large (Molinya-class) Russian missile boats. In 1996, the Philippines expressed its intention to buy Russian MiG-19s. All these transactions are indicative of the Russian intention to penetrate the Southeast Asian arms market and Southeast Asian interests to buy Russian military weapons and equipment.[98] A study even shows the extent to which Russia's arms sales efforts seem focused on Southeast Asia.[99]

China, on the other hand, has been pursuing self-sufficiency in arms production since 1949. With China's opening to the world in 1979, it has accelerated the development of its defence industry. At present, the Chinese defence industry plays a major role in modernizing the People's Liberation Army (PLA).[100] China is not only producing arms to meet its domestic needs. It is also manufacturing weapons to sell abroad. It is not, however, easy to describe China's arms sales because it does not publish any information about arms transfers abroad and has not submitted any data to the United Nations Register on Conventional Arms in the last several years. According to the study made by Amnesty International in June 2006, China's arms exports have reached an excess of US$1 billion a year.[101] Another study shows that the value of China's arms transfers to developing nations has averaged around US$600 billion annually.[102] It has been reported that China is fast emerging as one of the world's biggest arms exporters to developing nations.[103] In Southeast Asia, Indochinese states such as Cambodia, Laos, and Myanmar have been the top countries acquiring weapons from China.[104]

In Cambodia, China used to supply massive arms to the Khmer Rouge. But with the formation of a new coalition government in 1993, China ceased its arms transfers to the Khmer Rouge in order to forge defence ties with the post-1993 Cambodian government. In July 2000, Cambodia released its defence White Paper, claiming that it received military engineering and transportation equipment from China. Laos has also been identified as a recipient of China's military trade. In 1991, Laos even requested China to provide the Laotian armed forces with spare parts, assistance in the maintenance of weapons systems, training support, and supplies of ammunition.[105] In 2001, Laos and China signed a defence agreement in which China promised to provide equipment, weapons and ammunition to Laos.[106] Despite their strategic differences, Vietnam and China have also engaged in arms transfers. It was reported that China supplied Vietnam with weapons and other military equipment between 1992 and 1993. Yet among the countries of Indochina, or what S.D. Muni calls "the New ASEAN," China's defence cooperation with Myanmar has been the most extensive and varied.[107] China supplied Myanmar with an assortment of armaments that included F-7 fighter planes, Jianghu frigates, armoured personnel carriers, and main battle tanks. China did not supply these weapons as grants but as purchases.[108]

As part of its desire to strengthen defence ties with Southeast Asian countries as a whole, China has also explored the possibility of exporting arms and military equipment to the original ASEAN countries. The Philippines received military engineering equipment (six bulldozers and six graders) from China in 2005 as part of their defence cooperation agreements. China has even expressed an intention to assist the Philippines in its force modernization programme and to conduct joint military exercises in the maritime area, although the American factor is a major constraint in this plan. China has also established defence ties with Thailand with the intention of selling more arms and military equipment.[109] From the early 1980s into the late 1990s, Thailand received conventional weapons from China, which included items such as Type-59 and Type-60 main battle tanks, 130-mm towed artillery, armoured personnel carriers, multiple launch rocket systems, HQ-2B and HN-5A surface-to-air missiles, Jianghu-class frigates and C-801 anti-shipping missiles.[110]

Concluding statement

With exception of Singapore, and to a certain extent Indonesia and Malaysia, ASEAN countries have failed to develop their domestic defence industries because they prefer to purchase rather than to produce arms and military equipment. Moreover, the globalization of defence production is making the indigenization of defence industry less economically attractive. Though ASEAN countries have increased their defence spending in the aftermath of 9/11, the spending was used to purchase externally produced weapons rather than to manufacture arms for the development of national defence industries. Rather than being suppliers of weapons, ASEAN countries continue to be arms recipients, making ASEAN an important market for global defence producers. The persistent lack of transparency in Asian defence procurement is even resurrecting fears that arms purchases could have a destabilizing effect.[111] As one analyst asserts, "Without more white papers and open-ended discussions about what countries are buying and why, the situation will always be tense and riddled with suspicion."[112] Even amongst themselves, Southeast Asian countries are suspicious of one another's defence spending patterns.

Southeast Asian countries have responded to the globalization of defence industry in various ways. Globalization has helped ASEAN countries to diversify their sources of military weapons and equipment. Beyond the US, ASEAN countries are now making deals with other major powers like China and Russia as sources of arms acquisition. Globalization has also provided ASEAN with opportunities to pursue regional cooperation in defence production, although efforts will have to be sustained in order to realize this. Despite that, the globalization of defence industry has offered ASEAN states a golden opportunity to encourage foreign investors. ASEAN states may invite foreign defence industries to invest in the production of military products. Cheap labour and raw materials could encourage international defence industry to invest in defence industrial production. Singapore, for example, has utilized tax incentives to attract foreign firms to invest in the aerospace sector. To expand their embryonic DIB, Thailand and Malaysia have adopted aggressive offset policies through skills training and infrastructure developments.[113]

It is clear that defence industry touches the sensitivities of ASEAN states. But in order to face the challenges and opportunities of defence industry globalization, there is little doubt that ASEAN states will have to overcome their sensitivities on issues related to defence and security by promoting greater transparency in these areas.

Notes

* This chapter represents the personal view of the author and not the official position of the Department of National Defence, the National Defence College of the Philippines or any agency of the Philippine government. The author is grateful to Dr. Tim Huxley for the valuable comments on the earlier version of this chapter.

1 For an excellent discussion on this issue, see Eamon Surry, "Transparency in the Arms Industry," *SIPRI Policy Paper*, No. 2 (Stockholm: Stockholm International Peace Research Institute, January 2006).

2 Tim Huxley, "Discussion on Globalization's Impact on Defence Industry in Southeast Asia" delivered at the International Conference on Globalization and National Security organized by the Institute of Defence and Strategic Studies (IDSS) held at The Sentosa Resort and Spa, 2 Bukit Manis Road, Singapore, on 16 March 2006.

3 John Lovering, "The Defence Industry as a Paradigmatic Case of Actually Existing Globalization" in Judith Reppy (ed.), The Place of the Defence Industry in National Systems of Innovation (Cornell: Peace and Studies Programme, Cornell University, 2000).

4 Gong Chuanzhou and Ali Hua, "The Development of China's National Defence Industry in the Globalization Process" (Artillery Institute of the People's Liberation Army, Nanjing Army Command Institute, 15 May 2001), p. 1.

5 These two major theoretical traditions are excellently described in Adrian Kuah and Bernard Loo, "Examining the Defence Industrialization – Economic Growth Relationship: The Case of Singapore," *IDSS Working Paper*, no. 70 (Singapore: Institute of Defence and Strategic Studies, 2004).

6 Ibid., p. 7.

7 Ethan B. Kapstein, *The Political Economy of National Security: A Global Perspective* (New York: McGraw Hill, 1992), p. 91.

8 See US Department of Commerce, Pacific Rim Diversification and Defence Market

Guide, online, available at www.bis.doc.gov/DefenceIndustrialBaseProgrammes/ OSIES/ExportMarketGuides/PacRimMktGuideIndex.html accessed on 3 March 2006.

9 Adrian Kuah, "Globalization and Singapore's Defence Industrial Base," *IDSS Commentaries* (14 January 2004), p. 1.

10 Keith Krause, *Arms and the State: Patterns of Military Production and Trade* (Cambridge: Cambridge University Press, 1992).

11 Andrew L. Ross, "The International Arms Trade, Arms Imports, and Local Defence Production in ASEAN," in Chandran Jeshurun (ed.), *Arms and Defence in Southeast Asia* (Singapore: Institute of Southeast Asian Studies, 1989), p. 29.

12 Bilveer Singh, "Singapore's Defence Industries," *Canberra Papers on Strategy and Defence*, no. 70 (Canberra: Strategic and Defence Studies Centre, Australia National University, 1990), p. 38.

13 Kuah and Loo, "Examining the Defence Industrialization – Economic Growth Relationship: The Case of Singapore," p. 10.

14 Bilveer Singh and Kwa Chong Guan, "The Singapore Defence Industries: Motivations, Organization, and Impact" in Chandran Jeshurun (ed.), *Arms and Defence in Southeast Asia* (Singapore: Institute of Southeast Asian Studies, 1989), p. 98.

15 Todd Sandler and Keith Hartley, *The Economics of Defence* (Cambridge: Cambridge University Press, 1995).

16 For brief analysis of the dilemma of developing states in the area of arms industry, see Luis Bitencourt, "The Problems of Defence Industrialization for Developing States" in Sverre Lodgaard and Robert Pfaltzgraft (eds), *Arms and Technology Transfers: Security and Economic Considerations Among Importing and Exporting States* (Geneva and New York: United Nations, 1995), pp. 167–176.

17 Ross, "The International Arms Trade, Arms Imports, and Local Defence Production in ASEAN," p. 35.

18 For detailed discussion, see Rommel C. Banlaoi, *Defence Policies in Southeast Asia: A Comparative Study* (A research funded by the National Defence College of the Philippines, 2005).

19 Susan Willett, "East Asia's Changing Defence Industry," *Survival*, vol. 39, no. 3 (Autumn 1997), p. 118.

20 See Muthiah Alagappa (ed.), *Asian Security Practice: Material and Ideational Influences* (Stanford: Stanford University Press, 1998).

21 N. Ganesan, *Bilateral Tension in the Post-Cold War ASEAN* (Singapore: Institute of Southeast Asian Studies, 1999).

22 See Amitav Acharya, "Collective Identity and Conflict Management in Southeast Asia" in Emanuel Adler and Michael Barnett (eds), *Security Communities* (Cambridge, UK: Cambridge University Press, 1998), pp. 198–227.

23 See Amitav Acharya, "A Regional Security Community in Southeast Asia?" *Journal of Strategic Studies*, vol. 18, no. 3 (September 1995), pp. 175–200 and Yuen Foong Khong, "ASEAN and the Southeast Asian Security Complex" in David A. Lake and Patrick M. Morgan (eds), *Regional Orders: Building Security in a New World* (Pennsylvania: The Pennsylvania University Press, 1997), pp. 318–342.

24 See David Wright-Neville, "Southeast Asian Security Challenges" in Robert Ayson and Desmond Ball (eds), *Strategy and Security in the Asia Pacific* (New South Wales: Allen & Unwin, 2006), pp. 210–225.

25 See Rommel C. Banlaoi, "Southeast Asian Perspectives on the Rise of China: Regional Security After 9/11," *Parameters*, vol. 33, no. 2 (Summer 2003), pp. 98–107.

26 See Andrew Tan and J.D. Kenneth Boutin (eds), *Non-Traditional Security Issues in Southeast Asia* (Singapore: Institute of Defence and Strategic Studies, 2001).

27 See Alan Collins, *Security and Southeast Asia: Domestic, Regional and Global Issues* (Singapore: Institute for Southeast Asian Studies, 2003). Also see Alan

Collins, *The Security Dilemmas of Southeast Asia* (Singapore: Institute for Southeast Asian Studies, 2000).
28 Huxley, "Discussion on Globalization's Impact on Defence Industry in Southeast Asia," op. cit.
29 Kuah and Loo, "Examining the Defence Industrialization – Economic Growth Relationship: The Case of Singapore," p. 17.
30 Singh, "Singapore's Defence Industries," p. 38.
31 Huxley, "Discussion on Globalization's Impact on Defence Industry in Southeast Asia," op. cit.
32 Richard Bitzinger, "Towards a Brave New Arms Industry?" *Adelphi Paper*, No. 356 (London: International Institute for Strategic Studies, 2003), p. 13.
33 Singh and Kwa, "The Singapore Defence Industries: Motivations, Organization, and Impact," p. 96.
34 "Defence Technology To Be Singapore's Cutting Edge: Defence Minister," *Agence France Presse* (6 September 2000).
35 Ibid.
36 Ibid.
37 Narayanan Ganesan, "Singapore: Realist Cum Trading State" in Muthiah Alagappa (ed.), *Asian Security Practice: Material and Ideational Influences*, (Palo Alto, CA: Stanford University Press, 1998), p. 579.
38 Ministry of Defence, *Brunei Darussalam Defence White Paper 2004: Defending the Nation's Sovereignty* (Brunei Darussalam: Ministry of Defence, 2004), p. 42.
39 US Library of Congress Country Study, "Indonesia Defence Spending and Industry." Online, available at lcweb2.loc.gov/cgi-bin/query/r?frd/cstdy:@field(DOCID+id0174). Accessed on 4 November 2006.
40 Willett, "East Asia's Changing Defence Industry," p. 112.
41 See "Indo Defence 2008 Expo & Forum." Online, available at www.indo defence.com/.
42 Jon Grevatt, "Indonesian Navy Commission Four Ships," *Jane's Defence Industry* (20 October 2006).
43 US Library of Congress Country Study, "Indonesia Defense Spending and Defense Industry." Online, available at www.photius.com/countries/indonesia/economy/indonesia_economy_defense_spending_and~56.html accessed on 4 November 2006.
44 Anil R. Pustam, "SE Asian Defence Industry: Quo Vadis?" *Military Technology* (March–April 2002), p. 74.
45 Ibid.
46 See Malaysian Defence Industry Council. Online, available at mdic.mod.gov.my/mdic/english/eng_mdic.html.
47 For a good background on the SRDP, see Carolina G. Hernandez, "Arms Procurement and Production Policies in the Philippines" in Chandran Jeshurun (ed.), *Arms and Defence in Southeast Asia* (Singapore: Institute of Southeast Asian Studies, 1989), p. 125–151.
48 US Library of Congress Country Study, "Philippine Defence Spending and Industry." Online, available at lcweb2.loc.gov/cgi-bin/query/r?frd/cstdy:@field(DOCID+ph0157). Accessed on 4 November 2006.
49 Ibid.
50 For an excellent analysis of force modernization programme in the Philippines, see Renato Cruz De Castro, "Societal Forces of Military Doctrine and Posture: The Case of the AFP Modernization Programme, 1991–2003," in Amitav Acharya and Lee Lai To (eds), *Asia in the New Millennium* (Singapore: Marshall Cavendish Academic, 2004), pp. 195–228.
51 For more discussion on the PDR, see "Philippine Defence Reform." Online, available at www.dnd.gov.ph/. For a constructive critic of the PDR, see Rommel C.

Banlaoi, "Security Sector Governance in the Philippines" (paper presented to the Workshop on the Challenges of Security Sector Governance in Southeast Asia organized by the Friedrich Ebert-Stiftung, Geneva Centre for the Democratic Control of the Armed Forces and the Institute of Defence and Strategic Studies at Hotel Plaza Parkroyal, Singapore, on 14–15 February 2006).

52 Department of National Defence, *Defence Planning Guidance 2006–2011* (Quezon City: Office of the Secretary of National Defence, 2004).

53 US Library of Congress Country Study, "Thailand Domestic Defence Industry." Online, available at lcweb2.loc.gov/cgi-bin/query/r?frd/cstdy:@field(DOCID+th0141). Accessed on 4 November 2006.

54 Pustam, "SE Asian Defence Industry: Quo Vadis?" p. 74.

55 "Thailand Domestic Defence Industry," op. cit.

56 Surachart Bamrungsuk, "Role of the Royal Thai Armed Forces in the New Century and Military Self-Reliance" (paper delivered in the workshop Military Reform: Military Self-Reliance, Defence Industry and Cooperation between Public and Private Sectors, sponsored by Friedrich Naumann Foundation Thailand Project and the Thai Senate Standing Committee on Military Affairs at the Shangri-La Hotel, Bangkok on 14 December 2005).

57 Ministry of Defence, *Vietnam's National Defence in the Early Years of the 21st Century* (Hanoi: Ministry of Defence, 2004), p. 67.

58 Ibid.

59 Willett, "East Asia's Changing Defence Industry," p. 112.

60 Ann Markussen, "Should We Welcome a Transnational Defence Industry?" in Judith Reppy (ed.), *The Place of Defence Industry in National Systems of Innovation* (Cornell: Peace Studies Programme, Cornell University, 2000).

61 K. Hayward, "The Globalization of Defence Industries," *Survival*, vol. 43, no. 2 (June 2001), pp. 115–132.

62 See David Gold, "The Internationalization of Military Production" in Manas Chatterji, Jacques Fontanel and Akira Hattori (eds.), *Arms Spending, Development and Security* (New Delhi: Ashish Publishing House, 1995), pp. 105–114.

63 Markussen, "Should We Welcome a Transnational Defence Industry?" op. cit.

64 Gong and Ali, "The Development of China's National Defence Industry in the Globalization Process," p. 2.

65 Jurgen Brauer, "The Arms Industry in the Developing Nations: History and Post-Cold War Assessment" (paper presented at the conference on Military Expenditures in Developing and Emerging Nations at Middlesex University, London on 13–14 March 1998).

66 Ibid., p. 12.

67 *The Defence Industry in the 21st Century* (United Kingdom: Pricewaterhouse Coopers Aerospace and Defence Leader, 2005).

68 Ibid., p. 11.

69 Sheldon W. Simon, *The Economic Crisis and ASEAN States' Security* (Carlisle, PA: Strategic Studies Institute of the US Army War College, 1998), p. 8.

70 Ibid.

71 Russ Swinnerton, "The Strategic Environment and Arms Acquisitions in South-East Asia," in Bates Gill and J.N. Mak (eds), *Arms, Transparency and Security in South-East Asia* (Oxford: Oxford University Press and Stockholm International Peace Research Institute, 1997), p. 35.

72 "Defence Spending in Southeast Asia is Bouncing Back," *Voice of America*. Online, available at voanews.com/Korean/archive/2002–07/a-2002–07–19–19–1.cfm. Accessed on 2 February 2006.

73 Robert Hartfiel and Brian Job, "Raising the Risks of War; Defence Spending Trends and Competitive Arms Processes in East Asia," *Working Paper*, no. 44 (March 2005), p. 14.

74 Ibid.
75 "War and Terror Send Defence Spending Soaring: Mahathir," *Arab News*. Online, available at www.arabnews.com/?page=4&section=0&article=32868&d=1&m=10&y= 2003. Accessed on 2 February 2006.
76 Martin Broek, "Arms are not Tomatoes, Arms Production and Trade among the ASEM Countries" in Paul Scannell and Brid Brennan (eds), *Asia Europe Cross-points* (Amsterdam: Transnational Institute, September 2002).
77 Richard Bitzinger, "The Globalization of the Arms Industry: The Next Proliferation Challenge," *International Security*, vol. 19, no. 2 (Autumn 1994).
78 Willet, "East Asia's Changing Defence Industry," p. 121.
79 Kuah, "Globalization and Singapore's Defence Industrial Base," p. 1.
80 Huxley, "Discussion on Globalization's Impact on Defence Industry in Southeast Asia," op. cit.
81 See *Globalization and Defence* (report organized by the Institute of Defence and Strategic Studies at Sentosa Resort Spa, Singapore on 15–16 March 2006), p. 23.
82 Ibid.
83 Willett, "East Asia's Changing Defence Industry," p. 121.
84 Derek Da Cunha, "Renewed Military Buildups Post Asian Crisis: The Effect on Two Key Southeast Asian Bilateral Military Balances," *International Politics and Security Issues*, no. 3 (Singapore: Institute of Southeast Asian Studies, 2001).
85 N. Ganesan, *Bilateral Tension in the Post-Cold War ASEAN*, op. cit.
86 Da Cunha, "Renewed Military Buildups Post Asian Crisis," p. 6.
87 Ibid., p. 8.
88 Andrew Tan, "Force Modernization Trends in Southeast Asia," *IDSS Working Paper*, no. 59 (Singapore: Institute of Defence and Strategic Studies, 2004), p. 19.
89 Ibid., p. 4.
90 Collins, *The Security Dilemmas of Southeast Asia*, p. 107.
91 Singh and Kwa, "The Singapore Defence Industries: Motivations, Organization, and Impact," pp. 96–97.
92 Singh, "Singapore's Defence Industries," p. 17.
93 Richard Grimmet, "Conventional Arms Transfers to Developing Nations, 1997–2004," *CRS Report for Congress* (29 August 2005), p. 5.
94 Ibid., p. 7.
95 Dmitry Vasiliev, "Russian Arms Trade with Southeast Asia and the Republic of Korea," *Moscow Defense Brief* (June 2006).
96 Ibid.
97 Ibid.
98 See Alexander A. Sergounin and Sergey V. Subbotin, *Russian Arms Transfers to East Asia in the 1990s* (Oxford: Stockholm International Peace Research Institute, 1999).
99 Grimmet, "Conventional Arms Transfers to Developing Nations, 1997–2004," p. 8.
100 Evan Medeiros, "Analyzing China's Defence Industries and the Implications for China's Military Modernization" (testimony presented to the US–China Economic and Security Review Commission on 6 February 2004).
101 Amnesty International, *China: Sustaining Conflict and Human Rights Abuses* (New York: Amnesty International, 2006).
102 Grimmet, "Conventional Arms Transfers to Developing Nations, 1997–2004," p. 8.
103 Richard Norton Taylor, "Chinese Arms Fuel Conflicts, Amnesty Says," *Guardian* (12 June 2006).
104 See S.D. Muni, *China's Strategic Engagement With the New ASEAN: An Exploratory Study of China's Post Cold War Political, Strategic and Economic Relations with Myanmar, Laos, Cambodia and Vietnam* (Singapore: Institute of Defence and Strategic Studies, 2002), pp. 72–88.
105 Ibid., p. 72.

106 Ibid., p. 74.
107 Ibid., p. 77.
108 Ibid., p. 79.
109 R. Bates Gill, "China Looks to Thailand: Exporting Arms, Exporting Influence," *Asian Survey*, vol. 31, no. 6 (June 1991), pp. 526–539.
110 Daniel Byman and Roger Cliff, *China's Arms Sale: Motivations and Implications* (Santa Monica, CA: RAND, 1999), p. 21.
111 Shawn W. Crispin, "Military Spending is Back on ASEAN Countries' Agendas After Being Stalled by the Financial Crisis," *Far Eastern Economic Review*, (5 October 2000).
112 Ibid.
113 Willett, "East Asia's Changing Defence Industry," p. 122.

12 Globalization and the defence economy of South Asia

Two views

Vijay Sakhuja and Deba R. Mohanty

VIJAY SAKHUJA

The relationship between globalization and the defence economy has emerged as a significant issue in the growing debate on globalization and national security. Propelled by rapid changes in technology and communications, globalization is essentially an effort at integration of trade, markets and economies. Perceptions of how globalization opens the economies of nation-states to global integration, and what its implications are for the national security of states that are considered monolithic entities of state sovereignty, have become issues of debate.

Globalization apparently seeks to provide equal access to the global economic pie, though not necessarily on an equal distribution basis. Thus it has an important implication for the security of developing countries. Alternatively there are apprehensions, maybe misplaced, that globalization generates a new form of hegemonic domination by the developed world over the developing world. The apparent apprehensions are that the developed world is attempting to exercise hegemonic control through the architecture of regimes of fiscal cartels, intellectual property rights and the development of new weapons technologies.

A historical perspective of the state and national security in the international arena would reveal that national defence and security have always been embedded in the international economy. States have depended on external sourcing for developing indigenous military technology infrastructure and the international arms industry has always remained eager to sell weaponry and also transfer technology. This has led to a widespread diffusion of modern weapons, particularly among the developing countries. Therefore, the defence economy is not a closed national system but an integral part of the global economy.

On average, countries spend around 3–4 per cent of GDP on military expenditures. However, this average falls within a wide variation of ratios that would range from 0.1 per cent to 46 per cent. The complex causality behind economic growth and defence spending suggests that the correlation between economic growth and defence spending cannot be generalized across countries. The relationship between sectors of the defence economy may vary from one country to another due to differences in the politico-socio-economic structure and type of government in each country. Besides, this relationship is further dependent on the dynamics of internal and external security challenges that shape the allocation of fiscal resources for defence.

Factors shaping military expenditure

Military expenditure is driven by several factors. First, and in most cases, the perceived need for national security shapes the allocation of fiscal resources for the military. National security is fundamental to states and they would do everything within their capabilities to safeguard territorial integrity.[1]

Second, financial resources available to the government drive military expenditure. However, for some, security appears to be a luxury and there is no reason to expect that military spending rises proportionately with per capita income. Although security may be a necessity, it may not rise proportionately with income.

Third, the intense effort to secure allocation of resources by the stakeholders of national security is through the lobbying of interested parties, particularly the military, and this shapes the allocation of fiscal resources. A high level of expenditure enables a large force, resulting in better prospects for promotion and higher salaries. While the interest of the military in military expenditure is probably broadly similar, the ability of the military to influence budgetary decisions differs considerably in various governments. This factor would be an important issue in shaping the allocation of budgetary resources for the military. The greater the political power of the military, the higher the military expenditure will be.

Fourth, the dynamics of an arms race may lead to higher military spending. Collier and Hoeffler's regression analysis suggests that military expenditure is driven by neighbourhood arms races.[2] Using global data for the period 1960–99, Collier and Hoeffler estimated that an 'arms race multiplier' can result in an increase in military expenditure that can be more than doubled in both the originating country and its neighbour. An implication is that military expenditure is, to an extent, a 'regional public bad'.

Fifth, there is a demand and supply factor determining the fiscal resources that are made available to the military. The demand is based on several determinants such as (a) neighbourhood tensions and disputes; (b) alliances and treaty obligations; (c) internal security, insurgency and militancy; (d) compulsions of modernization and new technology acquisition; (e) doctrinal changes; and (f) global commitments such as UN Peacekeeping, humanitarian missions and commitments to transnational issues such as terrorism. Meanwhile, the supply side of defence spending is driven by (a) economic growth and prosperity resulting in surplus funds; (b) demands from the military-industrial complex; (c) assistance to alliance partners and commitment to treaties; and (d) joint development of military projects.

Finally, military expenditures can also be subject to external shocks in the event of an international war. Thus there is a consensus that the quantity of fiscal resources made available to a country's military is determined by several factors and varies depending upon the needs of national security, the economic condition of a government, types of government and international commitments.

This chapter focuses on the argument that the impacts of globalization have not been uniform throughout the world. In some regions, states continue to pay more attention to the traditional national security function than in others. Therefore the hypothesis that globalization and economic expansion have led to positive spin-offs in the defence economies of states cannot be universal and can, at best, be described as generic.

The rationale for my argument lies in the fact that the defence economies of South Asia, including their defence production and procurement processes, are largely driven by the traditional matrices of threat perceptions: (i) strategic assessments of national and regional security perceptions; and (ii) the impact of the immediate and extended neighbourhood strategic security environments on the defence policy process. Crucially, it is primarily the conventional processes and matrix of external and internal threat perceptions that drive the defence economies of countries within this region, which I have taken to include India, Pakistan, Bangladesh, Sri Lanka, Nepal, Maldives and Bhutan.

Pakistan

Since independence, governments in Pakistan – both military and democratically elected – have formulated the national defence policy to a large extent on the perceived security threat from India. Interestingly, Pakistan's defence decision-making process views India as a hegemonic state and a primary causal factor behind the constant rise in its defence budget. In particular, Pakistan has used the Kashmir issue to gain public support, and much propaganda has been generated concerning this 'threat' to serve political purposes. This threat perception has always been the primary argument supplied by Pakistan to foreign aid donors to prevent a cut in the defence expenditure.

Also, Pakistan's domestic situation has witnessed periodic upheavals, military coups and political takeovers. The praetorian control of state and economy provides for the complete control and orchestration of national security decision-making process. The Pakistani situation showcases a polity that is premised on an intense political divide; exacerbated economic problems; chronic sources of Islamic fundamentalism and terrorism; plus the associated factors of drug trafficking, gun culture and increasing societal violence premised on sectarianism. In such a situation, the military is the only institutional interest group that has seized the reins of political and economic control, and even constitutional legitimacy, over the decision-making process in Pakistan. Having scaled the commanding heights of the policymaking and decision-making processes, the Pakistani military enjoys absolute exclusivity in the formulation of a military budget with no peer to rival it.

Be it an elected civilian or an army chief who seizes power through a *coup d'état*, the President of Pakistan – as its top constitutional functionary – has always accorded top priority to the interests of the military. Any interference from the Prime Minister in military planning has never been allowed by the military. The military has consistently justified a high defence budget in the interest of the state and has dominated the decision-making. For instance, the military was in power for more than 30 years and, even when it was not, has played a significant role in national decisions.

Defence spending in Pakistan has witnessed continuous increase despite high budget deficits, declining development expenditure, and increasing debt services on account of public debt. High levels of defence expenditure have impacted the Pakistan economy negatively. There have been several studies on the impact of defence spending on the economy. According to one study,

> [D]efence expenditure in Pakistan has a negative impact on GDP when it increases to over 6.5 percent of the GDP for a decade and more. During the 1978–88 decade, this threshold had already been crossed with defence expenditures averaging 6.8 percent.[3]

The study concluded that, 'an examination of a budgetary trade-off in Pakistan found that economic services as a whole were adversely affected by military expenditure'.[4] Over the decades, persistent high defence spending has had a decidedly negative impact on the economic condition of the country.

These factors, together with Pakistan's pursuit of nuclear capability and constant impetus to achieve parity with India's forces, have prompted Pakistan to allocate larger funds for defence. This has exacerbated the prevalent poverty levels. Pakistan has constantly attracted the attention of the International Monetary Fund (IMF) in view of these polarized contradictions and systemic defaults. The IMF has been constantly exhorting Pakistan to curb further increases in

Table 12.1 Defence expenditure in Pakistan

Year	Defence expenditure
1995	112,085
1996	123,550
1997	131,803
1998	139,818
1999	146,931
2000	153,795
2001	169,761
2002	188,426
2003	208,031
2004	228,996

Sources: *Pakistan Economic Survey*, Islamabad, Pakistan; *The Military Balance 1995–96, 1996–97, 1997–98, 1998–99, 1999–2000, 2001–2, 2002–3, 2003–4* (London: IISS, for those years); *Military Technology*, 23:1 (1999), as cited by Pervaiz Iqbal Cheema; Jasjit Singh, 'Defence Expenditure in South Asia: An overview', *RCSS Policy Studies 10* (Colombo: RCSS, 2000), pp. 53–54; Shalini Chawla, 'Trends in Pakistan Defence Expenditure', *Indian Defence Review*, October 2004.

defence spending. In February 2001, Pakistan agreed to freeze the budget and thus not increase the allocation for defence in the budget for 2001–2; in that fiscal year, out of the total budget of Rs.752 billion, defence was allotted Rs.131 billion.[5]

Pakistan is an agrarian economy, with the agricultural sector accounting for a 25 per cent share in the nation's GDP. Unfavourable climatic conditions, floods and droughts, have therefore had a particular impact on the economy. For instance, the Pakistan Economic Survey 2000–1 indicated that the fiscal impact of the drought was estimated to be as high as Rs.25 billion. Furthermore, poor crops, political instability and social unrest have also tended to make the economy more vulnerable.

Pakistan's economic vulnerabilities aside, the renowned Pakistani economist Shahid Javed Burki has observed that Pakistan's GDP in 2004–5 grew by 8.4 per cent over the estimate for 2003–4.[6] He notes that although this reflected a healthy economic situation, there would be some temptation to spend an increasing amount on defence. This is corroborated by the fact that the budget for 2005–6 has increased the outlay on the military by 15 per cent in nominal terms, from Rs.194 billion ($3.25 billion) budgeted for 2004–5 to Rs.223.5 billion ($3.75 billion).

From a Pakistani perspective, the persistence of the Kashmir conflict issue and the dedication of resources to military expenditure have resulted in a slowdown in the rate of economic growth. Shahid Javed Burki has argued that, in the absence of the Kashmir dispute, military expenditure as a proportion of GDP would have been lower in the case of Pakistan.[7] He also argues that the cordiality or hostility of relations between states in any region would determine the scope of defence expenditure outlays. Shahid Javed Burki cites the example of Bangladesh, which has uneasy relations with India, yet spent only 1.1 per cent on defence. He argues for the need to conserve Pakistan's resources and suggests that

[I]f Pakistan had spent 2.5 percent on defence, a proportion roughly equivalent to that of India, it could have saved as much as three percent of GDP a year. Compounded over this period, the amount saved is equivalent to four times the country's gross domestic product.

The persistence of the Kashmir conflict has also impacted Pakistan's Foreign Direct Investment (FDI). In 2002, Pakistan received $823 million in FDI

Table 12.2 Selected macroeconomic indicators growth rates (in per cent)

Year	2001	2002	2003	2004	2005	2006
GDP Growth	1.8	3.1	4.8	6.4	6.6	7.0

Source: State Bank of Pakistan, Annual Report 2004–5.

compared to \$3 billion for India, a low figure compared to figures in East Asia.[8] Foreign investors preferred to stay away, partly because of the less open economy, but also because of deep concern about security. In the absence of such a situation,

> [B]oth India and Pakistan would have attracted amounts of capital to the order of perhaps \$10 billion for the former and \$2 billion a year for the latter. Two billion dollars of foreign flows would be equivalent to three percent of Pakistan's GDP.[9]

In sum, Pakistan has paid a very high economic, social and political price for continuing to keep its defence spending India-centric. This has largely prevented it from reaping the dividends of a globalized economy, which India is attempting to obtain.

Nepal

Tucked deep inside the Himalayas, Nepal is sandwiched between India and China, the two Asian giants. It has a 1,000-km open border with India (southern, western and eastern borders), with China to the north. Nepal's economy is partially integrated with India's economy and the geography prevents it from conducting a large volume of trade with any other country.

Nepal's experience of globalization and market reforms presents a mixed picture. Poverty is widespread in rural Nepal while the opposite is true in urban areas. Economic growth shows a similar pattern. Over the last 15 years, Nepal's annual economic growth rate has averaged about 5 per cent.[10] A close look into the components of economic growth reveals that Nepal's overall growth has derived largely from the growth of the non-agricultural sector, which now contributes about 60 per cent of GDP. This has transformed the economy's structure. However, about 78 per cent of the Nepalese workforce still works in the agricultural sector and is poverty-stricken.

The ongoing Maoist insurgency finds it roots in both the poverty of the nation that is 85 per cent rural, and the failure of the government to institute land reform measures following the restoration of representative government in 1990. Over the past two years the Royal Nepal Army has beefed itself up to 100,000, but this has not been large enough to win a war against the Maoists who have 4,000 core members and 15,000 or so militia supporters. The Royal Nepalese Army (RNA) is recruited and trained in India, and India is still the primary source of weapons for the Nepalese military. Interestingly, the founding father King Prithvi Narayan Shah was careful to choose India over China. Some of his successors have since attempted to collaborate with Beijing against New Delhi, after China's annexation of Tibet in 1950 and India's defeat by China in 1962. But the Nepalese have feared India traditionally and this psyche is still intact.

Nepal is totally dependent on foreign military assistance. For instance, India has undertaken modernization of the RNA in 1950s and in 1990 at Nepal's request. Military equipment and stores amounting to Rs.500 crore have been supplied to Nepal, which include 50,000 rifles, mines, bulletproof jackets, mine-protection vehicles, night-vision equipment, mortars and rocket launchers.[11] The RNA has trained with the Indian Air Force for the first time, and has been attached to various schools of instruction and field formations for a first-hand feel of tackling insurgency.[12]

Post 9/11, the United States has shown increased interest in economic and defence co-operation with Nepal. US military hardware support includes 20,000 M-16 rifles and two Huey Cobra helicopters. Likewise, the UK has given two helicopters, 35 land rovers and other logistic equipment. China, too, has supplied military equipment worth US$1 million, free of charge.[13] These include communication and night vision equipment. Similarly, in 2004, Pakistan had offered to supply military hardware against a 20-year line of credit amounting to US$5 million. Likewise, Russia and Poland have agreed to supply helicopters and fixed wing aircraft.

In August 2005, the Nepalese Ministry of Defense (MOD) was set to acquire the first-ever loan of Rs.1.1 billion from a consortium of commercial banks to finance the procurement of four MI-17 helicopters for the RNA.[14] The consortium of commercial banks has asked 8 per cent interest per annum, whereas the MOD has offered 7 per cent. Helicopters would be bought directly from the manufacturer, Joint Stock Company of Kazakhstan, and the total cost of four helicopters, including insurance premium interest for ten years and spare parts, would be around Rs.2 billion. Interestingly, the Prime Minister Sher Bahadur Deuba warned in January 2005 that the government would be compelled to spend all government revenue on security bodies if the peace process did not move forward.[15]

However, after the royal takeover in 2005, India stopped supply of all lethal weapons to Nepal, although some non-lethal weapons were still provided at one time. The government of Nepal has now asked India to resume its supply of weapons.

Bhutan

There are several similarities between Bhutan and Nepal. Like Nepal, Bhutan is also a Himalayan kingdom. There is a distinct asymmetry between Bhutan and the Asian giants in terms of geography, economy, military, natural resource and development. In its long history, Bhutan has never been colonized and has managed to maintain its sovereignty and territorial integrity despite attempts by the Tibetans and Mongols from the north, and British India from the south. Also it has been able to ward off any attempts at integration by its larger neighbours, as had been the case with Tibet and China (1959) and Sikkim and India (1976). As a result, Bhutanese society has been traditionally sensitive to the issues of security, and preserving its sovereignty, independence and territorial integrity has been a constant challenge historically.[16]

This sensitivity has had a beneficial impact on Bhutan and resulted in political stability. The country has been able to avoid colonial domination, the Cold War and regional rivalries. On the other hand, Bhutanese foreign policy has focused clearly on forging a close relationship with India while broadening Bhutan's links with the international community.[17]

The 1962 conflict between India and China led Bhutan to modernize the Royal Bhutan Army. This conflict brought to the fore the new strategic reality in the Himalayas, and Bhutan decided to seek convergence of its strategic interest with India. Bhutan views its relationship with India as a source of deterrence against other foreign powers. The prospect of shared security arrangements has generated a sense of assurance for its territorial security, as well as better prospects for rapid development. The developmental concerns were the only natural outlet for Bhutan to interact with the international trading system. Access could be obtained either through China, whose ports were remote along its east coast, or the more viable alternative of India through the port of Kolkata, which offered better opportunities to Bhutan for trade with the world.

Evidently, Bhutanese strategic thinking has a measured acceptance of overall Indian security arrangements as a means of protecting and strengthening its sovereignty. India provided the required weaponry and training through the Indian Military Training Team (IMTRAT) in 1963, and this was perhaps the seminal moment in the history of the Himalayan kingdom to have accepted India's concept of broad security perimeter, which continues to the present time.[18]

Given the geographical reality, Bhutan has limited resources, and its capacity to grow exports or speed-up domestic economic development is limited by its lack of natural resources, capital, labour and other factor endowments. Resources are limited to the extent that Bhutan seeks to deepen its integration with the Indian economy as a conduit for its own development. Essentially, diminutive geographical size and relative political and economic insignificance in the international system severely condition Bhutan's ability to engage with the global market and global economic system. The need to gain physical access through India remains a constant and inevitable reality.

Besides, 'Gross National Happiness' (GNH) has been the overarching development philosophy of Bhutan. As a concept it has guided development policies and programme. GNH suggests that happiness is the ultimate objective of development. It recognizes that 'there are many dimensions to development other than those associated with Gross National Product (GNP), and that development needs to be understood as a process that seeks to maximize happiness rather purely economic growth'.[19] Quintessentially, the premium placed on the happiness of a sovereign people lies at the heart of national security strategy in the Kingdom of Bhutan. Thus Bhutan offers a new paradigm of national power and index of the quality of human life.

Like any other developing country, Bhutan remains wary of globalization. It is believed that the sovereignty of the Bhutanese state will be diminished and compromised due to the impact of globalization. Globalization of Bhutan's economy may also restrict the degree to which Bhutan can pursue good governance, one of the objectives of GNH. There is an ingrained perception that Bhutanese culture has to be invigorated through education – such as knowledge of the humanistic and consciousness of values – which imparts the resilience to withstand the onslaught of cultural change borne by the winds of international trade.[20]

Bangladesh

A democratically elected government has been ruling Bangladesh since 1991. The Army has stayed away from active politics, thus imbibing an apolitical ideology, and this trend has reinforced democratic practices and institutions in Bangladesh. Meanwhile, the armed forces have grown into a professional force dedicated to the defence of the country and protection of its people from external aggression and internal subversion. The military has been providing invaluable services to nation building, particularly in times of natural disaster such as floods and cyclones. It also contributes to national development by providing services that build up infrastructure such as roads, bridges, railway tracks and ports.[21]

In Bangladesh, defence expenditure is a sensitive subject because it takes a sizeable share of limited resources. But Bangladeshis believe that there could be no true development without adequate internal and external security, and they argue that defence spending by Bangladesh remains at a very low level. Interestingly, Bangladesh's low defence spending has been acknowledged by international financial institutions such as the World Bank. The Asia Development Bank Document entitled 'Bangladesh Public Expenditure Review' (May 2003) notes that 'Bangladesh has a relatively low level of defence outlays, representing 1.3 per cent of GDP, less than the half the average for low-income countries and considerably lower than those for the rest of South Asia'.[22]

There is a strong belief that the military's role in nation building has a profound impact on the socio-economic development of the nation. Most of the money spent under the defence budget gets recycled into the civilian economy. For instance, military salaries and allowances, or expenditure on account of military stores like foodstuff or clothes, is fed back directly to the mainstream economy. Defence pensions provide social security to ex-servicemen and their families; and the benefits received by people dependent on members of the Bangladesh Armed Forces, if measured in economic terms, are also found to be reinforcing civil economy. In addition, job opportunities among different United Nations missions have been created at the initiative of the Armed Forces. By some estimates, Bangladesh has earned US$800 million on account of UN Peacekeeping operations. The income generated from these activities is helping to improve the living standards of the family members concerned as well as wider social development.

The Armed Forces of Bangladesh are equipped with predominantly Chinese military hardware: about 85 per cent of army equipment, and 50 per cent of naval and air force hardware. Chinese arms, though not very sophisticated, are

an attractive option due to their relative ease of availability (owing to good political relations) and also their low prices. The Chinese supply weapons to
Bangladesh on the basis of 'friendship prices' as well as long-term low rate
repayment arrangements. There has, however, been substantial controversy in
recent years over the appropriateness of purchasing frigates from the UK and
Republic of Korea, along with eight MIG-29s from Russia and fighter jets
from China in 2000, which might amount to a case of unwarranted public
expenditure.

Given the low revenue effort and the imperative to invest in health, education
and rural infrastructure, tight control is being maintained on defence outlays.
Besides, the slow rate of agricultural growth, prevalence of unemployment and
occurrence of natural disasters altogether compound the challenges that a
country like Bangladesh faces as it pursues the benefits of globalization.[23]

Sri Lanka

Uncertainty amidst a crumbling ceasefire, frequent suicide-bomber attacks, continued assassination attempts and ever-elusive peace talks: this sums up the
prevalent socio-economic and security environment in Sri Lanka. The years
1949–2005 have seen the eruption of at least three inter-ethnic wars and many
lesser skirmishes between the Sinhalese majority and the Tamil and Muslim
minorities. They have also witnessed a violent uprising in the Sinhalese-
speaking south against the (Sinhala-dominated) Sri Lankan state, even as militant Tamil groups continue to fight government forces.

Sri Lanka has suffered two abortive coups (1962 and 1966), two insurrections
(1987 and 1989) against the Government by the Janatha Vimukti Peramuna
(JVP), and now the ongoing civil war between the government and the Liberation Tigers of Tamil Eelam (LTTE). In the early days of nationhood, Sri Lankan
defence spending did not see any appreciable rise. Just after independence, the
Sri Lankan government allocated a small amount of about 0.24 per cent of
the budget to defence spending, which rose to 1.09 per cent in 1977.[24] However,
the figure continued to rise, and by 1986 it had reached 1.68 per cent. A notable
rise in the cost of defence occurred in 1991 after the departure of the Indian
Peacekeeping Force: a sum of Rs.10.61 billion, amounting to 8.85 per cent of
the total budget (or 2.85 per cent of the GDP) was incurred. By 1999, defence
spending in Sri Lanka was taking 6.63 per cent of the budget; and by 2000, cost
Rs.65.40 billion or 5.3 per cent of the country's GDP.

Inevitably, the unending secessionist war has compelled the government to
spend in order to overcome it. Sri Lanka sources its military equipment from the
US, Ukraine, Israel, Pakistan and China. Direct military expenditure on the war
by both the Sri Lankan government and the LTTE has been calculated to be as
much as Rs.295 billion. In 2001, President Chandrika Kumaratunga told her
government parliamentary group that the military expenditure for the year 2000
had exceeded the budgeted amount by Rs.30 billion (around US$365.85
million).[25]

A considerable portion of public expenditure continues to fund the purchase of sophisticated weapons to meet the needs of government forces locked in conflict against separatist Tamil Tiger rebels. As such, the military-fiscal costs of the ongoing civil war in Sri Lanka have proved damaging to the country's democratic political system and socio-economic development.

Maldives

Maldives, a small developing island state, is heavily dependent on just two main industries – fisheries and tourism – for its fiscal revenues, foreign exchange earnings, employment and growth. Fishing has traditionally been the main occupation and source of income for the ordinary citizens of Maldives. Despite tourism, most people outside the tourism zones depend on fishing for both subsistence and a source of income. On the other hand, tourism in Maldives is a global industry and has witnessed a fair amount of the impact of globalization, leading to development of sectors such as banking and finance, telecommunications and transport.

Maldives is thinly populated: 270,000 people spread over 200 islands. The country remains extremely vulnerable both environmentally and geographically, and there is considerable poverty. As a result, the markets are small and the natural resource base is narrow, fragile and prone to disruption by natural disasters such as the recent tsunami. Thus it faces a number of constraints in seeking to integrate into the global economy, having to manage its fragility in terms of size, geography, trade and above all, biodiversity.

Maldives has not engaged in any international conflicts since independence in 1965. However, there was one attempt to overthrow the government of President Maumoon Gayoom in 1988.[26] The country maintains a paramilitary police force called the National Security Service, which is made up of 3,500 personnel. They undertake security duties, including coastguard operations. Maldives spends 5.5 per cent of its GDP, approximately $41.1 million, on military expenditures.[27] The NSS has some light armour and sea attack capabilities that include two modified Dovra-class fast attack craft of Israeli origin.

India

The current economic boom in India has created euphoria in the global markets. There is a strong belief that India will be among the top economies in Asia and can be the second leader after China to lead the Asian economic boom. With an expected annual growth rate of 8 per cent, it would be the highest in Asia after China, which has been experiencing growth rates of over 9 per cent. Indian companies are on an acquisition spree in distant lands, in fields such as oil and gas, pharmaceuticals, information technology, infrastructure and a host of other areas. Indian giants such as Bharat Forge, Infosys, Ranbaxy, Birla Group and Reliance Group lead these acquisitions; and, as a result, a number of Indian companies can now be seen as significant commercial entities on the global economic canvas. The rising stock market has brought confidence to investors. Also, a vast pool of highly learned and skilled Indian professionals is in demand in the international market. India is home to a uniquely creative, highly talented, qualified, skilled and cheap manpower that supports silicon valleys the world over. These are indeed signs of a globalized India.

While this may provide a collective image of a 'shining and globalized India', the flipside shows the highest number of people living in dismal conditions and abject poverty, with a lack of nutritive food, medicine and basic amenities. Basic education and healthcare are still neglected sectors, leading to under-nutrition and higher child mortality rates in rural areas. On average, 23.3 million people sleep hungry, and 40 million children do not have access to primary education, which is more than one-third of the world's total child population.

Nonetheless, India is positioned at a critical juncture, experiencing globalization that accounts for 1 per cent of global GDP, affects 20 per cent of the world population, and arms a growing regional military power. The Indian leadership has been supportive of building a strong and modern military in order to safeguard national security, serving as a deterrent and supplying a force commensurate with India's size and interests. During the Indian Military Commanders' Conference in 2005, Prime Minister Manmohan Singh assured commanders that the government could allocate about 3 per cent of India's GDP for its defence needs if the economy continued to grow at 8 per cent annually.

India's defence budget has averaged between 2.3 and 2.6 per cent of GDP for almost a decade. This has, however, been insufficient for modernization and new acquisitions of military hardware required for military-strategic relevance in changing times. For nearly two decades, defence modernization has been stagnating in terms of the design completion of existing weapons systems, or the replacement of old worn-out ones.

Components of national power are inextricably linked to a nation's grand strategy, which represents the desire of a state to achieve its rightful place in the international system. Trends in defence expenditure therefore tend to 'objectively assess aspects of a state's military capability, although lacuna still remains as even the very concept of military capability is often value-laden'.[28] In the Indian context, it has been argued that the trends in allocation of fiscal resources for defence provide one key index – the military component – of a state's national power.[29]

It will be useful to locate India's defence expenditure in the overall context of India's grand strategic vision vis-à-vis its military capability and fiscal resources. In 2000, the Indian Defence Minister George Fernandes noted that 'India's area of interest extends from the north of the Arabian Sea to the South China Sea'.[30] Pranab Mukherjee, the current Defence Minister, has voiced similar sentiments and noted:

> Our location on top of the Indian Ocean between the sea routes from the Cape of Good Hope and the Mediterranean and the energy sources of

the Gulf to the strategic Malacca Straits gives us a vantage point and responsibility to safeguard the security of our energy supplies and shipping in the Indian Ocean region.[31]

At a time when India's growing economic prowess and beyond-region strategic vision are well acknowledged, India is spending the kind of money that could yield future dividends in terms of achieving its strategic ambitions.

A closer look at trends in India's defence expenditure offers some pointers. The government allocated Rs.89,000 crore to the defence establishment for 2006–7, Rs.6,000 crore more than budgetary allocations for the previous year.[32] However, the defence budget as a percentage of GDP was lower than last year's, and was pegged at 2.27 per cent of GDP against 2.5 per cent for 2005–6. A percentage of 3 per cent has been promised if an economic growth rate of 10 per cent is achieved. India's defence spending has seldom crossed 3 per cent of its GDP and has, in fact, been floating around 2.5 to 2.6 per cent for the past decade.

The primary argument for an increase in defence budget is based on the fact that India has an active border with Pakistan, and the two sides have fought three major wars in the last 60 years or so. Similarly, India has to maintain deployments along the Chinese border despite the fact that the two sides have signed an agreement of peace and tranquillity along their boundaries. The Indian Army is also engaged in internal security responsibilities in Kashmir and Northeast India. Unlike India, China and Pakistan have been spending relatively larger sums for national defence. Trend analyses for the past 15 years suggest that China's defence budget has been witnessing an increase of 10–11 per cent per annum, in real terms; and similar figures are true of Pakistan, which has witnessed a 13 per cent increase annually.

There also remains a pressing need to transform the relative backwardness of India's indigenous military-industrial complex, still considered rudimentary when compared against Western standards. There is a huge gap between India's domestic defence production efforts and her weapons requirements, resulting in a situation where almost 70 per cent of actual requirements are met through imports. India's investment in military R&D has never crossed 7 per cent since its independence in 1947.[33] Insufficient funding in the past in the area of military R&D has undoubtedly had a negative impact on India's long-term defence production efforts.

Yet, with growing security interests beyond South Asia, India has been even more determined to enhance its military capabilities, especially in terms of long reach deployments. Such capabilities have arisen partly due to strategic vision, and partly due to enhanced fiscal resources arising from economic liberalization and globalization of the Indian economy.

Concluding remarks

South Asia's experience of globalization and market reforms presents a mixed picture. The region continues to face major challenges from the forces of globalization, and in many cases, the integration of national economies into the global economy is still a distant dream. The regional countries are conscious of co-operative and mutually beneficial economic benefits that accrue from global-ization, but would equally do anything to prevent any forces that question the sovereignty of the state. They also resent the fact that they are, in fact, excluded from multilateral negotiations; and believe that the negotiations by the world's industrial powers are simply going to force concessions and, in the end, extract more favourable terms of trade over against them.

Yet the linkages between globalization and the defence economy are more apparent and forceful in the case of India. In fact, in India, the security function has increased with its liberalizing economy. India's rendezvous with globaliza-tion has been a singular case in which the factors of technological growth, GNP growth and defence expenditure growth have had some direct correlation with defence industrialization, defence transformation, and the export of defence hardware as contributors to the defence economy and overall economic develop-ment of India.

To a significantly lesser degree, Pakistan may have made some gains from globalization but its defence economic expansion continues to be driven by traditional animosity with India and more than three decades of military govern-ment. In the case of Bangladesh, Sri Lanka, Nepal, Bhutan and Maldives, the relative impact of globalization has been varied, and there is no tangible evid-ence to prove that the expansion of defence economies has been a factor in the globalization process.

At another level, South Asia is still mired in conflicts and pervaded by a 'par-tition mentality'. In this context, Pakistan cannot look beyond Kashmir and Islamabad has often accused New Delhi of being a hegemon. Bangladesh also shares similar views of Indian dominance in the region. There is a general belief that as India grows in economic and military capability, it will attempt to exer-cise a leadership role and prevent any peaceful mechanism for the resolution of regional conflicts. Conversely, there is a distinct possibility of conflict escalation in the region. In the case of Nepal and Sri Lanka, ethnic violence, insurgency and terrorism continue to pose as major challenges, and economic development remains severely hampered.

DEBA R. MOHANTY

Introduction[34]

The defence industry,[35] traditionally considered as a critical 'national asset', has long been one of the more protected parts of national industries of many coun-tries. Most countries prefer self-sufficiency in defence production and hence indigenous defence industries have been treated as critical to a country's secur-ity than simply as one more manufacturing sector. Even in market economic conditions, many of the states have preferred to keep their defence industries under state control. It is surprising then, how the forces of globalization as well as the end of the Cold War have challenged this once sacrosanct notion about autarky in defence production.

Globalization is a process of increasing cross-border integration of relationships through interaction of activities between companies, governments, other organizational entities and individuals. This process creates cross border dependencies since events in one part of the world increasingly have impacted on people and communities elsewhere. Primarily driven by global spread of information and communication technologies, deregulation of domestic financial markets and free trade arrangements, the relative power and influence of the state are increasingly becoming dependent on their position in international networks. These networks and interdependencies between states, however, are not symmetric.[36]

But suffice to argue here that the national defence industries of many countries are now heavily impinged by processes of globalization, a transition well established by empirical and other evidences cited by scholars and analysts across the globe.[37]

In less than a quarter century, considered fairly 'short span' in recorded history, the global defence industry has already undergone two distinct yet contrasting phases of spectacular changes and is currently witnessing a third phase of transformation. This is puzzling as well as worrisome. During the 1980s, considered peak time of the Cold War, the global defence industry witnessed the culmination of an era, marked by an unprecedented level of military efforts by two rival super powers, cumulative impacts of which had been felt the world over. The international arms bazaar was perhaps the most attractive business place for the two super powers as well as other major arms producers during the Cold War period.

The end of the Cold War and consequent disintegration of the Soviet Union threatened to bring down the weapons emporium to the nadir, it nearly did. A cursory glance at available indicators suggests that military expenditure plummeted from a high of $1,260 billion in 1987 to $704 billion in 1996. The same period between 1987–96 witnessed an almost 35 per cent decrease in operational expenditure, 20 per cent reduction in equipment procurement, nearly 25 per cent decrease in military R&D investments and an almost 30 per cent reduction in demand for military weaponry. According to the Bonn International Centre for Conversion (BICC), worldwide employment in defence industry fell from 17.5 million workers to 11.1 million during the same period. The so-called 'peace dividend' was perhaps visible in attractive diminishing figures, yet resultant difficulties witnessed in major centres of defence production necessitated changes in the military sphere in general and the defence industry in particular.[38]

The global defence industry tried to adjust itself to the new environment. marked by considerable reductions in almost every aspect of military efforts. The adjustment process was most visible in the United States. The US defence industry went in for a massive drive toward concentration, primarily through merger and acquisition (M&As) among defence manufacturers. It also adopted diversification strategies where many defence-dependent companies entered the civil market while quite a few became defence-dependent. Structural and other restructuring processes resulted in the emergence of a few giant defence manufacturers, while many medium-sized and small units either merged with their bigger counterparts or were wiped out from the defence market altogether.[39] What is most striking is the fact that many of the companies, that were earlier concentrated within the United States, went beyond national boundaries to forge partnerships of different types, either in order to expand their business activities so as to grow further in the competitive defence business, or just to survive in the contemporary market.[40]

Although slower to follow suit in comparison to its US counterpart, the European defence industry also witnessed significant changes during the whole of the 1990s and beyond. Both vertical and horizontal concentration efforts witnessed in the US defence industry were also witnessed in the European defence industry, which had been otherwise struggling with issues like structural and institutional processes related to the European Union, greater transatlantic military-industrial cooperation, formation of a single European defence industry and a common security and defence policy (known as ESDP).[41] At the same time, many European firms have been engaged in not only transatlantic military-industrial partnerships (especially the British defence firms) but also expanding their collaborative and joint-venture activities into other regions including Africa, Asia and elsewhere. Reforms have been underway in a Russian defence industry that had witnessed near chaotic conditions during the whole of the 1990s.[42] China had been implementing much needed reforms to reorganize its defence industrial sector during the same period – processes that are still underway well into the twenty-first century. Elsewhere, Israel, South Africa, Brazil, Australia and others have also undertaken a series of reform initiatives to adjust to the new international defence market conditions.[43]

Sometime during the late 1990s, the available indicators started suggesting a different trend. Military spending started looking up again. The near decade-long peace dividend paved the way for renewed efforts toward military modernization, force restructuring and military production. Evidence suggests that roughly from 1997–8 onward, the decreasing trends slowed down fast and were consequently translated into a real term increase in a span of just a few years. This is attributed primarily to renewed military efforts by the United States, the impacts of which have been felt the world over.

What do all these pointers suggest for the defence industry? Have challenges of consolidation, diversification and globalization been fully realized by the defence industry? How has the global defence industry responded to such challenges? And, what challenges and opportunities lie in the future for the global defence industry? These are some of the extremely complex questions that analysts and industry watchers the world over have been pondering. This chapter tries to explain some of the major challenges faced by the defence industry in the era of globalization and to assess what kind of impact it holds for the Indian defence industry. The chapter argues that relative consolidation, diversification and internationalization efforts witnessed in the defence industry during the whole of the 1990s are likely to continue well into the future, which in turn demands corresponding responses to such challenges from major arms producers. It argues further that a high degree of consolidation efforts by the US defence industry has also witnessed spill-over effects, especially in Europe, although the latter has been witnessing a slower pace of restructuring efforts.[44] Such a scenario has prompted smaller producers like India to contemplate and undertake structural and policy related reforms in the defence industrial sector.

Deconstructing the defence industry in the new age

The end of the Cold War drastically altered the international security scenario, which impinged on almost every major aspect of military efforts. Defence industry was perhaps among the worst affected in this rapidly changing scenario. As stated before, major centres of defence production, primarily the United States and the West Europe, started initiating a long, painful process of restructuring, which invariably included rapid consolidation efforts. The restructuring of the US defence industry during the early 1990s was aimed primarily at reducing the size and overall structure through rapid consolidation efforts. A comparison between the US defence industry during the height of the Cold War and the decade thereafter presents a dramatic contrast. In 1986, the top ten US defence firms were General Dynamics, General Electric, McDonnell Douglas, Rockwell, General Motors, Lockheed, Raytheon, Boeing, United Technologies and Grumman. In the decade since 1986, General Electric and Rockwell have divested their defence businesses, and General Dynamics has sold the core of its 1986 defence business, aircraft and missiles. Grumman was saved from near bankruptcy through a purchase by Northrop, Lockheed merged with Martin Marietta, and Boeing purchased McDonnell Douglas. While Raytheon, Boeing and United Technologies remain in the defence business, they have undergone dramatic transformation. In the early 1990s, the consolidation process in the US defence industry was most pronounced in the aerospace sector, which continued till the late 1990s.

The process of consolidation and diversification in the US defence industry has been supported by the US Department of Defense (DOD) with the aim of achieving savings in weapons costs through rationalization of production. Since 1993, the US DOD has therefore provided the opportunity for companies to write off their restructuring costs against military contracts. During the period 1993–7 the US DOD share of certified restructuring costs for seven major M&As was $765 million, with the forecast that this would result in US DOD savings in weapon acquisitions of more than $4 billion over a period of five years.[45] Such positive assessments have however been contested. Savings in weapon costs through rationalization measures must be weighed against the negative effect of tendencies to monopolistic pricing. The overall impact on competition in defence production is still not possible to assess. However, one possible negative impact is that the dominant market position of single arms producer is likely to increase their strength in relation to the US DOD. This is evident in the sense that the dominant position of top defence companies among the US DOD prime contractors has increased. Five companies receiving the largest US DOD prime contract awards accounted for nearly 30 per cent of total contract awards in 1998 as compared to 20 per cent in 1990, and the single company receiving the largest award accounted for 10 per cent in 1998 as compared to 6.2 per cent in 1990.[46]

Since the early 1990s, consolidation and diversification efforts have occurred in the European defence industry. Concentration efforts have occurred at two levels – national and intra-European. At national level, the creation of big competitive companies within single states has been witnessed.[47] This has taken place in countries like France, Germany, Italy, Sweden and Spain. National level concentration and restructuring efforts in defence industry were, during the same period, accompanied by cross-country joint ventures (hereafter, JVs) and various armament collaborations. These efforts were largely carried out within and among various European countries. Formation of large corporate structures paved the way for the reorganization of sectors like aerospace, missiles, radar systems, land-based systems and naval systems.

Apart from national and intra-European level concentration efforts, the European defence industry was also engaged in a series of what are commonly known as transatlantic military industrial links. Although such efforts were underway since the late 1980s and early 1990s, things really moved at a faster pace during the mid-1990s. Major British and German companies were involved in large-scale merger activities with the United States. Prominent cases that deserve mention here are Daimler–Chrysler and GEC–Tracor mergers. Companies like Daimler–Chrysler, BAe, GEC and others showed keen interest in acquiring units, left over from companies like Northrop Grumman and others. Even the proposed merger between Northrop Grumman and Lockheed Martin, which at the time of writing, is yet to be carried out prompted many European firms to look for acquisition of subsidiaries of these companies.[48]

European companies have also shown willingness to go beyond the Atlantic. Many instances denote such desire. For example, Thomson–CSF and Transport Holding have bought ADI, one of the largest arms manufacturing companies in Australia. Similarly a French Consortium led by Dassault Aviation (including partners like Thomson–CSF, Aerospatiale Matra and SNECMA) agreed to acquire a 20 per cent share in Embraer, the largest aerospace company of Brazil in spite of stiff opposition from the Brazilian Air Force. BAe systems along with Saab have acquired a 20 per cent share in Denel Aviation of South Africa. Companies like DASA, Celsius, Vickers and others have also gone into various acquisition and collaboration deals with many South African companies. Major European companies are still looking for opportunities in other countries.

In sum, the global defence industry has shown a set of major trends whose impacts have been felt directly or indirectly on defence industries of major countries in general, and the Indian defence industry in particular. They are:

- Led primarily by the United States, the global defence industry has witnessed a period of consolidation and diversification. It has shown increasing inclination toward internationalization of defence production efforts mainly through co-production and co-development, joint ventures and transnational M&As. Emerging patterns in arms trade offsets have also provided challenges and opportunities for the second-tier as well as smaller defence industries.

*   The global defence industry is witnessing a period of increased competition among manufacturers, thanks primarily to its shrinking size, demand and supply in both qualitative and quantitative terms. This, among others, has necessitated countries like Israel, Brazil, South Africa and India to strive for relevance in the international arms market.

*   The global defence industry has strived to adjust to the new international security conditions, where, among others, many traditional recipients have significantly reduced their acquisitions (for example, countries in Europe) while a host of countries have either sustained or even increased their equipment requirements (examples include countries such as Japan, South Korea, Saudi Arabia and others). Such a fluid international arms market entails some possibilities for second-tier suppliers to boost their export records.

*   The global defence industry has created scope for more technology and military goods diffusion, and hence readjustments in security priorities by many states. In other words, strategic and diplomatic considerations have come to play a major role in arms trade, a process that impacts international relations in contemporary times.

*   Emerging trends in internationalization of defence production efforts suggest that both 'autarkic' and 'going global' trends have, to a considerable extent, impacted on state decision-making in strategic areas. Although retention of key critical technologies has always been emphasized by the state for strategic reasons, beyond national boundary interactions among defence manufacturers have nevertheless brought down the earlier inertia associated with state control over defence industries.

The Indian defence industry: from self-sufficiency to self-reliance

Since India's independence, every successive Indian leadership has sought self-sufficiency in defence production, hence the urge to establish a comprehensive defence industrial infrastructure. While this is primarily attributed to substantive security considerations, it is also due to an inherent desire from within to aspire to become a great power.[49] Self-sufficiency in defence was adopted as a major policy goal since India gained independence in 1947, but as years passed and demands for security grew, India found it difficult to create and nurture an industrial base, which was hit by two major factors – lack of sufficient funding and access to defence technologies. Catering to the demands of the armed forces whose size was vast made the matter worse, which resulted in a situation of imbalance in defence requirements and production.

As Indian defence industry started maturing, self-reliance, instead of self-sufficiency in defence became a key policy objective some time since the late 1960s, which among others denoted, apart from its own production base for support, a degree of dependence on reliable foreign sources for access to technologies, supply of components and complete systems. From the early 1960s till the mid-1980s, licensed production and direct purchase and acquisitions remained the predominant form of equipment supply for the Indian defence forces. Analysts like Ajay Singh argue that there was a gap of nearly three decades in India's effort toward indigenous production.[50] This gap was especially evident in the fields of design and development, which constitutes the upper spectrum of self-reliance.

Production patterns during the 1980s and 1990s show that India has been able to an extent to initiate a number of projects for indigenous development in the defence sector. This has been partly possible due to increased allocation of funds for these projects as well as for R&D efforts. It is expected that increase in defence R&D, which has been increasing for some years and is likely to increase further in future, will boost indigenous effort.[51] However, the proportion of allocations for R&D still remains well under 10 per cent. Although licensed production has been seen as a stable form of production efforts, it has not made India self-reliant in terms of the upper-ends of defence production, especially in the field of design and development. With indigenous effort having its own weaknesses, especially in financial and lack of, or difficulties to access, foreign military technologies, another alternative to fill the technology gap has been contemplated for some time. This is where efforts toward joint design and development, and co-production come in, an opportunity largely created in the global defence industrial scenario in recent times.

Several new projects, to be jointly designed and developed with foreign firms, are coming up in the Indian defence industrial sector and India is keen to tap this opportunity to the fullest possible extent.[52] HAL has led the way in this effort. After successful integration of several electronic components in the Su-30MKI by the Indian scientists and technicians in recent times, the Russians are keen to offer a partnership, initially in licensed production of the aircraft by HAL but incrementally substituted by joint production in the future, which is a new experience in this kind of fourth generation aircraft project. A new simulator making it possible to train pilots for the Su-30MKI is on the cards for India.[53] Russia, in addition to this, has also proposed to become a partner in the ambitious fifth-generation combat aircraft project with India. They have proposed to jointly design, develop and produce by sharing costs.[54] Brahmos, another example, is a joint venture between India and Russia, three versions of which are nearing readiness for serial production and exports. This cruise missile project started in 1998 and is considered to be one of the major steps by India toward international collaboration. India's recent search for Advanced Jet Trainer (AJT) has also benefited its quest for collaboration partners. The US aviation giant Lockheed Martin is keen to offer technology transfer for the indigenous project.[55] This is the first time that, except for Russia, more and more front line arms producing countries are showing interests, not in exports but more importantly in joint ventures and other forms of industrial participation. Indian defence industry, especially since the last couple of years, has been experiencing noticeable changes. It is gearing up to grab this opportunity which was previously quite limited. Industry watchers believe that such changes in production policies are going to benefit Indian defence industry in many ways.

Reforms in higher defence management: impacts on defence industry

India's defence industry has entered a new phase of self-reliance in recent times, which is bound to impinge upon its future directions. Since the mid-1990s, several initiatives have been undertaken by the government to effect changes in the defence industry. Soon after the liberalization of the Indian economy, the defence industry started stressing the importance of civil–military interaction in the industrial sector within India and beyond its national boundaries. The private industries in India, which were thus far debarred from entering into defence production and whose role in the defence sector was limited to supply of spare parts and other minor contributions, started demanding a slice in defence production efforts. Initial efforts came up after the Kargil conflict erupted in 1999, when the Indian government constituted a committee to look into problems related to national security, which brought out the 'Kargil Committee Report'. This Report, among other recommendations, highlighted the importance of reforms in higher defence management and reforms in institutional processes in the security sector. Consequent to this report, the Government constituted a Group of Ministers Committee to look into matters related to national security and higher defence management. The committee submitted its report to the government in 2001, which is known as GoM Report on 'Reforming the National Security System'.[56] This Report has, among other things, emphasized the importance of self-reliance in India's defence industry and has recommended several steps to effect institutional changes into the defence industrial decision-making bureaucracy.

Coupled with changes at institutional and organizational levels, India's defence industry entered a new era after the Government announced a major change in policy by outlining codes of conduct for, and inviting private participation in, the defence industry in early 2002. This is seen as by far the most important policy shift in the defence industrial sector in the last 50 years. By doing so, the Government, through an official notification, No. 5(37)/2001-FCI, allowed private sector participation of up to 100 per cent and permitted foreign direct investment (FDI) of up to 26 per cent.[57] This decision, considered a major policy initiative, has been hailed by both the private industry and the government owned defence industry as the beginning of a new direction for the Indian defence industry, which has otherwise been considerably impinged by global trends.

In tune with the objectives of India's defence industry becoming self-reliant, the Government has initiated a series of structural and institutional changes in matters related to defence production. Earlier, procurement procedures were considered cumbersome and there were overlaps in organizational responsibilities of respective bodies responsible for procurement.[58] Such problems have been addressed by the Government, which has come out with three new Defence Procurement Procedures (hereafter, DPP) in the last four years. Following the GoM Report, the first DPP came out in 2002, which broadly laid out procurement procedures for outright equipment purchases from abroad (broadly known as 'Buy' category). The second DPP, a revision of the earlier version, came out in 2005, which enlarged its scope to include both outright purchase as well as purchases from within with collaborative efforts (known as 'Buy and Make' category). The latest DPP came out in late August 2006 (known as DPP-2006),[59] which provides comprehensive guidelines for all capital acquisitions for the Armed Forces. Some of the important features of the new DPP-2006 are: (a) all major decisions pertaining to the procurement process are to be taken simultaneously for reducing the time frame for acquisitions; (b) enhanced transparency by placing generic requirements of the services on the Ministry of Defence website and generating vendor registration through Internet; (c) increased transparency in the conduct of field trials; (d) 'Integrity Pact' made compulsory for all contracts above Rs.100 crore; (e) an 'Offset' obligation for all contracts above Rs.300 crore; (f) actively encouraging the Indian industry in development of defence equipment and systems on a cost-sharing basis with the government; and (g) provide a level playing field between foreign and Indian vendors.

Under the new system, the Services Headquarters have been integrated into the Ministry of Defence to provide closer interaction. Procurement structure is now made a three-tier structure with the recent establishment of Defence Acquisition Council (DAC) at the apex.[60] Its primary role will be to accord approval in principle, of long-term perspective plans (15–20 years), and capital acquisition plan (five years), as well as identify 'Make', 'Buy' and 'Make and Buy' projects and monitor progress of the three Boards under it – Defence Procurement Board, Defence Production Board and the Defence R&D Board. The Defence Procurement Board under the Defence Secretary will have the primary role of capital procurements and co-ordination. The Defence Production Board will be headed by the Secretary of Defence (Production and Supplies) and will oversee all activities related to indigenous manufacture, progress in 'Make' projects and will provide support to DAC. The Defence R&D Board will be headed by the Secretary of Defence (R&D) and will oversee progress, monitor and report on all R&D proposals in consultation with the user service and production board. Other measures at institutional level include direct linkages between armed forces and the Ministry of Defence through integrated headquarters, which include respective perspective planning branches. In sum, organizational and institutional changes brought about recently seem to complement policy changes within the overall defence industrial sector, which in turn is heavily influenced by global defence industrial conditions.

In tune with globalization: Indian defence industry in the twenty-first century

India's quest for self-reliance in defence has thus far produced mixed results. Some of the lessons that India has learnt in the past 50 years are worth noting here. First, the technology gap has facilitated scope for the acquisition of production technology rather than design technology. This in turn has created a licensed production regime at the cost of indigenization efforts. During the 1990s, the effort to encourage joint ventures and co-production with foreign firms in the Indian defence industrial sector is largely seen as a step to reduce license regime and boost indigenous industrial capabilities. A more globalized defence industrial order has proved to be helpful to India in this context. Second, private participation in the defence industrial sector has come after a long delay. Although it is too early to predict the nature and future direction of the role of private industry in defence production, its likely contribution is considerable in future. Third, the government has emphasized measures to enhance the defence industry to cope with future challenges occurring out of reform initiatives. Fourth, the government is now encouraging the defence industry to have more independent joint-design and development and production collaborations to reduce dependence on imports. Fifth, the government is also contemplating a viable strategy for exports of arms. The recent announcement by the Indian government to give export related incentives, including subsidies, to the industry is an example of this strategy. If current efforts at indigenized products, especially in the fields of electronics, aerospace, missiles are taken into consideration, it is assumed that by the end of the current decade, India might be able to save some quantum of foreign exchange through import substitution. On the other hand, products like Brahmos and Advanced Light Helicopters promise enough potential to be likely global products in the future. International arms markets being extremely competitive, it is too early to project or expect success. But, on the other hand, an incremental approach to entering the market is perhaps viable as India is currently gearing up to entering the regional market as a first step. It is too early to expect miracles but the industry seems upbeat about crossing the national boundary.

Trends in the global defence industry have unleashed a set of challenges and opportunities for the Indian defence industry. While challenges range from adjusting to the competitive nature of arms trade, especially in the context of India's current and future weapons procurement, opportunities have come in terms of multiple choices for partnership in production. Products at competitive prices along with a bigger package, which may include technology transfers and offsets, are the most preferred option for India. India's diplomatic efforts must play a proactive role in the international arms market. Signs of this new venture are already showing, where India is seen wooing several countries to advance its core interests. A twin strategy – fostering reliable long-term partnerships with countries like the US and bargaining for technological and associated benefits in arms transactions – should be in place for the future. India's diplomacy has another core area of responsibility in the field of arms exports. Although at a nascent stage, India's export potential is likely to grow in the future. This, in turn, will test its diplomatic skills to sell its products. This way, India's aspirations to become at least a viable second-tier defence producer could be realized, although much homework needs to be done in this regard. Reforms in Indian higher defence management with emphasis on defence production, a step in the right direction keeping global trends in mind, must continue. A comprehensive evaluation should also be done in the next couple of years to assess the first round of reforms in defence industry that has been underway since 2002. Self-reliance in defence technologies,[61] including critical technologies, must be accorded top priority, whereby a twin strategy is seemingly underway – developing systems through indigenous routes as well as gaining knowledge from technology diffusion and international collaborative efforts. The role of DRDO and other scientific institutions will be extremely critical in coming years. Major defence industrial units in India must carry on structural and organizational level reforms, in keeping with the changing developments taking place at international levels. The Indian government must find ways to give them enough independence as well as encourage them to go flat out in the global market. Aerospace, electronics and missiles being the core future market, conglomerates like Hindustan Aeronautics Limited, Bharat Electronics Limited and Bharat Dynamics Limited, which have shown commendable performance in recent times, must be unleashed to tap the global opportunities. India's entry into the future global market should be through a 'pockets of excellence' approach, which should be the future defence industrial strategy for India. The role of private participation in military efforts must also be further expanded to include involvement in complex, high-tech futuristic systems development. An incremental approach may include controlled private management of sick or non-profit state controlled defence industrial units.

Notes

1 Paul Collier and Anke Hoeffler, 'Military Expenditure: Threats, Aid, and Arms Races', World Bank Policy Research Working Paper No. 2927 (November 2002).
2 Ibid.
3 Jasjit Singh, 'Trends in Defence Expenditure', in *Asian Strategic Review, 1998–99* (New Delhi: Institute for Defence Studies and Analyses, 1999), pp. 71–73.
4 Ibid.
5 Mushahid Hussain, 'Pressure Put on Pakistani Spending', *Jane's Defence Weekly*, 10:2 (16 July 1988), p. 70.
6 Shahid Javed Burki, 'Kashmir: A New Strategy', *Dawn*, Internet edition, 5 July 2005.
7 Shahid Javed Burki, 'High Cost of the Conflict', *Dawn*, Internet edition, 12 July 2005.
8 Ibid.
9 Ibid.
10 Globalisation and Nepalese Economy', online, available at www.gefont.org/research/bigbuss/html/part1.htm.
11 Major-General (Ret) Ashok Mehta, *The Royal Nepal Army: Meeting the Maoist Challenge* (New Delhi: ORF-Rupa, 2005), pp. 66–75.

12 Ibid.
13 Ibid.
14 Prem Khanal, 'Govt Buying 4 Choppers with Bank Loans', online, available at www.nepalresearch.com.
15 'Security Costs will Spiral: PM', online, available at www.nepalresearch.com.
16 Tashi Wangyel, 'Rhetoric and Reality: An Assessment of the Impact of WTO on Bhutan', in *The Spider and The Piglet: Proceedings of the First International Seminar on Bhutanese Studies* (Thimphu: The Centre for Bhutan Studies, 2004).
17 Ibid.
18 Karma Ura, 'Perceptions of Security', *Journal of Bhutan Studies*, online, available at www.bhutanstudies.org.bt/journal/vol5/vol5-dz-a.htm.
19 A detailed view on the concept of 'Gross National Happiness' online, available at www.discoverbhutan.biz/pages/yana/y_devphilo01.html#dev.
20 Mark Mancall, 'Bhutan's Quadrilemma: To Join or Not to Join the WTO', *Journal of Bhutan Studies*, online, available at www.bhutanstudies.org.bt/journal/vol9/v9–5.
21 The armed forces have been successfully managing some losing state-owned enterprises such as the Bangladesh Machine Tools Factory (BMTF) and the Khulna Shipyard. Since BMTF's handing over to the Bangladesh Army management on 4 July 2000, the factory has turned into a profit concern repaying its outstanding debt of Tk 443.48 crore (The *New Nation*, 11 June 2003). Khulna Shipyard Limited, which incurred a loss of Tk 57 crore in 15 years since 1984, was similarly handed over to the management of the Bangladesh Navy on 3 October 1999. According to one report, this enterprise was able to make a profit of Tk 17 crore in the first three years under the effective management of the Bangladesh Navy (The *Daily Manav Zamin*, 27 July 2002).
22 Md. Nazrul Islam, 'Benefits of Defence Spending', online, available at www.bangla.net/newage/2003/july4th03/250703/oped.html.
23 Wahiduddin Mahmud, 'Bangladesh Faces the Challenge of Globalization', online, available at yaleglobal.yale.edu/display.article?id=2662.
24 Bertram Bastiampillai, 'Governance and Defence Spending in South Asia: Assessing Policy Implications in Sri Lanka', Regional Centre for Strategic Studies Policy Paper (2001).
25 'Rising Military Expenditure is Deterrent to Development in Sri Lanka: President', 10 January 2001, online, available at english.people.com.cn/english/200101/10/eng20010110_60065.html.
26 In November 1988, two trawlers carrying 150 PLOTE (People's Liberation Organization of Tamil Eelam) mercenaries landed in the Maldives. They quickly overpowered the Maldivian Militia using rockets and machine guns and attacked the President's residence. A 'panicked' Maldivian Government sent out calls asking for assistance and India responded.
27 CIA World Fact Book, online, available at www.cia.gov/cia/publications/factbook/rankorder/2067rank.html.
28 Deba R. Mohanty, 'Defence Budget: Hard Choices Ahead for India', article no. 38, 6 June 2005, online, available at www.sspconline.org/article.
29 Ibid.
30 'India Challenges China in South China Sea', *Stratfor.com*, 26 April 2000, online, available at stratfor.com.
31 Commodore R. S. Vasan, 'Milestones in Growth of Indian Navy: Strategic Dimensions and Their Relevance in the IOR', online, available at www.saag.org/papers13/paper1270.html.
32 'Shopping at Hand, Defence Allocation Jumps by Rs.6,000 crore', *Indian Express*, 1 March 2006.
33 Mohanty, 'Defence Budget: Hard Choices Ahead for India'.
34 The region South Asia includes eight states – India, Pakistan, Bangladesh, Nepal,

Bhutan, Sri Lanka, Maldives and Myanmar. Defence industries of the region are heavily concentrated in India, and to some extent in Pakistan. For purposes of convenience, this chapter addresses globalization of defence industry only from an Indian perspective.

35 Terms like 'defence industry', 'arms industry', 'military industry' and 'military-industrial complex' have been employed interchangeably by scholars and analysts around the world from time to time. This is primarily attributable to lack of a universally agreeable definition on the term. While attempts by scholars have been focused on the exclusivities associated with the subject, consistent changes in the nature and character of the subject of study make it difficult for scholars to formulate a precise definition. For definitional and theoretical problematique associated with such terms, see, James A. Blackwell, Jr. 'The Defense Industrial Base', *The Washington Quarterly*, Autumn 1992, pp. 189–206. All aforesaid terms have been used interchangeably in this book. I prefer to use the term 'defence industry', which I define as

> [A] cumulative aggregation of production and related organizations (including units, subsidiaries, marketing agencies, etc.) of a country engaged in producing goods and services primarily for national military purposes (the national armed forces, paramilitary and police forces) and secondarily for commercial purposes commensurate/ in tune with national politico-strategic and economic considerations.

36 A comprehensive narration of linkage between globalization and defence industry can be found in Mattias Axelon and Andrew James, *The Defense Industry and Globalization* (Stockholm: Defence Research Establishment; December 2000).
37 For example, see, Richard A. Bitzinger, 'Globalization in the Post-Cold War Defense Industry: Challenges and Opportunities', in Ann Markusen and Sean S. Costigan (eds), *Arming the Future: A Defense Industry for the 21st Century* (New York: Council on Foreign Relations; 1999). Also see, Keith Hayward, 'The Globalization of Defense Industries', *Survival*, vol. 42, no. 2, Summer 2000.
38 For a detailed account of the global defence industrial scenario in the early 1990s, see, introductory chapter in *Conversion Survey 1996* (Oxford: Oxford University Press, 1996).
39 Details of restructuring processes witnessed during the 1990s, see, *SIPRI Yearbook 2003* (Oxford: Oxford University Press; 2003).
40 Aggressive diversification drive by the prime and semi-prime defence companies from the United States has been well documented in successive yearbooks brought out by SIPRI during the 1990s.
41 Jocelyn Mawdsley and G. Quielle (eds), *The EU Security Strategy: A New Framework for ESDP and Equipping the EU Rapid Reaction Force* (Brussels: Bonn International Centre for Conversion and International Security Information Service, 2003). Also, see, European Commission, 'European Defence Industrial and Market Issues: Toward an EU Defence Equipment Policy', Communication from the Commission to the Council, the European Parliament, Brussels, March 2003, available at www.europa. eu.int. For an assessment of the EU defence industry, see, Deba R. Mohanty, 'Trends in European Defence Industry in the 1990s: An Assessment', *Strategic Analysis*, vol. xxviii, no. 4, October–December 2004.
42 For details of reforms underway in the Russian defence industry in current times, see, Julian Cooper, 'The Arms Industries of Russian Federation, Ukraine and Belarus', in *SIPRI Yearbook 2004* (Oxford University Press; 2004).
43 See, *SIPRI Yearbook 2004*, chapter on 'Arms Production'.
44 There are many scholarly studies available on restructuring in European defence industry. For a comprehensive survey of the European defence industry, see, Terrence Guay and Robert Callum, 'The Transformation and Future Prospects of Europe's Defense Industry', *International Affairs*, vol. 78, no. 4, October 2002, pp. 757–776.
45 Details online, available at www.acq.osd.mil.

46 For a detailed survey of trends in European defence industry, see, Deba R. Mohanty, 'Trends in European Defense Industry in the 1990s: An assessment', *Strategic Analysis*, vol. xxviii, no. 4, October–December 2004.

47 Thomas Lansford, 'Security and Market Share: Bridging the Transatlantic Divide in the Defense Industry' *European Security*, vol. 10, no. 1, Spring 2001, pp. 1–21.

48 India is keen to play the role of a strategic stabilizer at the world stage, which otherwise suggests that its military power ought to possess capabilities for bigger responsibilities beyond the Indian sub-continent. See, Deba R. Mohanty, 'Arming the Arsenal', *The Pioneer* (New Delhi), 24 February 2007.

49 Realist explanations suggest that states strive to increase their comprehensive military strength to sustain their security in an anarchic system. Desire to maximize security through military power often leads states or groups of states to compete with each other, thus leading to 'arms race'. Such a desire, even though translated in terms of arms race, nevertheless in many cases also flows out of an urge from domestic sources, especially from the state elites of a particular state. Both dynamics have been debated by international relations specialists from time to time. For an excellent account, see, Barry Buzan and Eric Herring, *The Arms Dynamic in World Politics* (London: Lynne Rienner Publishers, 1998). See, especially chapters on 'Action-Reaction Model' and Domestic Structure Model'.

50 Ajay Singh, 'Quest for Self-Reliance', pp. 125–156.

51 Deba R. Mohanty, 'Future of Indian Defence Industry', in N. S. Sisodia and C Uday Bhaskar (eds), *Emerging India: Security and Foreign Policy Perspectives* (New Delhi: IDSA & Promilla, 2005).

52 'India Keen on International Collaboration: Fernandes', The *Times of India*, 5 February, 2003.

53 'Sukhoi Family Will be Present in Strength', The *Hindu*, 4 February, 2003.

54 'Russia Offers India Partnership in 5th Generation Combat Aircraft Project', The *Hindustan Times*, 10 February, 2003.

55 'Lockheed Looking for Technology Transfer', The *Hindu*, 4 February, 2003.

56 This Report is considered to be one of the most important contemporary reports on national security. For details, see, 'Reforming the National Security System: Recommendations of the Group of Ministers', report of the GoM on National Security, National Security Council Secretariat, New Delhi, February 2001.

57 For detailed guidelines for private participation in the defence sector, see, Press Note no. 2, SIA FC Division, Department of Industrial Policy and Promotion, Ministry of Commerce and Industry, Government of India, dated 4 January 2002, online, available at dipp.nic.in. The policy decision to open up the private sector in defence production was taken in May 2001.

58 For a comprehensive description of procurement process and production, see, Lt. Gen Chandra Sekhar (Retd.), 'Defense Procurement and Production Systems', *Journal of the United Services Institution of India*, vol. cxxxi, no. 546, October–December 2001, pp. 524–539. Also see, Lt. Gen Vinay Shankar, 'India's Defense Procurements', *Indian Defense Review* (New Delhi), vol. 16, no. 4, October–December 2001, pp. 18–22.

59 All the policy documents related to defence procurement are available on the Ministry of Defence website www.mod.nic.in.

60 Members of DAC include the Defence Minister, Minister of State for Defence, Chief of Staff Committee, Service Chiefs, Vice Chiefs of Defence Staff, Secretary Defence, Defence Production and Supplies and Special Secretary Acquisition.

61 For a comprehensive analysis of defence technologies for future needs for India, see, Amitav Mallick, 'Self-Reliance in Defence Technologies' in Satish Kumar (ed.), *India's National Security: Annual Review 2003* (New Delhi: India Research Press; 2003). Also see, V. Siddhartha, 'Technology in the Future Needs of Our Armed Forces' in Satish Kumar (ed.), *India's National Security: Annual Review 2001* (New Delhi: Vikas Publishers; 2001).

13 Conclusion

Geoffrey Till

Introduction: globalization

The first conclusion that comes out clearly from the chapters in this book about the shape and effects of globalization in the Asia-Pacific is that it is very difficult to come to one. This is for two evident reasons. First, the term and nature of globalization continues to be variously understood and so its effects on the Asia-Pacific will be variously interpreted simply for that reason. Many of the chapters above have made this point explicitly or implicitly. Second, the Asia-Pacific emerges from this study as a vastly diverse area in which individual countries respond to the phenomenon of globalization in very different ways, and these do not permit easy generalizations. Readers who have worked through the pages of this book in the expectation of finding an answer at the end, may therefore be disappointed – but, arguably, so they should be!

Nonetheless, a few concluding observations may still be possible. There is general agreement that globalization is *not* a new phenomenon, a case made particularly by Chew and Ding. It may be helpful to review the matter chronologically. Perhaps three broad chronological eras in the wider world environment can be discerned and these are associated in large measure with the phenomenon of globalization. These have been called the 'pre-modern' and the 'modern', with a third, the 'post-modern' era now beginning to emerge.[1] Very crudely, the first period is characteristic of agricultural states with limited economic interdependence and insufficient surpluses to invest in further development, the second by the 'Realist' interactions of states shaped by industrial mass production and operating in a Westphalian international system. The third period is animated by aspirations for a cooperative world system of openness and mutual dependence operated by states moulded by, and for, the contemporary information economy that is such a characteristic of contemporary globalization. Only in a very rough sense is the transition from one period to another linear. Nearly all countries exhibit characteristics that blend all three paradigms, at least to some extent. But the phenomenon of globalization affects them all and, in return, their behaviour. Pre-modern states may be portrayed as its victims; modern states see it as an opportunity to advance their own interests and moderate their policies accordingly in response to it; post-modern states accept it as a source of universal benefit and seek to support it.

The trend towards state post-modernism is clearly accelerated by increasing globalization. The more globalized countries become, the more open their economies, the more likely is their manufacturing capacity to be relocated elsewhere, the more outward-looking their interests and the more likely they are to advocate and support free trade. All these are the characteristics of the post-modern, rather than modern states which, by contrast, will be warier about the implications of globalization for their own security and sovereignty, more protectionist in their economic policy, and less inclined to collaborate with others in the maintenance of the world's trading system. Either way, such attitudes will inevitably have their effect on the security policies of states, be they modern or post-modern.

Today, some of these basically pre-modern states are still to be found in Africa; most states in the Asia-Pacific are predominantly modern, while most essentially post-modern states are located in North America or, most especially, Western Europe. These categories are all matters more of degree than of kind and, as the chapters in this book have shown, some 'modern' Asia-Pacific states have markedly 'post-modern' tendencies, some of them – such as Australia, Singapore and Japan – quite strongly.

Of course, these modernist and post-modernist paradigms of national state behaviour are very crudely drawn; the differences between them are fuzzy matters of degree and decidedly not pole opposites. Most states exhibit a blend of the two sets of behaviours and characteristics and their armed forces might therefore be expected to, and indeed do, illustrate the same thing. But where should the countries of the Asia-Pacific be plotted on this spectrum of possibility, and to what extent does the development of their security policy and armed forces demonstrate and affect the impact of globalization on the Asia-Pacific – and vice versa?

The increasing extent to which the burgeoning economies of the Asia-Pacific seem likely to dominate the world economy of the twenty-first century suggest that the countries of the region certainly *ought* to be developing the trappings of globalization and post-modernism. Some countries clearly are, most obviously but in no particular order, Australia, Taiwan, Singapore, South Korea, Japan, China, India and New Zealand. Several of them, indeed, have been utterly transformed by the process of globalization, especially Taiwan, Singapore and South Korea. Given the development of ASEAN and other collective Asia-Pacific regional fora, and the manner in which long-standing issues such as the South China Sea dispute and concerns over the Straits of Malacca are being 'de-territorialized' it is easy to see why some should conclude that in the Asia-Pacific area, 'traditionalist and realist strategic cultures, with military power as their central focus and balance-of-power tactics as their main "game", are becoming less relevant'.[2]

The Singapore case, however, shows that things are not quite so simple. It is true that in Singapore, there has been, in recent years, a marked acceleration in the achievement of S. Rajaratnam's 1972 aspiration for Singapore to become a Global City embedded in an international trading system.[3] Singapore is one of the world's most globalized cities and clearly intends to remain so. It is investing heavily in the infrastructure and the institutions needed to sustain an expanding global maritime role, and it also puts a high premium on the kind of multilateralism that it thinks will stabilize relationships in the Asia-Pacific region.[4] Its military forces have operated in combination with others against common threats, such as international terrorism, including *Operation Enduring Freedom* and it is proud of its achievements in the East Timor crisis and the Tsunami relief operation.

Nevertheless, initially, it '...traditionally viewed its neighbours with caution, even suspicion'. After the traumatic experience of being abandoned by the British. first in defeat in 1942, and then again in their precipitate scuttle from 'East of Suez' announced in 1967, it has developed a strong preference for self-reliance and robust, if notably opaque, national defences.[5] These 'somewhat provocative military plans' have indeed sometimes produced adverse reactions in the region[6] and are an expression of a determination to defend national interests as well as collective ones.[7] Moreover, it is hard to imagine a mainstream European politician articulating, as did Prime Minister Gok Chok Tong, the following:

> I say to all Singaporeans: You have to feel passionately about Singapore. Being Singaporean should resonate in our hearts and minds. We built this country. We live, work and raise our children here. We will fight and, if we must, we will die to defend our way of life and our home.[8]

This kind of thinking illustrates the point that globalization in certain circumstances is by no means antithetical to a strong sense of nationalism, and that in those circumstances what Europeans would regard as old fashioned nationalism may still be a very significant policy determinant. The potential tensions between modern, post-modern and in some cases pre-modern tendencies is even more obvious elsewhere in the region.

Sometimes indeed, globalization has actually increased this. Its differential impact on communities within states has led to secessionist issues, and a consequent emphasis on national integrity at governmental level – as in the case of Indonesia, Thailand, the Philippines and Myanmar for example. The absence of collective cooperation in dealing with the currency crisis of 1997 illustrated the abiding strength of neo-mercantilist beggar-my-neighbour approaches in economic policy. Nor can there be much doubt from continuing issues over the ownership of the South China Sea, the safety and security of the Straits of Malacca, the future of Taiwan, and a host of other disputed jurisdictions over the region's islands and land and sea borders and an abiding suspicion of 'interference' by external powers, that most countries in the region continue to place a particularly high value on sovereignty and national independence.[9] Malaysia's then Prime Minister Mahatir illustrated this well in a speech in July 1997:

We are told we must open up, that trade and commerce must be totally free. Free for whom ? For rogue speculators. For anarchists wanting to destroy weak countries in their crusade for open societies, to force us to submit to the dictatorship of international manipulators.[10]

Clearly, the countries of the Asia-Pacific region, as elsewhere, exhibit a range of blends of the modern and the post-modern in their attitudes towards defence but, it seems fair to say, they are, overall, rather more tilted to the first approach than to the second.

So to summarize, the contributors to this volume have explored the impact of globalization on the Asia-Pacific, they have shown the diversity of the responses of the countries of the area, thereby demonstrating that the two-way relationship between globalization and the state is deeply complex, variable and does not permit easy conclusions. In some ways, the state shapes globalization: some for example argue that globalization can and indeed should be governed, with a designed shift from free trade in the direction of fair trade. This would, they say, significantly reduce the disparities between states, and between groups in states, which would in turn limit the prospects for instability and conflict. This assumes that the system remains state centred and that globalization can in fact by governed by action at the national level. Others argue that the size and capacity of states determines how the they react to, and help shape the direction of, a globalized world. Arguably, the 1990s was the era when small states like Singapore benefited most from the system, but now it is the era when larger countries like India, China, Brazil and a resurgent Russia, with the resources to project, as well as accumulate, power will benefit the most.[11] All of these approaches suggest that globalization needs to be seen essentially as a dependent variable, something that is shaped by inter-state and intra-state relationships and circumstances, rather than their determinant.

On the other hand, as Hughes has argued earlier, the processes of globalization may actually weaken the capacity of weaker states to maintain internal order and indeed their sovereignty. It may severely limit the operational freedoms even of the system's hegemons, let alone other powers. All this, if true, would tend to validate Adam Smith's contention that the system is based on blind and ungovernable economic forces in which states meddle at their peril.

A second fairly safe observation to be drawn from this book might well be an often unspoken assumption underlying most of the contributions to this book that since it depends absolutely on the free flow of trade – and this goes largely by sea – globalization itself needs to be seen essentially as a maritime phenomenon. This has always been the case, but the invention of the container has revolutionized the process. Indeed,

It is no exaggeration to say that the shipping container may have transformed the world, and our daily lives, as fundamentally as any of the other more glamorous or complex inventions of the last 100 years, the internet included.[12]

The regular arrival of a container ship like the *Emma Maersk* half a mile long, stacked 200 feet high with containers carrying 45,000 tons of manufactured goods, probably mainly from China, which is expected to be turned around in 24 hours, illustrates the sheer scale of this revolution. Not only does the modern shipping industry make globalization possible; it is itself profoundly globalized. Over 60 per cent of ships fly flags different from the nationality of their owners. In many cases these owners are in fact multinational corporations. A ship's crew, cargo and itinerary will be totally international and quite possibly insured, brokered and operated in still other countries too.[13]

Accordingly, the whole concept of globalization appears profoundly maritime. Low and decreasing sea-borne freight rates mean that the shipping costs of a $700 TV set from China to Europe is no more than about $10. This helps keeps European costs of living and rates of inflation down, encourages China to industrialize – improving thereby life for its citizens – and makes possible industrial re-location, most obviously from Europe and North America to the Far East, and the diversification of production lines around an increasing number of countries.[14]

Sea-borne commerce therefore produces a mutually dependent community of industrial production and consumption. The world has increasingly to be seen as a tight, interconnected nexus of countries and regions with high degrees of mutual economic, and therefore political, interdependence. As already noted, post-modernists would conclude that this is likely to reduce the likelihood of conflicts between states and to increase levels of international cooperation against anything that seems likely to threaten a system on which all depend.

International shipping, especially in the shape of the container, underpins the prospect of further beneficial growth in world trade. But to have that effect it needs to be predictable, traceable, compliant with detailed pick-up and delivery schedules and secure. This provides both an opportunity and a challenge, not least because sea-based globalization is potentially vulnerable to disruption. In itself, this is not new, for Mahan warned us of this over a century ago:

> This, with the vast increase in rapidity of communication, has multiplied and strengthened the bonds knitting together the interests of nations to one another, till the whole now forms an articulated system not only of prodigious size and activity, but of excessive sensitiveness, unequalled in former ages.[15]

Implications for security policy

This leads us into the third fairly safe observation from this book, that globalization has considerable security implications that will shape the security policy of the states in the system. Because of its effect on the state, and state practices, globalization is arguably the central fact of the strategic environment of the early twenty-first century. Many of the chapters in this book have pointed to both the security enhancing and the security eroding aspects of globalization for the countries of the Asia-Pacific.

Some, in the traditions of the nineteenth-century Manchester school, continue to welcome the onset of globalization, hoping that it will usher in an era of peace and plenty by replacing earlier, competitive, aggressive balance-of-power politics with a much greater sense of international community and shared interest. They make the point as does Hughes above, that growing economic interdependence tends to affect the costs and therefore the incidence of the use of force between countries. Governments of this persuasion will tend to see globalization as something to defend. As Sukma argues, moreover, many of the external and domestic challenges to security that come with systemic change of this sort may need to be handled cooperatively by the countries of the region. However the fact that there is not a single view of what globalization means is of consequence here. Even if the countries of the Asia-Pacific think they should defend globalization, it is not at all clear that they are actually defending the same thing or would use the same methods. Some see it largely as a matter of defending free trade and the security conditions that make it possible – a military task; others see the need to defend the system's durability, perhaps by making trade fairer – a political–economic task.

Others will be concerned with more traditional, 'modern' preoccupations. As Delamotte shows, countries like Japan react both to a host of local and regional issues, as well as to global campaigns, against, say terrorism, weapons proliferation or environmental degradation. They may be concerned that globalization may empower rather than limit stronger countries like China or India into dominating their regions to the possible disadvantage of their smaller neighbours. There is, as Ding has pointed out in regard to China, a balance to be struck between the positive and negative consequences of globalization for the security of the area. Many of the chapters above have pointed to the fact that globalization can adversely affect domestic security particularly if their countries contain people who see globalization as undermining their way of life, their independence, their beliefs and their future prospects. It can threaten such countries' sovereignty and the role and capacity of their governments.

A third group might dispute assumptions about globalization's longevity and worry, on the contrary, about its prospective if not imminent collapse. Either way, the present and future state of globalization will be a major determinant of the shape and nature of the world politics of states. Governmental attitudes to globalization will in turn be a major determinant of strategy and defence policy and therefore of the size, shape, composition and function of the armed forces of the Asia-Pacific and of the industries which support them.

Globalization encourages the development of a 'borderless world' in which the autarchy of the national units of which it is composed is gradually being whittled away by the development of a variety of transnational economic and technological trends. The focus will increasingly be on the system, not its components; military plans and strategy will, the post-modern argument goes, need to serve that system as a whole. Nations will become relaxed about their borders because they have to be. But this cuts both ways; they will be relaxed about the borders of other nations too. In a globalizing world, systems thinking pulls strategists forwards geographically. This forwards leaning approach to the making and implementation of strategy has been a marked characteristic of European and American defence thinking for a decade now. Thus Tony Blair in early 2007,

> The frontiers of our security no longer stop at the Channel. What happens in the Middle East affects us. ... The new frontiers for our security are global. Our Armed Forces will be deployed in the lands of other nations far from home, with no immediate threat to our territory, in environments and in ways unfamiliar to them.[16]

Globalization is a *dynamic* process since, amongst other things, trade and business produces a constantly changing hierarchy of winners and losers and, historically, conflict seems to be particularly associated with economic volatility.[17] New players in the game have to be accommodated, its victims supported and future directions anticipated. The defence of the system has therefore to be constant, and proactive rather than merely intermittent and reactive. This calls for continuous cooperative action along all the diplomatic, economic, social and military lines of development, with the latter's requirements based on the need to 'shape the international security environment' in order to prevent problems arising.

The incentive at the level of the state to take action either to defend the globalization system or to take precautions against its ultimate failure, may also be increased by the sense that such threats are serious and may presage the decay or collapse of globalization. As Jeffery Frieden reminds us,

> As was the case a hundred years ago, many people now take an integrated world economy for granted, regard it as the natural state of things, and expect that it will last forever. Yet the bases on which global capitalism rests today are not very different from what they were in 1900, and the potential for their disruption is as present today as it was then. ... The apparent stability of the early 1900s was followed by decades of conflicts and upheavals. Today's international economic order also seems secure, but in historical perspective it may be only a brief interlude.[18]

The threats that globalization faces are serious and may prove fatal, however. It is worth remembering that in many ways the world of the late nineteenth century was, in its own terms, as globalized as ours is today, but that the system collapsed in the face of commercial rivalry, the discontent of the disadvantaged and growing nationalism.[19] In some ways, indeed, these problems were actually a by-product of globalization, especially in regard to the kind of inequality of benefit that bred nationalism. The result of this was a World War which, as Niall Ferguson has observed,

[S]ank globalization – literally. Nearly 13 million tons of shipping went to the bottom of the sea as a result of German naval action, most of it by U-boats. International trade, investment and emigration all collapsed. In the war's aftermath, revolutionary regimes arose that were fundamentally hostile to international economic integration. Plans replaced the market; autarky and protection took the place of free trade. Flows of goods diminished; flows of people and capital all but dried up.[20]

This is indeed a chilling historical example of the way in which war can, to borrow Thomas Friedman's phrase, 'unflatten' the world. If it is indeed true that 'War and warfare will always be with us; war is a permanent feature of the human condition', then it is far from inconceivable that globalization might collapse again.[21]

A Marxist might even argue that all of this is a result of the 'inherent contradictions' of global capitalism and, accordingly, are historically inevitable.[22] Repeated shocks of the 9/11 sort, in conjunction with a sustained down-turn in economic activity would certainly strain the sea-based trading system on which globalization depends. Shippers point out that we are now passing through the most sustained period of economic growth in history and wonder how long this can go on.

Accordingly, at the level of the state, the prudent defence planner might well feel the need to bear this lesson of history in mind, especially given the fact that our kind of globalization faces an extra range of threats – most obviously international terrorism, resource depletion and environmental degradation – that theirs did not.[23] This could reinforce the tendency in the Asia-Pacific for nation-based rather than system-based strategic thinking and a focus on the immediate and the local threat rather than the more distant, both geographically and temporally.

Should this analysis be right, and should globalization either collapse or enter a period of terminal decline, we would face a bleaker, harder, much less communal world of increased levels of competition in which coercive military force and power politics resume their dominance of the strategic horizon. We would indeed have 'a warlike future'.

The 'excessive sensitiveness' that Mahan had in mind derives from the fact that interdependence, and indeed dependency of any sort, inevitably produces targets for the malign to attack. But there is special point in his warnings now, partly because the extraordinary extent and depth of today's version of globalization depends on a supply-chain philosophy of 'just enough, just in time' that increases the system's vulnerability to disruption. Moreover, there have emerged various groups and situations that could exploit or exacerbate that increased vulnerability. Such threats include, obviously, direct attack by groups or states hostile to the values and outcomes that the system encourages. Less obviously, international maritime crime in its manifold forms – piracy, drugs and people smuggling – and the unsustainable plundering of marine resources all threaten to undermine the good order on which the safe and timely passage of shipping depends. Conflict and instability ashore, moreover, can have disruptive effects in neighbouring seas, as was demonstrated all too clearly in the Tanker War of the 1980s or, more recently off Somalia, for example.[24] In some cases these threats may be posed against sea-based trade itself; more commonly, the conditions, both ashore and at sea, that make that trade possible are at risk.

Moreover, some of these threats to the system are also globalizing; insecurity in fact has become globalized too. The menace of international terrorism is the most obvious example of this but various other forms of maritime crime also seem to be following this path. To take just one illustrative example, it was reported in February 2006 that the Russian Mafia was involved in large scale poaching by Norwegian trawlers under a Russian flag from cod reserves in the Barents Sea; the fish were sent to China for filleting and then returned to Grimsby and Hull for sale in the British market. The consortium responsible for this had Swedish, Russian, Norwegian and Hong Kong connections; the consequence was the depletion of cod reserves and considerable financial benefit to Russian Mafia and other criminals, whose existence and success threatens good governance, domestic stability and the good order at sea upon which, it is worth repeating, the safe and timely passage of shipping depends.[25]

So how will the Asia-Pacific react to such threats to globalization and to the threats and opportunities that globalization itself represents? Although in many ways at the heart of the globalization process, this area has been authoritatively described as 'an exemplar of traditional regional security dynamics found largely in the military-political mode ... Old fashioned concerns about power still dominate the security agenda of most of the regional powers, and war remains a distinct, if constrained possibility'.[26]

This seems to come out quite strongly in the Asia-Pacific's developing requirement for energy security. In the last great age of globalization, manufacturing industry's reliance on raw materials that had to be extracted in other areas seemed to necessitate the control of territory that exacerbated the relations between states and led to conflict. These days, some analysts argue that our comforting optimism about the future of globalization depends on the assumption of sufficient resources. They go on to say that this is proving an illusion, most obviously in the availability of oil. A steep rise in oil demand especially from China, Japan and the rest of the Asia-Pacific is coinciding with a terminal fall in the discovery of new reserves.[27] These views are dismissed as alarmist by those who point to the system's capacity to easily weather previous oil-flow disruptions, such as the 1980s Tanker War between Iran and Iraq. They conclude from this that the 'market will look after itself'. Pessimists may respond by saying that while this may have be true in a time of plenty, the same may not apply in times of shortage.

Anticipating that they shall soon have to start scraping the bottom of the barrel, states are already manoeuvring so they can cope with a less secure energy future and even now this is exacerbating relations between them. China and Japan, for example, are in dispute over islands which straddle potentially important marine oil fields. They are both competing for stocks in the volatile

Middle East. The Chinese are heavily engaged in regimes which the US regards as dangerous and disreputable – Sudan, Venezuela, Zimbabwe and Iran – and are moving into the Indian Ocean, watched warily by India. This suggests the possible emergence of a kind of globalization with a harder, more competitive, more mercantilist edge.

Moreover, many analysts would point out that beneath all the collaborative rhetoric, national behaviour in the Asia-Pacific still reflects the 'modern' Westphalian state system with its assumptions of unending competition between states for power influence, land and resources, ideological supremacy and its preoccupations with military power.[28] Nor should we expect nationalism to wither as a result of globalization. 'Nationalism,' says Fred Halliday, 'is not an alternative to globalization, but an intrinsic part of it'.[29]

Defence industrial implications

The justification for the state is often held to be the protection of the security, widely defined, of the individual citizen. Indeed defence and the concept of the nation-state are completely bound up with one another. Defence is the ultimate 'public good' since everyone in a country benefits from it – even if they do not contribute to it – and no private organization can supply it. Accordingly security is one of the main justifications for the nation-state and a significant driver of the international system. For this reason, the approach of the book has been to explore the relationship between the state and globalization in the Asia-Pacific area with a particular focus on security policy, and, within that, on the development in the region of differing policies towards the defence-industrial base. This has seemed to us to be a particularly effective case study for the broader question of the impact of globalization on the Asia-Pacific generally. But in this final chapter perhaps one more refinement can be added: that maritime policies have a special salience as globalization itself can be seen as a sea-based phenomenon.

The chapters above have shown that for China, Japan, South Korea, India and much of Southeast Asia globalization has increased the capacity of individual states to spend on defence and in many cases has improved their technological capabilities too. Indeed across the region generally, the market for new naval material is expected to reach some $15 billion by the end of 2008, which doubles the 2003 total and is half as much again as the expected market in 2008 for both the United States and the European Union.[30] To this extent globalization can be said to have indirectly contributed to the capacity of the countries of the area to be masters of their own destiny. Globalization, in other words, on the surface at least has actually strengthened the search for self-reliance and often the power of nations. But this may be a matter of size. Smaller countries such as those of Southeast Asia have been slower than larger countries such as China and India to build up indigenous capability. Others, such as Pakistan have been shown in this book to have attempted to make up for deficiencies in their defence industrial resource base by a policy of strategic alliance with better endowed outsiders.

But a closer examination of this relationship shows the tensions and complexities that lie beneath this evident truth. It suggests that globalization in some ways may be not much more than a set of common problems and issues to which states have to respond in their own particular ways, but which, largely because the problems and issues are common, may well result in various forms of inter-state cooperation. These problems include severe spending constraints on the one hand alongside a recognition that changes in the global environment demand radical and probably expensive shifts in strategic outlook. Moreover, the unit costs and technical sophistication of platforms, sensors and weapons are increasing in ways which make building up and even sustaining force numbers increasingly difficult. More and more, nations – no matter how big they are – that are confronting global challenges face choices that force them to 'to juggle high technology, great expectations, tight funds and low volumes'.[31]

Moreover these tendencies are by no means restricted to the Asia-Pacific. Even in the United States after a period of considerable defence expenditure there is a downward pressure on future budgets and fleet numbers, a recognition that the future may demand different defence priorities from the present. Accordingly the Americans are thinking more in terms of open architecture solutions, in the adoption of commercial rather than naval standards in shipbuilding, in the acquisition of commercial-off-the shelf equipment and in greater acceptance of the need for partnership with foreign firms in, for example, the Joint Strike Fighter and Littoral Combat Ship programmes.[32] In Europe too, there are many countries, such as Sweden, for instance, which face similar pressures and, in their case, a radical shift from an operational focus on anti-invasion strategies and self-reliance to an expeditionary focus in concert with others and the development of rapidly deployable capabilities.[33] This has resulted in major changes in Sweden's defence industrial base, the creation of a defence industrial strategy, inspired by, but not a copy of the UK's example, the prioritization of critical defence manufacturing capabilities, and of the acceptance of partnership with foreign enterprises – such as BAE Systems with Saab for the Gripen fighter programme – and the conscious selling of some enterprises to foreign companies – such as the Kockums submarine capacity to the German HDV Group.[34]

Like their counterparts in Europe and North America, the countries of the Asia-Pacific have to respond to problems that are partly set by the results of globalization, by looking to other forms of globalization for solutions. Most obviously this demands the development of relationships with foreign equipment suppliers. In many cases, as we have seen, this takes the form of simply acquiring platforms, weapons or sensors – mainly from Western or Russian manufacturers but to some extent from newer countries in the field such as Israel or Brazil as well.

But there are clear problems with this. The material available might not be entirely fit for particular national purposes, and as India has discovered in the course of its close association with Russian defence manufacturers, projects can be slow to mature and much more costly than originally anticipated.[35] Moreover, this policy does imply the state losing control of its own defence entrepreneurs, arguably some degree of its sovereign foreign policy (since in some circumstances at least reliance on other countries could restrict its freedom of action), and it limits the country's ability to retain or build up indigenous capacity.

Hence the reviving attempt to create or recapture strategically sufficient national autonomy in the defence industrial sector through the development of a defence industrial strategy at governmental level, through heavy governmental investment in research and development, through sometimes covert protectionism and whenever necessary through strategic alliance. The widespread use of 'offsets' – the compulsory inward investments imposed on foreign defence suppliers by a purchasing government – illustrates the region's search for ways of reducing costs while building up indigenous industrial capacity at the national level.

But such advances in defence capability have in many cases only been made possible by the deliberate rationalization of a country's defence industry, by freeing it from government control and by opening it up to access from the wider world. In post-modern Europe, the Commission and the European Defence Agency are keen to develop a shared European defence industry and encourage defence industrial cooperation between its member states. Even so, at the national level, there has been a slowing down in efforts to restructure the defence industry across the continent, not least because of a marked reluctance to accept the need for large-scale industrial closures at home and a strong sense that solutions must be found that balance national outcomes. The 27 unit FREMM – Frigate European Multi Mission – collaborative programme between Italy and France for example ensures that both countries will share R&D costs but will essentially do their own building at home. Nonetheless it is 'the largest European naval programme for the next decade and the benchmark for future cooperation programmes'.[36]

The same arrangement applies to similar partnership deals between foreign and domestic suppliers in Europe and the Asia-Pacific such as the French DCN and Spanish Navantia's agreement to supply technology transfer and assistance in the building of six Scorpene submarines in India's Mazagon docks. This is but a small part of an overall Indian programme, aimed at making the best use of the globalized arms manufacturing industry, in order to rationalize and make more efficient its indigenous industrial capacity, to acquire a set of platforms, weapons and platforms that will make it an increasingly formidable player on the world ocean and eventually, in all likelihood, a significant arms producer in its own right.[37] Australia is evidently seeking to follow exactly the same path, as indeed are others in the region, to a greater or lesser extent.[38] Such developments may eventually correct one very noticeable aspect of such defence cooperation – namely that the countries of the Asia-Pacific, in striking contrast to those of the European Union are engaging in it much more with outsiders than they are with each other, despite the commonality of the problems they face.

To summarize, a glance at the region's defence industrial sector demonstrates that the impact of globalization on the countries of the Asia-Pacific reinforces the impression given by earlier chapters in this book that its effects vary widely from country to country but that in the main globalization provides solutions and opportunities as well as challenges to national integrity and power, and that there is in most countries in the region a widespread, and indeed growing, determination at the national level to make use of globalization rather than simply succumb to its influence.

Final conclusions

Partly because defence is a sensitive area, perhaps especially in the commercial sector, much of the data on which sound conclusions must be based remains elusive, especially in the Asia-Pacific area – a point made by Banlaoi above. This aggravates the more general problem of coming to definite conclusions about the impact of globalization on the Asia-Pacific since the debate about what globalization means anyway is far from resolved. Furthermore, the depressingly high levels of complex variability that distinguish the Asia-Pacific area make persuasive generalizations and attempts to apply the concept to it, especially difficult. Nonetheless it seems possible to conclude that, at least in this area, and even in the face of globalization, the nation-state appears alive and well. More generally, in this volume, we have tried to sketch out some of the questions on the relationship between globalization and the nation-state particularly in the defence sector. While we may not have been able to arrive at definite and agreed answers to all, even any, of them we feel that at least we can say that we know a little more about what we don't know. We hope that in that, at least, we have made a useful contribution to the debate.

Notes

1 Robert Cooper, *The Breaking of Nations: Order and Chaos in the Twenty-first Century*, London: Atlantic books, 2004, pp. 37–43. Barry Buzan and Ole Waever, *Regions and Powers: The Structure of International Security*, Cambridge: Cambridge University Press, 2003, pp. 22–26.
2 C.L. Chiou, 'Taiwan' in Ken Booth and Russell Trood, *Strategic Culture in the Asia-Pacific Region*, London: Macmillan, 1999, p. 66.
3 Richard A. Deck, 'Singapore: Comprehensive Security – Total Defence' in Ken Booth and Russell Trood, eds, *Strategic Cultures in the Asia-Pacific Region*, Basingstoke: Palgrave, 1999, pp. 252ff.
4 Tim Huxley, *Defending the Lion City: The Armed Forces of Singapore*, London: Allen Unwin, 2000, p. 33.
5 Deck, op. cit., p. 258.
6 Chandran Jeshurun, 'Malaysia; The Delayed Birth of a Strategic Culture' in Booth and Trood, op. cit., p. 227.
7 Huxley, op. cit., pp. 25, 45.
8 Cited in Leo Suryadinata, *Nationalism and Globalization: East and West*, Singapore: ISEAS, 2000, p. 94. See also David Brown, *Contemporary Nationalism in Civic, Ethnocultural and Multicultural Politics*, London: Routledge, 2000.

9 Booth and Trood, op. cit., offer a useful compendium of the array of attitudes in the Asia to defence and globalization.
10 Speech of 24 July 1997, cited in Frieden *Global Capitalism: Its Fall and Rise in the Twentieth Century*, New York: W.W. Norton, 2006, p. 392.
11 Harold James, 'Empire and its Alternatives', *Orbis*, Summer 2007, p. 403.
12 Oliver Burkman, 'The Shipping News', *Guardian*, 27 Jan 2007. See also Marc Levinson, *The Box*, Princeton: Princeton University press, 2006, pp. 264–278.
13 Daniel Y. Coulter, 'Navies and Globalization: An Estranged Couple' in Robert H. Edwards and Ann L. Griffiths, *Intervention and Engagement: A Maritime Perspective*, Halifax, NS: Dalhousie University, Centre for Foreign Policy Studies, 2003.
14 Facts and arguments of this sort may be found in 'Shipping and World Trade' reports, online, available at www.shippingfacts.com and the OECD's report, *The Role of Changing Transport Costs and Technology in Industrial Relocation*, May 2005.
15 Alfred Thayer Mahan, *Retrospect and Prospect*, London: Sampson, Low, Marston, 1902, p. 144.
16 Tony Blair, *Reflections on 21st Century Security*, Speech on HMS *Albion*, Plymouth, 12 Jan 2007.
17 Niall Ferguson, *The War of the World*, London: Allen Lane, 2006, pp. lix–lxii.
18 Jeffrey A. Frieden, op. cit., pp. xvi–xvii.
19 Frieden, op. cit., p. 16.
20 Ferguson, op. cit., p. 73.
21 Thomas L. Friedman, *The World is Flat; The Globalized World in the Twenty-first Century*, London: Penguin, 2005, p. 458; Colin S. Gray, *Another Bloody Century: Future Warfare*, London: Phoenix, 2005, p. 370.
22 Timothy Garton Ash, 'Global Capitalism has no Serious Rivals. But it Could Destroy Itself', *Guardian*, 22 Feb 2007.
23 Some analysts, though, argue that today's globalization is deeper and so more resilient than in earlier periods because manufacturing is not merely relocated; it is *redistributed* amongst a number of countries in ways which increases mutual dependence. Using the computer industry as an example, Friedman calls this the 'Dell effect'. Friedman, op. cit., pp. 529–536.
24 These are detailed in my *Seapower: A Guide for the 21st Century*, London: Frank Cass, 2004, pp. 310–378. In many ways this article is a development of the last chapter of that book.
25 'Cod Sold in Hundreds of Chippies Linked to Russian Black Market', the *Guardian*, 20 Feb 2006.
26 Buzan and Waever, op. cit., p. 93.
27 Jeremy Leggett, 'Dark Secret: What They Don't Want You to Know About the Coming Oil Crisis', *Independent*, 20 Jan 2006.
28 It is worth pointing out that with all our current focus on *transnational* terrorism, state-sponsored terrorism and localized ethno-nationalist terrorism are still distressingly common.
29 Fred Halliday, 'Nationalism' in John Baylis and Steve Smith, *The Globalization of World Politics: An Introduction to International Relations*, Oxford: Oxford University Press, pp. 521–538.
30 'Naval Market in Asia Pacific on a Rising Tide', *Jane's Defence Weekly*, 25 May 2005.
31 'Australia Juggles High Technology, Great Expectations, Tight Funds and Low Volumes', *Jane's International Defence Review*, Mar 2007.
32 Otto Kreisher, 'Use of COTS in Naval Ships', *Naval Forces*, IV/2006.
33 Rear-Admiral Anders Grenstad, Interview, *The Navy* (NZ) Feb/Mar 2008, pp. 20–22.
34 Tony Skinner, 'Changing Tactics', *Jane's Defence Weekly*, 11 Apr 2007.
35 'Russia Hikes Price of INS Vikramaditya', *Jane's Defence Weekly*, 5 Dec 2007.

36 Alexander Nicoll, 'The Changing Face of Prime Contracting', *World Defence Systems*, Autumn 2005; 'Europe's Naval Industry Must Co-operate to Compete', *Jane's Defence Weekly*, 5 Dec 2007. On the FREMM programme see report in *Jane's Navy International*, Dec 2006.
37 Rahul Bedi, 'Eying the Prize', *Jane's Defence Weekly*, 17 Jan 2007.
38 'Australia's New Arms Export Unit Sets Strategy', *Jane's Defence Weekly*, 5 Sep 2007; 'Seoul Aims for $2bn of Defence Exports by 2022', *Jane's Defence Weekly*, 26 Sep 2007.

Index

For Product Safety Concerns and Information please contact our EU
representative GPSR@taylorandfrancis.com
Taylor & Francis Verlag GmbH, Kaufingerstraße 24, 80331 München, Germany

www.ingramcontent.com/pod-product-compliance
Ingram Content Group UK Ltd.
Pitfield, Milton Keynes, MK11 3LW, UK
UKHW021831240425
457818UK00006B/162